Contents

Part Four
THE FINANCE DECISION

Acknowledgements

The production of the final text, with all its diagrams and tables, would not have been possible without the skilled assistance of Sue Brown and Nicola Smorowinski of the Leicester Business School. I am also indebted to John Cushion at Financial Times Management whose guidance at critical stages of preparation produced significant improvements.

Finally, I would like to acknowledge the unstinting generosity of John Alexander and Roy Thody at De Monfort University throughout gestation periods of research and development. Roy Thody deserves a special mention for his patient preparation of the study questions which eventually underpinned Chapter 11 and Chapter 12.

Dedication

To Jumbo, Hendle, Nomis, Nod and Tess for treading on eggshells.

PART ONE

Introduction

1

Corporate decision-making and the contemporary finance function

1 INTRODUCTION

Irrespective of the time horizon involved, the financial decision-maker is concerned with the allocation of funds between competing claims. Whilst not wishing to underestimate the element of social responsibility involved, this requires that, in the corporate sector of mixed economies, firms exist to convert resource inputs of money and physical capital into outputs of goods and services which satisfy consumer demand and, thereby, generate cash profits.

Since most economic resources are finite but society's demand seems unlimited, the corporate finance function can be perceived as the future allocation of scarce financial resources with a view to maximising aggregate consumer satisfaction. And because money capital (as opposed to labour) is typically the controlling factor, the problem ultimately is one of how society chooses to allocate limited funds between alternative uses.

In mature market economies a solution is attempted through the capital market. As Figure 1.1 reveals, companies come into being financed by external investor capital, which may include equity and debt finance plus an element of government aid. If they satisfy market needs, firms tend to make profits. These may be either distributed to the providers of capital or retained to replenish or enhance the internal asset base. The continued ability to sustain and increase operating capability through a search for investment opportunities in turn attracts further capital and individual companies expand. Given an efficient capital market, demand for their shares, based upon future profit expectations, may then exceed supply and, thus, the market value of equity will rise above the market value of tangible assets.

Of course the price of shares can fall, as well as rise. Companies engaged in inefficient or irrelevant activities are gradually starved of finance because of a shortage of cash, or the capital market's unwillingness to sustain their

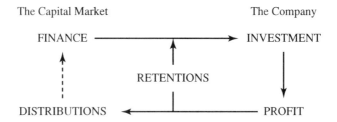

Fig 1.1 The mature market economy

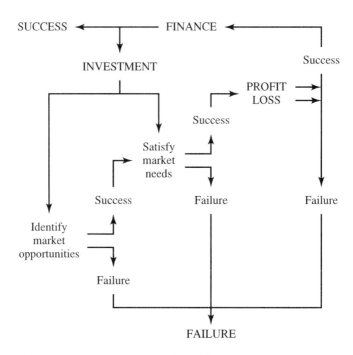

Fig 1.2 Corporate economic performance

investment base. As Figure 1.2 demonstrates, such companies will either fall prey to takeover or eventually disappear from the economic scene, unlike their profitable counterparts.

2 RETURN, RISK AND CAPITAL COSTS

Successful corporate decision-making thus includes two distinct, but nevertheless interrelated, aspects:

- The investment function, which identifies and selects investment opportunities which maximise anticipated net cash inflow and hopefully share price.

- The finance function, which earmarks potential funds sources required to sustain investment, evaluates the return expected by each and selects the optimum mix which minimises their overall capital cost.

As a corollary, the uncertainty associated with the acquisition and disposition of funds under changing market conditions must also be related to the expected returns from investment. What is of ultimate concern to the firm is not profit *per se* but also the likelihood of it occurring. An acceptable relationship between risk and return may elicit a level of periodic profit, which may be constrained and unique to that company, yet optimal since it satisfies investor expectations.

The firm's investment function and finance function are interrelated via the company's cost of capital. From a financing viewpoint it represents the costs incurred in the employment of funds. A complex concept, it does not only concern explicit interest on borrowings or dividends paid to shareholders. Companies also finance their operations by utilising funds from a variety of sources, both long and short-term, at an implicit or opportunity cost. By definition, these should be identified and included in any overall cost of capital calculation because they represent money which firms have at their disposal in order to generate output. Such funds include trade credit granted by suppliers, deferred taxation, as well as retained earnings without which companies would presumably have to raise funds elsewhere. In addition, there are implicit costs associated with depreciation and other non-cash expenses. These too represent retentions which are available for reinvestment. In terms of the investment decision, the cost of capital represents an opportunity cost criterion which

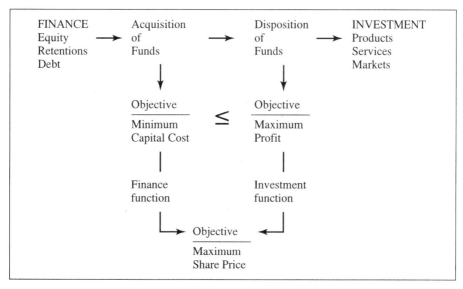

Fig 1.3 Corporate financial objectives

justifies the deployment of funds. Explained simply, a company wishing to make money profits would not wish to employ funds unless their marginal yield at least matched the rate of return its investors can earn elsewhere. This is illustrated in Figure 1.3.

3 FINANCIAL DECISION STRUCTURES

The foregoing suggests that corporate financial management should have as its objective the determination of a maximum inflow of cash profit and hence corporate value, commensurate with acceptable levels of risk associated with investment opportunities, having acquired capital in the most efficient (i.e. least costly) manner.

Decisions themselves can be subdivided into two broad categories: longer-term (strategic or tactical) and short-term (operational). The former may be unique, typically involving significant capital expenditure but uncertain future gains. Without sophisticated forecasts of required outlays and associated returns, period by period, which incorporate time value of money techniques and an allowance for risk, the subsequent penalty for error can be severe; in the extreme, corporate death.

Conversely, operational decisions tend to be repetitious, or infinitely divisible, so much so that funds may be acquired piecemeal. Costs and returns are usually quantifiable from existing data with any weaknesses in forecasting easily remedied. The decision itself may not be irreversible.

However, irrespective of the time horizon, the decision process should still involve:

(*i*)   The continual search for investment opportunities.

(*ii*) The selection of the most profitable opportunities, in absolute terms.

(*iii*) The determination of the optimal mix of internal and external funds required to finance those opportunities.

(*iv*) The establishment of a system of financial controls governing the allocation and use of funds.

(*v*)   The analysis of financial results as a guide to future decision-making.

Needless to say, none of these functions is independent of the others. All occupy a pivotal position in the decision-making process and naturally require co-ordination at the highest level. And this is where corporate financial management comes into play.

4 THE SCOPE OF CORPORATE FINANCE

The contemporary role of corporate financial management is best understood through an appreciation of its historical development. Chronologically, four main features can be discerned:

- Traditional
- Economic
- Systematic
- Behavioural

Traditionalists characterised pre-war thinking. Positive in approach (which means a concern with what is, rather than what should be) the discipline was Balance Sheet dominated. Financial management was presented textually as an essential classification and description of long-term sources of funds with instructions on how to acquire them, and at what cost. Any emphasis upon the use of funds was very much restricted to fixed asset investment using the established techniques of payback and accounting rate of return with their emphasis upon liquidity and profitability respectively. Unfortunately, like financial accounting to which it looked for inspiration, the subject lacked any normative objective or theoretical rationale for disposition of funds.

During the 1940s, however, there developed an awareness that numerous wide-ranging techniques (mathematical, statistical, logistical and behavioural) could be successfully applied to business. Spurred on by post-war recovery and the advent of computing, an increasing number of academics, preponderantly American, also began to refine and to apply the work of earlier economists, particularly discounted revenue theory and classical statistics, to the corporate environment. By the 1960s, this emphasis upon investor and shareholders' welfare produced competing theories of share price maximisation, optimal capital structure and the pricing of securities generally, all of which were subjected to exhaustive empirical research. Rigorous analytical techniques, based upon the random behaviour of economic variables, investor rationality and stock market efficiency, supplanted the conventional wisdom of accounting professionals in the finance literature. As a consequence, there emerged an academic consensus that the maximisation of shareholders' welfare, achievable through the maximisation of the net present value (NPV) of all a company's prospective capital investments, represents the prescribed objective of normative corporate finance.

Since the 1970s there has also been a significant awareness that the ebb and flow of finance through investor portfolios, corporate environments and global capital markets cannot be analysed in a technical vacuum characterised by equilibrium. Purposeful financial management, so the argument goes, must relate to all other functions within the chaotic system that it serves. Only then will it optimise the benefits which accrue to the system as a whole.

Proponents of this systematic approach, whose origins lie in management science, still emphasise the financial decision-maker's responsibility towards the maximisation of corporate value. However, their most recent work focuses upon the interaction of financial decisions within imperfect markets; more specifically, it questions the veracity of stock market efficiency which depends upon the recognition of simultaneous, interrelated flows of information and non-financial resources, as well as cash, throughout the system under scrutiny. Behavioural scientists, particularly communications theorists, have developed the approach still further by analysing the reaction of irrational individuals, firms and markets to the impersonal elements: cash, information and resources. Emphasis is placed upon the role of competing goals, expectations and choice in the decision process. The objective of current research is a better understanding of how the adaptive process determines investment, corporate and market performance, and *vice versa*.

Needless to say, none of the developments outlined above should be seen as mutually exclusive; all are discernible in corporate finance today. It is true that a particular development may be more appropriate for a particular area of management decision. Increasingly, however, various theoretical elements are being selected to provide a more eclectic approach to the decision process. Moreover, an historical perspective of the developments and changes that have occurred in the discipline can provide fresh insights into long-established practice.

Consider, for example, shareholders who unquestioningly utilise historical published accounting data without any adjustment in order to assess their corporate holdings. In one respect the approach can be defended, since evidence from the areas of share price determination suggests that variable dividend distributions are used by companies to convey information (sometimes falsely) concerning anticipated future profits. Whatever the truth of the matter, if a sufficient number of shareholders and potential investors believe these signals, it is likely that the demand for the company's shares will change. In the absence of any subsequent capital issues, the market valuation of equity will then follow suit, based only on market sentiment without any commensurate revision to tangible asset values or other trading fundamentals!

5 THE PLAN OF THE TEXT

The displacement of traditional academic degree structures by modularity and semester-based courses, all too often accompanied by a reduction in formal class contact, has created problems for teachers and students generally. The substantive content of corporate finance is also in the process of change, necessitating a reassessment of the fundamental assumptions that cut across the traditional boundaries of the subject. As a consequence, a number of texts on corporate finance have become too broad in scope *vis a vis* these new taught courses, whilst scholarly journal material and edited books of readings are now so academically refined as to confound an expanded university readership approaching the subject for the first time.

This study seeks to bridge the gap through a select coverage of the discipline's major components presented in the following order:

- The Investment decision
- The Dividend decision
- The Finance decision
- The Portfolio decision.

This sequence may depart from convention but it is believed by the author to make the subject much more accessible. It can also (and will) be defended academically.

For a more advanced readership, the text may also be viewed as a series of separate self-contained studies which can be combined to provide a coherent whole, thereby facilitating a flexible up-to-date treatise of current thinking on corporate finance.

The emphasis throughout is on a strong thematic structure which encompasses a normative analysis of corporate financial decisions with reference to classical and contemporary research. As a corollary, mathematical expositions are operationalised through simple numerical examples, uncluttered by unnecessary technical accounting detail, as well as more sophisticated study problems which articulate with the text.

PART TWO

The investment decision

2

Capital budgeting under conditions of certainty

Chapter profile

This chapter is concerned with the capital budgeting decisions which confront the firm and the means of evaluating proposed investments against a criteria of wealth maximisation. Four common techniques for selecting capital projects are explained:

- Payback
- Accounting Rate of Return (ARR)
- Internal Rate of Return (IRR)
- Net Present Value (NPV).

Incidentally, the concepts of annual benefit, the profitability index and discounted payback will also be discussed. However, the focus of attention will be on the time value of money and two common discounted cashflow (DCF) techniques used in project appraisal: IRR and NPV.

The mathematics of compound interest and discounting are presented. The concept of an investment's net terminal value (NTV) and its relationship to IRR and NPV as a key to understanding DCF analyses is explained. Procedures for ranking proposed investments under conditions of capital rationing, or where projects are mutually exclusive, are also introduced.

At a more technical level, certain practical problems associated with producing an economic appraisal based on incremental cashflows, rather than accrual accounting data, are described. These include the derivation of relevant cashflows using the opportunity cost concept, the impact of depreciation on corporate taxation and the incidence of predetermined rates of inflation and specific price changes.

The reader should appreciate, however, that the chapter's emphasis is *normative* in approach. The object is to explain how the decision-maker should behave, rather than to provide *positive* solutions to detailed investment decisions. For those concerned with what project managers do in practice, the text

Investment Appraisal by Mott (1997) referenced at the end of this chapter should serve as a useful introduction. The disparities which exist between theory and practice as revealed by empirical evidence, however, will be considered in Chapter 4.

1 INTRODUCTION

If it is assumed that the objective of corporate financial management is the maximisation of shareholders' wealth, the firm requires a consistent mechanism for measuring proposed investments and an appropriate criterion for their acceptance or rejection. Given this normative stance, the actual decision-maker is also perceived as a rational being who carefully assesses the net benefit to the shareholders of pursuing one course of action, rather than another.

Decisions themselves may be sub-divided into two broad categories: long-term (strategic or tactical) and short-term (operational). The latter are subsumed under the former, since they 'operationalise' strategy. Operational decisions are further distinguished by their tendency to repetition and divisibility. Their costs and revenues are also more amenable to quantification from historical data, with any weaknesses in forecasting frequently remedied. The decision itself may be reversible without any loss of goodwill.

In contrast, long-term investment decisions, which are the focus of this chapter, may be unique, irreversible, typically involve more significant capital expenditure, plus uncertain future gains. Without sophisticated forecasts of the required outlays and expected net returns, period by period, which incorporate inflation and an allowance for risk, the subsequent penalty for error can be severe; in the extreme, corporate death.

The strategic decision itself may be classified as follows:

(a) *Replacement*
The maintenance of operations at least at the *status quo* without compromising profitability. The decision may relate to the savings resulting from lower operating costs or the profit from additional volume produced by technological improvement compared with the cost of the investment.

(b) *Improvement*
Intended to generate additional revenue which would yield a satisfactory return on investment from alternative available technology.

(c) *Expansion*
Long-term comparisons of long-term returns inherent in increased profitable volume.

(**d**) *Buy or Lease*

Again, long-term profitability comparisons but in terms of alternative financing schemes.

(**e**) *Diversification*

Defined in terms of products, markets or alternate core technologies, set against the test of long-term profits.

With regard to each classification the distinguishing features are therefore:

- Long-term investment
- Large financial outlay
- Uncertainty

Of course, uncertainty is part of any decision, long or short, but the larger the investment and the further into the future its benefits are projected the greater its impact. When combined with inflation which may not be anticipated its effects are further magnified. Because of these added complexities the treatment of risk will be deferred until Chapter 4. What follows is an initial exposition of the investment decision process which concentrates upon the operational significance of capital budgeting techniques under conditions of certainty.

2 TRADITIONAL METHODS OF PROJECT EVALUATION

The term capital embraces physical and financial assets expressed in monetary terms. Budgeting may be defined as detailed quantified planning for commercial profit which requires management to make choices, if only because projects are mutually exclusive. A combination of the two terms relate, therefore, to the selective financing and deployment of capital assets for the purposes of maximum monetary benefit.

Typically, money capital is the controlling factor in any capital budgeting decision. Because funds are scarce, various projects are likely to be in competition. The existence of such *capital rationing* means, therefore, that each project must be ranked in terms of the relative long-term advantages it promises. To arrive at a decision, two conceptually simple methodologies are still in common usage: payback and the accounting rate of return.

Payback

The length of time required for a stream of cashflows to equal the original cost of an investment is termed its payback period. Assuming annual cashflows are constant, the formula is given by:

$$(1) \qquad P = \frac{I_0}{C_t}$$

where:

P = payback in years
I_0 = investment at time period 0
C_t = net cash inflow per annum.

Management then compare the payback period to some predetermined period of time within which they feel any investment should recoup its cost. This yardstick is a reflection of management's subjective attitude towards risk, and may differ from firm to firm. As an investment criteria, payback exclusively perceives the quality of an investment as an inverse function of time. The shorter the payback period the better the investment. However, consider the following investment decisions which confront a company with a payback criteria of three years.

Cashflows (£000s)	Year 0	Year 1	Year 2	Year 3
Investment A	(10,000)	5000	5000	5000
Investment B	(1000)	500	500	500

Both these investments have the same payback period of two years and would thus rank equally for acceptance. The criteria for payback is the sooner an investment is recovered the less any uncertainty regarding its worth. Intuitively however, Investment A is preferable. Whilst it delivers an identical rate of return in excess of cost after the payback date, its profit is higher in absolute terms.

Now consider two investments of equal size which elicit the same percentage rate of return and absolute profit in cash terms.

Cashflows (£000s)	Year 0	Year 1	Year 2	Year 3	Year 4
Investment A	(1000)	700	200	100	100
Investment B	(1000)	100	200	700	100

Again these investments have the same payback period but surely Investment A should still be preferred? To the recipient £700,000 in the first year has greater utility than £700,000 in the final year. Explained simply, payback not only emphasises liquidity at the expense of profitability but by emphasising total liquidity it also fails to take into account the timing and size of individual cashflows *prior* to the payback date.

Accounting rate of return

This ratio relates annual post-tax accounting profit (net of depreciation) to the cost of an investment, profitability being determined by historical accrual methods of financial accounting. Designed to overcome the deficiencies of payback, with which it is often used, a basic formula, where profits and depreciation are constant throughout the life of the project, is given by:

$$(2) \quad \overline{R} = \frac{P_t - D_t}{I_0}$$

where:

$\overline{R}$ = average accounting rate of return
P_t = annual book value profits before depreciation, net of tax
D_t = annual depreciation
I_0 = original investment at cost.

The ARR is then compared with a cut-off rate for investment (hurdle rate) predetermined by management as an acceptance criteria for capital projects. This rate may differ from company to company and be subject to revision, depending upon prevailing economic conditions.

Consider the following project data, where management employ a 10 per cent cut-off rate:

P_t = £20,000 per annum
D_t = £12,000 per annum
I_0 = £60,000.

Assume depreciation is calculated on a straight-line basis over the project's five year life, then

$$\overline{R} = \frac{£20,000 - £12,000}{£60,000} = 13.3\%$$

If there are no other projects in competition and an availability of funds, the project is acceptable.

When profits and depreciation vary from year to year over n periods, Equation (2) may be rewritten:

$$(3) \quad \overline{R} = \frac{\sum_{t=1}^{n}(P_t - D_t)/n}{I_0}$$

where the numerator represents the average post-tax profits, net of depreciation.

Of course, Equations (2) and (3) overstate the ARR to the extent that their denominators use the original cost of the investment, rather than the net book value of the project, as it moves forward in time. So, both equations can be modified by substituting the average undepreciated balance of the investment's cost into their respective right-hand terms to yield:

(4) $$\overline{R} = \frac{P_t - D_t}{\sum\limits_{t=0}^{n} I_t/n} = \frac{P_t - D_t}{I_0/2} \qquad \text{if depreciation is straight line}$$

or

(5) $$\overline{R} = \frac{\sum\limits_{t=1}^{n}(P_t - D_t)/n}{\sum\limits_{t=0}^{n} I_t/n} = \frac{\sum\limits_{t=1}^{n}(P_t - D_t)/n}{I_0/2} \qquad \text{if depreciation is straight line}$$

Using the figures from the previous example, the net book values for the investment I_t are:

Year	I_t(£000s)
0	60
1	48
2	36
3	24
4	12
5	–
$\sum\limits_{t=1}^{n} I_t$	$\underline{180}$

Thus

$$\sum\limits_{t=0}^{n} I_t/n = £180,000/6 = £30,000$$

or alternatively, given straight line depreciation (rather than the sum of the digits, declining balance or some other method):

$$I_0/2 = £60,000/2 = £30,000$$

and from either Equation (4) or (5) the ARR for this example is equivalent to:

$$\overline{R} = \frac{£8000}{£30,000} = 26.7\%$$

If a project exhibits a residual value, S_n, at the end of its useful life (i.e. scrap or salvage) this too should be incorporated into the appropriate ARR calculation. For example, Equation (4), which is applicable to the illustration, becomes:

(6) $$\overline{R} = \frac{P_t - D_t}{(I_0 - S_n)/2}$$

such that if the project's residual value $S_n = \pounds12,000$:

$$\overline{R} = \frac{\pounds8000}{\pounds48,000/2} = 33.3\%$$

As a complement to payback, the advantages of the various ARR methods are their simplicity and utility. Each successive equation is designed to reflect more accurately the average undepreciated cost of an investment, based on generally accepted accounting principles. However, therein lies their downfall.

Two firms considering an identical investment project in cashflow terms, which is acceptable using shared payback criteria, could arrive at different accept or reject decisions, simply because their preferred accounting procedures may differ. It will be recalled from the previous example that, by substituting the depreciated balances for the original cost of the investment, the ARR doubled from 13.33 per cent to 26.7 per cent for the same project, without any change in its efficiency.

The ARR also relies on historical cost accounting (HCA) methods developed for the purposes of determining accrued income within the context of the stewardship function of management. This may bear little relation to either the true cashflow position of the project or the decline in the value of the investment throughout its life. Even in the absence of overall inflation, accounting income will rarely equal economic income, nor cost equal *value*, to the extent that supply and demand factors and individual price changes specific to the project are ignored.

Of course, for the purposes of corporate decision-making, the use of a rate of return, however defined, is not without defect, irrespective of the weaknesses associated with financial accounting data. An emphasis upon indices of performance, rather than the corresponding absolute measures, raises the question of whether a larger return on say a small asset base is preferable to a smaller return on a larger amount, a familiar problem to those acquainted with the literature on divisional performance measurement.

The defect of any rate of return is that it may be increased by reducing the denominator, as well as by increasing the numerator. Moreover, it is possible to increase profits and reduce return on investment if the denominator grows more rapidly than the numerator. Thus, if a firm wishes to maximise its ARR, and capital can be varied, it will only increase its asset base if the marginal

19

profitability of new investment at least equals the last project's rate of return. In the extreme, the ARR would be maximised by reducing investment until all that remained was the single highest yielding project. By contrast, if absolute profits are the relevant measure, they would be maximised providing any new project showed any positive return, however small. Only if a firm's investment is fixed will maximising its rate of return become equivalent to maximising absolute profits. This assumption is unrealistic, however, except possibly for divisions within a company with little autonomy, since increases in the asset base are inherent in the investment decisions of most firms.

Further caution is required concerning the interpretation of an ARR because capital projects take place in a time continuum. By averaging the periodic rates of return on an investment, regardless of how far into the future they are realised, the ARR not only fails to discriminate between projects of different duration, but also introduces bias into individual projects.

As a simple average of its periodic returns, a project's overall ARR for n periods can be determined by calculating:

(7) $$\overline{R} = \sum_{t=1}^{n} r_t/n$$ where r_t = the periodic return on investment

Consider then two projects, A and B, with equal lives which are *mutually exclusive*, i.e. the acceptance of one precludes the acceptance of the other. The company's cut-off rate for investment is 10 per cent. Their ARRs are calculated using Equation (7) as follows:

$$ARR_A = (5\% + 10\% + 15\%)/3 = 10\%$$
$$ARR_B = (15\% + 10\% + 5\%)/3 = 10\%$$

Ignoring any problems associated with interpreting the rates of return for projects of different size, if the firm's objective is ARR maximisation, both projects are equally acceptable. Yet, project B delivers the bulk of its return earlier than A. In other words, either ARR_A is overstated, or ARR_B is understated, or both are incorrect!

The point is that the ARR shares the same fundamental weakness as payback. If they are to have any economic significance at all, both must attach a weighting to the timing of their respective costs and benefits, period by period throughout the life of a project.

3 THE TIME VALUE OF MONEY CONCEPT

The economic concept of *present value* (PV), based upon the principles of compound interest and discounted revenue theory contained in Irving Fisher's classic text (1930), recognises the importance of time in assessing investment opportunities. Even in a world of complete certainty without purchasing power risk (neither inflation nor deflation), £1.00 today is still worth more than £1.00 received after one year. Because money is a scarce economic commodity, its supply and demand characteristics manifest themselves in a market rate of interest over time. If you possess more than you need, £1.00 today can be invested to produce capital growth next year. Conversely, when you need more than you possess, you can borrow. Thus, the present value (PV) of £1.00 repayed in one year's time is worth less than £1.00 lent today. The repayment includes the principal plus interest. The loan is the principal or capital only.

The derivation of an appropriate rate of interest (borrowing) or a rate of return (lending) is a complex phenomena which will be introduced later in the chapter and developed throughout the remainder of the text. However, it is important to distinguish at the outset between borrowing or lending rates, as opposed to the cost of funds.

The cost of funds is a function of three variables:

(*i*)   the amount borrowed
(*ii*) the market rate of interest (the lender's desired rate of return)
(*iii*) the repayment period.

£100 borrowed at six per cent for one year requires repayment of £106. In other words, £100 today is equivalent to £106 one year hence, under the conditions stated. The value of money has changed with time simply because of what one can do with it. Reformulating the problem, the net cash benefits from an investment may be defined as the value today of sums of money to be received in the future. The present value of a six per cent investment yielding £106 one year from now is £100. In both cases the cost of funds is £6.00.

But what if a second mutually exclusive investment proposal exhibited the same monetary values multiplied by a factor of 1000 (say). The interest rate (rate of return) would still be six per cent but the interest repayment (cost of funds) would be £6000, juxtaposed against a loan of £100,000. Would the reader be indifferent between this and the original investment, either as a borrower or a lender? This is mentioned not only because it readdresses the problem of using relative measures of performance in the form of percentages *vis a vis* absolute values but also because it introduces the concept of an individual's changing attitude towards the magnitude of an investment.

4 THE MATHEMATICS OF PRESENT VALUE

It will be shown in due course that, correctly applied, the time value of money concept formally acknowledges that different cash amounts paid and received at different points in time possess different present values which can measure their utility to the parties to a transaction.

For the moment, using the techniques of compound interest, a future value (the repayment) may be regarded as equivalent to a present sum (the loan) invested at a constant compound rate of interest over a number of periods. Expressed mathematically:

(8) $FV_n = PV(1 + r)^n$

where:
   FV_n = future value at time period n
   PV = present value at time period 0
      r = rate of interest (expressed as a proportion and not a percentage)
      n = number of periods

Conversely, the present value of an investment is determined by reducing the sum of money to be received in the future to a present value using the following formulation:

(9) $PV_n = \dfrac{FV_n}{(1 + r)^n}$

which is simply a rearrangement of Equation (8).
   The following examples should clarify matters:

(a) The future value (FV) of £1.00 invested per annum over five years at 10%; Equation (8):

	Formulae	£
Year 1	$(1.1)^1$	1.1000
Year 2	$(1.1)^2$	1.2100
Year 3	$(1.1)^3$	1.3310
Year 4	$(1.1)^4$	1.4641
Year 5	$(1.1)^5$	1.6105

(b) The present value (PV) of £1.00 receivable at future dates, assuming a rate of interest of 10%; Equation (9):

	Formulae	£
Year 1	$\dfrac{£1.00}{1.1000}$	0.9091
Year 2	$\dfrac{£1.00}{1.2100}$	0.8264
Year 3	$\dfrac{£1.00}{1.3310}$	0.7513

Year 4	$\dfrac{£1.00}{1.4641}$	0.6830
Year 5	$\dfrac{£1.00}{1.6105}$	0.6209

So what if various sums of money are to be received (or repayed) annually, rather than as a lump sum at the end of a period of time?

The link between a PV and periodic future sums is still the rate of interest. Using an appropriate interest rate, future income can be reduced to a present value as follows:

$$(10) \qquad PV_n = \sum_{t=1}^{n} \frac{C_t}{(1+r)^t}$$

where:

PV_n = present value of future cashflows
r = rate of interest
n = number of future years, with $t = 1, 2 \dots n$
C_t = cash inflows receivable in the future at time period t.

The equation is again a mirror image of compound interest, because if ΣC_t represents the variable sum of cashflows receivable in the future, then their PV must be the principal invested at the requisite rate of interest.

When equal annual amounts are to be received at regular annual intervals, i.e. an *annuity*, the future value of £1.00 per period for n periods is given by:

$$(11) \qquad FV_{An} = \sum_{t=1}^{n} (1+r)^{n-t} = \frac{(1+r)^n - 1}{r}$$

Conversely, the present value of a regular annuity of £1.00 per period for n periods is:

$$PV_{An} = \frac{1}{(1+r)} + \frac{1}{(1+r)^2} + \frac{1}{(1+r)^3} \dots + \dots \frac{1}{(1+r)^n}$$

$$= \sum_{t=1}^{n} \frac{1}{(1+r)^t}$$

which is equivalent to:

$$(12) \qquad PV_{An} = \frac{1 - 1/(1+r)^n}{r} = \frac{1 - (1+r)^{-n}}{r}$$

Thus, the present value of a 10 per cent annuity produces £1.00 annually for five years:

$$PV_{A5} = £0.9091 + £0.8264 + £0.7513 + £0.6830 + £0.6209$$

$$= \frac{1 - 1/(1.10)^5}{0.10} = £3.79$$

The analysis can also be extended to determine the present value of £1.00 to be received in perpetuity. The equation for a perpetual annuity is given by:

(13) $$PV_{A\infty} = \frac{1 - 1/(1 + r)^{\infty}}{r}$$

However, the present value of £1.00 received at infinity ∞ is very close to zero. Algebraically:

$$\frac{1}{(1 + r)^{\infty}} \longrightarrow 0$$

so that Equation (13) reduces to:

(14) $$PV_{A\infty} = 1/r$$

For a perpetual annuity of £1.00 at an annual interest rate of 10 per cent:

$$PV_{A\infty} = 1/0.1 = £10.00$$

For a perpetual annuity representing any sum of money, C_t, to be received annually at a rate of interest, r, the general equation is given by:

(15) $$PV_{A\infty} = C_t/r$$

5 DISCOUNTED CASHFLOW (DCF) TABLES

The general mathematical procedure of dividing an income stream by a rate of interest (or return) to determine value is termed *capitalisation*. As a concept, its comprehension provides the key to understanding corporate finance. For example, the derivation of a constant rate of return in perpetuity is based on a reformulation of Equation (15) which solves for r:

(16) $$r = C_t/PV_{A\infty}$$

It also follows that if one has observations for the present value and r, the annuity can be determined as follows:

(17) $$C_t = PV_{A\infty} \times r$$

These simple techniques based upon the capitalisation concept will, therefore, resurface throughout the remainder of the text.

The reader should also be aware that the process of reducing any future sums to a present value by reference to a rate of interest over the appropriate period is also termed *discounting*. Thus, a discounted present value is represented by Equation (10): the equivalent of an amount invested today at an interest rate, r, to yield such future sums at the time periods specified.

Unlike payback and ARR the discounting concept provides methods of capital budgeting which take into account the timing of monetary inflows and monetary outflows over the entire life of a project. Moreover, to facilitate their use, instead of working with the formulae, the decision-maker can consult *discounted cash flow* (DCF) tables of varying degrees of sophistication. These reverse the logic of compound interest. Appendix 3 at the end of this text contains four tables which provide compound interest and DCF *factors* for the following four equations:

(18) $\quad FV_n = (1 + r)^n$ $\qquad$ Future value of £1.00 invested at alternative compound rates of interest at the end of n periods

(19) $\quad PV_n = \dfrac{1}{(1 + r)^n}$ $\qquad$ PV of £1.00 received after n periods discounted at an interest rate r

(20) $\quad FV_{An} = \dfrac{(1 + r)^n - 1}{r}$ $\qquad$ Future value of £1.00 invested annually for n periods at an interest rate r

(21) $\quad PV_{An} = \dfrac{1 - (1 + r)^{-n}}{r}$ $\qquad$ PV of £1.00 received annually for n periods discounted at an interest rate r.

The determination of the present value of any amount at a given *discount rate* for a given number of years consists of selecting the appropriate factor from the DCF tables and multiplying by the number of future £s being discounted.

Consider a situation where a bank agrees to lend an amount today at 10 per cent provided it is repaid £121,000 in two years time. The size of the original loan (the PV) can be determined as follows.

Using Equation (9):

$$PV = \frac{£121,000}{(1 + 0.1)^2} = £100,000$$

Using the PV table showing the value of £1.00 *after n* periods (Table 2):

$$PV = £121,000 \times 0.826 = £100,000$$

If the bank were considering a 10 per cent loan with equal annual repayments of £1000 pa over four years the amount borrowed would conform to Equation

(10):

$$PV = \frac{£1000}{1+0.1} + \frac{£1000}{(1+0.1)^2} + \frac{£1000}{(1+0.1)^3} + \frac{£1000}{(1+0.1)^4} = £3170$$

or using the appropriate factor from Table 4, which is a cumulative version of Table 2, showing the present value of £1.00 received *annually*:

$$PV = £1000 \times 3.170 = £3170$$

The latter problem can also be reformulated as a mortgage decision. If the bank were willing to lend £3170 today at 10 per cent how much would the borrower be required to pay in four equal instalments?

The cashflow annuity which when discounted is equivalent to a present value is termed the *annual benefit*. Algebraically, it may be determined by reference to the fundamental equation:

(10) $$PV = \sum_{t=1}^{n} \frac{C_t}{(1+r)^t}$$

where the annual benefit $C_t = C_1 = C_2, \ldots = C_n$ such that:

(22) $$PV = C_t \left(\frac{1-(1+r)^{-n}}{r} \right)$$

Using the figures:

$$£3170 = C_t(3.170)$$

and solving for C_t:

$$C_t = £1000$$

Alternatively using the appropriate factor from the annuity table:

$$C_t = £3170/3.170 = £1000$$

To visualise better the impact of the time value of money upon future cashflows the annual present values of £1000 are given below over four years discounted at 10 per cent.

Year	1	2	3	4
PV	£909	£820	£751	£683

These reveal that £1000 received annually is worth progressively less at present as realisation becomes more remote. This fact becomes very important in a situation of capital rationing when investments are being ranked in order of preference so that one may be selected. The total cashflows over their entire life may be identical, but their individual timing may be different with the result that one has a higher present value.

Consider the following:

Cashflows (£)	Year 1	Year 2	Year 3
Investment A	1000	900	500
Investment B	500	900	1000

With a common capital investment and discount rate, intuitively A would be preferable since:

PV A > PV B

The reader may care to confirm this.

6 INTERNAL RATE OF RETURN

There are two basic DCF approaches to investment appraisal: the internal rate of return method (IRR) and net present value (NPV).

In its simplest form the IRR method assumes that the annual cash inflows, cash outflows and life of a project are known with certainty. It then solves for a rate r which discounts future net cashflows for the appropriate number of periods back to a present value which equals the cost of the investment from which they arise. Using earlier notation:

$$(23) \qquad I_0 = \sum_{t=1}^{n} \frac{C_t}{(1+r)^t} \qquad (\text{or } PV - I_0 = 0)$$

where:
I_0 = cost of the investment today
C_t = net cash inflows receivable in the future at time period t
r = IRR
n = number of periods under observation, with $t = 1, 2 \ldots n$
PV = present value of future cash inflows discounted at r = IRR.

Projects are accepted if they satisfy the following conditions:

- IRR ⩾ Target rate of return
- IRR > Cost of capital.

By equating future cashflows to the cost of the investment, the IRR may be viewed as a break-even point, i.e. the maximum rate of interest required to finance a project if it is not to make a loss.

As an investment criterion, the IRR is analogous to a time-adjusted ARR based on anticipated cashflows, rather than accrual accounting data. Compared with a cut-off rate for investment (a hurdle rate), projects are selected according to the size of their IRRs under conditions of capital rationing or where a choice must be made between mutually exclusive alternatives. IRR maximisation is often favoured in practice where time value of money concepts are employed because investment decisions can be assessed by reference to percentages which are universally understood. Moreover, where the annual cashflows from an investment are equal in amount, the IRR may be approximated directly from PV annuity tables, quite simply, using the following formula:

(24) I_0/C_t

which represents a factor corresponding to the discount rate for the appropriate number of years.

Consider a decision to invest £60,000 to yield £20,000 net of tax per annum over five years:

$$I/C_t = \frac{60,000}{20,000} = 3.0$$

From the annuity table where $n = 5$, it can be seen that the project's IRR lies between 19 per cent (3.058) and 20 per cent (2.991). Thus, if the firm's cost of capital was 15 per cent the project would be acceptable.

Unfortunately, the IRR is not always so easy to compute and apply. Even where cashflows are equal in amount, because the factor may not correspond exactly to an appropriate figure in the PV annuity table, it may require a precise method of interpolation if projects are to be ranked accurately. And where cashflows are uneven, the factor computation cannot be used without smoothing the stream, which defeats the object of the exercise. Establishing the correct IRR must be determined either by repeatedly solving for r using Equation (23), preferably using a software program, or again by recourse to a method of interpolation. Even then, the IRR may be indeterminate, or not a real number.

Computational difficulties apart, as a relative measure of performance expressed as a percentage, the IRR shares the same weaknesses as the ARR. Maximising the IRR may cause a company to restrict itself to small rich projects which, for the reasons already given, can run counter to the objective of absolute wealth maximisation (a point further explored in the next chapter). The IRR model also assumes, quite restrictively, that under conditions of certainty:

(i)   Intermediate net cash inflow will be reinvested at a rate of return equal to the project's IRR.

(ii) All financing will be undertaken at a cost equal to the project's IRR.

In other words, reinvestment rates and capital costs are assumed to equal the

IRR. Moreover, these rates are assumed to remain constant over the life of the projects. Relax any of these assumptions and the IRR will change.

To illustrate the point, consider a project costing £1,952,000 yielding net cash inflows of £1,000,000 per annum over three years. The reader may care to confirm that this produces an IRR of 25 per cent. However, for this to equal the project's actual return, the pattern of borrowing and reinvestment which equates total cash inflows with total cash outflows must conform to the bank overdraft formulation in Table 2.1, which produces a cash balance of zero at the end of three years.

Summarising Table 2.1 (£000s):

Total cash inflows	1152
Total cash outflows	(1152)
Net terminal value	–

Thus, the break-even characteristic of the IRR equation is confirmed, i.e.

(23) $PV - I = 0$

Table 2.1 The bank overdraft formulation

Project (£000s)	Year 0	Year 1	Year 2	Year 3	
Outflow	(1952)				
Inflow		1000	1000	1000	
Borrowing (25%)					
Inflow	1952				
Outflow					
Interest		(488)	(488)	(488)	
Capital				(1952)	
Net Outflow				(1440)	
Net Inflow		512	512		
Reinvestment (25%)					
Inflow		512	512		
Interest					
t_{1-2}			128	128	(25% of 512 pa)
t_{2-3}				160	(25% of 512 + 128)
Outflow				(1440)	
Net Cashflow		512	640	(1152)	

Clearly, if funds had been borrowed at a rate in excess of 25%, the terminal bank balance or *net terminal value* (NTV) of the project would have been negative. Conversely, if reinvestment rates had exceeded 25%, the NTV would have been positive. However, the NTV is zero because capital costs and investment rates are assumed to equal the overall project return, which equates the cash inflows with cash outflows, i.e. the project's IRR.

7 NET PRESENT VALUE

Because of the computational difficulty frequently associated with the IRR, the use of *net present value* (NPV) techniques has emerged since the 1960s as an alternative approach to investment appraisal.

Rather than solve for a discount rate, the NPV method actually incorporates one into the PV calculation of Equation (23). This is also logical. An IRR in isolation has no meaning, since it is a relative measure calculated independently of any observable rate of return or cost of capital figure. It is also an averaging technique which depends only on the arithmetic relationship between cash inflows and outflows. To inject economic meaning into the model, the IRR itself has to be compared with a company's desired rate of return or capital cost. Far better, therefore, to discount future net cash inflows using one of the latter rates based on real world conditions to determine whether their present value today is greater or less than the cost of an investment. Clearly, if a positive NPV emerges, sometimes termed an *excess present value* (EPV), the project must be acceptable, since the amount represents a return expressed in absolute cash terms over and above the desired rate of return which is already incorporated in the discounting process.

Under conditions of certainty, the NPV model shares a number of assumptions with the IRR. The project's life and all cashflows are known and will not change. However, NPV further assumes that the discount rate (either the rate of interest or desired rate of return) can be correctly defined and will not change. More realistically than the IRR, the NPV model also assumes that:

(*i*)   Intermediate net cash inflows can be reinvested at the project's discount rate.

(*ii*) All financing is undertaken at the discount rate.

Of course, in common with the IRR, if any of these assumptions are relaxed the NPV so calculated becomes invalid.

Using earlier notation, the present value of net cash inflows less the cost of investment may be expressed mathematically as follows:

$$(25) \qquad NPV = \sum_{t=1}^{n} \frac{C_t}{(1+r)^t} - I_0 \qquad (\text{or } PV - I_0 = NPV)$$

where:

r = the discount rate, rather than the IRR which solves for a zero NPV.

Projects are accepted if:

- NPV > 0 where r is a cost of capital rate
- NPV $\geqslant$ 0 where r is a desired rate of return.

They are then ranked according to the size of their NPV under conditions of capital rationing or where a choice must be made between mutually exclusive alternatives. Thus, the model's objective function is NPV maximisation and not IRR maximisation.

Again, recourse can be made to DCF tables in order to calculate an NPV. Returning to the earlier decision to invest £60,000 to yield £20,000 net of tax per annum over five years, assume that management require a 15 per cent after tax return. Using the annuity table the NPV computation is a simple two-stage process:

(*i*)   Compute the PV of all future cash flows.
(*ii*)   Subtract the cost of investment from (*i*) above.

Thus:

C_t	DCF factor	PV	I_0	NPV
£20,000	3.352	£67,040	(£60,000)	£7040

This reveals that if they desire 15 per cent after tax, management would be willing to pay £67,040 for the pattern of cashflows promised when in fact they are paying only £60,000. The £7040 NPV is the amount by which the present worth of future cashflows exceeds the cost of the initial investment.

It is conceivable, however, that if there were enough smaller richer projects, albeit with smaller NPVs, which are not mutually exclusive these could be preferable to the one above when taken together. To facilitate comparisons between investment proposals of different magnitudes, NPV computations may, therefore, be expressed in percentage terms by using an NPV or EPV *index* which measures the NPV per £1.00 invested, i.e.:

$$(26) \qquad NPV \text{ index} = \frac{PV}{I_0}$$

So

$$\frac{PV}{I_0} = \frac{£67,040}{£60,000} = 1.117 \text{ or } 111.7\%$$

This might be compared with an alternative where:

$$\frac{PV}{I_0} = \frac{£12,000}{£10,000} = 1.2 \text{ or } 120\%$$

One can see that with £60,000 to invest the replication of the latter is preferable to the adoption of the former.

Conversely, in a situation of capital rationing, where money is the limiting factor, the NPV index is also a useful guide to the order in which projects should be selected if wealth is to be maximised, particularly if individual projects are divisible. For example, if a company has £16 million to invest and the following investments are being considered:

	A	B	C	D
I_0(£000s)	(4000)	(10,000)	(2500)	(8000)
NPV (£000s)	2320	1920	660	1760
NPV Index	0.58	0.19	0.26	0.22

their rankings in terms of NPV and the index subject to a single capital constraint would be:

	NPV (£000s)		NPV index (£000s)
A	2320	A	2320
B	1920	C	660
D (0.25)	440	D	1760
C	–	B (0.15)	288
	4680		5028

Thus, the selection of projects by the NPV index, rather than the NPV, produces a higher increase in corporate wealth. However, the reader should note that the index approach only applies to capital budgeting with a single constraint. When considering investment by stages or instalments over a period of years, then if capital is rationed in more than one year, it will be necessary to use linear programming techniques to arrive at the optimal investment decision. For a lucid introduction to the subject, see Brealy and Myers (1996).

8 NPV, IRR AND NET TERMINAL VALUE (NTV)

It is important to note that, like the IRR, the NPV (although expressed in monetary terms) is still an abstract concept, whose fundamental assumptions concerning borrowing and lending rates are frequently misunderstood.

Consider the project cashflows from the earlier bank overdraft formulation:

Time period	t_0	t_1	t_2	t_3
Cashflows, £000s	(1952)	1000	1000	1000

The reader can now affirm that, if the project's desired rate of return is 25 per cent, the project's NPV is zero. However, using the bank overdraft formulation, this is only true if both the borrowing and reinvestment rates associated with the project are also 25 per cent throughout the project's life. If not, the NPV will differ, just as it would if the project's discount rate was different to 25 per cent.

It is also apparent that, because the project's NPV is zero, the discount rate must equal the project's IRR, provided all the conditions of both models are satisfied. Remember that the IRR solves for a discount rate which equates the present value of future cashflows with the cost of an investment.

From Equation (23):

(23) $PV = I_0$ where $r = IRR$

Rearranging terms, it therefore follows that:

(27) $PV - I_0 = NPV = 0$ where $r = IRR$

To clarify matters further, it will also be recalled from the IRR discussion that the cash balance at the end of a project's life is defined as its *net terminal value* (NTV). This is zero if the project has been discounted at its IRR. Thus, from Equation (27)

(28) $NPV = NTV = 0$ where $r = IRR$

So what is the relationship between NPV and NTV if the discount rate does not equal the IRR?

As stated earlier, the NPV of a project is an abstract monetary concept. What it represents is the cash surplus at the end of a project's duration expressed in today's terms. Discounting the NTV back to a present value over the life of the project, at either the appropriate cost of capital or desired rate of return, must, therefore, produce its NPV. Expressed mathematically:

(29) $NPV = \dfrac{NTV}{(1 + r)^n}$

Conversely, using the techniques of compound interest, the NPV is equal to a sum of money today which, if invested at the project's discount rate over its life, would produce its NTV. This is given by:

(30) $NPV(1 + r)^n = NTV$

It should now be obvious why a project with a NPV of zero has a NTV of zero. If there is no cash surplus at the end of its life there can be no NPV. However, if, for example, a project with a life of three years, discounted at 10 per cent, produces a cash balance of £944 its present value must be £709.30. This can be ascertained either by reference to Equation (29), or the appropriate DCF factor contained in the Appendix.

$$NPV = \frac{£944}{(1.1)^3} = £944 \times 0.7513 = £709.30$$

Conversely, using the mathematics of compound interest or the factor from Table 1 in the Appendix:

$$NTV = £709.30(1.1)^3 = £709.30 \times 1.3310 = £944$$

Of course, the preceding analysis does not negate the fact that NPV remains an abstract concept. But it does explain a common source of confusion associated with its use. So should decision-makers avoid the problem altogether and construct a capital budgeting model which explicitly compares closing cash balances with an objective function which maximises NTV?

The answer is not so simple. Because money is a scarce commodity with a present value which is inversely related to its future receipt, it is not possible to rank the NTVs for different projects with different lives without invoking the time value of money concept. To illustrate the point, consider two projects, A and B, only one of which can be chosen, which exhibit the following characteristics: based on a bank overdraft formulation:

Project	Year 3	Year 5
NTV_A	£944	
NTV_B		£1000

Since $NTV_B > NTV_A$, project B would seem preferable. Unfortunately, this may conflict with wealth maximisation criteria.

Assume that over the five-year period the prevailing discount rate which is applicable to both projects is 10 per cent (i.e. intermediate borrowing and reinvestment rates also equal 10 per cent). This means that at time period three the firm has the opportunity to reinvest £944 at a 10 per cent compound rate of interest for two years. From Equation (8) or tables it now becomes apparent that project A is more valuable than project B because:

$$£944 \times 1.1^2 = £944 \times 1.21 = £1142.24 > £1000$$

But the direction of this inequality is precisely what NPV would reveal. Rather than extend the original analysis to a common *terminal* date, NPV expresses future values in terms of a uniform *present* date using a one-stage process. Of course, the project manager may wish to confirm the NTV's either by Equation (30) or compound interest factors. In the example, the basis of the calculations would be NPVs of £709.30 and £620.90 for A and B respectively. This is corroborated by our prior knowledge of the NTVs for A and B and the application of Equation (29) since:

$$NPV_A = £944/(1.1)^3 = £944 \times 0.7513 = £709.30$$
$$NPV_B = £1000/(1.1)^5 = £1000 \times 0.6209 = £620.90$$

The point is that because $NPV_A > NPV_B$, wealth is maximised by selecting project A because this will produce a higher cash surplus at the end of five years.

9 RELEVANT CASHFLOWS: AN OVERVIEW

So far, this chapter has explained how the basic DCF techniques of IRR and NPV represent a significant improvement over the more traditional methods of payback and accounting rate of return (ARR) for the purposes of capital budgeting. Based upon the time value of money concept, the DCF techniques analyse the value today, of sums of money to be received in the future, with certainty, from a current investment in productive resources.

However, reservations have been expressed concerning the computational difficulties associated with IRR and its use as a wealth maximisation criteria in relation to NPV. If a company is to maximise its wealth on behalf of the shareholders through an inflow of long-term cash profit, it should do so in *absolute* terms. This is because an investment is probably worth undertaking if the periodic present value of total revenue less total costs exceeds the initial capital outlay, irrespective of its rate of return. Under conditions of capital rationing, though, management should only select projects which contribute to the maximisation of the net present value (NPV) of all a company's prospective capital investments.

Opportunity costs

It is also important to realise that, even under conditions of certainty, NPV maximisation not only requires the determination of the explicit, physical cashflows which enter into a decision but also the implicit or opportunity flows in real terms.

A complex concept, opportunity value and cost identifies either those benefits which are sacrificed or those costs which are unavoidable if a project is undertaken. Thus, if there are revenues or expenses which are unaffected by any new decisions they do not enter into the NPV calculation. The key phrase is 'what difference does it make', i.e. are they incremental?

It follows, *inter alia*, that the historical cost concept developed for the stewardship function of external financial reporting upon which the ARR depends, is irrelevant for decision purposes and not simply because a summation of monetary values from different periods may have little economic meaning.

Historical cost, net book values derived thereof and associated expenses are 'sunk' costs. Even replacement costs (net or otherwise) may not be strictly aggregable in situations where an item is used jointly with others to provide a single revenue flow. The measure to use for any input into a decision is that of its next best alternative use or, alternatively, the profit foregone.

Hence, if current stocks of inventory have no realisable value but can be used for a specific project, then their cost must be incorporated into any calculation as nil. Equally, if a firm has alternative uses for a factor which is not available on the open market then this might place the opportunity cost above market price.

For example, equipment costing £40,000 a year ago may be worth only £10,000 currently, due to obsolescence. Yet, it might be substitutable for something else which could reduce costs by £20,000. Thus, its value to the firm is £20,000.

Likewise, where there is a capital item worth say £1 million, which can be used for projects A, B and C, the higher profit foregone on A and B, if C is to be taken up, must be incorporated into the calculation of the latter's opportunity cost.

Depreciation and corporate taxation

Since the test for opportunity cost as an operational concept focuses upon what is incremental or otherwise, it also follows that depreciation should be added back to accounting profit in all DCF calculations. By definition, it does not represent a separate cash outlay over the life of a project. It is merely a form of retained earnings designed to recoup the cost of an investment.

However, since depreciation, or more correctly capital allowances, reduces accounting profit for tax purposes, and taxation represents a cash outflow, it must be taken into account when calculating net of tax cash inflows.

By way of illustration consider a five-year investment project where:

Capital investment = £60,000
Depreciation   = £12,000 per annum
Accounting profit = £8000 per annum, net of tax and depreciation.

Assuming that corporation tax is 50 per cent and a 100 per cent capital allowance is spread over five years, the conventional accounting profit for tax purposes may be compared with the true cash flow as follows:

	Taxable income £	Cashflow £
Gross profit	28,000	28,000
less capital allowance	12,000	
Pre-tax profit	16,000	
Corporation tax	8,000	(8,000)
Post-tax profit	8,000	20,000

Had depreciation or capital allowance not been deducted from the first column the tax liability would have been £14,000 (50 per cent of £28,000) and net cashflow £14,000. As it is, £6000 of the cashflow is retained because the 50 per cent tax rate is applied to the depreciation-adjusted profit figure. In other words, depreciation acts as a *tax shield* by reducing the company's corporate tax liability.

There is of course another aspect of taxation which has a bearing upon DCF calculations, namely the timing of the tax payment to the fiscal authorities. In the UK this can occur between nine and twenty one months after income has been earned. Assuming a twelve month delay, an accurate picture of the cashflow pattern relating to the £60,000 investment which determines the project's NPV would not be represented by net receipts of £20,000 per annum over five years but by the following schedule:

Time period	t_0	t_1	t_2	t_3	t_4	t_5	t_6
Inflow (£)	–	28,000	28,000	28,000	28,000	28,000	–
Outflow (£)	(60,000)	–	(8,000)	(8,000)	(8,000)	(8,000)	(8,000)
Net flow (£)	(60,000)	28,000	20,000	20,000	20,000	20,000	(8,000)

Working capital

Within the context of PV analyses, the timing of the incremental cash receipts and payments relating to the amount of working capital which is required to sustain a project must also be considered.

Working capital should be included as a cash outflow in year 0 with adjustments in subsequent years for the net investment required to finance inventory, debtors and precautionary cash balances, less creditors caused by acceptance of the project. At the end of the project's life the funds still tied up in working capital are released for use elsewhere in the business. This amount should therefore be shown as a cash inflow in the last year or thereafter, when made available. The net effect of these working capital adjustments is to charge to the project the interest foregone (opportunity cost) on the funds which are invested throughout the entire life of the project.

10 INFLATION AND DCF

Whilst it is absolutely essential that project data is cast in incremental (opportunity cost) cash terms, another common mistake in investment appraisal is to calculate the NPV using current (nominal) cashflows without any adjustment for changing price levels. Yet it has long been appreciated, particularly by investors, that to draw up a list of assets and liabilities in a Balance Sheet when the individual items may be expressed in money at different dates or to compare revenues and expenses in an Income and Appropriation Account, may be likened to an attempt to add or subtract amounts which are expressed in different currencies.

This arises for two quite distinct reasons. First, the value of money may change, irrespective of how it is spent; the phenomenon known as inflation. Second, the value of money may change over time when it is spent on particular items. It is also important to realise that inflation only manifests itself when a sufficient number of specific goods and services increase sufficiently in price. By contrast, the price of a particular item might change even in the absence of inflation and for quite different reasons, such as technological innovation. Moreover, this individual price change may have little, or no effect on the overall rate of inflation.

Applied to capital budgeting:

- A predetermined inflation rate represents an anticipated reduction in the overall purchasing power of money reflected in a general price index such as the RPI. This can be reinstated by an upward revision of a discount rate based on the *real* (nominal) rate of interest which reflects zero inflation to the *money* rate of interest which compensates for this. Alternatively, the company can refer to *market* rates of interest which are also money rates because they already incorporate purchasing power losses anticipated by investors.
- Specific price changes affect a firm's future individual cashflows. Current (real) cashflows must be inflated by an appropriate index of specific prices to arrive at their forecast money cashflows.

It is worth recalling the fundamental concept of the time value of money. Even with zero inflation and constant prices, £1.00 today is worth more than £1.00 received in one year's time because money is a scarce commodity. The link between the two is the real rate of interest. By foregoing current consumption of goods and services generally, in favour of investment, an individual can consume more in the future. However, as Fisher noted (1930), this extra future consumption which stems from investing at real rates of interest will be eroded if there is a rise in general prices. Investors will require even more money in the future to buy the same quantity of goods and services.

To compensate for this phenomenon, Fisher defined a general model of the relationship between the money rate of interest (market rate), denoted by m, and the real rate of interest r, when i is the general rate of inflation. This is given by:

(31) $(1 + m) = (1 + r)(1 + i)$

So, if the real rate of interest is 10 per cent and the rate of inflation is 5 per cent: the market rate of interest is derived from:

$$(1 + m) = (1 + 0.1)(1 + 0.05) = 1.155$$
$$m = 15.5\%$$

Within the context of capital budgeting the NPV is now found by discounting money cashflows at the money market rate of interest.

To illustrate the *Fisher effect* consider a company with £5 million to invest subject to capital appreciation of 10 per cent in present value terms (i.e. an NPV index of 1.1). The incremental cash revenues over the next four years relating to a project in terms of current prices are expected to be £2 million per annum. The discount rate, representing the real cost of capital, is 20 per cent. The NPV is calculated in the usual way:

Year	Cashflow £000s	Discount factor	Present value £000s
0	(5000)		5000.0
1–4	2000	2.5887	5177.4
NPV			177.4
NPV index			0.035

Whilst the project delivers a return in excess of cost, on the strength of the profitability index of 3.5 per cent in relation to a 10 per cent NPV criteria per £1.00 invested, the proposal would be rejected.

Now assume that for the duration of the project the rate of inflation is estimated to be 10 per cent per annum but that all the individual cashflows are expected to be affected by an annual rise in specific prices of 20 per cent. The investment proposal should be reformulated as follows:

With a money rate of interest of 32 per cent given by:

$$(1 + m) = (1 + 0.2)(1.1) = 1.32$$

Year	Current cashflows	Specific price index (20%)	Money cashflows	Money cost of capital factor (32%)	PV
0	(5000)	1.0	(5000)	1.0	(5000)
1	2000	1.20	2400.0	0.7576	1818.24
2	2000	1.44	2880.0	0.5739	1652.83
3	2000	1.7280	3456.0	0.4348	1502.67
4	2000	2.0736	4147.2	0.3294	1366.02
NPV					1339.83
NPV index					0.26

The original decision has now been reversed. Since the 26 per cent NPV index exceeds the investment criterion of 10 per cent, the project would be accepted.

Rather than discount money cashflows by the money rate of interest, there is an alternative way of approaching the problem. Money cashflows can be discounted by the general rate of interest to produce real cashflows which are then discounted at the real rate of interest.

Expressing the information contained in the previous table algebraically, the NPV of money cashflows is given by:

(32) $$NPV = \sum_{t=1}^{n} \frac{M_t}{(1 + m)^t} - I_0$$

where:
M_t = actual money cashflows
$(1 + m) = (1 + r)(1 + i)$.

Thus, it follows that using the second procedure:

(33) $$NPV = \sum_{t=1}^{n} \frac{M_t/(1 + i)^t}{(1 + r)^t} - I_0$$

So which method is preferable? All one can say is why bother to discount twice when the first method represents a single-stage process?

However, it is interesting to note from the preceding equations that if specific price changes shadowed the rate of inflation the two would cancel each other out. The specific price index (a compound factor) which is applied to the real cashflows would conform to the inflation component, $(1 + i)$, of the money discount rate. Thus, the price-adjusted NPV equation would simplify and be equivalent to the original NPV formulation in the presence of zero inflation and constant prices.

$$(25) \quad NPV = \sum_{t=1}^{n} \frac{C_t}{(1+r)^t} - I_0$$

The reader may care to confirm that if the specific price index in the original example was compounded at 10 per cent per annum, rather than 20 per cent, but the rate of inflation was still a uniform 10 per cent per annum, the money NPV would equal the original NPV based on current prices discounted at the real rate of interest.

Finally, the reader should appreciate that, for the purposes of exposition, the preceding analysis has been undertaken under restrictive conditions. If each specific price is expected to rise at a differential rate, each component cashflow must be adjusted accordingly. Similarly, differential inflation rates are best incorporated into the capital budgeting process by combining money cashflows which are subject to the same inflation rate. Next establish the particular discount rates corresponding to each rate of inflation. The PV of each cashflow can then be determined separately and combined to give an NPV figure. (The numerical example in Appendix 1 should clarify matters.)

11 SUMMARY AND CONCLUSIONS

This chapter has explained how the basic DCF techniques of internal rate of return (IRR) and net present value (NPV) represent a significant improvement over the payback and accounting rate of return (ARR) methodologies for the purposes of capital budgeting. Based upon the time value of money concept, both the IRR and NPV analyse the value today of sums of money to be received in the future with certainty from a current investment in productive resources.

Table 2.2 Capital budgeting models

Model	Objective	Investment criteria
Payback	Minimise payback (Maximise liquidity)	Time
ARR	Maximise ARR	Profitability percentage
IRR	Maximise IRR	Profitability percentage
NPV	Maximise NPV	Absolute profits

Table 2.2 summarises the objective functions and measurement criteria of the four approaches.

The data requirements of the ARR differ from payback, IRR and NPV, being accrual rather than cashflow based. Whilst payback in its rudimentary form ignores the time value of money it can be calculated using discounted cashflows to provide a more realistic assessment of a project's liquidity. Unfortunately it still ignores profitability beyond the payback date.

Neither payback nor ARR maximise wealth. As a relative measure of performance expressed as a percentage rather than absolute profits IRR, too, shares the same dysfunctions as the ARR. Faced with a choice, if the incremental (opportunity) money cashflows for a project are correctly defined, an NPV analysis is therefore preferable. By incorporating discount rates which are based on money (market) rates of interest into present value (PV) calculations, it is free from the computational difficulties associated with the IRR, which solves for such rates.

Although mathematically complex on first acquaintance, it must be emphasised that the NPV approach to capital budgeting (like the IRR, ARR and payback) is still a financial decision model which is an abstraction of the real world. By selecting appropriate data from complex situations there is an inevitable loss of detail. Moreover, under conditions of complete certainty NPV assumes that for a particular project:

- The cost of the investment is known.
- The investment life is known and will not change.
- Cashflows are known.
- Price level changes are predetermined.
- Discount rates based on market rates of interest can be correctly defined and will not change.
- Borrowing and reinvestment rates equal the discount rates.
- A firm has access to unlimited cash resources, since once existing funds are exhausted the firm can borrow at the market rate of interest.

Relax any one of these assumptions and the result of a NPV calculation is invalidated. A number of techniques based upon probability theory, utility theory, sensitivity analysis and computer simulation (which are all explained in Chapter 4) can reduce, if not eliminate, uncertainty. The derivation of desired rates of return and market rates of interest is a more contentious matter on which there is still no unanimity of opinion. It will, therefore, resurface throughout the remainder of this text. To bring the current discussion on NPV to a satisfactory conclusion, however, it remains to consider why the normative objective of corporate finance, namely the maximisation of shareholders' wealth, is synonymous with the maximisation of the NPV of all a company's investments. This will be addressed in Chapter 3.

References

(1) Brealy, R.A. and Myers, S.C., *Principles of Corporate Finance,* McGraw Hill, 1996.

(2) Fisher, I., *The Theory of Interest,* Macmillan, 1930

(3) Mott. G., *Investment Appraisal,* Financial Times Pitman Publishing, 1997.

3

Net present value versus internal rate of return

Chapter profile

This chapter begins with the presentation of the Separation Theorem which explains why corporate investment decisions need not conflict with the normative objective of shareholder wealth maximisation. The fundamental provisos are that capital markets are perfect and the discount rate is defined as an opportunity cost of capital.

Although attention is still restricted to a consideration of decision-making under conditions of certainty, it is also shown how the two rival methods of project appraisal based upon the time value of money, IRR and NPV, may elicit different ranking and acceptance signals in the presence of capital rationing, or where projects are mutually exclusive and generate cashflows beyond a single period.

Unlike the IRR approach, which also suffers from a number of computational difficulties, the NPV methodology allied to NPV maximisation is shown to be entirely consistent with the stated objective of maximisation of shareholders' wealth, provided the correct discount rate (or rates) are incorporated into the firm's investment decision model under the conditions stated.

1 INTRODUCTION

In Chapter 1 a case was presented for the pursuit of shareholders' wealth maximisation, rather than any other stakeholders, as the fundamental objective of corporate management. The previous chapter also suggested that, under conditions of certainty, the use of NPV maximisation as an investment appraisal criteria appears entirely consistent with this objective, since it maximises profit in absolute terms. Under a number of economic conditions, notably capital rationing, its main rival IRR was found to produce conflicting accept or reject signals when applied to the same project proposals. The purpose of this chapter is to explain why.

As a precursor to this discussion, however, it is first necessary to expand upon why, even in a world of certainty, if ownership is divorced from control, a company's investment decisions can be determined independently from the personal preferences of a multiplicity of shareholders.

2 INVESTOR WEALTH AND UTILITY

Wealth maximisation criteria enable individuals (or the management of firms) to maximise their consumption preferences by adjusting their income streams over time. If an individual's income stream exceeds the optimal pattern for current consumption that person can invest in productive assets, or lend the income surplus. Alternatively, if the desire for current consumption exceeds the income stream, the individual can either reduce their current stock of wealth (forego the future consumption of income) by realising assets, or borrowing to obtain the necessary funds.

Ignoring for the moment borrowing and lending opportunities, Figure 3.1 illustrates the choice of productive investment opportunities available to an individual relative to their preference for current consumption which maximises utility.

The curve W_0–W_1 is termed the *physical investment line* and plots their current wealth against future wealth over a single period. W_0 represents maximum consumption from a given stock of wealth (zero investment), W_1 represents maximum wealth at the end of the period (zero consumption). Between the two, the opportunity locus, W_0–W_1, represent the numerous more realistic combinations of consumption and investment which confront the individual. Point E represents an assumed preferred (optimum) combination for

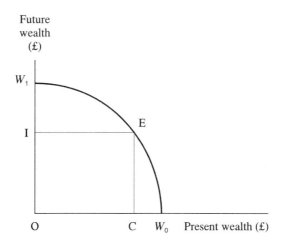

Fig 3.1 Wealth, consumption and investment

that individual. O – C on the horizontal axis represents current consumption in monetary terms. $C-W_0$ represents current consumption foregone (investment) to produce a stock of wealth at the end of the period, given by O–I on the vertical axis.

It is important to note that the physical investment line is a curve and not a straight line. Assuming that the individual is rational, the first investment selected would be that which produces the highest future yield (i.e. incremental income stream). Thereafter, if the economic law of *diminishing returns* sets in, the marginal productivity of further investment opportunities declines. This explains why companies should select capital projects which maximise absolute profits if they wish to maximise wealth.

So how is the individual's preference for current consumption *vis a vis* future consumption calibrated? Figure 3.2 superimposes different utility *indifference* curves for the individual over the physical investment line, W_0-W_1, from Figure 3.1. Each point along the curves corresponds to a combination of present and future wealth which the particular individual would accept with equanimity. Higher curves (upwards and to the right) correspond to higher levels of satisfaction for the various combinations plotted. Point E on the utility curve denoted U–U', which is tangential to W_0-W_1, is the optimum mix of consumption and investment for this individual. Utility is maximised by consuming a proportion of beginning period wealth, W_0 which corresponds to O–C, and investing the balance, $C-W_0$, to elicit a closing period stock of wealth which is measured by O–I. Indifference curves which do not impinge upon the physical investment line are not feasible given the investor's periodic wealth profile.

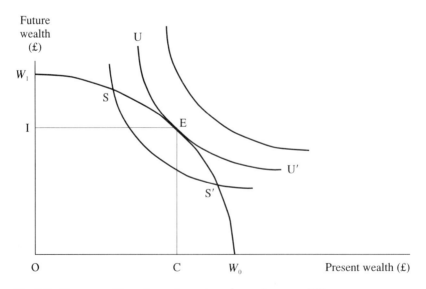

Fig 3.2 Consumption, investment and maximum utility

Those which intersect W_0–W_1 are also sub-optimal. For example, points S and S' are feasible propositions, but neither would maximise the individual's utility preference for consumption and investment, since the curve U–U' (with point E) represents a higher level of satisfaction.

3 WEALTH MAXIMISATION WITH BORROWING AND LENDING OPPORTUNITIES

If the preceding single period model is now extended to incorporate the possibility of lending consumption surpluses or borrowing to finance a deficit *via* the capital market, the individual's time preferences for consumption and investment are also widened.

Figure 3.3 introduces the time value of money concept into the analysis. The line L–B represents the possibilities for different investors either to utilise their stock of wealth and access the capital market exclusively, or to avail themselves of its facilities in conjunction with the consumption and investment opportunities associated with non-financial markets. This is still represented by the physical investment line, W_0–W_1.

It is assumed that borrowing and reinvestment rates are equal, such that if an individual lent W_0 at an interest rate r it would compound to the following future value at the end of one year:

(1) $W_1 = W_0(1 + r)$

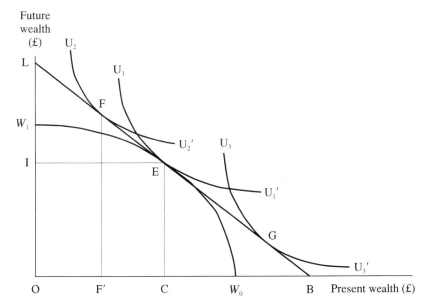

Fig 3.3 The capital market, consumption, investment and investor utility

Conversely, if an amount were borrowed at the same rate and an amount W_1 was repayable in one year's time, its present value (PV) is given by:

(2) $W_0 = W_1/(1 + r)$

From Equation (1) it follows that:

(3) $\dfrac{W_1}{W_0} = (1 + r)$

where $(1 + r)$ represents the slope of the lending and borrowing opportunity line, L–B. Solving for r, under the conditions stated, also produces the *market rate of interest*.

Note also that the discussion is now focusing upon investors, rather than the individual. This is because a capital *market* has been introduced, which by definition requires a plurality of buyers and sellers. By implication it is assumed to be *efficient* because borrowing and lending rates conform to a uniform market rate of interest which facilitates money transactions.

However, each individual is permitted to express consumption and investment preferences which may be unique, so their particular sets of indifference curves in terms of slope and position could well differ from those presented in Figure 3.2.

Let it be assumed that there are three investors within the market with identical sums of money to invest but a different set of consumption priorities which exhibit unique sets of utility indifference curves, one of which is tangential to the lending and borrowing line, L–B. Armed with their common productive investment opportunities, represented by the physical investment curve, W_0–W_1, Figure 3.3 indicates the optimum trade-offs between their current and future consumption in relation to the universal opportunities for either borrowing or lending at a uniform market rate of interest.

As before, the point E on the curve U_1–U_1' represents maximum satisfaction for the original investor considered in Figures 3.1 and 3.2, who neither needs to borrow nor lend. The tangent $U_2 - U_2'$ with the line L–B above W_0–W_1 (point F) maximises utility for an investor with funds surplus to requirements. The balance can be reinvested at the market rate of interest r to enhance end of period wealth. Conversely, the U_3–U_3' tangent (G) represents the optimum position for a financially embarrassed investor on the physical investment curve. Because the desire for current consumption exceeds their original stock of wealth, the individual is forced to borrow.

It is important to appreciate, therefore, that individual investors can increase their satisfaction still further by either borrowing or lending, thereby moving along the line L–B. For example, any individual whose time preferences (utility) are matched by point F can invest up to point E on the physical investment line W_0–W_1, consume O–F' and then lend F'–C. Irrespective of the shape of the individual utility indifference curve all investors would deploy funds up to point E and then maximise their respective utility by either lending or borrowing along the line, L–B, at the market rate of interest.

4 THE SEPARATION THEOREM

Theoretically, the wealth maximisation criterion enables an individual or firm to maximise the satisfaction derived from their consumption. However, it is possible to conceive of real market imperfections which would prohibit such a course of action. For the purpose of exposition, the preceding analysis therefore assumed implicitly that if investors are to adjust their income streams to preferred consumption patterns there must exist a *perfect capital market* which exhibits the following characteristics:

- Large numbers of buyers and sellers, none of whom is large enough to distort the market by their singular actions (i.e. perfect competition).
- All investors have the freedom to borrow or lend or to buy and sell assets on their own accounts.
- There are no transaction costs which restrict these decisions.
- The tax system is neutral.
- The market for information is available to all and costless.

Whilst the assumptions of a perfect capital market can be criticised and indeed will be throughout this text (culminating in Chapter 13) they represent the bedrock of corporate finance. It will be shown how market perfection permits the development of models of investor behaviour, such as the one presented, that reduce much of the mathematics to simple linear differential equations with unique solutions under conditions of equilibrium.

However, the wealth maximisation criteria under the conditions stated has another advantage. As Irving Fisher noted in his classic book (1930) and Tobin reconfirmed (1958), in an era where ownership is divorced from control it permits the firm to remain aloof from the need to measure the consumption preferences of a multiplicity of shareholders. Although the preceding analysis employed a method of utility measurement based upon the subjective time preferences of the individual, under the assumption of perfect capital markets the firm that wishes to maximise its shareholders' wealth can concentrate upon their own investment decision under consideration using NPV criteria. The owners then adjust their individual income streams to personal preferred patterns of consumption quite separately, by either buying or selling their shares, borrowing or lending to invest elsewhere.

Assume that a shareholder has an attractive opportunity to invest in a new company. Further assume that by retaining funds to invest in capital projects their existing firm's dividend distribution is insufficient to allow the individual to take advantage of this. The shareholder is confronted with two options. One is to borrow funds at the market rate of interest. The other is to liquidate all or part of their holding in the existing company. Conversely, a shareholder who is still receiving dividends in excess of their consumption preferences may reinvest funds in the firm by purchasing additional shares, or look elsewhere.

These examples are simply illustrations of the consumption investment model presented earlier. However, they demonstrate what Fisher termed the *Separation Theorem*, which decouples the consumption decisions of the owners from their company's investment decisions. If firms wish to maximise shareholders' wealth the shareholders can adjust their desired income streams to the requirements of their optimal patterns of outside investment, if necessary buying and selling the shares of the firm itself. This leaves the firm to accept capital projects whose rate of return represents that which shareholders can earn on comparable alternative investments by borrowing at the market rate of interest. In other words, the firm's discount rate should reflect outside investment opportunities foregone by shareholders since they are free to borrow or lend to maximise the satisfaction that they derive from consumption.

Thus, if the firm maximises its own wealth by maximising the NPV of all its projects, using the shareholders' opportunity cost of capital as the discount rate, the maximisation of shareholders' wealth should not be compromised in an efficient capital market.

The Separation Theorem also has a number of further implications, even if the capital market is assumed to be perfect:

- The maximisation of shareholders' wealth relates to the maximisation of the market value of a company's shares, which will be shown to mean the market price per share and not the aggregate market value of all shares.
- The maximisation of share price requires explicit consideration of the firm's dividend (consumption) decision in relation to the retention (investment) decision as a determinant of equity values (wealth).
- Because the corporate discount rate is a function of the shareholders' opportunity cost of capital (which *inter alia* reflects a market rate of interest), if shareholders prefer current dividends (consumption) rather than future capital gains which are financed by retentions (investment), different multiple discount rates may readily apply to individual projects if share price is to be maximised.
- Thus, any proposed corporate investment decision might not be independent of its financing decision and the preferred consumption patterns of the providers of capital.
- Finally, if the funds required for investment proposals extend beyond retained earnings, or a further issue of shares, to other sources of finance, each of which reflects a different market rate of interest, the question

arises as to how these are combined to define an opportunity cost of capital rate applicable to individual projects.

Thus, significant difficulty may be encountered in attempting to implement the rationale of the Separation Theorem, even at a conceptual level. The issues raised will therefore underpin Parts 3, 4 and 5 of this study. For the moment, suffice it to say that the relevance of the theorem is that, if a definitive choice is to be made between two investment projects, the use of a capital budgeting model which incorporates a correctly defined opportunity cost of capital rate is preferable to any other. To be more emphatic, under conditions of certainty, and perfect markets, NPV maximisation is entirely consistent with the normative objective of shareholders' wealth maximisation. IRR maximisation may frustrate this purpose.

5 COMPUTATIONAL DIFFICULTIES AND THE INTERNAL RATE OF RETURN (IRR)

Assume an investment promised £1 million next year, £2 million in two years, £4 million in three years and £3 million the following year. The current economic value of this earnings stream would equal its PV, i.e. the sum of the individual PVs. Given a prevailing interest rate of 14 per cent, the PV may be calculated using the appropriate factors from DCF tables as follows:

Year	Earnings	Discount factor (14%)	PV
	£000s	$\dfrac{1}{(1+r)^t}$	£000s
1	1000	0.8772	877.2
2	2000	0.7695	1539.0
3	4000	0.6749	2699.6
4	3000	0.5921	1776.3
			6892.1

So the earnings stream's economic value is £6,892,100.

In other words, if an individual deposited £6,892,100 today at 14 per cent per annum, it would permit annual withdrawals of £1 million, £2 million, £4 million and £3 million respectively, leaving nothing on deposit.

Reformulating the example, if corporate management were considering an investment project which yielded the same income pattern and they desired a 14 per cent rate of return, then £6,892,100 would represent the maximum amount which they would invest. The PV equals the cost of the investment, i.e. NPV is zero, and 14 per cent represents the project's IRR.

Likewise, if a company were to exhibit a similar income stream and the earnings yield of its competitors was 14%, then its current stock market valuation should be £6,892,100. Hopefully, this would also exceed the market value of its tangible assets, since the former incorporates goodwill.

Expressed mathematically, it will be recalled from Chapter 2 that the IRR method of investment appraisal solves for a discount rate, r, which reduces future sums, C_t, back to a present value, PV, equal to the cost of the investment, I_0, for an appropriate number of periods, n.

$$(4) \qquad I_0 = \sum_{t=1}^{n} \frac{C_t}{(1+r)^t} = PV - I_0 = NPV = 0$$

Hence, the IRR is the discount rate which reduces the net present value of a project to zero.

Projects are accepted if:

- IRR $\geqslant$ the target rate of return
- IRR $>$ the opportunity cost of capital.

In a situation of capital rationing, or where a choice must be made between mutually exclusive alternatives, if the company's objective function is IRR maximisation, investments would be ranked and selected according to the size of their IRRs. So if:

$$IRR_A > IRR_B > IRR_C$$

project A would be selected, rather than B or C, subject to the proviso that it at least matched the previous project's IRR.

Leaving aside the questionable assumptions which underpin the model, the IRR unfortunately suffers from a number of mathematical complexities. Whilst it is often favoured in practice because investment decisions can be assessed by reference to a percentage (and if cashflows are equal in amount the IRR may be interpolated from PV annuity tables), it is rarely easy to compute.

If investment proposals exhibit uneven cashflows throughout their lives (a typical situation):

(*i*) The IRR cannot be solved using the factor computation, I_0/C_t, explained in Chapter 2.

(*ii*) The IRR may not be determinate.

(*iii*) The IRR may not be a real number.

6 THE IRR AND UNEVEN CASHFLOWS

Where cashflows are uneven, solving for an IRR requires a combination of NPV and linear interpolation techniques, instead of the simple factor computation. In the absence of a scientific calculator or a software program the solution is a four-stage process whereby:

(1) DCF factors for a single but quite arbitrary interest rate for each year under observation are selected from the PV table of £1.00.
(2) A NPV is computed.
(3) If positive, the NPV is recomputed using a higher discount rate and hence a lower factor, so as to produce a negative NPV (or *vice versa* if the reverse holds).
(4) A zero NPV is then established by linear interpolation in order to obtain the project's IRR, which conforms to Equation (5).

(5) $PV - I_0 = NPV = 0$ where $r = IRR$

By way of illustration, consider the following project where NPVs have been computed at 20 per cent and 21 per cent respectively:

Year	Cashflow £	DCF factor 20%	PV £	DCF factor 21%	PV £
0	(100)		(100)		(100)
1	25	0.8333	20.83	0.8264	20.66
2	35	0.6944	24.30	0.6830	23.91
3	40	0.5787	23.15	0.5645	22.58
4	40	0.4823	19.29	0.4665	18.66
5	34	0.4019	14.07	0.3855	13.49
NPV			1.64		(0.70)

Using linear interpolation one now solves for the discount rate where NPV is equal to zero. This is at a point represented by the fraction 1.64/2.34 between 20 per cent and 21 per cent. Thus

$$IRR = 20\% + \frac{1.64}{2.34}(21 - 20)\% = 20.7\%$$

Clearly, if discounting had been conducted between 18 per cent and 27 per cent, then interpolation would have been conducted between those limits.

Unfortunately, the greater the disparity between discount rates, the less accurate the method. This is because the PV equation is not a linear progression. Graphically, NPV computations for the above project are shown in Figure 3.4 with the straight line between the two points representing an approximation to the curve provided by linear interpolation at 18 per cent and 27 per cent respectively (which is obviously less accurate than the proportional difference between 20 and 21 per cent).

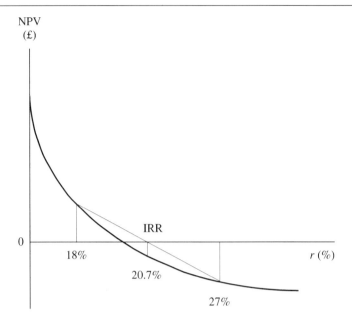

Fig 3.4 NPV at different discount rates

It is for this reason that in the absence of computer facilities IRR is frequently criticised for its time-consuming trial-and-error methodology. Initial NPV computations must be repeated until they become sufficiently close to zero to make interpolation worthwhile.

However, this is not strictly true. As a basis for interpolation a simple approach is to divide total cash inflows by the number of years, and to adjust the resultant average downward if larger cashflows occur in the later years of a project (recognising that they are less valuable when discounted). This average annual cashflow is then incorporated into a factor computation in order to provide an initial discount rate. Interpolation is subsequently conducted in the usual manner.

Using the previous example:

$$\frac{\text{Total cash inflows}}{\text{Number of years}} = £175/5 = £35$$

Assuming that cash inflows equal an annuity of £33 the basic formula, I_0/C_t yields:

$$£100/£33 = 3.030$$

This corresponds to a discount rate between 19 per cent (3.0576) and 20 per cent (2.9906). Interpolation can therefore commence at 20 per cent since this elicits a low NPV of £1.64.

7 THE IRR AND INDETERMINACY

Some projects have more than one IRR where there are cash outflows *during* the life of the project. Consider the following:

Year	Cashflows	DCF (10%)	DCF (25%)
	£	£	£
0	(1000)	(1000)	(1000)
1	2350	2136	1880
2	(1375)	(1136)	(880)
NPV		0	0

As a general rule, where a project has only an initial cash outflow there will be a unique IRR solution. However, each subsequent net annual outflow during the life of a project will generate a further IRR. With n changes in sign for the cashflows there may be n solutions for the IRR. Moreover, some IRRs may be positive and others negative.

To overcome this problem and generate a unique IRR, the following procedure may be adopted. Using the company's cost of capital rate, discount back from the most distant cash outflow, year on year, and offset the resultant amount each year against inflows until all cashflows are positive. Then proceed with the IRR computation, in the usual manner. For example, given a 7 per cent capital cost and the following cashflows:

Initial outflow	£4277
Inflows	£1000 years 1 to 9
Subsequent outflow	£2000 year 10

a unique IRR of 14.6 per cent can be determined from column three below using the techniques outlined earlier.

Year	Cashflows	Discounted outflow 7%	Net cashflows
	£	£	£
0	(4277)		(4277)
1	1000		1000
2	1000		1000
3	1000		1000
4	1000		1000
5	1000		1000
6	1000		1000
			(*continued*)

Continued from p. 55

Year	Cashflows £	Discounted outflow 7% £	Net cashflows £
7	1000		1000
8	1000	minus $\left\{\dfrac{(869)}{1.07} = (812)\right\}$	188
9	1000	minus $\left\{\dfrac{(2000)}{1.07} = (1869)\right\}$	(869)
10	(2000)		

Expressed mathematically, the proposal may be written:

$$£4277 = \sum_{t=1}^{n=7} \frac{£1000}{(1+r)^t} + \frac{£188}{(1+r)^8} = \text{NPV} = 0$$

where r = IRR.

Solving for r:

IRR = 14.6%

8 WHEN THE IRR IS NOT A REAL NUMBER

A serious conceptual feature of an IRR computation is that the solution for r might not represent a *real* number. It may occur only rarely, but it makes the IRR methodology redundant. Consider the following example:

Year	Cashflow £
0	(1000)
1	2000
2	(2000)

Using Equation (5), the investment proposal is represented by:

$$£1000 + \frac{£2000}{(1+r)^2} = \frac{£2000}{(1+r)} \qquad \text{where } r = \text{IRR}$$

Dividing by 1000 and multiplying out by $(1+r)^2$ gives

$$(1+r)^2 + 2 = 2(1+r)$$
$$(r^2 + 2r + 1) + 2 = 2r + 2$$

Simplifying:

$$r^2 + 1 = 0$$
$$r^2 = -1\%$$

Since the square root of a minus number is imaginary, the IRR is not real.

9 RANKING AND ACCEPTANCE UNDER IRR AND NPV

Under NPV, uneven cashflows present none of the mathematical problems associated with IRR, except that individual discount factors must be applied to each cashflow, rather than an annuity factor. As a consequence, NPV is generally regarded as computationally superior.

Using earlier notation, the present value of net cash inflows (outflows) less the cost of the investment may be expressed mathematically as:

$$(6) \qquad NPV = \sum_{t=1}^{n} \frac{C_t}{(1+r)^t} - I_0 = PV - I_0$$

where:

r = the discount rate, as measured by the opportunity cost of capital.

Under conditions of certainty it will be recalled that the model assumes that capital costs, cashflows and the discount rate are known, correctly defined and will not change over the life of the project. It is also assumed (with important consequences) that intermediate cashflows are financed or reinvested at the discount rate and not the project's IRR.

Investment proposals are only accepted if:

- NPV $\geqslant 0$, where r is a desired rate of return.
- NPV > 0, where r is the opportunity cost of capital.

In a situation of capital rationing, or where a choice must be made between mutually exclusive alternatives, investments would be ranked and selected according to the size of their NPVs if the firm's goal is NPV maximisation.

So if:

$$NPV_A > NPV_B > NPV_C$$

the company would select project A in preference to B and C under the conditions stated. According to Fisher's Separation Theorem, in a world of complete certainty characterised by perfect capital markets, the firm's objective function would also conform to the maximisation of shareholders' wealth, expressed as the market price per share.

In the absence of capital rationing and mutual exclusivity, it should be emphasised that IRR will produce the same accept, break-even and reject decisions as NPV for a *single period* investment, i.e.

$$NPV > 0, \qquad IRR > r$$
$$NPV = 0, \qquad IRR = 0$$
$$NPV < 0, \qquad IRR < r$$

Even in a *multi-period* setting if a project is still being considered in isolation both methods will signal the same accept or reject decision if there is only one initial cash outflow followed by subsequent net annual inflows. To be more precise, given a positive NPV, the IRR will be greater than the project's discount rate r. This may be proved as follows. Let:

A = cash outflow
B = cash inflows discounted at the project's IRR
C = net cash inflows discounted at a rate r equal to either the company's opportunity cost of capital or desired rate of return

such that:

$$C > B = A$$

IRR would only signal the rejection of a project if it was less than either the cost of capital or the desired rate of return. In terms of inequalities, if:

$$IRR < r$$

then

$$B > C$$

the reason being that the cash outflows are discounted less heavily using the IRR rather than the discount rate, r. But this is logically impossible under the conditions stated since:

$$C > B = A$$

Hence, the project is acceptable using either IRR or NPV techniques and, given Fisher's Separation Theorem, both corporate and shareholder wealth is maximised.

10 CAPITAL RATIONING

So what if an investment's cashflows do not conform to a simple pattern of net cash inflows and a choice must be made between alternatives? This arises where proposals are mutually exclusive, i.e. the acceptance of one precludes another (such as the use of a piece of land). It also reflects the existence of capital rationing, where the firm must allocate limited funds between competing projects.

Where a choice must be made NPV may rank projects differently to IRR. Consider the following data where the opportunity cost of capital for discounting purposes is a uniform 10 per cent. NPV favours project A, whilst IRR criteria would select B. Yet, A is clearly the better project if the market rate of interest is 10 per cent, since it produces a higher net terminal value at the end of three years.

Project	Cashflows (£)				Investment criteria		
	t_0	t_1	t_2	t_3	IRR	NPV (10%)	NTV (10%)
A	(1000)	500	700	900	43%	709.3	944
B	(1000)	1000	500	500	54%	698.0	929

Figure 3.5 illustrates how NPV is affected by changes in the discount rate in relation to IRR which solves for NPV = 0, where r = IRR.

At one extreme, NPV is maximised when r equals zero, since cashflows are not discounted. At the other, IRR solves for zero NPV, maximising r at the intersection of the horizontal axis. If r was zero, the net terminal value at the end of each project's life (the actual cash balance which measures the increase in the firm's stock of wealth) would be the difference between either projects'

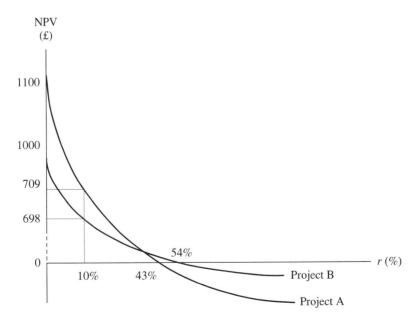

Fig 3.5 NPV and IRR compared and contrasted

undiscounted cashflows and their costs of investment, i.e.:

$$NTV_A = £2100 - £1000 = £1100$$
$$NTV_B = £2000 - £1000 = £1000$$

Solving for $r = IRR$, however, would produce zero cash balances in both cases. Wealth is unaffected.

Between these two extremes, differing discount rates determine the slope of the curves according to the timing and amounts of each projects' cashflows. In the example, a relatively low discount rate such as 10 per cent values more highly the more distant but larger cash inflows associated with project A. Higher discount rates eventually erode this advantage. Conversely, project B is less affected by high discount rates, since it delivers the bulk of cash inflows earlier. Clearly, any two projects exhibiting different patterns of cashflow in terms of timing and size will elicit different patterns of NPV with a slope and a point of indifference between the two projects (the intersection of the curves) corresponding to a discount rate which may be unique.

As a consequence, a project with a higher IRR is not necessarily the project with the larger NPV. Different patterns of cashflows produce different IRRs, but the IRR method produces a percentage result and does not deal in absolute terms like NPV. As an averaging technique it merely solves for a single discount rate which equates the net cash inflows of a project with the cost of an initial investment. In the above example, project B is therefore favoured because it delivers the balance of cash returns more quickly, even though their total is £100 less than that for project A.

There are two important corollaries to this analysis. One is that both NPV and IRR assume that borrowing and reinvestment rates are assumed to be equal to each other. The second is that they are assumed to be constant over the life of the project. Thus, as an averaging technique, the IRR approach to capital budgeting cannot accommodate reinvestment rates or future capital costs that differ from each other or vary over time. Moreover, the IRR assumptions are likely to be more unrealistic. In the previous example, it is highly improbable that the true costs of borrowing or reinvestment opportunities are 43 per cent or 54 per cent.

The NPV approach, using a single discount rate, may assume that reinvestment rates and future capital costs will be constant and equal for the duration of a project. This, too, may not always be realistic. However, it is doubtless a better reflection of economic reality than the IRR model, particularly if the company's opportunity cost of capital is used as a discount rate. Besides, if multiple discount rates prevail they can be incorporated into NPV analyses more easily.

11 DIFFERENTIAL PROJECTS

If a company's objective is to maximise shareholder wealth the IRR approach to capital budgeting can also yield misleading results when comparing multi-period projects of different size with regard to their cost of investment or future cashflows. As explained in Chapter 2, the difference between NPV and IRR rankings occurs because the former provides an *absolute* measure of wealth, whilst the latter is a *relative* measure expressed as a percentage.

Consider again two projects of identical size which differ only with respect to their net cash inflows. The opportunity cost of capital is a uniform 5 per cent.

Project	Cashflows (£)			Investment criteria		
	t_0	t_1	t_2	IRR	NPV (5%) £	NTV(5%) £
A	(10,000)	2,000	12,000	20%	2789	3075
B	(10,000)	10,000	3,125	25%	2358	2560

Again NPV favours project A, while IRR favours project B. Given the prevailing discount rate, the NTV approach confirms that the NPV criteria is consistent with wealth maximisation.

This discrepancy still arises because funds which are generated are assumed to be reinvested or raised at different rates; under IRR at the project's IRR, while under NPV at a different discount rate. In order to compare projects with equal investment costs but differential cashflows using the IRR approach, the incremental return from the incremental cashflows must therefore be computed. In terms of the previous example a *ghost* project or sub-project is created by taking the difference between the cashflows as follows:

Sub-project	t_0	t_1	t_2
(A minus B)	0	(£8000)	£8875

Solving for r using Equation (5):

$$\frac{£8000}{1+r} = \frac{£8875}{(1+r)^2}$$

The IRR equals 10.9 per cent.

Since the incremental yield on project A is greater than 5 per cent it can now be seen that it should be accepted. Notice also that this corresponds to the proof on acceptance shown earlier, namely that IRR would only signal rejection of a project if it is less than the appropriate discount rate.

Now consider two projects of different size, not only with respect to net cash inflows but also investment cost.

Project	t_0	t_1	IRR
A	(£10,000)	£12,000	20%
B	(£15,000)	£17,700	18%

Under IRR, the size of the project is ignored. The smaller investment is favoured because the method expresses a result by reducing all cashflows to average percentage terms. In other words, IRR would favour a £50 return on £100 to £100 on £500.

This leads back to the question originally posed in Chapter 2. Is a high return on low capital sums preferable to a low return on larger investments, even though the cash inflow of the latter exceeds the former? Put another way, should a firm maximise its IRR or its absolute cash inflows? Again the dilemma can only be resolved by calculating the incremental return on the sub-project. This requires an additional £5000 outflow but yields additional revenue of £5700 which is equivalent to an IRR of 14 per cent. If the company can obtain funds at less than 14 per cent then clearly this is preferable to project A. However if funds are scarce, such that their capital cost is greater than 14 per cent then the smaller rich project may be preferred. Both decisions would accord with the NPV criteria of wealth maximisation.

12 SUMMARY AND CONCLUSIONS

Without recourse to incremental yields and ghost project techniques it would appear that NPV is superior to IRR. By assuming certainty both models imply that:

(*i*)   The interest rate or rate of return can be correctly defined and will not change.
(*ii*) Cashflows are known.
(*iii*) Investment life is known.

Relax any one of these conditions and the results of either calculations are invalidated.

Computational difficulties apart, the validity of the models under the conditions stated, therefore, hinges upon their respective assumptions concerning reinvestment rates and capital costs. According to the Separation Theorem, in a perfect capital market the firm's investment decisions can be made separately from the investment decisions of its shareholders. The relevant rate of interest in project appraisal is the opportunity cost of capital earned on comparable investments outside the firm. This is consistent with the maximisation of share-holder wealth. However, under the IRR it is assumed that borrowing and rein-vestment rates equal the project's IRR, whereas under NPV the discount rate is the appropriate figure relating to these flows.

If their respective assumptions concerning reinvestment rates and capital costs are relaxed both NPV and IRR will not necessarily be correct and may give the wrong accept or reject decisions. With NPV for example, it depends very much on the relationship between the size of the NPV and the change in these rates. Consider the following PV computation:

Time period	t_0	t_1	t_2	t_3	NPV (20%)	IRR
Cashflow (£)	(1000)	500	500	500	53	23%

The project appears acceptable because the IRR exceeds the discount rate and NPV is positive. But now assume borrowing was undertaken at 20 per cent. The financing and net cashflow schedule incorporating interest on borrowings would be as follows:

	t_0	t_1	t_2	t_3
Financing (£):	1000	(200)	(200)	(1200)
Net flow (£):	–	300	300	(700)

Should the project be accepted? Assuming reinvestment occurred at only 6 per cent the true cashflow pattern would be thus:

	t_1	t_2	t_3
Net cash inflow (£):	300	300	
Interest (£): t_{1-2}		18	
t_{2-3}			18
			19
Net cash outflow:			(700)
	300	318	(663)

The bank overdraft formulation can now be summarised as follows:

Total cash inflows	£618
Total cash outflows	(£663)
Net terminal value	(£45)

Since the project under-recovers by £45 it would therefore be rejected.

Thus, the NPV method using a single discount rate, rather than multiple rates, does not necessarily give the correct acceptance signals compared to the NTV approach, if different borrowing and reinvestment rates (market rates of interest) apply to different cashflows during the same period.

On the other hand, NPV remains technically superior to its main rival, the IRR, which does not deal with multiple discount rates. Apart from its mathematical weaknesses, the IRR remains less meaningful precisely because it is calculated independently of *any* rate of return or cost of capital figure. It depends only on the relationship between cashflows and does not include a discount rate in its derivation. As stated earlier, to inject economic meaning into the model IRR has to be compared with a firm's rate of return or cost of capital. By contrast, NPV has immediate impact, since it utilises one of these figures in the form of a discount rate to determine an increase in wealth. Besides, a project's IRR may be significantly higher than prevailing discount rates. This may make it unrealistic with regard to rates of return and capital costs available not only to the firm but also the shareholders, thereby invalidating its use as a wealth maximisation criteria.

Logically, IRR should only be used if it at least equals the last project's discount rate (thereby maintaining a firm's rate of return or opportunity cost of capital) or, alternatively, if it can be assumed that if a project is not undertaken, funds can be invested on the market at that project's IRR.

References

(1) Fisher, I., *The Theory of Interest*, Macmillan 1930.
(2) Tobin, J., 'Liquidity preferences as behaviour towards risk', *Review of Economic Studies*, Vol. 25, February 1958.

4

The treatment of uncertainty

Chapter profile

This chapter examines the impact of uncertainty upon the capital investment decisions which confront the firm. Various methodologies which transform an uncertain situation into one of quasi-risk and the impact of risk-adjusted investment criteria upon corporate wealth maximisation are explained and illustrated.

The case for reducing multi-valued expectations to a single cashflow are discussed which introduces the statistical concept of the probabilistic normal distribution. An analysis of the variability of cashflows around their expected monetary value and the application of mean-variance analysis which uses the standard deviation as a measure of risk are presented. Confidence limits are explained within the context of risk attitudes. The sequential analysis of probabilistic cashflows, the use of sensitivity analysis and computer simulations as guides to managerial action are all described.

Finally, assuming shareholder wealth is to be maximised, the maximisation of the present value of certainty cash equivalents based upon the concept of expected investor utility is presented as an ideal but problematical managerial technique for dealing with risk. The derivation of an appropriate discount rate which utilises the opportunity cost concept is explained with reference to the inter-relationship between the investment, dividend and financing decisions which confront the firm.

The chapter concludes with a concerned review of recent empirical evidence on the mediocre interaction between corporate objectives, capital budgeting techniques and the treatment of risk in UK companies of varying size.

1 INTRODUCTION

In order to construct a normative model of the corporate investment decision the analysis so far has been undertaken under conditions of *certainty*. Certainty assumes that the expected incremental cashflows of a project proposal and its associated cost of financing are known in advance. In this chapter it is explained how a company can evaluate an individual project where more than one set of future cashflows are possible. The impact of alternative sources of finance will be deferred until Part 4, by which time the attitudes of financial stakeholders and management to the different income streams which may stem from an investment decision have been considered. The chapter should also be viewed as a precursor to Part 5, which analyses the consequences of accepting a proposal in relation to an existing portfolio of investments, where neither the intervening cashflows nor the expected returns of the portfolio's constituents are known with certainty. First, however a few more definitions.

2 RISK AND UNCERTAINTY DEFINED

Risk and uncertainty both refer to situations where the possible outcomes of a present investment decision are plural. However, *risk* implies that the dimensions and probabilities of these outcomes are known in advance, whereas *uncertainty* cannot be objectively forecast.

Probability defines the likelihood that a particular event will occur, expressed as either a percentage or a decimal number. An outcome that is certain is said to have a probability of 100 per cent or 1.0 and two possibilities that are equally likely would both have a probability of 50 per cent or 0.5.

Most investments undertaken by firms (and much of their financing) lie within the domain of uncertainty. The distribution of possible future cashflows incremental to each is not known in advance, nor is the likelihood of them occurring. What management require, therefore, is some technique whereby a situation of uncertainty may be converted to one of *quasi-risk* by projecting an assumed distribution of outcomes to which they subjectively assign respective probabilities. Henceforth, the terms risk and uncertainty will therefore be used interchangeably.

3 RUDIMENTARY APPROACHES TO THE TREATMENT OF RISK

Because it is a truism to state that firms operate in a world of uncertainty various reasons can actually be proposed for ignoring it. One is that in the long-run all firms are likely to confront the same uncertainties, so no competitive advantage is gained by incorporating it into an investment analysis. Another is that if a decision taken now subsequently proves to be incorrect remedial action can always be taken. Because decision-making is an iterative process it is also argued that future capital budgeting forecasts should improve with the benefit of hindsight.

Unfortunately, this 'head in the sand' philosophy creates its own problems. If a decision is taken on the basis of the best guess or *most likely* outcome the question arises as to how far a project can deviate from its original acceptance criteria as uncertainties accumulate before it should be abandoned. Given the interrelationships between projects, abandonment may not even be possible without bankruptcy. By ignoring the dispersion of possible outcomes there is also no reliable basis for the acceptance or rejection of projects where a choice must be made between mutually exclusive alternatives or in the presence of capital rationing. Even enforced choices may differ from individual to individual, depending upon their attitudes towards risk.

Moving from the simplest to the most sophisticated, six techniques which might be applied to investment appraisal under conditions of uncertainty in order to overcome these difficulties are invariably recommended:

- The arbitrary modification to acceptance criteria related to profitability or liquidity, according to a project's perceived risk.
- An analysis of the sensitivity of the individual variables contained in a project proposal to various degrees of error associated with their measurement.
- A three-point estimate of the proposal.
- A probability estimation of all the variables contained in the investment project which produces its expected or mean return.
- A statistical consideration of risk which analyses the dispersion of probable outcomes from the mean, i.e. the standard deviation.
- The derivation of a project's certainty cash equivalent, based upon investor utility.

Of these six, however, the following techniques should only be regarded as a precursor to more sophisticated analyses.

The modification of acceptance criteria

One method of coping with uncertainty is to classify proposed investments into categories according to their nature. The implication of this approach is that projects vary in their degrees of uncertainty according to the category into which they fall. The adjustment for uncertainty is made by varying the minimum return standard (or other acceptance criteria) that is required for projects in these several categories. In relation to the capital budgeting models previously considered, this would mean using either a shorter than normal period for payback, or a higher than normal hurdle rate in the form of an accounting rate of return (ARR), internal rate of return (IRR), or discount rate for net present value (NPV) calculations.

The classification of projects into categories according to their presumed degrees of uncertainty and the application of varying acceptance criteria to these categories constitutes a pragmatic and feasible approach to risk analysis. Unfortunately, it suffers from a number of weaknesses which leave the size of the adjustments unresolved:

- The actual level of uncertainty in a particular proposal is not examined.
- It fails to allow for different degrees of uncertainty among projects in the same category.
- It assumes that all projects in a given category are more uncertain (or less uncertain) than all the projects in another category.
- The assignment of acceptance criteria to the various categories of proposed investment must be arbitrary, otherwise it means that management already know the extent of the risk involved (which is clearly a tautology).

Sensitivity analysis

Sensitivity analysis is not a method of quantifying risk, but rather a technique for identifying the variables in an investment proposal which may have a significant impact on its expected return. In its most sophisticated form it is a powerful operation which may be performed using a *computer simulation* which:

- Deconstructs cashflow data into its major components such as the cost of the investment, the operating costs associated with production hours, wage rates, productive efficiency and forecast levels of demand, all juxtaposed against selling prices and total revenue.
- Analyses each variable sequentially by holding all others constant and measuring the impact of changes to the variable under scrutiny upon the payback period, the project's return or its NPV.
- Analyses likely combinations of changes to variables.

Three-point estimation

Another improvement upon the best guess or most likely outcome of an investment proposal is to forecast the optimistic and pessimistic possibilities as well. Unfortunately, the worst possibility in any particular project may be catastrophic, so it is unlikely to provide management with an appropriate acceptance criteria.

However, where project proposals are mutually exclusive, or in the presence of capital rationing, the method can provide a logical basis for a subjective decision based upon:

- The *minimax* criterion which considers the project which produces the best result under the most adverse circumstances.
- The *Laplace* criterion which considers the most favourable simple average of the best, most likely and worst alternatives envisaged, the implication being that each eventually occurs with equal probability.

- A *probability* estimation which attaches different probabilistic weights to the three events, if necessary to arrive at a modal figure for the anticipated payback, return or NPV.

Each criterion can be compared with similar calculations for competing projects and with any target requirement. The probabilistic estimate is clearly the best method, since it incorporates the possibilities of events occurring. However, it may be ineffectual, given the likelihood that the most optimistic or pessimistic situation arising might be so small as to have little impact on the most likely eventuality. An alternative procedure, therefore, would be to forecast the best and worst results which have a reasonable chance of occurring. This is akin to sensitivity analysis. The forecasts could then be combined into a weighted average figure. The difficulty of this approach, however, is that each variable might elicit a different set of probabilities which cannot be combined to give a final range of outcomes, only a weighted average.

The concept of expected monetary value

Expected monetary value (EMV) analysis is a methodology which provides management with a weighted average based upon a multiplicity of probabilistic outcomes associated with an investment decision, rather than a three-point estimation. Explained simply, the monetary value of each possible annual cashflow C_i is first multiplied by an assigned probability P_i, based upon management's subjective assessment of each occurring. The products $C_i P_i$ are then summated to yield an annual EMV for the spectrum of possible cashflows at time period t as follows:

$$(1) \qquad \text{EMV}_t = \sum_{i=1}^{n} C_i P_i$$

Management then establishes the acceptability of the investment using NPV criteria in the usual manner. By obtaining the present value of the sum of the EMVs by discounting over the appropriate number of years at their desired rate, from which the investment's cost is subtracted, the *expected net present value* is given by:

$$(2) \qquad \text{E(NPV)} = \sum_{t=1}^{n} \frac{\text{EMV}_t}{(1+r)^t} - I_0$$

To illustrate, consider a firm with a proposed investment requiring an initial outlay of £1000. The future cashflow will consist of only one inflow at the end of one year. Management assess the distribution of possible outcomes, their judgmental probabilities and the resultant products to be:

| C_i | ΣP_i | $\Sigma C_i P_i$ |
£		£
4000	0.10	400
3000	0.35	1050
1000	0.22	220
0	0.16	0
(1000)	0.09	(90)
(2000)	0.06	(120)
(3000)	0.02	(60)
	1.00	1400

The EMV of the future cashflow from the investment is therefore £1400. If the company's cost of capital is 15%, the present value of the investment is:

$$PV = £1400/1.15 = £1217$$

So that using Equation (2):

$$E(NPV) = £1217 - £1000 = £217$$

Thus, the project delivers an expected return of £217 in excess of cost, which presumably is acceptable if considered in isolation.

The concept of EMV represents an improvement over cruder methods of characterising a situation of multiple possible outcomes. It considers all such outcomes together with their probabilities and thus provides a useful means of representing multi-valued expectations by a single NPV figure. Note in particular that the use of the 'most likely outcome' as a measure of the distribution does not necessarily provide the same answer as E(NPV). As can be seen from the above distribution the most likely cashflow is £3000. However, this does not mean that a firm can simply reduce multi-valued expectations to their EMVs and then proceed to make its investment decision as it would under conditions of certainty to satisfy wealth maximisation criteria. To do so ignores the variable depth of cashflows around the EMV, as well as different management and shareholder attitudes toward risk.

4 MEAN-VARIANCE ANALYSIS

An implicit assumption of EMV analysis is that the cashflows for a project are normally distributed, that is with a symmetrical frequency distribution which conforms to the well known bell-shaped curve based on the Law of Large Numbers. The Law's *Central Limit Theorem* states that as a sample of independent, identically distributed random (IID) numbers approaches infinity its probability density function will conform to the normal distribution. Thus, if a project's cashflow estimates are assumed to behave in this way, then for each variable for each year a probability curve can be constructed as shown in Figure 4.1.

Whilst the question of whether real economic variables, such as a project's cashflows, are normally distributed is deferred until Chapter 13, the proposition is extremely attractive. The assumption permits corporate management to use standard computer programs for taking random samples and to make a sufficient number of sampling runs from innumerable probability curves to construct a probability distribution for the project as a whole. This may be expressed in terms of the E(NPV) in a multi-period context by:

$$(3) \qquad E(NPV) = \sum_{i=1}^{i=n} (NPV_i)P_i = E(NPV_1)P_1 + E(NPV_2)P_2 + ... + E(NPV_n)P_n$$

subject to the summation of the probability of occurrences being unity:

$$\sum_{i=1}^{n} P_i = 1.0$$

Thus, management now has a much more realistic assessment of the project proposal. Faced with a significant probability of mediocre E(NPV)s the company would wish to assess the risks of insolvency. If the project is marginal a significant chance of losses may be viewed as merely inconvenient. With large incremental investments, however, such a situation would be disastrous. This is where management's attitude towards risk comes into play when considering the most appropriate course of action. But where does this leave the shareholder?

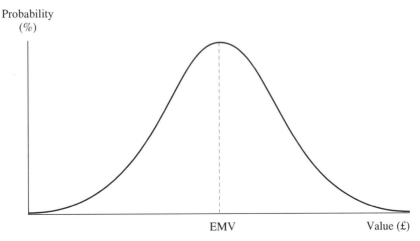

Fig 4.1 Normal distribution

Good managers should know more about their company than any other stakeholder (or so it is argued). Furthermore, as employees of the company management's interactions between insolvency, the threat of bankruptcy and job security should work in other stakeholders' favour. On the other hand, if a shareholder's financial interest in the firm is small relative to their total investment elsewhere, they may still view the risk of corporate bankruptcy associated with the adoption of a major project as only a minor inconvenience, particularly if there is a probability (however small) of significant gains.

A similar anomaly arises if the maximisation of E(NPV) is the criterion of choice between more than one project in cases of capital rationing, or where a selection must be made from mutually exclusive alternatives. Here EMVs alone are not a sufficient measure of risk. The depth of variability associated with EMV also becomes important. Consider the choice between the two following alternatives:

(*i*)   the certainty of no gain or loss
(*ii*) a 50–50 chance of winning £1 or losing 90p.

Many people would prefer the latter because it has an EMV of 5 pence compared with an EMV of zero for the first alternative.

But suppose the choice is between:

(*i*)   the certainty of no gain or loss
(*ii*) a 50–50 chance of winning £100,000 or losing £90,000

Here again there is a positive EMV of £5000 for the second alternative and a zero for the first. But in this instance many individuals would prefer the first alternative because of their unwillingness to risk the loss of £90,000.

To eliminate the paradox it is therefore suggested that managerial investment decisions should be analysed within the context of mean-variance analysis which uses the standard deviation as a measure of risk.

The approach assumes that periodic cashflows, which are normally distributed, may be summarised by the following parameters:

(4) $$EMV = EMV_t = \sum_i^n C_i P_i$$

(5) $$\text{Variance} = VAR\,(C_i) = \sum_i^n (C_i - EMV)^2 P_i$$

(6)   Standard deviation (square root of the variance) $= \delta(C_i) = \sqrt{VAR\,(C_i)}$

The variance of a random periodic cashflow C_i is a statistical *measure of dispersion*. It is equal to the weighted summation of the squared deviations of each observable cashflow from its EMV, where each weight is represented by the probability of occurrence. The deviations are squared because a normal distribution is symmetrical and the total probabilities equal one. To use the sum of the unsquared deviations of a large sample which are self-cancelling and always equal to zero would defeat the object of the exercise.

The scale change in relation to the expected value introduced by squaring the deviations is removed by calculating the square root of the variance, which gives the standard deviation. As a measure of the dispersion of all possible outcomes (their deviations around the mean) it provides a summary measure of risk. However, it also contains another convenient property.

In general, the probability that any expected cashflow will lie within a given number of standard deviations above the mean is calculated by the *z statistic*. This measures the actual deviation from the mean, divided by the standard deviation. In terms of the earlier cashflow notation:

(7) $z = (C_i - \text{EMV}_t)/\delta(C_i)$

Since a normal distribution is symmetrical the probability of a cashflow deviating above or below the mean is given by $2z$. With this information it is possible for management to assess the insolvency implications relating to a particular project and the possible threat of bankruptcy.

From any statistical table of z statistics for the standard normal distribution (see Appendix 4), the distribution of cashflows about the EMV conforms to confidence levels expressed as a percentage. Figure 4.2 plots the intervals one, two and three standard deviations from the mean.

$2z$ for $-\delta$ to $+\delta = 68.26\%$

$2z$ for -2δ to $+2\delta = 95.44\%$

$2z$ for -3δ to $+3\delta = 99.74\%$

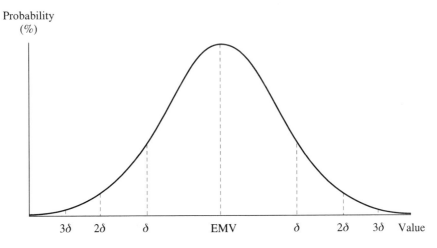

Fig 4.2 The confidence limits of mean-variance and analysis

Thus, the probability density function of the cash returns will allow EMV, $\delta(C_i)$ to represent the risk associated with the project. The objective of E(NPV) analysis is to reduce the variability of cashflows for a given EMV, or alternatively maximise the EMV for a given degree of variability. Thus, for any one year within a project proposal:

(8)   Max: EMV_t given $\delta(C_i)$

(9)   Min: $\delta(C_i)$ given EMV_t

It should also be noted that, just as EMV alone can prove an unreliable criterion of choice, so, too, risk is not equivalent to variability *per se*. The depth of variability from an EMV is clearly important. For example, two investments A and B might display the following inequality:

$$\delta(C_i)_A < \delta(C_i)_B$$

Yet, one could not categorically state that A's cashflows are less riskier than those of B. Indeed:

$$EMV_A < EMV_B$$

might more than offset the variability in cashflows.

To remove this anomaly it is therefore suggested that management should predetermine some desired minimum discounted cash return, (NPV) expressed as a profitability *index*, which they can compare with the expected NPV indices from proposed investments adjusted for risk using the standard deviation.

The latter would correspond to a level of confidence which they desire. Thus, the objective function of the NPV selection process under conditions of uncertainty becomes:

(10)   Max: $\dfrac{E(NPV) - n\delta E(NPV)}{I_0} \geq \dfrac{Min\ (NPV)}{I_0}$

where:
    n = the number of standard deviations
    I_0 = the cost of investment.

The variance of the E(NPV) is given by:

(11) $VAR\ E(NPV) = \delta^2 = \displaystyle\sum_{i=1}^{i=n} (NPV_i - E(NPV)^2\ P_i)$

The standard deviation is the square root of the variance:

(12) $\delta\ E(NPV) = \sqrt{VAR\ E(NPV)}$

5 AN APPLICATION OF MEAN-VARIANCE ANALYSIS

To illustrate the application of mean-variance criteria within the context of capital budgeting consider a situation where a firm is deciding which of two investment opportunities to undertake. Management has generated the following data:

	Project A	Project B
Life of project	5 years	5 years
DCF factor 10%	3.79	3.79
	£	£
Initial investment	2500	2500
Likely annual cash inflow (net of tax)	650	700

Possibilities of the net annual cashflows differing from their most likely flows are given by the following probabilistic estimates:

one chance in		A £	B £
20	at least	800	–
50	not more than	450	–
25	at least	–	1700
$12\frac{1}{2}$	a loss of	–	(200)
100	a loss of	–	(600)

The chance of a loss on project A is considered to be insignificant. On the basis of the most likely outcomes the following analysis has also been produced:

Net present value of projects' likely flow discounted at 10%

	A £		B £
Inflow (£650 × 3.79)	2463	(£700 × 3.79)	2653
Outflow	2500		2500
NPV of project	(37)		153

It is therefore suggested that project B should be adopted.

However, this decision would be compared with an EMV analysis as follows:

	Probability (%)	Cashflows (£)	$C_iP_i(£)$
Project A	5%	800	40
	93%	650	604.5
	2%	225	4.5
		EMV	£649
Project B	4%	1700	68
	87%	700	609
	8%	(200)	(16)
	1%	(600)	(6)
		EMV	£655

It has been assumed that 'at least £800' and 'at least £1700' can be interpreted as £800 and £1700 respectively. 'Not more than £450' is taken to equal £225, since the probability of a loss is insignificant.

The E(NPV) of each project's EMV discounted at 10% is given by:

Project	'A'		'B'
	£		£
Inflow (649 × 3.79)	2459	(655 × 3.79)	2482
Investment	2500		2500
E(NPV)	(41)		(18)

The following conclusions are drawn:

(*i*) If project A earned the most likely cash inflow of £650 per year for 5 years, it would not give the required 10 per cent return. If project B earned the most likely cash inflow of £700 a year for 5 years it would provide a return in excess of 10 per cent.

(*ii*) When probability is taken into account, neither project earns the required return but project B is still to be preferred in the sense that it minimises losses.

However, closer analysis of the data reveals both statements to be misleading. While project A could well be ruled out, as it will probably not even earn 10 per cent, it might be preferred because of the 93% confidence level of making £650 compared with the 87% confidence level of projects B's £700. It also offers downside protection, unlike project B where possible losses may occur.

The true significance of this phenomenon is revealed by mean variance analysis. The riskiness of the cashflows measured by the standard deviations, $\delta(C_i)$, for A and B are calculated as follows:

(a) Given $\text{EMV}_A = £649$

$(C_i - \text{EMV})$	£	$(C_i - \text{EMV})^2$	P_i	Certainty equivalent (£)
$800 - 649$	151	22,801	0.05	1140.05
$650 - 649$	1	1	0.93	0.93
$225 - 649$	(424)	179,776	0.02	3595.52
				4736.50

$\text{VAR}(C_i) = 4736.50$
$\sqrt{\text{VAR}(C_i)} = \delta(C_i) = £68.82$

(b) Given $\text{EMV}_B = £655$

$(C_i - \text{EMV})$	£	$(C_i - \text{EMV})^2$	P_i	Certainty equivalent
$1700 - 655$	1045	1,092,025	0.04	43,681.00
$700 - 655$	45	2,025	0.87	1,761.75
$(200) - 655$	(855)	731,025	0.08	58,482.00
$(600) - 655$	(1255)	1,575,025	0.01	15,750.25
				119,675.00

$\text{VAR}(C_i) = 119,675$
$\sqrt{\text{VAR}(C_i)} = \delta(C_i) = £345.9$

The variability below the respective mean for each project may now be calculated:

(c)

$(\text{EMV} - n\,\delta(C_i))$	A	B	Confidence level
given $n = 1$	580.18	309	68%
given $n = 2$	511.36	(36.8)	97%
given $n = 3$	442.54	(382.7)	99%

It is now clear that although both projects under-recover at the end of five years:

$$\text{EMV}_A < \text{EMV}_B$$
$$\delta(C_i)_A < \delta(C_i)_B$$

such that project A would be preferred if insolvency is to be avoided in any one year.

6 DECISION TREES AND THE CONCEPT OF EXPECTED NET PRESENT VALUE

The decision tree technique provides management with alternative diagrammatic representations of the probabilities associated with a project's cashflows. This can facilitate their analysis and be more effective than a written report. It clarifies various courses of action where a project's outcomes can be deconstructed into a sequence of likely occurrences with *conditional* probabilities. Branches from the trunk stem from previous decisions made by the company (control factors) and chance (uncontrollable events), hence its name. An example best explains the application.

A company is considering a major investment in a new productive process. The total cost of the investment has been estimated at £2,000,000 but if this were increased to £3,000,000 productive capacity could be substantially increased. Because of the nature of the process, once the basic facilities have been established, it is prohibitively expensive to increase capacity at some future date. Another problem facing management is that the demand for the product is very uncertain. However, the following estimates are available:

Investment A (£3m)			*Investment* B (£2m)		
Demand probability	*Years*	*Annual net cash flow (£m)*	*Demand probability*	*Years*	*Annual net cash flow (£m)*
0.3	1–4	1.0	0.4	1–4	0.6
	5–10	0.7		5–10	0.5
0.5	1–4	0.8	0.4	1–4	0.6
	5–10	0.4		5–10	0.2
0.2	1–10	0.1	0.2	1–10	0.2
	Cost of capital	10%		Cost of capital	10%

Management's solution to the problem based on a decision tree analysis would reveal the information contained in Table 4.1.

The calculations which produce the figures contained in Table 4.1 are as follows:

Present value of £1.00 received for the requisite number of years (from DCF tables)

Years	PV factor
1–4	3.17
5–10	2.98
1–10	6.15

Present value of probabilistic cashflows

Years	PV factor	P_{iA}	PV_A	P_{iB}	PV_B
1–4	3.17	1.0	3.17	0.6	1.90
5–10	2.98	0.7	2.09	0.5	1.50
1–4	3.17	0.8	2.54	0.6	1.90
5–10	2.98	0.4	1.19	0.2	0.60
1–10	6.15	0.1	0.62	0.2	1.23

Table 4.1 An application of decision tree analysis

Investment	Probability	Years	Cashflow	Present value cashflow	Expected value
£(million)			£(million)	£(million)	£(million)

Decision tree:

A(3) branches:
- 0.3 → (1–4: Cashflow 1.0, PV 3.17 ; 5–10: Cashflow 0.7, PV 2.09) → 1.58
- 0.5 → (1–4: Cashflow 0.8, PV 2.54 ; 5–10: Cashflow 0.4, PV 1.19) → 1.87
- 0.2 → (1–10: Cashflow 0.1, PV 0.62) → 0.12

$\Sigma P_i = 1.0$
EMV 3.57
Cost 3.00
E(NPV) 0.57

B(2) branches:
- 0.4 → (1–4: Cashflow 0.6, PV 1.90 ; 5–10: Cashflow 0.5, PV 1.50) → 1.36
- 0.4 → (1–4: Cashflow 0.6, PV 1.90 ; 5–10: Cashflow 0.2, PV 0.60) → 1.00
- 0.2 → (1–10: Cashflow 0.2, PV 1.23) → 0.25

$\Sigma P_i = 1.0$
EMV 2.61
Cost 2.00
E(NPV) 0.61

Three points now emerge:

(*i*) The E(NPV) of both investments is almost identical but the smaller investment is marginally superior.

(*ii*) The analysis does not give clear guidance as to whether management should provide the additional capacity now or later. More information is required about the excess cost over and above the equivalent of £1 million today in the future to provide this.

(*iii*) The current degree of risk associated with each investment should be assessed by reference to the standard deviation. However, it can be seen that there is a greater range of possible outcomes with the larger investment, i.e. a greater chance of high cash flows and also a greater chance of low cash flows.

If the lowest estimate actually results the position will be:

	£3 *million investment*	£2 *million investment*
	PV £(million)	PV £(million)
Cashflow	0.62	1.23
Cost	(3.00)	(2.00)
NPV	(2.38)	(0.77)

If the best estimate materialises:

	£3 *million investment*	£2 *million investment*
	PV £(million)	PV £(million)
Cashflow	5.26	3.40
Cost	(3.00)	(2.00)
NPV	2.26	1.40

Proceeding to a statistical analysis of risk where:

$$E(NPV)_A = 0.51 < E(NPV)_B = 0.61$$

The standard deviation for each investment is calculated as follows:

£3 million investment

$(C_i - EMV)$	$(C_i - EMV)^2$	P_i	$(C_i - EMV)^2 P_i$
$5.26 - 3.57 = 1.69$	2.86	0.3	0.86
$3.73 - 3.57 = 0.16$	0.03	0.5	0.01
$0.62 - 3.57 = (2.95)$	8.70	0.2	1.74
		VAR_A	2.61

$$\delta_A = \sqrt{VAR_A} = \sqrt{2.61} = 1.615$$

£2 *million investment*

$(C_i - \mathrm{EMV})$	$(C_i - \mathrm{EMV})^2$	P_i	$(C_i - \mathrm{EMV})^2 P_i$
$3.40 - 2.61 = 0.79$	0.62	0.4	0.248
$2.50 - 2.61 = (0.11)$	0.012	0.4	0.005
$1.23 - 2.61 = (1.38)$	1.90	0.2	0.380
		$\mathrm{VAR_B}$	0.633

$$\delta_B = \sqrt{\mathrm{VAR_B}} = \sqrt{0.633} = 0.796$$

Clearly, the smaller investment minimises risk in relation to its E(NPV) at all confidence levels.

7 THE CONCEPT OF EXPECTED UTILITY

As stated earlier, the use of EMV criteria in isolation may prove unreliable under conditions of uncertainty, particularly in cases of capital rationing or where choices exist between mutually exclusive alternatives. Although mean-variance analysis is designed to overcome this defect, the ultimate acceptance of an investment proposal still depends upon the decision-maker's attitude toward risk. One decision-maker, less risk-averse than another, may accept a project which the other would reject because he is only focusing upon the possibility of future projects. Even though the monetary gains and losses associated with the project are identical to both it would be paradoxical for the gambler to perceive the project as risky. To overcome this defect, an alternative criterion of choice is therefore required which refers not to an individual's consumption preferences over time but to an individual's attitude toward monetary gains or losses under various conditions. Expected utility is such a criterion.

In effect, expected utility calibrates an individual's subjective attitude toward risk, in terms of units of utility rather than units of money. These units are then converted to their *certain cash equivalent* in order to quantify a risky decision. The process may be illustrated as follows.

Suppose a decision-maker is faced with an investment project which requires an initial outlay of £50,000. In return the following distribution of discounted cash inflows and their associated probabilities are calculated as follows:

Discounted gain/loss	ΣP_i	*EMV*
£		£
200,000	0.1	20,000
100,000	0.3	30,000
50,000	0.4	20,000
		(*continued*)

Continued from p. 81 Discounted gain/loss	$\sum P_i$	EMV
£		£
(10,000)	0.1	(1,000)
(15,000)	0.1	(1,500)
	1.0	67,500

Clearly E(NPV) signals acceptance since the expected present value of future cashflows exceeds the cost of the investment. But what of the individual's attitude toward the risk?

In order to ascertain this, the individual is first asked to choose between a series of complex hypothetical lotteries. Assume that he is asked to take part in a game offering a 50–50 chance of receiving nothing or £100,000, to which the respective values of zero and one are attached arbitrarily. These figures are assumed to represent points on a scale of utility. Next the individual is asked if he would prefer a figure less than £100,000, say £80,000, to be received with certainty, rather than partake in the lottery. Assuming that he would, smaller alternative certain amounts are offered until a figure is reached which expresses the individual's indifference between certain cash and the lottery.

Suppose the final amount is £40,000. Then a utility of 0.5 may be assigned to this by reference to the following equation:

$$U(40,000) = 0.5\ U(0) + 0.5\ U(100,000)$$
$$0.5 = 0.5(0) + 0.5(1.0)$$

Thus, three points on the individual's utility curve have now been calibrated in terms of utility and an associated certainty cash equivalent:

0, £0:0.5, £40,000:1.0, £100,000

Other points on the scale may be obtained by proposing other lotteries using amounts for which utilities have already been established. For example, the certainty equivalent conforming to a lottery with a 0.3 probability of £100,000 and a 0.7 probability of £40,000 might be £50,000. Hence the utility of £50,000 could be obtained by the following equation:

$$U(50,000) = 0.3\ U(100,000) + 0.7\ U(40,000)$$
$$0.65 = 0.3(1.0) + 0.7(0.5)$$

Utilities in excess of £100,000 may be obtained by using known utilities in equations representing indifference. Assume the individual is indifferent between a certain £40,000 (the utility of which has already been established as 0.5), and a lottery with a 0.3 probability of £200,000 and a 0.7 probability of zero. The equation is:

0.3 U(200,000) + 0.7 U(0) = U(40,000)

0.3 U = 0.5

U = 1.67

Negative cashflows can also be determined in the same manner. Assume the individual is indifferent between £50,000 or a lottery with a 0.8 gain of £100,000 and a 0.2 loss of £10,000. The equation of indifference may be solved as follows:

0.2 U(−10,000) + 0.8 U(100,000) = U(50,000)

0.2 U + 0.8(1) = 0.65

U = −0.75

If the above procedures are now repeated exhaustively, a utility schedule for the individual will emerge which may be graphed.

As Figure 4.3 reveals, the graph is consistent with the individual's attitude toward risk. Except for relatively small gambles he is risk-averse, as shown by

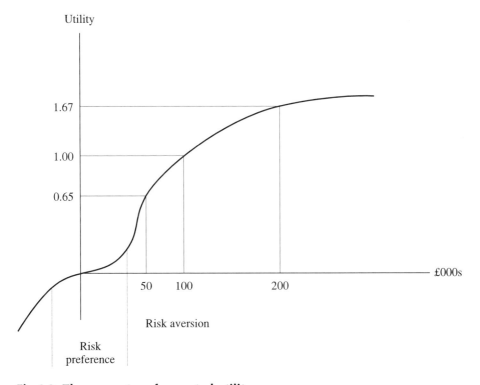

Fig 4.3 The geometry of expected utility

the concave shape of the function (looking from below). Near the origin the convex sector denotes risk preference. In particular it may be noted that the utility of £100,000 is less than twice that of £50,000 but more than half the utility of £200,000.

8 EXPECTED UTILITY AND CERTAINTY CASH EQUIVALENTS

Once an individual's utility curve has been established it is possible to compute the certain cash equivalent of the distribution of uncertain possible cash outcomes for any investment project.

The equivalent utilities of the discounted cashflows are multiplied by their respective probabilities, then totalled to obtain the expected present utility of the distribution. This expected utility may then be converted to its certain cash equivalent by reference to the individual's utility function. This in turn is compared with the cost of the initial investment.

Using the previous example (for an investment which costs £50,000) the following table may be produced for the likely cashflows:

Discounted gain/loss (£)	P_i	U_i	Weighted utility
200,000	0.1	1.67	0.167
100,000	0.3	1.00	0.300
50,000	0.4	0.65	0.260
(10,000)	0.1	(0.75)	(0.075)
(15,000)	0.1	(0.52)	(0.152)
			E(U) 0.5

Reference to the individual's utility function shows that the certainty cash equivalent for the expected utility of the distribution of discounted cashflows is £40,000. Clearly, the project should only be accepted if this is greater than the utility of the required investment. In this case, however:

U£40,000 < U£50,000

since $0.5 < 0.65$.

Hence, the project would be rejected. This, it will be recalled, overturns the original decision based upon EMV calculations and the E(NPV) acceptance criteria.

One final point should be emphasised. Decision tree analysis revealed that the probability distribution of anticipated cashflows in one period might depend upon the actual outcomes in previous years. Similarly, once determined, investor utility functions are not necessarily a constant. They might be conditional upon the impact of previous experiences upon wealth and thus determine attitudes toward risk which are transient. This being the case, they must be subject to periodic review if future certainty equivalents are to remain valid investment criteria.

9 THE CHOICE OF AN APPROPRIATE DISCOUNT RATE

The formal treatment of risk in capital budgeting so far suggests two different approaches based upon the time value of money and discounted cashflow analyses:

- The maximisation of expected net present value for a minimum level of risk, where risk is measured by the standard deviation of the E(NPV).
- The maximisation of investor utility which dispenses with the standard deviation altogether and discounts the certainty equivalents of a project's anticipated cashflows.

However, both approaches confront the decision-maker with two fundamental problems. First, expected monetary values must be derived from a subjective probabilistic estimate of future cashflows. Second, the discount rate must still be correctly defined. The solution to the former is essentially a question of management's forecasting abilities. The choice of an appropriate discount rate, however, is a conceptually more complex decision.

In Chapter 3 it was explained that in a perfect capital market under conditions of certainty the company's investment decisions can be made separately from the shareholders' consumption decisions, provided the discount rate represents a market rate of interest. Correctly defined, this equals the shareholder's opportunity cost of capital applicable to comparable investments undertaken elsewhere.

Under conditions of uncertainty but perfect markets it will be explained in Parts 3 and 4 how opportunity costs of capital (market rates of interest) reflect the total risk associated with an investment. Total risk may be subdivided further into two components:

- *Business risk*, derived from the selection of projects with differing uncertain, future cashflows.
- *Financial risk*, associated with how the investment is initially financed and how its earnings are ultimately packaged for distribution.

Both elements of risk impact upon a project's discount rate. Rational (risk-averse) investors will require a higher return than its certainty equivalent to compensate for total risk (although this suggestion will be critically examined later within the context of portfolio decisions).

For the moment, the important point to recognise is that, under conditions of uncertainty, the market rate of interest already includes a risk premium based on a consensus of investor sentiment concerning the future. To add a further premium for risk would, therefore, involve an element of double counting somewhere within a project appraisal if the cashflows to be discounted are already based upon probabilistic estimates. In the absence of an assessment based on the possibility of multiple expectations, such as the most likely NPV, a case can be made for using some form of risk-adjusted discount rate. However, this too introduces a general problem associated with multi-period asset investments. When a discount rate is adjusted for risk, whether it be from a risk-free rate on gilt-edged securities, or by the addition of a further premium, its impact on a project is much greater on distant discounted cashflows than upon those received earlier. If risk is assumed to be solely a function of time (the payback criteria) this facet of the DCF concept is acceptable. If not, it will either overstate or understate a project's net present value depending on the pattern of cashflows. This explains why the introduction of premiums to compensate for risk into portfolio investment decisions relate to single-period models.

With regard to mean-variance analysis and the calibration of expected utility based on the certainty equivalents of cashflows, there is a further problem. To use a market rate of interest which incorporates an allowance for risk still involves an element of duplication. This arises because reduction of multi-valued expectations to their expected monetary values as a basis for investment appraisal, which are then assessed by either the project's standard deviation or its certainty cash equivalent, both account for risk. Most texts on corporate finance, therefore, recommend that to avoid a duplication of the elimination of risk it is imperative that the adjusted gains or losses are not discounted by the market rate of interest, which also includes a risk premium. The correct figure is a default-free discount rate, such as the return on gilt-edged government securities with the same maturity (redemption) date as the project's cashflows.

The view taken here is that such a recommendation is far too simplistic. Projects which now should be rejected may be accepted by understating the *relevant* discount rates, thereby overstating their expected net present values.

10 THE OPPORTUNITY COST OF CAPITAL REVISITED

By definition, the risk-free rate under conditions of certainty contains no adjustment for the possibility of multiple expectations or investor attitudes toward risk under the assumptions of a perfect capital market. However, as explained in Chapter 3, this is a special case. It was also explained that, in a perfect capital market given the Separation Theory of Fisher (1930), the firm's investment decisions can be processed independently from the shareholders' consumption decisions. The principle applied was the best opportunity foregone. The relevant discount rate in project appraisal is the shareholders' opportunity cost of capital (to whom management are ultimately responsible) earned on comparable investments outside the firm.

Armed with knowledge of mean-variance analysis and the concept of a certainty cash equivalent, the opportunity cost precept can be reformulated under conditions of uncertainty. How much would an investor be willing to pay for a risk-return trade-off or a stream of cash equivalents of expected utility values that represent the maximum benefits to be derived from the ownership of a company's shares? Invoking the opportunity cost principle, the maximum price offered by a potential shareholder for a company's shares would be determined by the investment alternative foregone.

In the absence of capital rationing, an investor with access to unlimited funds at the risk-free rate may choose not to purchase the shares by borrowing at this explicit cost of capital. If this situation characterises the company's prospective, total shareholder clientele, the firm's discount rate applied to mean-variance analyses or the stream of expected utility cash equivalents which determines the maximum offer price is the explicit risk-free market rate of interest.

However, if capital rationing prevails, or the explicit incremental cost of borrowing is positively correlated to the size of the investment, individual decisions to purchase shares may preclude alternative opportunities for investment or consumption. These may be categorised as follows: for each prospective investor:

(*i*) the return on the best risk-free investment opportunity foregone
(*ii*) the explicit capital cost of the finance used
(*iii*) the time-preference rate of the most attractive alternative consumption opportunity.

The appropriate discount rate for any investor to incorporate into the maximum price calculation for the firm's shares would be measured by the highest of these three rates that would be foregone as a result of purchasing the shares. Thus, it follows that the market rate of discount which the firm applies to its capital projects is the highest 'rate of return' (opportunity cost of capital rate) foregone by the investor who pays the highest purchase price for all the company's shares, which might not be the return on gilt-edged securities.

However, this leads one to ask what precisely is the investor buying? Is it the prospect of current consumption in the form of dividends or increases in future wealth *via* retention financed investment and future capital gains? Moreover, under conditions of uncertainty, what factors might cause a change in the shareholder's market rate of discount and hence share price, as a result of the payment or non-payment of a dividend by the firm?

As in the case of the corporate investment decision, the answer should be a change in the distribution pattern of the future income stream in relation to shareholder expectations when their original decision to purchase the shares was made. Thus, it may be impossible to gauge the impact of corporate investment decisions upon the firm's discount rate and market value without explicit consideration of its dividend policy. The decision to pay a dividend rather than retain funds to reinvest in new projects also has implications for the firm's *overall* financial policy. Specifically, a company's recourse to debt capital rather than equity may alter the shareholders' perception of financial risk, causing them to revise, yet again, their market rate of discount. Because debt interest represents a prior contractual claim on the firm's incremental cash-flows (or assets in the event of liquidation), the shareholders may extract a premium return by way of compensation. Both matters will be given detailed consideration in Parts 3 and 4.

11 CORPORATE OBJECTIVES, INVESTMENT BEHAVIOUR AND RISK: SOME EMPIRICAL EVIDENCE

The maximisation of shareholders' wealth achievable through the maximisation of the expected NPV of a firm's prospective capital investments represents the prescribed objective of normative financial theory. Yet, the empirical research suggests that the goal inaccurately describes managerial utility functions: NPV is not the most popular measurement criteria and risk is treated simplistically.

Several UK surveys on corporate objectives, including Carsberg and Hope (1976), Hill (1982) and Pike and Ooi (1988), have long since confirmed that UK management prefer to adopt a short-run rate of return or profit target for decision-making purposes that is not necessarily related to market forces. A favoured criterion is the return on assets which can be derived from published company accounts prepared on a historical cost basis. Even in a sophisticated financial sector such as the insurance industry, where portfolio techniques are the rule, UK equity fund managers prefer not to look beyond a five-year time horizon (see Hill 1994).

The past twenty years has also provided considerable research into the methods of investment appraisal actually employed by UK companies. A study by Pike (1982), based on a sample of 100 drawn from the largest 300 UK firms, reveals the payback technique to be the commonest investment criteria by far, often used in conjunction with the accounting rate of return as a proxy for the rate of profit. Moreover, only 38 per cent of his respondents analysed risk in any way, half of whom remained sceptical of the results.

Revisiting the sample in 1986, Pike found that while the percentage of respondents using NPV had increased from 39 per cent to 68 per cent, less than half the latter group used it exclusively. Where discounting methods are applied to capital projects it would appear that NPV is making the greatest headway but it still falls behind IRR which is second only to payback, leaving the ARR to bring up the rear.

The more advanced standing of NPV in recent years is not surprising given that in relation to other capital budgeting techniques it was largely unknown prior to the 1960s, even in academia. Yet, over twenty five years later it was still being ignored by medium-size UK companies. According to the study by McIntyre and Coulthurst (1985) only 13 per cent of 141 respondents used any DCF technique, although the more recent surveys cited by Pike and Wolfe (1988), Pike (1992) and Drury, Braund, Osborne and Tayles (1993) suggest that NPV is gaining in popularity across the business spectrum.

Analysed in unison, research also reveals another interesting phenomenon. Whilst larger, sophisticated firms are obviously more likely to use NPV than smaller firms (which tend to favour payback), the use of multiple appraisal criteria such as payback allied to a profitability measure is endemic. One explanation is that many firms may actually pursue an ill-defined set of objectives based on rules of thumb and industry norms. When making and gauging their investment decisions, the use of more than one investment criteria is therefore designed to cover any eventuality. Another causal factor reported by Ho and Pike (1991) in their survey of 146 of the largest UK firms is that payback is invariably used to analyse risk. Summarising their findings, 87 per cent of sample respondents accounted for risk in some way (compared with 37 per cent in the 1987 survey results reported by Pike.) The methodologies, which are not inspiring, can be broken down as follows:

Classification of risky projects	*Respondents*
(*i*) Reducing payback	75%
(*ii*) Increasing the hurdle rate (discount rate, IRR or ARR)	77%

Formal risk assessment	*Respondents*
(*i*) Sensitivity analysis	85%
(*ii*) Use of probabilities	51%

One only hopes that, given the commercially available software, sensitivity analysis is being conducted using computer simulation and not a scientific calculator.

Turning to the American evidence, the IRR is also more popular than the ARR. As in the UK, payback is still most favoured. Whilst twenty five years ago NPV was the least popular technique in large US companies (see Petty, Scott and Bird (1975)), more recent evidence reveals that unlike the UK it has become more popular than IRR; see Moore and Reichert (1983), Levy and Sarnat (1988). A comparative study of UK and US investment practice by Scapens, Sales and Tikkas (1982) has long since confirmed that DCF techniques are more widespread in the US, but, like the UK, the classification of risky projects and formal risk assessment, the treatment of inflation and capital rationing in investment appraisal are all poorly handled.

That a number of UK firms use very sophisticated DCF techniques is undeniable. Nevertheless, there remains a considerable disparity between normative theory and industry practice. In the survey by Pike and Ooi (1988) concerning the relationship between investment behaviour and corporate objectives and constraints, based on 100 large UK firms, the following conclusions are worthy of note:

- The importance of shareholders' wealth maximisation was not correlated with the use of NPV techniques; indeed senior managers pay little attention to how financial goals are translated in performance measurement terms, tending to rely on payback and traditional accounting rate of return measures.
- Management attach more importance to short-term profit-related investment objectives in terms of profitability, i.e. return on assets, despite a significant increase in the perceived importance of the shareholders' wealth maximisation objective over the period of study.

Also of interest are Pike and Ooi's behavioural explanations for these anomalies, particularly how the judicious use of payback and short-run profitability criteria might actually resolve conflict between shareholder and managerial objectives. For example, shareholders could be indifferent between two investment proposals with differing payback but an identical NPV, because they have recourse to the capital market for the sale of shares and hence the present value of future cashflows via capital gains. As a consequence, rational management should select the more liquid project, if their promotion and bonus prospects were determined by annual cashflows. Even in the presence of remuneration packages linked to long-run profitability, individual managers may still prefer short-run liquidity, since they might expect to leave the firm before investment projects have run their course, an observation confirmed by the author (op. cit.).

Whatever the truth of the matter, there is clearly still much to explain concerning the investment behaviour of companies and those interested in their performance. What is not in doubt is the empirical support managerial actions lend to the vast body of economic evidence concerning theories of the firm, cost-plus pricing and managerial utility functions. This has long suggested that if firms pursue any long-term objective at all they tend to do so in an evolutionary manner by trying to maintain or increase their current profits within their practicable horizons.

12 SUMMARY AND CONCLUSIONS

This chapter has suggested a rational approach to the solution of capital invest-ment decisions under conditions of uncertainty, namely the maximisation of the present value of the cash equivalents of expected utilities. Rather than max-imise a project's expected NPV for a minimum level of risk (as measured by the standard deviation), the model incorporates the plurality of outcomes that exist under conditions of uncertainty, subjective estimates of their probabilities *and* the risk attitudes of those involved in the decision making process.

However, a number of reservations must be expressed concerning certainty equivalents:

- Equivalent utilities and hence certainty cash equivalents can only be obtained with difficulty and will differ from individual to individual. Hence they are highly subjective.
- Even if risk functions for individuals are obtained they may be susceptible to change over time. Moreover, where more than one person is involved in an investment appraisal the problem arises as to how different utility func-tions can be combined to obtain an overall measure of risk attitudes in the group decision-making process.
- The utility approach calibrates two different aspects of risk which may also be suspect:
  (*i*)   The uncertainty attached by an individual to a project via probabilities using *Gaussian* techniques. These are based upon the classical tools of statistics, even though the probabilities themselves are subjectively assessed.
  (*ii*) The psychological attitudes of individuals towards risk who may actually act differently from the predictions of classical probability theory.

It will be recalled that it is in relation to individual's differing perceptions of a risky project where mean-variance analysis falls short. Hence a need for an alternative methodology. The question to be asked, however, is if the subjective probabilities of the former methodology do not always provide a unique solution, then how can their incorporation into the latter approach improve matters?

Finally, it should be emphasised that both mean-variance analysis and the use of expected utility and certainty cash equivalents are all variants or exten-sions to the basic NPV model first encountered in Chapter 2 under conditions of certainty and perfect capital markets. Accordingly, they also suffer from the limitations of that method, particularly with regard to assumptions concerning capital costs and reinvestment rates. As such, these various approaches to investment appraisal under risk and non-risk conditions should be used with caution. Properly perceived they are the keys which may open a Pandora's box creating more problems than they can solve.

References

(1) Carsberg, B.V. and Hope, A., *Business Investment Decisions Under Inflation: Theory and Practice,* ICAEW, 1976.

(2) Drury, C., Braund, S., Osborne, P. and Tayles, M., *A Survey of Management Accounting Practices in UK Manufacturing Industries*, CACA (London) 1993.

(3) Fisher, I., *The Theory of Interest*, Macmillan, 1930.

(4) Hill, RA., 'Facts and theory in measuring divisional performance', *Accountancy*, Vol. 93, No. 1064, April 1982.

(5) Hill, R.A. and Meredith, S., 'Insurance institutions and fund management: a UK perspective', *Journal of Applied Accounting Research,* Vol. II, No. 2, 1994.

(6) Ho, S.S.M. and Pike, R.H., 'Risk analysis in capital budgeting contexts: simple or sophisticated', *Accounting and Business Research*, Vol. 21, No. 83, 1991.

(7) Levy, H. and Sarnat, M., *Principles of Financial Management*, Prentice Hall, 1988.

(8) McIntyre, A.D. and Coulthurst, N.J., 'Theory and practice in capital budgeting', *British Accounting Review*, Autumn, 1985.

(9) Moore, J.S. and Reichart, A.K., 'An analysis of the financial management techniques currently employed by large US corporations', *Journal of Business Finance and Accounting*, Vol. 10, No. 4, 1983.

(10) Petty, J.W., Scott, S.F. and Bird, M.M., 'The capital expenditure decision-making process of large corporations', *Engineering Economist,* Spring, 1975.

(11) Pike, R.H. and Ooi, T.S., 'The impact of corporate investment objectives and constraints on capital budgeting practices', *The British Accounting Review*, Vol. 20, No. 2, August 1988.

(12) Pike, R.H., *Capital Budgeting in the 1980s,* CIMA (London) 1982.

(13) Pike, R.H., 'Owner-manager conflict and the role of the payback method', *Accounting and Business Research,* Winter 1985.

(14) Pike, R.H. and Wolfe, M., *Capital Budgeting in the 1990s*, CIMA (London) 1988.

(15) Pike, R.H., 'Capital budgeting survey: an update', *Bradford University Discussion Paper,* 1992; cited in Pike, R.H. and Neale, C.W., *Corporate Finance and Investment,* Prentice Hall, 1993.

(16) Scapens, R.W., Sale, T.J. and Tikkas, P.A., *Financial Control of Divisional Capital Investments*, CIMA (London) 1982.

PART THREE

The dividend decision

5

Equity valuation and investment ratio analysis

Chapter profile

This chapter's purpose is to consider the relevance of discounted revenue theory, examined in Part 2, with respect to the pricing of ordinary shares, i.e. equity. The analysis of stock market performance, utilising published financial ratios, is also introduced. Since it is based on logical argument, the reader is not burdened with any references at this stage.

Armed with the capitalisation concept, the simple mechanisms of share valuation, utilising dividends and earnings under various growth conditions, are outlined. The special case of capitalising a perpetual annuity, so as to calculate the dividend yield, the earnings yield and its reciprocal the price/earnings (P/E) ratio, is explained. Other financial indicators, based upon dividends, earnings and their inter-relationships, are also defined.

Finally, their interpretation is illustrated numerically. This provides a foundation for a more detailed consideration, in the ensuing chapters, of the differential influence of dividend policies and financial structures which impinge upon corporate values, investor returns and the maximisation of shareholders' wealth.

1 INTRODUCTION

There is more to financial analysis than the interpretation of historical data which is contained in company accounts, as the economic discourse of Part 1 revealed. Accountants, auditors, government, the tax authorities and even management may defend published financial statements, by proclaiming that the price paid for assets and the income which they apparently generate are accountable facts. In this sense, the reports are objective: they are composed of 'real' figures which purport to present a 'true and fair view'. Whether their data has utility for any stakeholder, other than the Inland Revenue, however, is questionable. Suppose a company with turnover of £25 million and profits of

£5 million shows in its balance sheet the following:

	£000s	
Land	20,000	(Bought 5 years ago)
Buildings	80,000	(60,000 spent 5 years ago, the balance representing the cost of subsequent additions at various dates)
Plant	40,000	(Various equipment bought on average 2 years ago)
Stock	5,000	(Many different items, bought on average 3 months ago)
Debtors	4,000	(All expected to be good and to repay on average 3 months hence)
Cash	2,000	(Held for 2 months)
	151,000	

At least five significant points emerge:

- Each item in the list is a fact, i.e. a record of transactions which have actually taken place. Every one represents actual money, or money receivable. Except to the extent that there might be error or misrepresentation (for example, equipment might have been bought and charged against current revenue, thus reducing profit and the asset figure below total cost), the list is a factual statement of assets owned and prices paid.
- However, the total of £151 million has no real meaning. It is a summation of sterling at different values, i.e. now, five years ago, three months hence, and so on, which equals the nominal value of authorised and issued share capital plus the historical cost of reserves, debenture stocks and other liabilities. It has about as much validity as saying that four apples and three pears equal seven fruit.
- Even if the figures were adjusted for inflation (i.e. average price change), the list of assets gives no indication of their specific worth. The land might be in a development area and saleable for £50 million. The specific cost of replacing the buildings and equipment in their present form might be £250 million. Moreover, the assets might have a high current market value or a low current value compared with only a year ago. As a consequence, a significant disparity may exist between the nominal and market value of equity plus reserves, as well as debt. Yet none of this is revealed by the accounts.
- Similarly, but to opposite effect, the £5 million profit is an accrual-based subtraction of various historical costs from current revenue which does

not correspond to the net inflow of cash (to the extent that goods and services have been bought and sold on credit and the figure also includes depreciation which is a non-cash expense).

- In the long run, a company's wealth is the amount it can first earn and subsequently distribute. If one adopts this criterion of value, however, there is a conflict between a tangible asset figure, net of all liabilities (even current cost based), and either a profitability or a dividend valuation which reflects the market price of equity, based on discounted revenue theory. The former ignores human resources and intangible items, which incorporate such items as goodwill and brand names. The latter are forward looking and embrace the whole structure of the firm, based upon present value analyses of projected cashflows, relative to a company's desired rate of return (which may bear no relation to the accountants' familiar return on capital employed).

In other words discounted revenue theory presupposes an objective: the NPV maximisation of all a firm's investments, which, *inter alia*, implies shareholder wealth maximisation and the satisfaction of all other stakeholders. In contrast financial accounting statements provide neither an objective nor a model. Costs are held constant, market conditions are an unknown and the recipients are left to rely upon their normative judgement concerning corporate performance.

Leaving aside the accountants' mentality, this dichotomy arises because of the necessity for up-to-date information which dictates the need to relate the income of the firm to arbitrary reporting periods which do not necessarily conform to the cycle of its operations. If all inputs into the productive process were converted into output and sold within a single accounting period there would be little problem; the only asset held by the firm would be cash. Since business is a continuous process, however, at the end of each accounting period there are normally significant amounts of input, each at various stages of conversion into output, all of which should be valued. It is this fact of asset valuation which poses the greatest problem for the accounting profession. Even the admission of current values rather than historic costs into accounting statements (let alone present value analysis) represents a departure from their stewardship role, i.e. the simple recording of transactions which have actually taken place, and a move towards the estimation of periodic cashflows explained in previous chapters.

Despite an academic pedigree in excess of fifty years, the requirement that financial accounting data should reflect current values has only gained fleeting and desultory formal recognition from the UK accounting profession comparatively recently. Yet, since the 1930s, it has long been appreciated by financial theorists and analysts that at an operational level, market valuations, which are based upon discounted revenue theory and incorporate intangible items such as goodwill, are crucial to any assessment of a company's stockmarket efficiency. Dividend yields, price earnings (P/E) ratios and other financial measures are, therefore, published in the financial press daily in order to facilitate such analyses. Unfortunately, they are rarely explained, it being assumed that readers are fully conversant with their use.

What follows is an introduction to rudimentary models of share price determination which underpin investment ratio analysis. Various procedures are examined whereby ordinary shares are valued based on dividends per share and earnings per share (EPS), assuming nil, constant and split growth. Given these assumptions, both dividend and earnings valuations of equity are shown to be entirely consistent if the shareholders' return is correctly defined.

The controversy concerning the influence that different dividend or reinvestment policies exert upon equity prices, dividend yields and earnings yields, via the shareholders' risk return trade-off under conditions of uncertainty, is not considered until Chapter 7. The relevance of changes in the capitalisation rate *vis à vis* financial policy and theories of capital structure is also deferred to Part 4 of the text, where the valuation and costs of alternative sources of finance–debt, retained earnings and other implicit funds–are also explained.

The immediate aim is to provide an understanding of the simple mechanics of equity pricing so that the rationale for a series of definitions of the commonest investment ratios relating to share valuation can be presented as a precursor to their practical application and theoretical foundation in the following chapters.

2 THE CAPITALISATION CONCEPT AND DIVIDEND VALUATION

It will be recalled from Chapter 2 that, under conditions of certainty, a fundamental proposition of capital market theory defines the value of an asset as its future net receipts discounted back to the present at an appropriate rate. Expressed mathematically:

$$(1) \qquad P_0 = \sum_{t=1}^{n} \frac{1}{(1+r)^t} C_t$$

where:

P_0 = the present value or price
C_t = the net cash flow for each time period
r = the interest rate (or rate of return)
n = the number of periods under observation.

If the annual cash receipts from an investment, C_t, are constant over time and tend to infinity then the price paid for that investment P_0, based upon the present value of those receipts, is the simpler equation for a perpetual annuity:

$$(2) \qquad P_0 = \frac{C_t}{r}$$

where:
$$C_t = C_1 = C_2 = C_3 = \ldots = C_n$$
$r =$ the interest rate or required rate of return which is assumed not to change.

Explained simply, a 10 per cent return of £100 in perpetuity implies an investment of £1000 today.

The term r is known as the *capitalisation rate*. This is because if one has observations for r and C, then the utilisation of Equation (2) in order to arrive at a present value is termed 'capitalisation', i.e. one is capitalising cashflows in order to arrive at a value.

It also follows from above that, given observations on price and the capitalisation rate, cash receipts can also be determined. Rearranging terms:

$$(3) \qquad C_t = P_0 r$$

Given observations on C_t and P_0 one can also solve for r as follows:

$$(4) \qquad r = \frac{C_t}{P_0}$$

These simple operations are crucial to an understanding of share valuation theories. Assume an investor holds a share for one year, at the end of which a dividend is paid. The share is then sold *ex div*, which means the new investor does not receive the dividend, as opposed to *cum div* where the dividend would be incorporated into price.

For the purposes of exposition, ignoring taxation, transaction costs and the fact that dividends are paid biannually, the current share price is given by the expected year end dividend, D_1, plus the expected share price at the end of the year, P_1, discounted at k_e, the investors' desired rate of return for shares in that risk class. This is the *single-period dividend valuation model:*

$$(5) \qquad P_0 = \frac{D_1}{1 + k_e} + \frac{P_1}{1 + k_e}$$

If it is assumed that the rate of return k_e is 10 per cent per annum, the expected dividend per share and share price one year hence are 10 pence and £1.00 respectively, then the current share price is:

$$P_0 = \frac{£0.10}{1.1} + \frac{£1.00}{1.1} = £1.00$$

On the basis of a 20 pence dividend and a 90 pence share price in two years' time, the share price at the end of the first year is:

(6) $$P_1 = \frac{D_2}{1 + k_e} + \frac{P_2}{1 + k_e}$$

$$= \frac{£0.20}{1.1} + \frac{£0.90}{1.1}$$

$$= £1.00$$

If the original investor holds the share for two years, current share price can be calculated by discounting the annual dividends, plus the share price at the end of year two, as follows:

(7) $$P_0 = \frac{D_1}{1 + k_e} + \frac{D_2}{(1 + k_e)^2} + \frac{P_2}{(1 + k_e)^2}$$

such that:

$$P_0 = \frac{£1.10}{1.1} + \frac{£0.20}{(1.1)^2} + \frac{£0.90}{(1.1)^2}$$

$$= £1.00$$

If it is assumed that the cost of equity k_e is correctly defined and will not change, then the price of a share held for a finite number of years, n, is equal to:

(8) $$P_0 = \frac{D_1}{1 + k_e} + \frac{D_2}{(1 + k_e)^2} + \cdots + \frac{D_n}{(1 + k_e)^n} + \frac{P_n}{(1 + k_e)^n}$$

Rewritten, this defines the *finite-period dividend valuation model:*

(9) $$P_0 = \sum_{t=1}^{n} \frac{D_t}{(1 + k_e)^t} + \frac{P_n}{(1 + k_e)^n}$$

Since the value of the share at time period n is determined by the discounted sum of dividends thereafter:

(10) $$P_n = \frac{D_{n+1}}{(1 + k_e)^{n+1}} + \frac{D_{n+2}}{(1 + k_e)^{n+2}} + \cdots$$

The *general dividend valuation model* based upon distributions where n tends to infinity is given by:

(11) $$P_0 = \sum_{t=1}^{\infty} \frac{D_t}{(1 + k_e)^t}$$

A full discussion of how the appropriate equity capitalisation rate, k_e, is determined will have to wait until Chapter 7. For the moment, it is important to note that the shareholders' desired rate of return is an opportunity cost of capital. To reiterate, the term 'cost of capital' is actually a misnomer, since it is the 'return' that can be earned elsewhere if funds were invested at a rate commensurate to an appropriate degree of risk. Thus, it also corresponds to the company's cost of equity capital because it represents the minimum expected return required by shareholders from their financial investment in a company which acts responsibly. If management cannot maintain this return, funds should be returned to the shareholders, for example in the form of dividends. The same argument also applies if operating profits and reserves are surplus to a company's investment requirements. And this introduces the special model of constant annual dividends.

It will be recalled from Equation (2) (where P_0 equals C_t/r), that a 10 per cent rate of return in the form of a £100 perpetual annuity is valued at £1000. An analogous case exists in share valuation. If the annual dividend, D_t, is constant in perpetuity, Equation (11) now reads:

$$(12) \qquad P_0 = \frac{D_1}{1 + k_e} + \frac{D_1}{(1 + k_e)^2} + \frac{D_1}{(1 + k_e)^3} + \cdots$$

Since D_1 is equal to D_2 which is equal to D_3 through to D_∞, Equation (12) reduces to:

$$(13) \qquad P_0 = \frac{D_1}{k_e}$$

Equation (13) represents the *constant dividend valuation model*. So, a company which pays a 10 pence dividend per share in perpetuity with an equity capitalisation rate, k_e, of 10 per cent has a current share price:

$$P_0 = \frac{D_1}{k_e} = \frac{£0.10}{0.1} = £1.00$$

This price is *ex div*, since Equation (13) assumes the current dividend, D_0, has been paid. A *cum div* price is equal to:

$$(14) \qquad P_0 = D_0 + \frac{D_1}{k_e}$$

$$= £0.10 + \frac{£0.10}{0.1}$$

$$= £1.10$$

Cum div or *ex div*, one should also note that the assumption of a constant dividend in perpetuity implies that the company never retains any of its annual net cash flow, but distributes it all as a dividend. To be more precise, the company's annual net cash flow which is surplus to its investment requirements is a constant in perpetuity. Having retained sufficient funds to maintain the shareholders' desired rate of return in the future, it is, therefore, paid out as a dividend each year. This is a very important proviso, but it is obvious once the notion that the equity capitalisation rate is in fact an opportunity cost of capital, as explained earlier.

3 DIVIDEND GROWTH MODELS AND CAPITAL GAINS

Whilst the special model of constant dividend valuation provides a rationale for full dividend distributions, the presentation of the general model does not specify either growth in dividends or how other dividend policies are determined.

Assume, therefore, that companies who decide to pay only a proportion of their distributable profits as a dividend do so in order to finance growth through retentions. How does this impact upon share price?

Applying a mathematical construction termed the constant growth formula, it is assumed that dividends grow at a constant annual compound rate in perpetuity and the *ex div* current share price can be defined as:

$$(15) \qquad P_0 = \frac{D_1}{k_e - g}$$

where:

g = the annual growth rate in dividends.

If the dividend which has just been paid, D_0, is assumed to grow at an annual rate, g, Equation (15) may also be rewritten:

$$(16) \qquad P_0 = \frac{D_0(1 + g)}{k_e - g}$$

Equations (15) and (16) are termed the *constant-growth dividend model*. They are derived by first writing the *ex div* current share price as the discounted sum of future dividends based on a constant compound annual growth rate:

$$(17) \qquad P_0 = \frac{D_0(1 + g)}{(1 + k_e)} + \frac{D_0(1 + g)^2}{(1 + k_e)^2} + \cdots + \frac{D_0(1 + g)^n}{(1 + k_e)^n}$$

The numerator of each successive right-hand term $(1 + g)$ is multiplied by its predecessor but is discounted for an extra year. So, for the series to converge and P_0 to be finite, discounting must more than compensate for the growth in dividends. This limiting assumption is crucial to the operation of the model. If k_e equals g, the share price would be infinite. If k_e is less than g the share price would be negative. If k_e exceeds g, Equation (17) may be usefully rewritten:

(18) $$P_0 = \frac{D_1}{1 + k_e} + \frac{D_1(1 + g)}{(1 + k_e)^2} + \cdots + \frac{D_n(1 + g)^{n-1}}{(1 + k_e)^n}$$

This has a special mathematical structure that permits rearrangement to produce a much simpler form for the right-hand side.

First, multiply both sides of Equation (18) by the ratio, $(1 + g)/(1 + k_e)$, so that:

(19) $$P_0\frac{(1 + g)}{(1 + k_e)} = \frac{D_1(1 + g)}{(1 + k_e)^2} + \frac{D_1(1 + g)^2}{(1 + k_e)^3} + \cdots + \frac{D_1(1 + g)^n}{(1 + k_e)^{n+1}}$$

Now subtract Equation (19) from Equation (18):

(20) $$P_0 - P_0\frac{(1 + g)}{(1 + k_e)} = \frac{D_1}{1 + k_e} - \frac{D_1(1 + g)^n}{(1 + k_e)^{n+1}}$$

If the equity capitalisation rate, k_e, is larger than the growth rate, g, the right-hand term of Equation (20), $D_1 (1 + g)^n/(1 + k_e)^{n+1}$, approaches zero as the number of periods, n, approaches infinity. Thus, Equation (20) simplifies to:

(21) $$P_0 - P_0\frac{(1 + g)}{(1 + k_e)} = \frac{D_1}{1 + k_e}$$

Multiplying both sides of Equation (21) by $(1 + k_e)$ and solving for P_0:

$$P_0(1 + k_e) - P_0(1 + g) = D_1$$
$$P_0[1 + k_e - (1 + g)] = D_1$$
$$P_0(k_e - g) = D_1$$

which is equivalent to Equations (15) and (16):

$$P_0 = \frac{D_1}{k_e - g} = \frac{D_0(1 + g)}{k_e - g}$$

Therefore, the current *ex div* share price is determined by capitalising next year's dividend at the amount by which the desired rate of return on equity exceeds the constant rate of growth in dividend.

Assume that the dividend next year is 10 pence, the shareholders' rate of return is 10 per cent per annum and the annual growth rate is five per cent in perpetuity, conforming to $k_e > g$. From Equation (15):

$$P_0 = \frac{D_1}{k_e} = \frac{£0.10}{0.10 - 0.05} = £2.00$$

Of course, this growth model is still naïve. It is only applicable to an all-equity company. If debt capital is involved (a case considered in future chapters) its impact upon how earnings are packaged for distribution and the consequences for k_e would cause problems for constant growth rates financed by retentions. Consider, therefore, a 'split-growth' rate in dividends.

Assume that constant growth is unsustainable but expected to change at the end of time period n. Using Equation (9), the finite dividend valuation model:

$$P_0 = \sum_{t=1}^{n} \frac{D_t}{(1 + k_e)^t} + \frac{P_n}{(1 + k_e)^n}$$

The dividend series from time period one to time period n inclusive is defined by setting D_1 equal to $D_0 (1 + g)$, D_2 equal to $D_1 (1 + g)$, through to D_n equal to $D_{n-1} (1 + g)$. The right-hand term, the discounted *ex div* share price at time period n, can be calculated by adapting Equation (15) such that:

$$(22) \qquad P_n = \frac{D_{n+1}}{k_e - g}$$

Assume again that the dividend next year is 10 pence, the required rate of return is 10 per cent per annum, but the 5 per cent annual growth in dividends is expected to fall to 4 per cent after the third year.

The current *ex div* share price is the discounted sum of future dividends for two years, plus the present value of the *ex div* price at the end of year two. Substituting Equation (22) into Equation (9) produces the *split-growth dividend model*:

$$(23) \qquad P_0 = \sum_{t=1}^{n} \frac{D_t}{1 + k_e} + \frac{D_{n+1}/(k_e - g)}{(1 + k_e)^n}$$

So that in terms of the example:

$$P_0 = \frac{D_1}{1 + k_e} + \frac{D_2}{(1 + k_e)^2} + \frac{D_3/(k_e - g)}{(1 + k_e)^2}$$

$$= \frac{£0.10}{1.1} + \frac{£0.10(1.05)}{(1.1)^2} + \frac{£0.10(1.05)^2/(0.1 - 0.04)}{(1.1)^2}$$

$$= £0.0909 + £0.0867 + £1.5185$$

$$= £1.6961$$

Note that share price has fallen from £2.00 in response to a reduction in the growth rate in dividends.

To conclude this introduction to growth rates, consider now the impact of capital gains on equity valuation. If a share price grows at the annual rate of G then:

$$(24) \qquad P_1 = P_0(1 + G)$$

Recalling Equations (15) and (16), the current share price:

$$P_0 = \frac{D_1}{k_e - g} = \frac{D_0(1 + g)}{k_e - g}$$

and the share price one year hence:

$$(25) \qquad P_1 = \frac{D_2}{k_e - g} = \frac{D_1(1 + g)}{k_e - g}$$

It follows from Equations (15) and (25) that:

$$(26) \qquad P_1 = P_0(1 + g)$$

A comparison of Equations (24) and (26) reveals that the share price grows at the rate G, which is equal to the annual growth rate in dividends, g. Substituting G equal to g into Equation (15) produces the equation for a *dividend-capital gain model*:

$$(27) \qquad P_0 = \frac{D_1}{k_e - g}$$

In other words, Equation (27) redefines the current price of a share as next year's dividend capitalised at the amount by which the desired rate of return on equity exceeds the percentage capital gain.

For example, if next year's dividend is 10 pence per share, share price is expected to grow at 5 per cent per annum and the equity capitalisation rate is 10 per cent:

$$P_0 = \frac{£0.10}{0.10 - 0.05} = £2.00$$

which is identical to the share price previously calculated using Equation (15).

4 EARNINGS VALUATION MODELS

As an alternative to the various dividend and capital gain models, shareholders' equity can be valued using a company's post-tax earnings, ideally on a cash flow basis.

Over one period the current price is given by the anticipated earnings, E_1, at time period one, plus the *ex div* price, P_1, at the end of the year discounted at k_e, the investors' desired rate of return for shares. This represents the *single-period earnings model*:

$$(28) \qquad P_0 = \frac{E_1}{1 + k_e} + \frac{P_1}{1 + k_e}$$

If it is assumed that the cost of equity k_e is correctly defined (more of which later), then the *finite-period earnings model* is equal to:

$$(29) \qquad P_0 = \sum_{t=1}^{n} \frac{E_t}{(1 + k_e)^t} + \frac{P_n}{(1 + k_e)^n}$$

where the end period share price is again *ex div*.

If n tends to infinity, the *general earnings valuation model* is given by:

$$(30) \qquad P_0 = \sum_{t=1}^{\infty} \frac{E_t}{(1 + k_e)^t}$$

If annual earnings E_t are constant in perpetuity, Equation (30) simplifies to the *constant-earnings valuation model*:

$$(31) \qquad P_0 = \frac{E_1}{k_e}$$

since E_1 is equal to E_2 and so on through to E_∞.

Moving on, a *constant-growth earnings model* is equal to:

$$(32) \qquad P_0 = \frac{E_1}{k_e - g} = \frac{E_0(1 + g)}{k_e - g}$$

A *split-growth earnings model* can be derived by adapting Equation (29), the finite earnings model:

$$P_0 = \sum_{t=1}^{n} \frac{E_t}{1 + k_e} + \frac{P_n}{(1 + k_e)^n}$$

The right-hand term, the discounted *ex div* share price at time period n, can be calculated by adapting Equation (32) such that:

$$(33) \qquad P_n = \frac{E_{n+1}}{k_e - g}$$

Substituting Equation (33) into Equation (29):

$$(34) \qquad P_0 = \sum_{t=1}^{n} \frac{E_t}{1 + k_e} + \frac{E_{n+1}/(k_e - g)}{(1 + k_e)^n}$$

Equations (28) to (34) reiterate the salient mathematical logic of the dividend Equations (5) to (22). The only difference would appear to be the substitution of earnings terms for dividend terms in a parallel series of equations. However, this invites an immediate criticism.

Unless a company pursues a policy of full dividend distribution, such that D_t equals E_t, it is obvious that the respective figures for k_e must differ in the corresponding dividend and earnings models, if their current share price P_0 is to converge. To be more precise, if P_0 is identical throughout, not only must the capitalisation rates for dividends and earnings differ but a unique relationship must also exist between the two.

This still represents a fundamental point of disagreement among academics and practitioners alike, which will be explored later in the text. To clarify the current position, consider this chapter's original numerical example.

Let the shareholders' rate of return equal 10 per cent per annum with the expected dividend per share and the *ex div* share price one year hence set at 10 pence and £1.00 respectively. From Equation (5):

$$P_0 = \frac{D_1}{1 + k_e} + \frac{P_1}{1 + k_e}$$

$$= \frac{£0.10}{1.1} + \frac{£1.00}{1.1} = £1.00$$

Now assume that the earnings per share (EPS) at the end of year one is 20 pence. Solving for k_e in Equation (28):

$$P_0 = \frac{E_1}{1 + k_e} + \frac{P_1}{1 + k_e}$$

$$= \frac{£0.20}{1.2} + \frac{£1.00}{1.2} = £1.00$$

Thus, the equity capitalisation rate for earnings is 20 per cent, which is twice that for dividends. Nor is this accidental, since the dividend distribution (i.e. the dividend payout ratio) is precisely 50 per cent of earnings. In other words k_e, which can now be specifically termed the 'earnings yield', is twice that of the 'dividend yield'.

5 THE CAPITALISATION CONCEPT AND INVESTMENT RATIO ANALYSIS

To reiterate, if the annual receipts C_t from an investment are constant over time and tend to infinity then the price paid for that investment P_0, based upon the present value of those receipts, is the simple equation for a perpetual annuity:

(2) $\quad P_0 = \dfrac{C_t}{r}$

The term r is known as the capitalisation rate because if one has observations for r and C_t the application of Equation (2) in order to arrive at a present value is termed 'capitalisation'.

It also follows from above that, given observations on price and the capitalisation rate, cash receipts can also be determined.

(3) $\quad C_t = P_0 r$

Given observations on C and P one can also solve for r as follows:

(4) $\quad r = \dfrac{C_t}{P_0}$

These simple operations are crucial to an understanding of the application of share valuation theories which underpin investment ratios which are published in the financial press. From Equation (13) which assumed that share price is a function of constant dividend payments in perpetuity one can simplify:

(13) $\quad P_0 = \dfrac{D_1}{k_e}$

where:

$\quad P_0$ is the share's current market value

$\quad D_1$ is the constant maintainable dividend per share paid each period (based on current distribution)

$\quad k_e$ is the equity capitalisation rate of dividends (the dividend yield).

Rearranging terms, k_e, the *dividend yield*, is defined as:

(35) $\quad k_e = \dfrac{D_1}{P_0}$

Similarly, if share price is assumed to be a function of earnings, from Equation (31) it will be recalled:

$$P_0 = \dfrac{E_1}{k_e}$$

where:

$\quad P_0$ is the current share price

$\quad E_1$ is the constant maintainable earnings per share paid each period (based on latest reported profits)

$\quad k_e$ is the equity capitalisation rate of earnings (the earnings yield).

Rearranging terms, k_e, now an earnings yield, may be defined as:

(36) $\quad k_e = \dfrac{E_1}{P_0}$

so that the reciprocal of the earnings yield, termed the *price/earnings* (P/E) ratio is derived as follows:

$$(37) \qquad P/E = \frac{P_0}{E} = \frac{1}{k_e}$$

On the assumption that a firm's current post-tax profits are maintainable indefinitely, the P/E ratio provides a simple method whereby a company's distributable earnings can be capitalised to arrive at a total market value for its shares (the market capitalisation of equity). Thus:

$$(38) \qquad \text{Total market capitalisation} = (P/E) \times \text{total earnings after tax}$$

Given a company's latest reported profit figures, pre-existing P/E ratios for similar firms can be used to place a comparative value on that company's shares. This can then be compared with its actual current market price or total market capitalisation of equity in order to establish whether it is either undervalued, equitable, or overvalued. Undervalued, the market buys, equitable it holds, overvalued it sells.

A number of simple rules on a complex subject to be explored in future chapters:

- The P/E ratio (earnings yield reciprocal) shows how the company's value is rated in relation to the profit it earns. The higher the P/E ratio, the greater confidence there is that profits are going to rise, and the lower the P/E, the greater the concern that it might be unable to sustain profits.
- Conversely, a low P/E ratio could reflect the fact that a company's shares are undervalued by the market relative to its profit performance and thus make it attractive to speculative investors.
- Shares in companies that are expected to produce rapid growth in profits and hence capital gains offer low dividend yields, while higher dividend yields are offered by what are regarded as relatively mature and stable businesses with little prospect of increasing profits and dividend.
- Conversely, part of stock market law is 'the higher the yield the higher the risk'. This applies particularly to shares where a higher dividend yield usually signals uncertainty over whether the dividend can be maintained in future, particularly if earnings cover is low.
- In general, if any investment offers either a higher dividend yield or earnings yield (a low P/E ratio) than similar investments, it is advisable to be cautious.

6 INVESTMENT RATIOS

The commonest ratios relating to investment analysis may be defined as follows:

1 Ordinary share values

$$\text{Nominal value (or Par value)} = \frac{\text{Dividend yield} \times \text{Market value}}{\text{Dividend \%}}$$

$$\text{Market value} = \frac{\text{Nominal value} \times \text{Dividend \%}}{\text{Dividend yield}}$$

2 Dividend measures (before deduction of income tax)

$$\text{Dividend per share} = \frac{\text{Total dividend (gross)}}{\text{Number of shares}}$$

$$\text{or Nominal value} \times \text{Dividend \%}$$

$$\text{Dividend percentage} = \frac{\text{Dividend yield} \times \text{Market value}}{\text{Nominal value}}$$

$$\text{or} \frac{\text{Dividend per share}}{\text{Nominal value of an ordinary share}}$$

$$\text{or} \frac{\text{Total dividends (gross)}}{\text{Total nominal value of issued ordinary shares}}$$

$$\text{Dividend yield} = \frac{\text{Nominal value} \times \text{Dividend \%}}{\text{Market value}}$$

$$\text{or} \frac{\text{Dividend per share} \times 100}{\text{Market value of an ordinary share}}$$

$$\text{or} \frac{\text{Total dividend} \times 100}{\text{Total market value of ordinary shares}}$$
$$\text{(i.e. market capitalisation)}$$

3 Earning measures (net of corporation tax)

$$\text{Return on capital employed (ROCE)} = \frac{\text{Profits after tax minus preference dividend (gross)} \times 100}{\text{Balance sheet value of ordinary shares plus reserves}}$$

$$\text{Earnings per share (EPS)} = \frac{\text{Profits after tax and preference dividend (gross)}}{\text{Number of shares}}$$

$$\text{Earnings yield} = \frac{\text{Earnings per share} \times 100}{\text{Market value of an ordinary share}}$$

$$\text{or} \frac{\text{Profits after tax and preference dividends (gross)}}{\text{Market capitalisation}} \times 100$$

$$\text{Price/Earnings ratio (P/E)} = \frac{1}{\text{Earnings yield}}$$

$$\text{or} \frac{\text{Market value of an ordinary share}}{\text{Earning per share}}$$

$$\text{or} \frac{\text{Market capitalisation}}{\substack{\text{Profits after tax and preference} \\ \text{dividend (gross)}}}$$

4 The relationship between dividends and earnings

$$\text{Dividend cover} = \frac{\text{EPS}}{\text{Dividend per share}}$$

$$\text{or} \frac{\text{Profits after tax and preference dividends (gross)}}{\text{Total dividend}}$$

$$\text{Dividend payout ratio} = \frac{1}{\text{Dividend cover}} \times 100$$

$$\text{or} \frac{\text{Dividend per share}}{\text{EPS}} \times 100$$

$$\text{or} \frac{\text{Total dividends}}{\substack{\text{Profit after tax and preference} \\ \text{dividends (gross)}}} \times 100$$

7 CAPITALISATION: AN APPLICATION

Armed with the foregoing models and the measures derived from them, consider the following public information relating to a company:

Share capital: Authorised and Issued £1 shares   £500,000
Profits after tax and preference dividend   £50,000

Dividend percentage   5%

Market value of ordinary shares   £2

The following ratios may now be calculated:

$$\text{Dividends per share} = \frac{£25,000}{500,000}$$

$$\text{or } £1.00 \times 5\% = 5 \text{ pence}$$

$$\text{Dividend yield} = \frac{£1.00}{£2.00} \times 5\%$$

$$\text{or } \frac{£0.05}{£2.00} \times 100$$

$$\text{or } \frac{£25,000}{£1m} \times 100 = 2.5\%$$

As defined earlier, the dividend percentage is always calculated on the nominal value of the ordinary shares, the rationale being the intuitive simplicity of expressing a return on a constant amount. However, it does not follow that an improvement in a company's return percentage or a company with a relatively higher percentage than those of its competitors is more attractive to investors. Such an interpretation depends crucially upon market value which may, of course, fluctuate over time or differ between firms. This 'real' rate of the return on market value is termed the 'yield' by the financial press.

In the above example, it is precisely half the dividend percentage since market value is twice the nominal value. For shareholders comparing their investment over time or across different companies, or for potential investors contemplating investment now, the yield is clearly the more relevant measure.

It is also interesting to disclose the profitability of earnings. This is particularly true of companies which pay little or no dividend, or where dividends fluctuate erratically. Shareholders themselves may not be concerned with dividend payments alone, particularly marginal rate tax payers and financial institutions who are interested in the prospect of capital gains which may materialise from profits which are retained. In such cases, earnings measures are clearly appropriate. Using the information given:

$$\text{ROCE} = \frac{£50,000}{£500,000} \times 100 = 10\% \qquad \text{EPS} = \frac{£50,000}{500,000} = 10 \text{ pence}$$

$$\text{Earnings yield} = \frac{£0.10}{2.00}$$

$$\text{or } \frac{£50,000}{£1m} = 5\%$$

Like the dividend percentage, ROCE and EPS (which are familiar to accountants) should both be treated with suspicion, being based exclusively on historical cost accrual statements. In order to establish performance in real terms, earnings (ideally cash profits) must be related to a market value in the form of a yield, which hopefully exceeds the rate of inflation. Only then can a company's shares, either over time or in relation to other shares, be assessed.

However, this need not be undertaken by a direct comparison of yields. In fact, to avoid any confusion of terminology, yields in the financial press refer to dividends. For earnings' analyses, P/E ratios are published which compare share prices with annual profits (albeit accounting profits). In this example:

$$P/E \text{ ratio } = \frac{1}{5\%}$$

$$\text{or } \frac{£2.00}{£0.10}$$

$$\text{or } \frac{£1m}{£50,000} = 20$$

In other words, share price is 20 times the level of earnings.

Note that, because the P/E ratio is a reciprocal of the earnings yield, the higher the former the lower the latter will be. It will also be recalled that the product of the two measures must equal unity. In this case:

Earnings yield × P/E ratio

$$5\% \times 20 = 1$$

The final measures to be considered, namely the dividend cover and its reciprocal, the dividend payout ratio, measure the size of the annual dividend in relation to annual post-tax profits. A record of the former is said to provide some indication of a firm's ability to maintain dividends from earnings which may fluctuate over time. The latter reveals a firm's willingness or ability to maintain a given dividend distribution level, having regard to changing profit levels.

In the above example dividends are adequately covered since:

$$\text{Dividend cover} = \frac{10 \text{ pence}}{5 \text{ pence}}$$

$$\text{or } \frac{£50,000}{£25,000} = 2$$

$$\text{Dividend payout ratio} = \frac{1}{2} \times 100$$

$$\text{or } \frac{5 \text{ pence}}{10 \text{ pence}} \times 100$$

$$\text{or } \frac{£25,000}{£50,000} \times 100 = 50\%$$

These measures have a further convenient property in that they establish a link between the various dividend and earnings measures. For example:

Dividend per share	$\times$	Dividend cover	$=$	EPS
5 pence	$\times$	2	$=$	10 pence
Dividend yield	$\times$	Dividend cover	$=$	Earnings yield
2.5%	$\times$	2	$=$	5%

What this demonstrates, of course, is why just a few selected measures in the financial press (market price, P/E ratio, dividend yield and cover) are held up to encapsulate the essential rules concerning a company's market performance, as outlined earlier. If, in the above example, the information provided had related to only three variables from the financial press (say the P/E ratio, dividend cover and the market price of the company's shares) any unknown in the series of investment ratios previously defined could still be determined, given information from published accounting statements such as the dividend percentage, EPS and par value. Whatever demerits the use of historical earnings might have, it is certainly true to say that the distillation of performance in the form of P/E ratios, yields and the like, still provides experienced financial analysts with a more immediate intuitive feel for companies under their scrutiny, than any measures drawn exclusively from published financial statements.

8 SUMMARY AND CONCLUSIONS

The general dividend valuation model discounts future dividends and the net proceeds on the sale of a share to a current market price. The specific dividend valuation model discounts a constant stream of dividends in perpetuity. Assuming a constant annual growth in dividends the current value of a share is derived by capitalising next year's dividend at the difference between the equity cost of capital and the annual growth rate in dividends. Basic theory states that the dividend growth rate should equal the capital gains yield.

Current share price, based on either a finite earnings stream, in perpetuity, or under constant growth conditions, can also be calculated as an alternative to models based on dividends. Given unique relationships between the earnings yield (or its reciprocal the P/E ratio) and the dividend yield, corresponding equity valuations based on earnings and dividends should converge.

This 'law of one price', which will be discussed in future chapters, explains why a select few published financial ratios which capitalise perpetual annuities, based upon discounted revenue theory, are believed to impound all that is knowable about a share's performance. They may also be self-fulfilling indicators of equity values, to the extent that investment decisions are collectively based on such measures.

References

A guide to further reading is provided at the end of Chapter 6.

6

Valuation and takeover

Chapter profile

Having explained a number of universally available measures by which investors analyse stock market performance, this chapter comprehensively illustrates two of their practical applications. These provide the reader with an opportunity to reflect upon the practical relevance of dividend policy to investment and financial decisions before considering its theoretical and empirical significance in Chapter 7. The first case concerns an unlisted company coming to the capital market requiring an aggregate flotation value and 'offer for sale' price per share. Particular attention is paid to the dividend yield, dividend cover and price earnings (P/E) ratio required by potential investors. Secondly, the various methods of valuation which vindicate the motives for acquiring a business as a going concern in the event of a takeover are explained. Again, one of the distinctions drawn is between the use of the P/E ratio and the dividend yield as a basis for valuation. The reader is finally reminded that a derivation of share price which utilises DCF analyses of either prospective earnings or dividends, rather than actual data drawn from published financial accounts, still represents an ideal measure.

1 INTRODUCTION

If financial analysts could successfully measure the value of an asset in a business for all purposes at any one point in time, share valuation would present little difficulty. Unfortunately, published accounts upon which they initially depend, measure different assets in different ways so that a value cannot be placed on a company as a whole. With the exception of property, fixed assets are usually to be seen in balance sheets at historic costs less depreciation thereon, whereas current assets are valued at market value or cost whichever is the lower. Moreover, intangible items, including brand names, may be ignored. There is also the effect of synergy to consider.

However, as the previous chapter revealed, various approaches to share valuation exist, which are not asset based but dividend and earnings lead. These may utilise discounted revenue theory and the capitalisation concept of a perpetual annuity which can be made operational though familiar financial ratios. Each may assist the analyst when determining a price for a share or the total market capitalisation of equity. The purpose of this chapter is to develop the concept further through a series of practical illustrations which look at a business as a going concern in the event of:

- A company coming to the market for the first time
- A company which falls prey to takeover

Whereas a company which seeks a stock exchange listing is motivated primarily by the need to finance expansion, it must be emphasised that the rationale for mergers, amalgamations, conglomerations, acquisitions and takeovers is varied and complex, even though a precise terminology is available to distinguish each strategy. However, within the confines of this text, each are of only incidental concern. The terms will be used interchangeably and whilst an overview of the motivational factors which underpin the case for composite business entities and the problems which can ensue are necessarily provided, the prime objective is to consider common methodologies of equity valuation once a company has selected another for the purpose of acquisition. These are:

(i)   The net assets basis.
(ii) A going concern value incorporating goodwill.
(iii) Valuation based on the profitability of an enterprise, as revealed by its accounts, relative to dividend policy.
(iv) Valuation utilising future cashflows, the most sophisticated technique of all.

2 COMING TO THE MARKET: CAPITALISATION APPLIED

To appreciate why just a few selected measures published in the financial press, such as market price, the P/E ratio, dividend yield and dividend cover, are believed to capture the essential features of a company's market performance, first consider the case of an existing unlisted company wishing to finance expansion by having its shares marketed on the Stock Exchange. Previously, enjoying little documentation of its financial affairs under the company's legislation and secure from take-over, D Ltd seeks a valuation that will accord with a voluntary 'offer for sale'. In particular what it requires are:

(i)   A market value for the company.
(ii) A recommendation for the aggregate flotation value.
(iii) Knowledge of how many shares should be issued, and in what

denominations, having regard to the dividend yield and dividend cover required by investors.

(*iv*) The offer for sale price per share.

To assist the decision, the following information is available. A, B and C are listed companies engaged in the same type of business as D Ltd. Recent information on all four companies is given in Table 6.1.

In addition:

A: appears to have secure and advancing dividends, supported by gradually growing earnings.

B: shows solid dividends although earnings have failed to make progress.

C: reveals a pattern of dividends and earnings with negligible movement in recent years.

D: has a sound record, although it has made little headway in recent years. Its own forecast of profits before tax for year 4 is £810,000; although in view of its past record, this forecast should be treated with caution. The company has adequate liquid assets.

The rate of Corporation Tax may be assumed as 25% throughout.

In order to solve the problem, it is necessary first to produce comparative financial and investment profiles of all four companies (Table 6.2), so that D

Table 6.1 Primary data

	A £000s	B £000s	C £000s	D £000s
Profit after loan interest and before tax:				
Year 1	1315	734	359	799
Year 2	1361	734	370	805
Year 3	1405	736	364	801
Net capital employed, end of Year 3:				
Loan	1500	390	500	–
Equity				4700
Ordinary share capital	2000	1540	994	–
Reserves	2310	4260	1656	–
Total	5810	6190	3150	4700
	£	£	£	£
Nominal value per share	0.10	0.25	0.25	–
Current share price	0.80	1.40	0.90	–
Last dividend %	19.50	17.30	16.00	–

Table 6.2 Valuation and income profile

	A £000s	B £000s	C £000s	D £000s	Notes
Equity	4,310	5,800	2,650	4,700	Share capital plus reserves
Market value	16,000	8,624	5,578	–	See (a) below
Earnings	1,100	550	275	605	Profits after tax, see (b) below
Dividend	390	266	159	–	Percentage on ordinary share capital
Return on equity %	25.5	9.5	10.4	12.9	$\dfrac{\text{Profits after tax}}{\text{Capital employed minus loan}}$

can establish a capital structure and dividend policy which is attractive to potential investors. It is important to realise that as a listed company D Ltd will be judged by this structure and also compared with similar firms on the market. Such an exercise is clearly less problematical than say the privatisation of State-owned monopolies, such as British Rail. Nevertheless, the figures no longer reflect any known accounting exactitude but rather a feeling for anticipated events.

Calculations and assumptions

(a) Market value is derived by the following two-stage procedure:

(i) $\dfrac{\text{Share capital}}{\text{Nominal value}} = \text{Number of shares}$

(ii) Number of shares × Current share price = Total market value

Thus:

Company	Share capital	= Number of shares	× Current share price	= Total market value
A	£2,000,000/0.10	= 20,000,000	× £0.80	= £16,000,000
B	£1,540,000/0.25	= 6,616,000	× £1.40	= £8,624,000
C	£994,000/0.25	= 3,976,000	× £0.90	= £3,578,400

(b) Earnings have been calculated using the following approximations:

A, steadily increasing, to around £1.45 million ≃ £1,100,000 after tax
B, stable at £735,000 ≃ £550,000 after tax
C, stable at £365,000 ≃ £275,000 after tax
D, stable at £805,000 ≃ £605,000 after tax

Table 6.3 Investment ratio profile

	A £000s	B £000s	C £000s	D £000s	Notes
Nominal value	0.10p	0.25p	0.25p	–	Given
Current share price	0.80p	£1.40	0.90p	–	Given
Dividend %	19.3	17.3	16.0	–	Given
Dividend yield %	2.4	3.1	4.4	–	$\dfrac{\text{Nominal value} \times \text{Div \%}}{\text{Market value}}$
Dividend cover	2.8	2.1	1.7	–	$\dfrac{\text{Profit after tax}}{\text{Dividend (gross)}}$
Earnings yield %	7.0	6.4	7.7	–	$\dfrac{\text{Profit after tax}}{\text{Market value}}$
P/E ratio	14.5	15.7	13.0	–	$\dfrac{1}{\text{Earnings yield}}$

Table 6.2 itemises the salient features of the four companies' accounts as a basis for analysis. The 'unknown' variables are the required forecast of market value and dividend relating to D. These may be established by reference to the investment profiles of A, B and C which are given in Table 6.3. These profiles are simply a reformulation of the financial data contained in Table 6.2 into the familiar investment ratios.

With this information, the implications for D can now be assessed.

(a) Total market valuations

The simplest and typically most conservative valuation to be placed upon all the shares of D would be based upon its net assets calculated directly from the accounts. On the information available, this would take the form of assets minus liabilities, without any adjustment for current values as either a going concern (net replacement cost), surplus assets (realisable value), or intangible items, producing a figure of £4.7 million.

The disparities between nominal and market values for A, B and C suggest, however, that this figure is no more than a lower benchmark. Even if book values are still adhered to, a more sophisticated valuation based upon the capitalised value of D's earnings utilising a return on equity, based upon the ROCE of similar firms, provides a significantly higher figure. For example, ignoring the anomolously high return of A and taking an average return on capital plus reserves of 11 per cent for B, C and D provides a capitalisation of D's after-tax earnings of:

$$\frac{£605,000}{0.11} = £5.5 \text{ million}$$

Ignoring book values altogether, a more satisfactory current market valuation may be determined using the P/E ratios of Table 6.3. Clearly, D's growth does not match that of A. It is nearer that of company B. If D's earnings are therefore capitalised using the latter's P/E ratio the following market value would result:

$$£605,000 \times 15.7 \simeq £9.5 \text{ million}$$

However, if full subscription is to be ensured, financial prudence would dictate that the shares of D should be offered at a figure below their market value. To ascertain the aggregate flotation value for an offer for sale, a lower P/E ratio would thus be more applicable. Taking the figure for C, the following valuation may be determined:

$$£605,000 \times 13.0 \simeq £7.9 \text{ million}$$

It therefore seems reasonable to conclude that D should be floated on the market at an aggregate value of somewhere in the region of £8 million.

(b) Per share valuation

With regard to the number and denomination of shares to be offered, the dividend policies of similar companies now comes into force, since the firm cannot be floated at two different prices, one related to earnings and the other to dividend expectations. On the basis of the information relating to A, B and C, it appears that the dividend paid by D should be covered twice. Thus, the total dividend payout based upon the earlier estimate of D's after-tax earnings would be:

$$\frac{£605,000}{2} = £302,500$$

If the aggregate flotation value is taken as being £8 million then the dividend yield, i.e. the 'real' rate of return, on the shares of D will be:

$$\frac{£302,500}{£8 \text{ million}} \simeq 3.8\%$$

This should prove satisfactory to potential investors since it falls between the forecast yields of 3.1% and 4.4% for B and C respectively.

Proceeding one stage further, the market value per share is also constrained by the price of similar shares currently being traded on the market according to 'the law of one price'. The performance of B and C initially suggests that an issue made at 25 pence with a premium of 75 pence attached, providing a market value of £1.00 per share, might succeed. Given a total dividend payout of £302,500 on 8 million shares nominally valued at 25 pence each, this would then result in the following dividend percentage:

$$\text{Dividend \%} = \frac{\text{Dividend yield} \times \text{Market value}}{\text{Nominal value}}$$

$$= \frac{3.8\% \times £1.00}{£0.25}$$

$$= 15.2\%$$

When compared with the percentages for A, B and C, 15.2 per cent might be considered rather on the low side. A nominal value of 22 pence per share would improve this figure and could be justified, particularly if one considers the low value for A. The revised calculation would produce:

$$\text{Dividend \%} = \frac{3.8 \times £1.00}{£0.22}$$

$$= 17\%$$

which is more in line with D's other competitors.

It must be stressed that dividend yields rather than percentages are the real measure of a share's return and it is the yield of 3.8 per cent which should motivate rational investors to take up an offer for sale. However, one cannot ignore the dividend percentage, if only because it is published in company accounts, and might sway the investment decisions of uninformed shareholders.

(c) Conclusion

To avoid any confusion and to ensure success, it is, therefore, suggested that D should market its shares at 22 pence with a 78 pence premium attached. Table 6.4 now sets out the proposed capital structure in accordance with this recommendation having regard to all the dividend expectations of investors.

Readers may now wish to confirm that EPS and dividend per share are 7.6 pence and 3.8 pence respectively.

3 MOTIVATION AND ACQUISITION STRATEGY

If one considers the success of merged companies, the literature reveals that the failure rate is not insubstantial and often characterised by mediocre purchases undertaken by inept management. Post-merger indicators of investment performance, such as the return earned by shareholders, including cash dividends and

Table 6.4 Capital structure and investment profile

	D £000s
Ordinary share capital (8 million)	1760
Reserves (share premium)	6240
Flotation value	8000
Earnings (profits after tax)	605
Dividends	302.5
Dividend cover	Twice
Nominal value per share	£0.22
Premium per share	£0.78
Market value per share	£1.00
Dividend %	17%
Dividend yield	3.8%
Earnings yield	7.6%
Price/Earnings ratio	13

capital gains, are frequently worse than the average performance of other firms in respective industries. Conversely, a significant factor in determining the success of acquisitions is the establishment of a corporate strategy and a rigorous acquisition plan. A lack of pre-planning is a common theme throughout the American literature, as the work of Weston, Chung and Hoag (1990) reveals. Historically, this is also noted in the reports of the UK Monopolies and Mergers Commission, as well as its overseas counterparts, alongside a reluctance to quantify the benefits expected to be gained from a merger. For these reasons, a precursor to any acquisition strategy should be to consider the motivation for it.

The most obvious motive for an acquisition derives from a rational consideration of a company's financial objectives. However, there exists a variety of other possible motives that are not derived from commercial considerations. They are termed *subjective*, yet may be supported by elaborate rationalisation.

Two such motives relate to fear and obsolescence. The former is premised on the belief that, unless the company expands, larger companies will destroy it. This sets in motion a process of accretion. Obsolescence is connected with ageing organisations which display increasingly rigid and systematised bureaucracies. The scope for individual initiative and spontaneity are stifled, which results in both an obsolescent organisation and an obsolescent management. One solution to the problem is to buy in enterprise through corporate acquisition, even at Chief Executive level, as the 1991 study by Martin and McConnell found.

Unfortunately, both fear and obsolescence carry with them unconscious underlying attitudes. Fear initially leads to a denial of being afraid and then an attempt to 'tighten up' the company and to turn it around. Obsolescence produces a defensive attitude of superiority typically based on the firm's longevity and to a redoubling of effort. The effect of these underlying attitudes and the fact that in a merger the acquiring company will be the dominant party tends to produce a condescending attitude toward the acquired company and efforts to manipulate and to control it.

Controlling behaviour is the pivotal issue. The dominant organisation believes that it must incorporate the same processes and procedures in all of its components. But the imposed control systems may well stifle the very qualities of initiative and spontaneity that lay behind the initial acquisition. What may emerge are resentment, contempt and a loss of innovative personnel, all of which necessitates buying in yet another completely new management group. However, the replacement executive might be more bureaucratic given that their brief will be to re-control the organisation. This control focus on the part of the host organisation is, therefore, self-defeating.

Of course, fear and obsolescence are only partial explanations of the quest for corporate growth. As causal factors, they only apply to those companies who react to the growth of others. They do not explain the preoccupation with growth that has been characteristic of the 'fast track' corporate sector which is frequently associated with global conglomerate mergers, management buy-outs (MBOs) and the leveraged buy-outs (LBOs) of mature public companies since the 1980s. Here the desire for growth is premised on the belief that participation in several industries increases the chance of success. However, the *quid pro quo* is that it also increases the possibility of failure.

Given the separation of ownership and control and a lack of corporate governance, mergers are invariably instigated by management without consultation with shareholders. The former may be motivated primarily by growth, as measured by size criteria such as sales turnover, assets and number of employees, and a perception of increased power, prestige and security which this brings. Interest in the growth of earnings may be secondary or diffused by other personal or group goals which lead to managerial satisficing behaviour. On the other hand, shareholders who act rationally should be interested in their wealth maximisation, as evidenced by the growth of the market value of equity through improved earnings via dividends and capital gains. Thus, size and prestige are intermingled managerial goals which may be achieved in the short term by a policy of acquisitions but which conflict with the shareholders' long-term financial objectives.

Thus, subjective motivation may be supported by an elaborate rationale. However, it differs from the *objective* goals which relate to a merger. These are based on a comprehensive analysis of a company's strategic commercial considerations. Such an analysis should embrace:

- Business areas
- Resource areas
- Influence areas.

Areas of influence are those constraints upon the business and resource decisions of the firm which arise from legal limitations, societal pressures and the self-interest of internal and external non-managerial groups. Business areas are those sections of the environment which receive the company's output. Resources relate to the firm's inputs of finance, material and personnel.

Given an objective understanding of the strategic problems which confront the firm and the constraints imposed thereon, the common business motives which are advanced by management to support an acquisition programme are:

(*i*)   To establish a balanced diversified portfolio of investment which will either maximise or stabilise earnings commensurate with a degree of risk and/or balance product life cycles.

(*ii*)   To secure economies of scale and achieve synergy.

(*iii*) To avoid barriers to entry.

(*iv*)   To increase or maintain market share.

(*v*)   To increase or maintain the rate of growth.

(*vi*)   To reduce competition.

(*vii*) To secure new products or services.

(*viii*) To guarantee outlets for existing products and services.

The greatest problem to be considered in the case of resource areas is the risk of losing supplies, which may also be related to the company's degree of market dependence. Three threats can be envisaged. One is a supplier's failure which necessitates a rescue operation and even its acquisition. Secondly, there might be the possibility of a takeover by a competitor. Finally, a takeover might be envisaged with the intention of switching resources to a different activity.

Other resource factors which might justify an acquisition are the availability of excess funds from reserves, the sale of assets or working capital, the benefits of tax advantages and the procurement of valuable personnel.

Now, assuming that a strategic analysis of any or all of the above factors confirms that corporate objectives can only be achieved by radical means, this implies a need for investment. Having already come to the market, management's options are, therefore, an acquisition or internal investment. Two fundamental arguments favour the former:

- speed
- cost.

Obviously, there are trade-offs. Time must be juxtaposed against utility. Cost must be assessed in relation to potential benefits.

As explained elsewhere, the problem of a cost-based asset valuation is its evidence of earning power. An acquisition at the market value of assets, let alone their book value, may be interpreted as a 'bargain buy' but as a going concern the firm may be quite moribund. For companies with a stock exchange listing pursuing policies which produce a low market capitalisation of equity relative to the book value of net assets, *the valuation ratio*, the possibility of takeover increases. But if such an acquisition is not part of a carefully conceived corporate plan which reflects factors other than shareholders' earnings, for example asset stripping, the acquiree will inherit problems which are not dissimilar to takeovers premised upon the subjective managerial goals of growth, prestige and security outlined earlier.

The merger can elicit rising expectations on the part of shareholders and potential investors. And if these are not fulfilled, confidence can evaporate rapidly and equity prices will tumble.

4 ACQUISITION PRICING: THE NET ASSET BASIS

Assuming a company has completed a thorough analysis of its strategic capabilities and decided upon a potential acquisition as the most viable means of achieving its objectives, the question now arises as to the most appropriate method of valuation.

In the long run, the prime determinant of the market price of a share is the cash the company can first earn and hence pay out as a dividend. If one adopts this criterion of value, however, there is not only a conflict between cash and accounting profits but also profitability and an asset value, since the latter may ignore goodwill. However, an asset-based valuation cannot be dismissed altogether, because the nature and circumstances of a business may require reference to this method. The firm being taken over may be unprofitable or profits may be erratic. Distributions, too, may vary or be non-existent, so that there is no reliable basis for even a dividend valuation. In any event, reference to the assets is justifiable, if only as a benchmark in the form of the valuation ratio, since earning power must have a profound effect on capital value.

In determining the take-over valuation careful attention has to be given to the past history and present background of the company and financial details should be prepared in respect of the asset position at the valuation date, together with a review of the trading and profit and loss results over a period of years.

A record of the asset position probably disclosed by the last published accounts of the company, plus a summary of trading results for the determined period, will give some indication of the company's position. Equally, study of the assets may provide some of the evidence required to indicate any adjustments necessary to the figures. At worst however, all the asset valuations may be based on HCA with few notes or qualifications. If this is the case then the following procedures should be adopted:

(a) Fixed tangible assets

It is wise to have land and buildings revalued, irrespective of any professional valuation revealed by the accounts.

With regard to such items as plant and machinery, motor vehicles, fixtures and fittings, etc, which are not shown at current cost, the book values may require uplift. Depreciation rates employed during the period of review must be questioned as evidence most indicative of the closeness of the approximation of the net book value to a current value. These rates may be quite arbitrary and not produce either a value in use (net replacement cost) for operating assets, or value in exchange (realisable value) if assets are surplus to requirements.

(b) Investments

Listed shares and securities valued at middle price market value may be fine but unlisted shares, if the amount involved is material, must be the subject of a secondary valuation using methods similar to those used in the main valuation.

It is important to distinguish between investments which are necessary for the earnings capacity of the business (e.g. trade investments and investments in subsidiaries) which are long-term holdings and those investments which are really 'spare cash' items which although earning interest should really be regarded as current (surplus) assets.

(c) Current assets

Hopefully, the balance sheet values may be taken without extensive revision. However, some adjustment to current cost may become apparent when the trading results are reviewed which relate to HCA methods of stock valuation and the provision for bad debts.

(d) Intangible assets

The value of the business beyond tangible balance sheet items must also be taken into account by the valuer. The value given to 'goodwill' will be discussed separately; suffice it to say that it must enter into the calculation.

If such items as R and D, patents or brand names have a real or saleable value, which is material, an independent expert valuation may be necessary and the amount included with the tangible assets.

(e) Marshalling the assets

After consideration of all these balance sheet items on the lines suggested it is now necessary to marshal the assets into three groups in order to consider the company's going concern value:

(a) Tangible assets directly employed in the business made up of:
- Net fixed assets, i.e. fixed operating assets at net replacement cost, excluding fixed assets and investments not employed in the business for their earning power, minus long-term liabilities.
- Net current assets, i.e. current assets at market value less investments not needed, minus current liabilities.

(b) Tangible assets and financial investments not directly employed in the business, whether regarded as fixed or current. These must be included in the final value of the shares concerned at their realisable value because their acquisition will produce income which is independent of the earnings of the company from its trading operations. Excess, idle or 'surplus' assets may aid cash flow in the future, either for working capital or for distribution.

(c) Intangible assets, i.e. the value given to the business over and above the sum of the tangible assets, plus other investments. The amount may be computed by one or other of the various methods used for determining goodwill.

5   GOING CONCERN VALUATION INCORPORATING GOODWILL

The value of goodwill has concerned analysts for many years, not least because its 'real' value is ultimately what one can get for it and is a compromise between buyer and seller.

The methods evolved for the evaluation of goodwill are not particularly inspiring, even those standardised by the UK accounting profession. They are usually a variation on the right-hand term in the following equation:

$$(1) \qquad V = A + \frac{P - rA}{m}$$

where:

V = going concern value of the business

A = value of net assets

P = expected profits per annum

r = normal rate of return

$P - rA$ = superprofit

m = capitalisation rate of superprofit

$$\frac{P - rA}{m} = \text{value of goodwill}$$

subject to: $m > r$.

Superprofit is the difference between expected profit (P) and what economists term 'normal' profit defined as the average return on the assets (rA) in perpetuity, for the industry in question.

The inequality $m > r$ reflects the intangible nature of superprofit, i.e. its fragility or increased risk and, therefore, the higher capitalisation rate associated with that portion of anticipated profit attributable to goodwill.

The value equation can also be rewritten in a manner more amenable to accountants, namely:

$$(2) \qquad V = A + (P - rA)\,\frac{1}{m}$$

where:

$\dfrac{1}{m} =$ a number of years purchase of superprofit

the rationale being that the shorter the term the higher the capitalisation rate, i.e. the more risky and hence more fragile the goodwill.

To illustrate the application of Equations (1) and (2), consider a company with tangible assets of £100 million and expected profits of £19 million per annum. Using a variety of assumptions, goodwill and hence going concern values may be calculated as follows:

(a) If a reasonable return on capital is 10% then normal economic profit would be £10 million and the superprofits £9 million. Assuming these are capitalised at 20% which is equivalent to a five years purchase of goodwill:

	£ million
Tangible assets	100
Goodwill (9/0.2 or 9 × 5)	45
Going concern value	145

If a lower return on the intangible assets is expected because of less risk (say 15%) the goodwill would be more valuable, i.e. less transient, thus:

	£ million
Tangible assets	100
Goodwill (9/0.15 or 9 × 6.66)	60
Going concern value	160

(b) Since the purchase of a number of years superprofits is similar to a fixed-term annuity, its value can also be calculated using present value analysis. Assuming five years purchase, i.e. a discount rate of 20%:

	£ million
Tangible assets	100
Goodwill (PV of £9 million annuity for five years, 9 × 3.7907)	34.117
Going concern value	134.117

In their defence, it is argued that the above methods recognise the fact that tangible assets can be sold separately and are reasonably permanent. However, this may not be true. A piecemeal valuation of assets also seems more appropriate in the event of asset stripping or liquidation, rather than in the take-over of a company as a going concern. The methods cut across the concept of valuing a business as an entity, as opposed to its component parts. A further criticism is that two appropriate rates of return have to be assumed. One capitalisation rate may be arbitrary enough; two rates may defeat the object of the exercise and also widen the margin of error.

Despite these defects, either method may approximate to a valuation which is eventually agreed between buyer and seller. The fact is that the company is very profitable and may be more valuable than its total assets of £100 million. This suggests a final approach to the valuation of goodwill which is equivalent to capitalising a perpetual annuity but which avoids the superprofit calculation.

(c) Assuming that a rate of return of 10% is expected from investment in the company:

	£ million
Going concern value (£19m/0.1)	190
Tangible assets	100
Goodwill	90

If the goodwill is deemed to be fragile, a lower value may now be placed upon it. For example:

	£ million	£ million
Tangible assets		100
Goodwill: Profits capitalised at 10%	190	
Less tangible assets	100	
Mean value of:	90	45
Going concern value		145

Needless to say, none of the above methods are supposed to give the intrinsic valuation of the business but rather to suggest a valuation for the purposes of negotiation.

6 PROFITABILITY BASIS

If a take-over valuation is to be based exclusively on the past, present or anticipated accounting profits of a company, rather than the assets, great care should still be taken to ensure that the basis for capitalisation is entirely reasonable. Allowance must be made for all charges (including tax) and retentions or ploughback, because what interests the purchaser is what can be earned by at least leaving the business in the same position as it was prior to take-over. Note that the figure for profits after tax is unlikely to be the same as the dividend, because of the allowance for ploughback and may produce a different valuation (a point to be discussed later).

Matters which should be given particular attention in the accounts are:

(**a**) A P/E ratio applied to post-tax earnings.

(**b**) As a corollary to the above, a capitalised dividend valuation based upon dividend yield.

(**c**) Management remuneration which might be artificially high, not only in a bonus culture, but also to avoid corporation tax.

(**d**) Transactions which are not at arms length and therefore not available to the prospective purchaser.

(**e**) Cost of sales which should be in current terms.

(**f**) Adequacy of depreciation in order to provide funds for the replacement cost of assets. Note that depreciation rates could have been used to keep cash in the business in order to maintain a dividend distribution at the expense of reinvestment, as the following example reveals:

Company A(£000s) Balance Sheet at 2000				Company B (£000s) Balance Sheet at 2000			
Share capital	100	Assets	100	Share capital	100	Assets	100
Profits = 20 p.a.				Profits = 20 p.a.			
Depreciation over 5 years				Depreciation over 10 years			

(*continued*)

Continued from p. 131

Balance Sheet at 2004				**Balance sheet at 2004**			
Share capital	100	Assets (cost)	100	Share capital	100	Assets (cost)	100
		Depreciation	80			Depreciation	40
		Net book value	20			Net book value	60
		Cash	80			Cash	40
	100		100		100		100
No dividends				Dividends £40			

(**g**) The correct treatment of R and D as revenue or capital.

(**h**) The impact of future repairs and maintenance on profits.

(**i**) The inclusion of any non-recurring income or profits, such as those arising from the sale of excess or idle assets.

(**j**) Provision for bad debts.

After making adjustments to the post-tax profits, the valuer must then ascertain whether it is practicable to hold these over as a foundation for the estimate of current maintainable earnings at the valuation date. This may be difficult where there are fluctuations in past profits. Even where a steady growth is evident there is also the question of whether this will continue. However, having arrived at an appropriate figure this must now be capitalised by reference to an appropriate P/E ratio, i.e. the reciprocal of the desired earnings yield. If profits are constant in perpetuity:

$$(3) \qquad V = \Pi(1 - t) \times \text{P/E}$$

or:

$$(4) \qquad V = \frac{\Pi(1 - t)}{k_e}$$

where:

V = going concern value of the business
Π = expected profits for appropriation at valuation
t = rate of corporation tax
$\text{P/E} = 1/k_e$
k_e = earnings yield.

If profits grow at a constant rate in perpetuity, Equation (4) may be rewritten using the constant growth formula explained in Chapter 5, based on anticipated post-tax earnings one year after takeover:

$$(5) \qquad V = \frac{[\Pi(1-t)]\,(1+g)}{k_e - g}$$

where:

g = a constant rate of growth in earnings

$g < k_e$ (if V is to be finite).

In the absence of a suitable P/E ratio relating to, say, similar companies in a similar industry, one can assume that the minimum yield to be sought by a prospective purchaser is the rate of return obtained from gilt-edged stocks. To this yield one might add a premium for the risk inherent in acquiring the company. The amount of risk depends very much on the individual circumstances and the attitude of the buyer. For example, will management continue to function well in the purchased company? Does technical expertise reside with individuals, rather than in the nature of the business itself? In fact, will the nature of the business change?

The net asset position is still important in determining the amount of risk. If the assets 'cover' the price of the investment (i.e. the asset backing which is analogous to the valuation ratio) this may be compensatory in the event of corporate failure and liquidation. Consider the following acquisition:

	£ million
Share capital	50
Retained earnings	50
Going concern value	100
Represented by:	
Net assets at valuation	100

If the purchaser is willing to pay £120 million for the business because of strong earnings then the cover is £100 million divided by £120 million, in other words 0.83, which is reasonable unless the liquidation value is well below £100 million.

As a basis for valuation, distinction should also be drawn between the P/E ratio which is based upon the earnings yield after tax and the dividend yield. The P/E ratio is more important to investors wishing to acquire control of a company (as well as marginal rate tax payers who are attracted by the prospect of capital gains through their sale of shares). This is not to say that one can ignore how the earnings are to be packaged for distribution. On the contrary, adequate dividend yields may also be necessary to attract potential minority investors, now as well as in the future, who pay tax at the standard rate and seek regular income. But this should not be at the expense of ploughback.

Consider the following:

£ millions	Company A	Company B	Company C
Purchase price	1,000	1,000	1,000
Profitability: P/E ratio	8.3	11.1	16.7
Earnings yield	12%	9%	6%
Earnings before tax	160	120	80
Tax at 25%	40	30	20
Profits after tax	120	90	60
Dividend yield (5%)	50	50	50
Retained earnings	70	40	10
Ploughback %	58%	45%	16%

Dividend yields are identical but Company A offers the best prospects for growth and capital gains.

Capitalisation of the net maintainable earnings in accordance with the appropriate P/E ratio will produce an amount representing the total value of the net assets employed in the business. To this value may have to be added the 'surplus' assets at a realisable valuation, i.e. those assets the income from which has not been included in the net maintainable earnings figure. The resulting amount (termed the total market capitalisation) divided by the number of equity shares will give the per share valuation required.

This share valuation should be compared with a valuation based on anticipated profits available for distribution net of tax and an allowance for ploughback. Since dividends convey information concerning likely future earnings (dividend signalling) this forecast distribution may be taken as a proportion of the dividend level that would be expected, based upon either the dividend yields of similar firms or their return on nominal value (dividend percentage) multiplied by the shares' market value as calculated above. The result will give the highest valuation based on rational dividend expectations after acquisition.

Consider the following purchase:

	£ million
Share capital: 5 million shares of £10 each	50
Retained earnings	50
	100
Represented by:	
Net assets at valuation	100

where:
- (*i*)   Earnings before tax are expected to be £10 million per annum, i.e. zero growth.
- (*ii*)   The retention rate is 80%.
- (*iii*) The earnings yield required is 15%, the reciprocal of which represents a P/E ratio of 6.66.
- (*iv*) The dividend percentage of similar firms is 6%.
- (*v*)   Tax is at 25%.

Thus, one can calculate:

(a) *Valuation based on earnings yield (P/E ratio)*

- (*i*)   Post-tax earnings × P/E ratio = Total market capitalisation
  £20 million $(1 - 0.25) \times 6.66 = £100$ million

- (*ii*) $\dfrac{\text{Total market capitalisation}}{\text{Number of shares}}$ = Market value per share

  $\dfrac{£100 \text{ million}}{5 \text{ million}} = £20$

(b) *Valuation based on dividend yield*

	£ million
Pre-tax profits	20
Less taxation (25%)	5
	15
Ploughback (80%)	12
Distributable dividend	3

(*i*)

$\dfrac{\text{Actual dividend}}{\text{Expected dividend}} \times \text{Total market capitalisation} = \text{Forecast market value}$

$\dfrac{£3.0 \text{ million}}{£3.0 \text{ million}} \times £100 \text{ million} = £100 \text{ million}$

(where the expected dividend is 6% of the shares nominal value)

(*ii*) $\dfrac{\text{Total market value}}{\text{Number of shares}}$ = Forecast market value per share

$\dfrac{£100 \text{ m}}{5 \text{ m}} = £20$

Note that, whilst the return on nominal value (dividend percentage) is 6%, the return on market value (dividend yield) is 3%. Note also that the dividend cover is five since the forecast dividend payout ratio is 20%. This is not accidental. Unless a company pursues a policy of full distribution with an earnings yield (k_e) equal to the dividend yield such that:

$$P_0 = \frac{E_t}{k_e} = \frac{D_t}{k_e}$$

where:

P_0 = share price
E_t = constant EPS per period
D_t = constant periodic dividend per share
k_e = a common capitalisation of yield

it is obvious that the market price of equity (P_0) will be identical only if there exists a unique relationship between the P/E ratio (based on the earnings yield) and the dividend yield, relative to profits after tax (dividends plus retentions) and dividend distributions respectively; a point which will be addressed in Chapter 7.

The reader may also care to verify that if the dividend percentage of similar firms was 5% then the dividend signalling effect of an actual distribution of £3 million, rather than an expected dividend of £2.5 million, would cause share price after take-over to increase to £24 per share based upon:

$$\frac{£3 \text{ million}}{£2.5 \text{ million}} \times £100 \text{ million} = £120 \text{ million}$$

However, it must be emphasised that any suggestion that dividend policy *per se* determines share price still remains a fundamental point of disagreement among academics and financial analysts alike which is discussed in the following chapter. The most notable protagonists are Modigliani and Miller (MM) whose Nobel Prize winning contribution to capital market theory is 'the law of one price' (alluded to in Chapter 5 and elsewhere) for which there is considerable empirical support. MM (1958 and 1961) state that, under certain conditions, two identical assets cannot sell at different prices if their forecast level of earnings conform in an efficient market characterised by investor rationality. In other words, dividend policy is irrelevant (a debate which continues to this day).

7 CASHFLOW BASIS

In determining income and hence value using financial accounting data, the former depends upon the latter and *vice versa*. The assets have value only in as much as they will provide income in the future, and income can only be assessed by valuing the assets at two points in time. Thus, the exercise becomes circular! Moreover, income is accrual-based rather than cash-based and, therefore, highly suspect.

This circle can be broken by thinking entirely in terms of cash. Income is defined in terms of net cash inflows, rather than in allowing for accounting revenue minus historical costs which includes non-cash expenses such as an allowance for the maintenance of capital, i.e. depreciation. The replacement cost of assets still needs to be estimated (a negative cashflow) but to include accounting depreciation in as well would be to account for the cost of the asset twice.

The going concern value of the company will be equal to the present value of the future cash inflows (less cash payments) resulting from operations. To this may have to be added the realisable value of assets to the extent that 'surplus' assets may be sold and the sale price will form part of the future cash inflow. Conversely, if the total assets are inadequate, further investment (cash outflow) may have to be anticipated in the cashflow forecast.

It should be noted that an economic analysis is now being prepared, rather than stewardship-based accounts, in order that an acquisition decision may be made. This necessarily involves projections into the future and the result of the projection will be a cashflow for each year. Once the firm is acquired, accounting reports in the future will obviously be produced in accordance with accepted accounting principles, based on historical cost and the accruals concept, but these may well differ from the cash projections used in an investment analysis, even under conditions of certainty.

Despite this disparity, the whole process accords with a fundamental proposition of capital theory, namely that the value of an asset is the future payments it provides discounted back to the present at an appropriate rate. Expressed mathematically:

(6) $$P_0 = \sum_{t=1}^{n} \frac{1}{(1+r)^t} C_t$$

where:
   P_0 = the present value or price
   C_t = the net cash inflows for each time period
   r = the interest rate (or rate of return)
   n = the number of periods under observation

And if cashflows are constant and n tends to infinity Equation (6) simplifies to:

(7) $P_0 = C_1/r$

which is the familiar formula for capitalising a perpetual annuity. It will be recalled that r is termed the capitalisation rate, because if one has observations for r and C_t, then the use of Equation (7) in order to arrive at a value or price P_0 is termed 'capitalisation', i.e. one is capitalising cashflows in order to determine a present value.

If cashflows are not constant over time, but grow at a constant rate g, then the present value of future payments over n periods is as follows:

$$(8) \qquad P_0 = \frac{C_1}{1 + r} + \frac{C_1(1 + g)}{(1 + r)^2} + \frac{C_1(1 + g)^2}{(1 + r)^3} + \cdots + \frac{C_1(1 + g)^{n-1}}{(1 + r)^n}$$

If, however, n tends to infinity Equation (8) also simplifies to the constant-growth formula for a perpetual annuity as explained in Chapter 5, namely:

$$(9) \qquad P_0 = \frac{C_1}{r - g}$$

where:

$r > g$

if P_0 is to be finite.

It has already been demonstrated how these simple equations can be made operational by the application of actual P/E ratios and dividend yields to accounting data prepared on a non-cash basis. Consider, therefore, the previous example, where earnings and dividend yields of 15% and 3% respectively produced:

Total market value = £100 million
Market price per share = £20

Both figures were determined by capitalising a perpetual annuity based upon accounting conventions. Let it now be assumed that:

(*i*) On a cash basis, the prospective purchaser requires a forecast earnings yield of 18%.

(*ii*) First-year net cash income after charging depreciation of £8 million is anticipated to be £17 million.

(*iii*) Taxable accounting profits are £20 million.

(*iv*) The rate of corporation tax is 25%.

(*v*) Cashflows are expected to grow at 2% per annum.

Under conditions of certainty, a going concern value may be calculated based upon first-year cashflows as follows:

	£ million
Net cash inflow	17
add depreciation	8
	25
Less tax (£20 million × 0.25)	5
Cash inflow	20

Using Equation (9)

$$P_0 = \frac{C_1}{r - g} = \frac{£20 \text{ million}}{0.18 - 0.02} = £125 \text{ million}$$

so that with 5 million shares in issue the per share valuation is £25.

Note that this cashflow valuation is 25% higher than the accounting valuation, not only because the basis of capitalisation is higher but also because the income is assumed to grow. But what of the dividend valuation?

If, as originally stated, similar firms are currently yielding 3% then the first-year distribution is not £3 million (as before) but:

£125 million × 0. 03 = £3.75 million

Assuming the firm maintains a constant dividend payout ratio after take-over, then this dividend will also grow by 2% per annum. Thus, we have only one unknown, namely k_e the long-run dividend yield, in the now familiar equation:

$$P_0 = \frac{D_1}{k_e - g}$$

where:

D_1 = the first-year dividend distribution

Solving for k_e:

$$£125m = \frac{3.75 \text{ million}}{k_e - 0.02}$$

$$k_e = 5\%$$

As stated earlier, if dividends are not to affect share price there must be a unique relationship between the dividend yield and dividend policy. What the example reveals is a point cogently made by M J Gordon (1962), previously contested by MM (1961), that the long-run equity capitalisation rate used in the constant growth formula must be an increasing function of the growth rate. It will be recalled that in the original example with zero growth the dividend yield (k_e) was only 3%.

As Chapter 7 will explain, this does not conflict with the law of one price and the dividend irrelevancy hypothesis proposed by MM. They would suggest that the rationale behind the higher yield relates to the profitability of investment opportunities provided by the 2% growth of retained earnings over time, rather than any increase in dividend distributions.

8 STOCK MARKET DATA, INVESTOR BEHAVIOUR AND TAKEOVER STRATEGY

Armed with the financial methodology of takeovers, a number of pointers applicable to the selection of shares which were outlined in Chapter 5 now bear repetition in relation to corporate acquisition, whether cashflow or accounting based.

- The P/E ratio (earnings yield reciprocal) shows how the company's value is rated in relation to the profit it earns. The higher the P/E ratio, the greater confidence there is that profits are going to rise; and the lower the P/E, the greater the concern that it might be unable to sustain profits.
- Conversely, a low P/E ratio could reflect the fact that a company's shares are undervalued by the market relative to its profit performance and thus make it attractive to speculative investors.
- Shares in companies that are expected to produce rapid growth in profits and hence capital gains offer low dividend yields, while higher dividend yields are offered by what are regarded as relatively mature and stable businesses with little prospect of increasing profits and dividend.
- Conversely, part of stock market law is 'the higher the yield the higher the risk'. This applies particularly to shares where a higher dividend yield usually signals uncertainty over whether the dividend can be maintained in future, particularly if earnings cover is low.
- In general, if any investment offers either a higher dividend yield or earnings yield (a low P/E ratio) than similar investments, it is advisable to be cautious.

According to the legendary UK investor Jim Slater it pays, therefore, to specialise in growth shares for long-term reward. In his recent text *Beyond the Zulu Principle*, the golden rules for investment, albeit based upon published accounting data, are expanded upon as follows:

(i) Mandatory criteria
(a) A prospective P/E ratio no larger than 20 (a yield of 5 per cent).
(b) For large investments, a prospective P/E ratio which is less than a

company's future growth rate. For smaller investments a maximum P/E ratio of 75 per cent of growth rate.

(c) Avoid speculative shares, namely those with the highest P/E growth factor (PEG), calculated by dividing the prospective P/E ratio by the estimated future growth rate in EPS. These are the ones to sell to improve the average safety margin of an investment portfolio.

(d) Strong cashflow in terms of cash per share in excess of EPS for the last reported year and the average of the previous five years.

(e) Low gearing (the proportion of debt in the firm's financial structure), preferably under 50 per cent or, better still, positive cash balances.

(f) High relative strength in the previous 12 months coupled with high relative strength in the preceding month or three months. Avoid shares that are flagging on the market.

(g) A strong competitive advantage.

(h) No active selling of a company's shares by its directors.

(ii) Highly desirable criteria

(a) Accelerating EPS, preferably linked to a company's ability to replicate its successful activities.

(b) A number of directors buying shares.

(c) A market capitalisation in excess of £30 million.

(iii) Bonus criteria

(a) A low price-to-sales ratio (PSR).

(b) Something innovative.

(c) A low price-to-research ratio (PRR).

(d) A reasonable asset position.

According to Slater, 'These criteria may be looked on as an investor's quiverful of arrows. They need not all be fired and some may miss their targets, but you do need to score a substantial number of bullseyes.' They may also be refined and extended by experience and new ideas.

As applied to takeover activity, the lesson to be learned from his approach to investment confirms the earlier point that the likely rewards from an acquisition are determined by the analysis which precedes it. A company which selects another for the purpose of long-term growth by utilising a rigorous disciplined approach with in-built safety margins, such as asset backing, supported by strong financial criteria has little to fear. If the composite entity continues to grow profitably, patient investment will eventually be rewarded by an efficient stock market which reflects its progress.

Conversely, the earlier discussion of the motives for acquisition drew attention to the dangers associated with company takeovers for short-term benefits merely because their shares were priced low on the stock market. Even though the acquirer may be purchasing at less than book value (negative goodwill) the acquiree may be worth more dead than alive and the assets worth less than their stated book value.

It will also be recalled that the subjective reasons behind a takeover, based on managerial goals of growth, prestige and security, may be supported by an elaborate rationalisation without an objective analysis of the commercial factors involved. As with any investment, however, an acquisition strategy is the art of the specific, where preparation meets opportunity. In the absence of luck, let alone judgement, the likely consequence of takeovers motivated by factors which exclude the growth of shareholders' earnings from the equation is that post-acquisition equity prices may collapse. This explains why firms can develop a misguided interest in the effects of acquisitions upon their stock market performance.

By way of illustration, consider Table 6.5 which compares two takeovers.

In the first case, with lower-priced shares and financial indicators which are identical, the stock market data of the composite entity obviously remains unchanged after the acquisition. In the second situation, all else is equal except that half the number of shares are purchased for twice the price which also

Table 6.5 Acquisitions and stock market data

	Case One		Case Two	
	Pre-acquisition	*Post-acquisition*	*Pre-acquisition*	*Post-acquisition*
Acquired Company				
Number of shares	50,000		250,000	
Post-tax earnings	£500,000		£500,000	
Sale price	£5,000,000		£5,000,000	
Share price	£10		£20	
EPS	£1		£2	
Earnings yield	10%		10%	
P/E	10		10	
Acquiring Company				
Number of shares	1,000,000	1,500,000	1,000,000	1,250,000
Post-tax earnings	£1,000,000	£1,500,000	£1,000,000	£1,500,000
Market capitalisation	£10,000,000	£15,000,000	£20,000,000	£25,000,000
Share price	£10	£10	£20	£20
EPS	£1	£1	£1	£1.20
Earnings yield	10%	10%	5%	6%
P/E	10	10	20	16.66

corresponds to that of the acquiring company. As a consequence, the acquirer benefits from a 20 pence (20 per cent) increase in EPS, such that the earnings yield rises from 5 per cent to 6 per cent. In other words, the P/E ratio falls from 20 to 16.66. However, all this presupposes that as in Case One the share price remains constant following the acquisition.

First, it seems reasonable to assume that with a 20 per cent improvement in EPS, share price will rise by a similar proportion, i.e. £4.00. An increase in share price from £20.00 to £24.00 would, therefore, produce a resurgence in the P/E from 16.66 back to 20 (yielding 5 per cent). Second, it is conceivable that price will rise still further, not backed by trading fundamentals such as earnings but from extra *general* buying pressure.

The logic behind such crowd psychology is explained in Mackay's classic nineteenth century text *Extra-Ordinary Delusions of the Madness of Crowds* which can be applied to capital markets and is well documented in Chapter 13. The driving forces are either fear or, in this case, greed. The combined impact of increased EPS and a proportionally sharper increase in the price of equity produces a much higher P/E ratio than that which existed prior to takeover. Assuming share price stabilises at £28.00, the reader may care to verify that the P/E ratio will rise from 20 (pre-acquisition) to 28, which is equivalent to an earnings yield of approximately 3.57 per cent.

Now visualise the composite entity making another acquisition, this time with a share price of £28.00 as opposed to £20.00, with similar economic gains and then others, each with similar results. It would appear that a successful acquisition programme elicits vast capital gains for shareholders plus the growth, security and prestige which corporate management so desire.

Unfortunately, an element of what Mackay termed delusion is involved here. This stems from the confidence required on behalf of shareholders to sustain a high share price and, therefore, a high P/E ratio which is premised not only on a rising earnings trend but also reflects the extra buying pressure fed by the mania of eager investors. However, any factor that undermines this confidence can break the upward spiral and share price will fall. It may also precipitate a selling panic such that equity reaches a bargain basement level and the company itself falls prey to takeover.

At least three factors can be identified. The first is the shareholders' perception of their individual positions in the spiral. Was equity received upon acquisition or purchased subsequently? If the former, the shareholder might still gain; if much later, the shareholder loses. There is considerable evidence to support this (see Franks, Harris and Titman 1991). The second factor arises because each subsequent acquisition must have a discernible favourable impact upon the EPS of the composite entity. Since the company is growing by takeover, then either the size or the number of acquisitions must perpetually increase. Whichever applies, the strain on commercial competence grows and the probability of making an uneconomic decision increases. This final factor is crucial in the longer term. Both theory and evidence has long suggested that acquisitions are drawn from a limited spectrum; namely those companies with low P/E ratios (see Myers 1976).

It will be recalled that a low P/E ratio could reflect an undervaluation of equity by the market relative to profit performance, thus making the company an attractive investment proposition. Equally, however, the commercial viability of the merged entity may be dubious, inasmuch as a low P/E ratio can also portray investor concern that a company might be unable to maintain its profits. But in order to sustain the P/E ratio, EPS must be sustained year after year, what Myers termed the *bootstrap* game. Consequently, an entity acquired for essentially non-commercial reasons must produce profitable performance for an extended period, a requirement that may prove impossible.

So either shareholders' panic, or a bad acquisition, or declining financial performance may break the spiral. This is not to say that all spirals will break, but even composite entities which survive to acquire again and again can be accused of short-termism which is eventually doomed to failure. Recalling Case Two in the previous numerical example, they may be using a higher P/E ratio as leverage in relation to that of their acquisition merely to secure an immediate improvement in EPS. If this subsequently attracts speculative investors, share price may be climbing a wall of worry, which is not supported by trading fundamentals. The company will then find it difficult to discontinue its periodic addition of relatively low P/E candidates, even to provide an illusion of EPS growth which justifies its share price.

9 SUMMARY AND CONCLUSIONS

This chapter has explored some of the motives that underpin initial market placings and acquisitions. Each motive is rational but is not necessarily based on the long-term commercial viability of the enterprise. As an ideal, present value analysis utilising cashflows rather than accounting data was also presented as the most sophisticated technique for valuing a company as a going concern. However, for the purposes of simplicity it was necessary to assume that the following information was known with certainty:

(*i*)   All future cashflows in perpetuity, including an allowance for constant growth which is less than the rate of capitalisation.

(*ii*) A single rate of capitalisation, with capital costs and reinvestment rates equal to this (i.e. borrowing and lending rates are equal).

(*iii*) That sufficient funds were being retained to maintain the expected future cashflows without compromising dividend policy.

(*iv*) The timing and amounts of asset replacements.

(v)   The realisable value and timing of the sale of surplus assets

Future chapters will demonstrate that if any one of these assumptions are relaxed the valuation so derived becomes invalid. In view of this limitation, market placings and takeovers are likely to be confirmed at a practical level using publicly available information, primarily drawn from financial reports. Typically, this latter approach is based upon the following methods:

- Balance sheet values (relating to net assets).
- Expectations (relating to accounting income) in the form of:
    - (i)   a going concern value using a normal rate of return on net assets, plus a goodwill calculation based on the capitalisation of superprofits
    - (ii)   a profitability valuation using a P/E ratio applied to post-tax earnings
    - (iii) as a corollary to the above, a capitalised dividend valuation based upon dividend yield.

No one method is necessarily correct, rather they should be used when appropriate to provide a range of values for the purposes of negotiation. As a final illustration, consider the following information prepared for a takeover bid:

Adjusted Balance Sheet	(£000)
Ordinary shares of £10.00	800
Retained earnings	250
Liabilities	550
	1600
Represented by:	
Fixed assets	1000
Current assets	600
	1600

(i)   Future profits after tax are estimated at £200,000 (£0.25 EPS).

(ii)   Future dividends cannot fall below £120,000 per annum (£0.15 per share).

(iii) The market price of shares in companies doing an equally uncertain trade and financed by ordinary share capital suggests that the current P/E ratio is 7 (which is equivalent to a 14.5% return) and that the dividend yield is 10%.

A range of prices per share offered might be calculated as follows:

1. *Balance sheet valuation*

Net assets: £1.6 million minus £0.55 million = £1.05 million

Per share valuation $\dfrac{£1.05 \text{ million}}{80,000} = £16.31\text{p}$

2. *Expectations*

(a) *Going concern* (superprofits); using Equation (1) where:

$$V = A + \frac{P - rA}{m}$$

	Profits	*Capital equivalent*
	£	
Expected profits	200,000	
But a normal return (say of 12.5% on assets of £1.05 million)	131,125	£1.05 million
Superprofits (excess of expected profit over 'normal' profit)	68,875	
Capitalised value of superprofits at 25% (i.e. say four years purchase of goodwill)	$\dfrac{68,875}{0.25}$	
or	£68,875 × 4	£0.275 million

Going concern value = £1.325 million

$$\text{Per share valuation} = \frac{£1.325 \text{ million}}{80,000} = £16.56$$

(b) *Profitability*
Anticipated profits are given as £200,000 per annum and the expected P/E ratio is 7. Thus, using:

Profits after tax × P/E ratio = Total market capitalisation
£200,000 × 7 = £1.4 million

$$\text{Per share valuation} = \frac{£1.4 \text{ million}}{80,000} = £17.50\text{p}$$

(c) *Dividends*
If expected dividends are £120,000 and the yield is 10%, then capitalising a perpetual annuity:

$$V_0 = \frac{D}{k_e} = \frac{120,000}{0.1} = £1.2 \text{ million}$$

$$\text{Per share valuation} = \frac{1.2 \text{ million}}{80,000} = £15$$

Note, however, that if the bid price per share is to accord with an earnings valuation, then the actual dividend after takeover should be £140,000 such that:

$$V_0 = \frac{D}{k_e} = \frac{140,000}{0.1} = £1.4 \text{ million}$$

Since this uplift to dividends is well covered by profits after tax this should present little problem, provided that the company still has adequate retained earnings for reinvestment.

It should also be noted that the purchase value of the tangible assets provides considerable cover (asset backing) for the company as a going concern. The acquisition also appears attractive, since the valuation based upon the profit-earning capacity of the business exceeds that for net assets and confirms the existence of goodwill.

One could make an initial bid of around £16.50 per share based upon the minimum value arrived at by an estimate of the value of the net tangible assets. A fairer price might be £17.00, based upon an allowance for goodwill and the earning power of the assets capitalised at a reasonable rate of return, as evidenced by the appropriate P/E ratio. In order to ensure success, particularly in the event of a struggle (when the bid price might go further still), an offer of £17.50 would seem realistic.

Finally, if surplus assets with an immediate realisable value of £0.15 million had also been identified, over and above the operating assets of £1.05 million, the reader may care to verify that the going concern values would actually be as follows:

Basis	Net assets	Superprofits	Profitability	Dividends
Total value	£1.2 million	£1.475 million	£1.55 million	£1.35 million
Per share	£15.00	£18.44	£19.37	£16.87

What this reaffirms is that the sale of excess or idle assets (which provide a once-only benefit) can only enter into the calculation after annually recurring operating profits have been capitalised. And needless to say, if realisation is delayed, the eventual proceeds from the sale would also have to be discounted back to a present value at an appropriate interest rate in order to bring it in line with the main valuation.

References

(1) Franks, J.R., Harris, R.S., and Titman, S., 'The postmerger share-price performance of acquiring firms', *Journal of Financial Economics*, Vol. 29, March, 1991.
(2) Gordon, M.J. *The Investment, Financing and Valuation of a Corporation*, Richard D. Irwin 1962.

(3) Mackay, L.L.D., *Extraordinary Delusions of the Madness of Crowds*, Farrar, Straus and Giroux (New York) 1932 (originally published in 1841).

(4) Martin, K.J. and McConnell, J.J., 'Corporate performance, corporate takeovers, and management turnover', *Journal of Finance*, Vol. 46, June, 1991.

(5) Modigliani, F. and Miller, M.H., 'The cost of capital, corporation finance and the theory of investment', *American Economic Review*, Vol. XLVIII, No. 3, June, 1958.

(6) Miller, M.H. and Modigliani, F., 'Dividend policy, growth and the valuation of shares', *Journal of Business of the University of Chicago*, Vol. XXXIV, No. 4, October, 1961.

(7) Myers, S.C., 'A framework for evaluating mergers', in Myers S.C. (Ed.), *Modern Developments in Financial Management*, Frederick A. Praeger 1976.

(8) Slater, J., *Beyond the Zulu Principle*, Orion, 1996.

(9) Weston, J., Chung, K.S., and Hoag, S.E., *Mergers, Restructuring and Corporate Control*, Prentice-Hall 1990.

7

Dividend policy and earnings valuation

Chapter profile

Chapter 5 explained the relevance of discounted revenue theory to the pricing of ordinary shares and the analysis of stock market performance, using published financial ratios. Chapter 6 detailed various practical measures and conceptual approaches for the purpose of valuing a company, either coming to the market for the first time, or in the event of falling prey to takeover.

One distinction drawn was the application of either the P/E ratio (reciprocal of the earnings yield) or the dividend yield as a basis for capitalisation, ideally in cash terms. The purpose of this chapter is to reflect more rigorously upon the relationship between dividend distribution patterns, investment and financing decisions; in particular, whether a specific dividend policy, which conforms to an optimum retention rate, maximises the market value of equity.

Given the normative objective of shareholder wealth maximisation, based upon Fisher's Separation Theorem, dividend relevancy hypotheses under conditions of certainty and uncertainty which also incorporate growth, utilising the models explained in Chapter 4, are presented. The opposing view of dividend irrelevancy and the *law of one price*, as advocated by Modigliani and Miller (MM) based upon the pioneering work of Walter, is described.

Problems of statistical analyses are explained. Conflicting empirical evidence concerning the relationship between dividend yields and the market value of equity is chronicled. The fiscal treatment of dividends *vis á vis* capital gains, which gives rise to clientele theory, the informational content of distribution policies (dividend signalling), as well as the impact of transaction and issue costs, are further issues which are addressed.

1 INTRODUCTION

It is an oft-forgotten fact that, prior to the 1940s, accounting and financial analysis focussed upon cashflow and solvency. It is only since the Second

World War that those interested in corporate performance have become preoccupied with published financial statements, the so-called 'bottom line', and for those companies with a stock exchange listing, its important derivative, earnings per share (EPS). If proof be needed, EPS is, after all, the only financial indicator whose definition and calculation is regulated by the professional accountancy bodies of the UK, in their accounting standard, SSAP 3.

Yet, as explained in the previous chapter, accrual-based historical cost records of stewardship, compiled for ex-post reporting purposes (and any ratios derived thereof), may be underpinned by arbitrary accounting conventions which are entirely inappropriate for economic profit measurement and value analysis, ex-post or otherwise. Familiar criticisms of EPS are that:

- It ignores cashflow, the numerator being accrual based.
- It is a measure of profitability which utilises a historical cost denominator (nominal value), rather than the market price of equity.
- Both parameters are susceptible to creative accounting manipulation, particularly in the short-term.
- It makes no allowance for inflation and specific price level change.
- It ignores the time value of money.

The distillation of corporate performance in the form of price/earnings (P/E) ratios published in the financial press, which divide the current price of a share by the EPS, does not weaken these criticisms. It merely compounds the felony. A cost-based measure of profitability is now being mixed and matched with a market value of equity. As a consequence, investor decisions may not only be implemented on the intrinsic value of the company concerned, but also on any distortions caused by its choice of accounting policies. This implies that shareholder wealth may be determined by current accounting conventions at the expense of anticipated future cashflows; all of which naturally runs counter to the normative objective of corporate finance presented in this text.

To resolve the dilemma one could point to more recent accounting pronouncements, such as the UK financial reporting exposure draft on goodwill and the cashflow accounting standard (FRED12 and FRS1 respectively). For the purposes of investment analysis, however, more detailed, technical disclosure on a historical basis (even concerning cash and intangible items) is no substitute for an economic valuation.

One role of executive management should be to report publicly upon the relationship between all its investments undertaken on the shareholders' behalf and the timing and size of their uncertain future cashflows. Ideally, it should be expressed in NPV terms. The historical failure to do this is presumptuous. It implies that the equity investor (institutional or otherwise) is sufficiently sophisticated financially to see through any distortions created by the accrual accounting policies which management utilise to discharge their stewardship responsibilities, primarily for the benefit of the tax authorities, rather than corporate stakeholders. It is also an increasingly heroic assumption given the democratisation of share ownership through privatisation issues in the UK.

It was explained in previous chapters why the empirical evidence concerning the use of discounted cashflow analyses, even as an internal managerial control model, remains dispiriting compared to payback and the accounting rate of return. Not suprisingly, NPV therefore represents a global *non-sequitor* as a means of financial reporting. Consequently an inordinate number of non-institutional shareholders are left bewildered by a proliferation of conventional published data. To understand the factors, normative or otherwise, which may underpin the price of their shares and the reaction of even the most informed rational investor to a firm's dividend and investment policies, it is necessary, therefore, to return to first principles and to commence with a restatement of theory.

2 A BASIC VALUATION MODEL

A fundamental proposition of capital theory is that the value of an asset is the future cash payments it provides discounted back to the present at an appropriate rate. Expressed mathematically:

(1) $$P_0 = \sum_{t=1}^{n} \frac{1}{(1+r)^t} C_t$$

where:
P_0 = the present value or price
C_t = the cashflow for each time period
r = the interest rate (or rate of return)
n = the number of periods under observation

And if cashflows are constant and n tends to infinity Equation (1) simplifies to:

(2) $$P_0 = C_1/r$$

which is the familiar formula for capitalising a perpetual annuity. r is termed the capitalisation rate, because if one has observations for r and C_t, then the use of Equation (2) in order to arrive at a value or price P_0, is termed 'capitalisation', i.e. one is capitalising cashflows in order to determine a present value.

If cashflows are not constant over time, but grow at a constant rate g, then the present value of future payments over n periods is as follows:

(3) $$P_0 = \frac{C_1}{1+r} + \frac{C_1(1+g)}{(1+r)^2} + \frac{C_1(1+g)^2}{(1+r)^3} + \cdots + \frac{C_1(1+g)^{n-1}}{(1+r)^n}$$

If, however, n tends to infinity Equation (3) also simplifies to the constant-growth formula for a perpetual annuity, explained in Chapter 5, namely:

$$(4) \quad P_0 = \frac{C_1}{r - g}$$

These simple equations are crucial to an understanding of share valuation theories. Unfortunately, the precise definition and behaviour of the individual variables is a complex matter upon which there is still disagreement.

This can be illustrated, quite simply, using Equation (2). For example, if it is assumed that share price is a function of future earnings after tax (in cash terms) one can write the *constant-earnings valuation model:*

$$(5) \quad P_0 = E_1/k_e$$

where:

P_0 = the market price of ordinary shares (i.e. equity)
E_1 = the constant post-tax earnings per share paid each period
k_e = the market's equity capitalisation rate of earnings.

Rearranging terms, k_e, the prospective earnings yield required by ordinary shareholders, is:

$$(6) \quad k_e = E_1/P_0$$

The reciprocal of the earnings yield then defines the prospective price/earnings (P/E) ratio:

$$(7) \quad 1/k_e = P_0/E_1$$

In accordance with the operations explained in Chapter 6, the P/E ratio provides an alternative but familiar method whereby earnings can be capitalised to arrive at a market value for a company's shares, i.e. post-tax earnings multiplied by the P/E ratio equals share price. Thus:

$$(8) \quad P_0 = E_1(1/k_e)$$

However, what if share price is assumed to be a function of dividends? Again using Equation (2), one can write the *constant-dividend valuation model:*

$$(9) \quad P_0 = D_1/k_e$$

where:

D_1 = the constant dividend per share paid each period
k_e = the equity capitalisation rate of dividend.

Rearranging terms the dividend yield k_e is:

$$(10) \quad k_e = D_1/P_0$$

The dilemma is now obvious. Unless a company pursues a policy of full distribution such that E_1 equals D_1 with an earnings yield equal to its dividend yield, the market price of equity must differ using equations (5) and (9) in the absence of a unique relationship between dividend policy and dividend yield.

3 BASIC DIVIDEND THEORY

Porterfield (1965), among others, has attempted to resolve this dilemma by reasoning that ultimately dividends are all that shareholders receive from an equity investment. He acknowledged that they may experience capital appreciation (or depreciation) in market value if they sell their shares. However, the selling price itself is a function of future dividends at the time of sale, and if the company has engaged in no outside financing since its inception, increases in future dividends must be a consequence of a less than full distribution policy in previous periods.

This is best illustrated when the equity resides with shareholders at the time of a company's liquidation. All that is expected is the final *ex div* price, which represents the return of original capital invested plus capital appreciation. Capital appreciation may be defined as all earnings not previously paid as dividends, including those in the last period. Porterfield then explains how this valuation process may be extended back through the life of the company to define the share price, from shareholder to shareholder and period by period, until one arrives at the original price paid, the *finite-period dividend valuation model* explained in Chapter 5.

$$(11) \qquad P_0 = \sum_{t=1}^{n} \frac{D_t}{(1+k_e)^t} + \frac{P_n}{(1+k_e)^n}$$

In this basic statement of dividend theory, the stream of future dividends the share is expected to provide is taken as the future payments investors consider in arriving at the price or value of a share. Further, it is assumed that the company itself engages in no outside financing, in which case the dividend expectation is determined by the company's current earnings, its investment or retention rate (the two are the same with no outside financing), and its return on investment. The product of the return and retention rate equals the expected rate of growth in dividend.

The result is a growth model analogous to Equation (4) that predicts the value of a share on the basis of four variables:

(*i*)   Current earnings
(*ii*) The retention or investment rate
(*iii*) Rate of return on investment

(*iv*) The rate of return investors require on the share (the equity capitalisation rate).

Thus, the decision variable a company may use to influence share price is its retention rate and, given the value of the other three variables, the price of a share for any given retention rate may be determined. Moreover, if it is assumed that the objective of the company is to maximise its value, where value is a function of future earnings, which in turn are a function of investment, the task of the theory is to provide information on the nature of these two functions so that a model of share price determination may be developed to find the optimum investment (retention) rate which maximises corporate value.

And this has one provocative implication. It implies that the retention rate *per se* (i.e. apart from the profitability of investment undertaken) influences share price. In other words, the price of a share is a function of the dividend payout ratio.

The validity of this proposition therefore depends upon whether investors buy a share's future earnings or future dividends. As Porterfield states, the dividend expectation must be what the investors buy, since retentions are merely a proxy measure for future dividends. All that earnings advocates may logically maintain is that the distribution of earnings between dividends and retentions is irrelevant to share price. However, for this to be true it is necessary to demonstrate that the rate at which investors discount a dividend is independent of the expected rate of growth in the dividend.

Suffice it to say that, whichever behaviour postulate is correct, a solution to the problem would benefit both the investment decisions of companies and shareholders alike and aid the study of capital formation, in a free market economy. However, the usefulness of either proposition is severely restricted by the fact that the future is not certain and by the related assumption that funds are not always freely available.

4   THE GORDON GROWTH MODEL UNDER CONDITIONS OF CERTAINTY

Prior to Porterfield's exposition, M.J. Gordon (1962) took up this challenge by first identifying the following three alternative sources of income provided by a share investment in publicly listed companies:

(*i*) Future earnings per share
(*ii*) Future dividends per share
(*iii*) The future dividends for a finite number of periods, plus the price at the end of that time.

In the absence of a differential tax treatment of dividends *vis á vis* capital gains,

Gordon concluded that (*iii*) reduces to (*ii*), since the price at any future date may be expected to depend on subsequent income. The major issue therefore is between earnings and dividends and the theory which Gordon developed assumes that future dividends are what the investor buys in a share.

Consider first a world of certainty where:

(*i*) A company earns E_1 in the period ending at $t = 1$ and E_1 in each successive period (i.e. earnings are constant).

(*ii*) All earnings are paid out in dividends such that: $E_1 = D_1$, i.e. EPS is equivalent to dividends per share.

(*iii*) The company is expected to adhere to a full dividend distribution policy.

(*iv*) The company is expected to engage in no outside financing.

The company is therefore expected to earn and distribute E_1 in perpetuity.

If the rate of return which investors require on a share is k_e, the valuation of the share may be expressed in expanded form as:

(12) $$P_0 = \frac{E_1}{1 + k_e} + \frac{E_1}{(1 + k_e)^2} + \frac{E_1}{(1 + k_e)^3} + \cdots + \frac{E_1}{(1 + k_e)^n}$$

Thus, k_e is the discount rate which equates a dividend expectation of E_1 in perpetuity with the present share price P_0, i.e. the price of a share is a function of dividends, which is equivalent to:

(9) $$P_0 = D_1/k_e \quad \text{since } E_1 = D_1$$

However, if assumption (*ii*) is now relaxed, and the company announces at $t = 0$ that it will retain and invest E_1 during the first period and that it expects to earn a rate of return r on the investment such that $r = k_e = E_1/P_0$ and further that in each successive period it will pay out all earnings as dividends, the share price is now expressed as:

(13) $$P_0 = \frac{0}{1 + k_e} + \frac{E_1 + k_e E_1}{(1 + k_e)^2} + \frac{E_1 + k_e E_1}{(1 + k_e)^3} + \cdots + \frac{E_1 + k_e E_1}{(1 + k_e)^n}$$

since the shareholder receives nothing at $t = 1$.

The investor therefore relinquishes E_1 at $t = 1$ and receives instead $k_e E_1$ in perpetuity. Distribution of dividends over time has therefore changed. However, $k_e E_1$ in perpetuity discounted at k_e is exactly equal to E_1, since the retention investment rate r equals the equity capitalisation rate. Equation (13) simplifies to Equation (12), which in turn is equivalent to Equation (9).

For example, with an annual dividend of 100 pence per share in perpetuity and an equity cost of capital of 10 per cent per annum, Equation (12) would show:

$$P_0 = \frac{£1.00}{1.1} + \frac{£1.00}{(1.1)^2} + \frac{£1.00}{(1.1)^3} + \cdots$$
$$= £0.91 + £0.83 + £0.75 + \cdots$$

Alternatively, if the dividend payment at the time period one is retained by the company, reinvested at 10 per cent per annum and all the earnings are subsequently distributed, Equation (13) would reveal:

$$P_0 = \frac{0}{1.1} + \frac{£1.10}{(1.1)^2} + \frac{£1.10}{(1.1)^2} + \cdots$$
$$= 0 + £0.91 + £0.83 + \cdots$$

Thus, in perpetuity, Equations (12) and (13) conform to Equation (9) such that:

$$P_0 = \frac{£1.00}{0.1} = £10.00$$

Gordon, therefore, confirms that under conditions of certainty dividend policy is irrelevant. A company can be expected to retain and invest any fraction of earnings in any period without the share price being changed, so long as r (return on reinvestment) is equal to k_e (the equity capitalisation rate).

But what if r does not equal k_e? Using the following notation:

P_t = price of a company's shares at the end of period t
D_t = dividend per share paid by the company during t
E_t = income per share earned during t
r = return on investment the company is expected to earn in every future period
b = fraction of income the corporation is expected to retain in every future period
k_e = shareholders' required return on the company's shares.

where:

(i)   Time subscripts referring to a period in the future reflect the mean or expected value of a probability distribution of a random variable, which the investor is assumed to estimate subjectively.

(ii) r and b are only estimates of what the company will earn and retain in each future period.

(iii) r and b are not dated, reflecting the assumption that investors estimate the same value of each for every future period supported by the following real world considerations.

As Gordon states:

(a) Investors rarely have any clear notions of how r and b will change over time.

(b) Companies do quite frequently follow a policy of paying a stable fraction of their normal earnings in dividends.

(c) In the absence of information to the contrary, the assumption that r is expected to be the same in every future period seems to be reasonable and free of bias. It may not occur but investors will only have a broad idea as to the extent and timing of the change in r, and it is not clear how such expectations may be represented.

He then considers a company for which the following is true:

(i)   It engages in no outside financing.

(ii)   It has a quick ratio of one and no long-term debt.

(iii)   It will retain the fraction b of its income in every future period.

(iv)   It will earn the rate of return on investment r in every future period.

For this company, the dividend in any future period is certain. It will simply be:

(14) $D_t = (1 - b)E_t$

and the rate of growth in dividends will be rb. The price of the company's shares at $t = 0$ will be:

$$(15) \quad P_0 = \frac{E_1(1 - b)}{1 + k_e} + \frac{E_1(1 - b)(1 + rb)}{(1 + k_e)^2}$$
$$+ \frac{E_1(1 - b)(1 + rb)^2}{(1 + k_e)^3} + \cdots + \frac{E_1(1 - b)(1 + rb)^{n-1}}{(1 + k_e)^n}$$

so that from Equation (4) where n tends to infinity:

$$(16) \quad P_0 = \frac{(1 - b)E_1}{k_e - rb}$$

which may be rewritten as:

$$(17) \quad P_0 = \frac{D_1}{k_e - g}$$
$$= \frac{D_0(1 + g)}{k_e - g}$$

where:

D_0 = the current dividend

$g = rb$, the rate of growth in dividends, subject to the constraint that $k_e > g$ for the price of the share to be finite.

Rearranging terms, the equity capitalisation rate, which Gordon calls the *rate of profit*, is, therefore, defined as:

$$(18) \qquad k_e = \frac{D_1}{P_0} + g \qquad \left(\text{from } \frac{(1-b)E_1}{P_0} + br \right)$$

Equations (15), (16) and (17) represent the Gordon growth model in various guises. Each reveals that the price of a share is its forecast dividend divided by the amount that the rate of profit investors require on a share exceeds the rate of growth in the dividend. Under conditions of certainty, however, where k_e the rate of profit investors require is constant, a higher retention b will produce a lower numerator in the equations, thereby affecting share price adversely. Conversely, a higher b value will produce a lower denominator which has a beneficial effect on share price, particularly where the reinvestment rate r exceeds k_e, since the growth in dividends g is a function of r and b. Thus, for a given retention rate and in the absence of any external financing, if r exceeds k_e, P_0 will rise. If the reverse holds, P_0 will decline. This suggests that management should only retain funds for reinvestment if their rate of return at least equals the rate of profit which investors require, i.e.

$$r \geq k_e$$

If the reverse holds, funds should be returned to the shareholders all of which accords with Fisher's Separation Theorem explained in Part 2.

To prove the point, consider three companies, each with a uniform EPS of 100 pence, an equity capitalisation rate of 10 per cent per annum and an annual retention rate of 50 per cent. They only differ with regard to r, their periodic rates of return on reinvestment, which are 5 per cent, 10 per cent and 15 per cent respectively.

From either Equations (15), (16) or (17) share price is derived as follows:

$$(i) \quad P_0 = \frac{£0.50}{0.10 - (0.50 \times 0.05)} = \frac{£0.50}{0.10 - 0.025} = \frac{£0.50}{0.075} = £6.67$$

$$(ii) \quad P_0 = \frac{£0.50}{0.10 - (0.50 \times 0.10)} = \frac{£0.50}{0.10 - 0.05} = \frac{£0.50}{0.050} = £10.00$$

$$(iii) \quad P_0 = \frac{£0.50}{0.10 - (0.50 \times 0.15)} = \frac{£0.50}{0.10 - 0.075} = \frac{£0.50}{0.025} = £20.00$$

As Gordon, therefore, acknowledged under conditions of certainty and constant growth, the rationale behind such movements in share price relates to the profitability of investment opportunities (r) and not alterations in dividend policy.

5 THE GORDON GROWTH MODEL UNDER CONDITIONS OF UNCERTAINTY

Gordon proceeded to develop an analogous theory of corporate valuation and investment under conditions of uncertainty with respect to the future and an aversion to risk on the part of rational (i.e. risk-averse) investors.

To illustrate, assume that in an uncertain world a company announces that it will no longer distribute E_1 at time period one but will reinvest this amount to earn $k_e E_1$ in perpetuity. As a consequence, rational investors raise their subjective equity capitalisation rate k_e to k_e^* so that the discounted dividend stream becomes:

(19) $$P_0^* = \frac{0}{1 + k_e^*} + \frac{E_1 + k_e E_1}{(1 + k_e^*)^2} + \frac{E_1 + k_e E_1}{(1 + k_e^*)^3} + \cdots + \frac{E_1 + k_e E_1}{(1 + k_n^*)^n}$$

with the consequence that:

$P_0^* < P_0$ = the original share price

What in fact has happened? The near dividend was reduced and the distant dividends were raised. This elicits a rise in the discount rate on the part of investors. Gordon argues therefore that a change in dividend policy has affected share price. The question, therefore, is whether the behaviour of investors under conditions of uncertainty is correctly represented by a model in which the equity capitalisation rate or discount rate that equates a dividend expectation with a share price is a function of the dividend payout ratio.

Gordon does not state categorically that k_e is a function of the rate of growth in dividends, but he does maintain that it is plausible that:

(*i*) Investors have an aversion to risk.
(*ii*) Given the riskiness of a company, the uncertainty of a dividend expectation increases with the time in the future of the dividend payment.

In using the term risk notice that the *business risk* of the company, by which is meant the variability of its earnings (and hence their quality) inherent in its products and market characteristics, remains unchanged. Gordon is focusing upon the *financial risk*, i.e. how the earnings are packaged for distribution. It is in this sense that risk-averse investors prefer dividends now, rather than later, in the absence of differential income tax treatment *vis á vis* capital gains.

It therefore follows from the two propositions that an investor may be represented as discounting a dividend in time period t at a rate of k_{e_t} with k_{e_t} not independent of t. Moreover, if aversion to risk is large enough and risk is a rapid function of time k_{e_t} increases with t. It is therefore possible, but not certain, that investor behaviour is correctly approximated by the notion that the value of a dividend expectation is calculated using:

$$k_{e_t}$$

where $t = 1, 2, 3 \ldots n$ and

$$k_{e_t} > k_{e_{(t-1)}}$$

In this event, the single equity capitalisation rate used in share valuation models must be an increasing function of the rate of growth in dividends. In other words, dividend policy determines share price.

Thus rewriting Equation (12) where $D_1 = E_1$:

$$(20) \qquad P_0 = \frac{E_1}{1 + k_{e_1}} + \frac{E_1}{(1 + k_{e_2})} + \frac{E_1}{(1 + k_{e_3})^3} + \cdots + \frac{E_1}{(1 + k_{e_n})^n}$$

the k_e of Equation (12) is an average of the k_{e_t} of Equation (20) such that if the entire dividend expectation is discounted at this single rate it results in the same share price. The discount rate k_e (or more correctly $\bar{k}_e$) is therefore an average of the k_{e_t} with E_1 the weight assigned to each item.

Proceeding one stage further let the company retain E_1 and invest it to earn rE_1 per period in perpetuity. Using the same sequence of discount rates from Equation (20) the valuation of the new dividend expectation becomes:

$$(21) \qquad P'_0 = \frac{0}{1 + k_{e_1}} + \frac{E_1 + rE_1}{(1 + k_{e_2})^2} + \frac{E_1 + rE_1}{(1 + k_{e_3})^3} + \cdots + \frac{E_1 + rE_1}{(1 + k_{e_n})^n}$$

The shareholder forsakes E_1 and receives rE_1 in perpetuity, but the latter is now discounted at the dated rates:

$$k_{e_t}$$

where $t = 2$ and k_e rises as a function of time with a limit of infinity.

And it can be shown that rE_1 so discounted is less than E_1. Hence P'_0 is less than the P_0 of Equation (20), i.e. dividend policy influences share price. As a corollary, it can also be shown that $\bar{k}_e$, the new average of the k_{e_t}, is greater than the original k_e. In general, reducing the near dividends and raising the distant dividends (lowering the dividend rate) changes the weights of k_{e_t} and their raises average, thereby reducing share price. Thus Equation (17) must be rewritten as:

$$(22) \qquad P_0 = \frac{D_1}{\bar{k}_e - g} \qquad \text{from (16)} \qquad \frac{(1 - b)E_1}{\bar{k}_e - rb}$$

To illustrate the point, assume that:

(i)   A current dividend equity capitalisation rate of 10 per cent reflects the variability of post-tax earnings and a full distribution policy for a particular company (i.e. business and financial risk conform).

(*ii*) The constant forecast dividend per share is 80 per cent.

(*iii*) The equity capitalisation rate (k_e) for another industry constituent, consequential upon its exceptional retention rate b and a reinvestment rate r, is equivalent to 15 per cent per annum (reflecting a financial risk premium).

(*iv*) This company's next dividend per share is, therefore, lower, say 50 pence.

(*v*) The company's annual constant growth rate in dividends (g) comprises 5 per cent.

From Equation (22), the equity value of the full distribution company in perpetuity is:

$$P_0 = \frac{D_1}{k_e - g} = \frac{£0.80}{0.10} = £8.00$$

whilst the partial dividend (growth) firm's dividend valuation is equivalent to:

$$P_0 = \frac{D_1}{k_e - g} = \frac{£0.50}{0.15 - 0.05} = £5.00$$

6 THE OPTIMUM INVESTMENT AND RETENTION RATE

The discussion leading up to Equation (22) began with the plausible assumption that the value of a share is its expected future dividends discounted at k_e the investors' rate of return required on the expectation. It was then explained, given the assumptions that:

(*i*) the company engages in no outside financing

(*ii*) it is expected to earn r on investment and retain a fraction, b, of its income, E, in every period

that the entire dividend expectation D_1 may be represented by the current dividend D_0, from $(1 - b)E_0$, and its rate of growth $g = rb$:

$$D_1 = D_0(1 + g)$$

It was further shown that under conditions of uncertainty and investor risk aversion the value of a share is equal to its dividend expectation divided by the amount that the average rate of profit investors require on the share exceeds the rate of growth in dividend. Recalling:

(22) $\qquad P_0 = \dfrac{D_1}{\overline{k}_e - g}$ from (16) $\qquad P_0 = \dfrac{(1-b)E_1}{\overline{k}_e - rb}$

given:

$$\overline{k}_e = f(k_{e_t})$$

where:

f means 'is a function of' or 'is dependent on', i.e. $\overline{k}_e$ is determined by each individually weighted (dated) k_{e_t}

$t = 1$ with a limit of infinity

with

$$k_{e_t} > k_{e_{(t-1)}}$$

since:

(i) $\quad k_{e_t}$ is an inverse function of the dividend payout ratio, $(1 - b)$
(ii) $\quad k_{e_t}$ is a positive function of the discount period, t.

The attractiveness of the Gordon growth model is that the value of a share is predicted on the basis of the following four variables, the first three of which can be estimated from a company's financial history:

E_0 = current earnings
b = retention of investment rate
r = rate of return on investment
k_e = rate of return investors require on the share (the equity capitalisation rate or rate of profit).

However, Equation (22) is not only a valuation model, but also an investment model on the assumption that the objective of the company is to maximise its share price. By assumption, retention is the only source of funds to finance investment and the value of b, given E_1, r and k_e, that maximises P_0 is the optimum annual rate of investment. Assuming that r and k_e, as well as E_1, are independent of b, the derivative of P_0 with respect to b is taken in order to derive the investment rate that maximises share value:

(23) $\qquad \dfrac{\Delta P_0}{\Delta b} = \dfrac{E_1}{(\overline{k}_e - rb)^2}(r - \overline{k}_e)$

The first conclusion to note is that price is independent of the retention rate b when $r = k_e$. If $r > k_e$, price increases with the retention rate. If $r < k_e$, price falls as the retention rate increases. The implication, therefore, is that companies should either retain all of their earnings or go into liquidation and return capital to shareholders, depending on whether $r \gtreqless k_e$.

However, this dilemma is easily resolved by considering r, the average return on net investment to be a declining function of b. Retaining the assumption that k_e is independent of b, the variation in share price now suggests some finite b at which P_0 is maximised. If $r > k_e$ when $b = 0$, then $\Delta P_0 / \Delta b$ is positive at $b = 0$. However, as b rises, r falls, with a consequence that there is some finite b at which $\Delta P_0 / \Delta b = 0$ and P_0 is maximised.

If $r < k_e$ at $b = 0$, P_0 is maximised by a negative net investment. Of course, this is all very plausible if k_e is known and independent of b, since the functional relationships between r and b may be obtained by companies from internally available data. However, the crux of the Gordon hypothesis is that k_e varies with b. And this rate of return which shareholders require is not obtainable from internal company data. The function must therefore be established separately.

There is also one further problem. To predict the current level of a share's price, the profitability of all future investments must be considered, since future dividends depend on future investments. Suffice it to say, however, that this phenomenon is not unique to Gordon. All multi-period share price models contain, by design or default, a prediction of future investment and its profitability.

7 EARLY EMPIRICAL EVIDENCE

Although the equity capitalisation rate is not available internally, Gordon presents a plausible hypothesis that under conditions of uncertainty the variable is an increasing function of the expected rate of growth in dividend. Hence, the model should be operational.

In testing the model empirically, Gordon (1962) reported poor results when it was assumed that k_e was independent of the growth rate $g = br$. However, his belief on theoretical grounds that k_e was an increasing function of br led him to test this hypothesis more successfully but not enough to settle the matter statistically. Gordon (1963) therefore concluded that the relevance of dividend policy to share price required further study.

Certainly, prior to the 1960s the financial literature on the subject was inconclusive. Graham and Dodd (1951) argued positively that the shareholders' valuation of equity must be determined by dividends rather than earnings, a position which they reaffirmed in Graham, Dodd and Cottle (1962). Lintner (1956) revealed, on the basis of interviews with US companies, that dividend decisions also represent an active rather than a passive variable for managerial decision-making. Management were more concerned with the likely changes in dividend distribution, as opposed to their absolute level. Management were also averse to short-term increases in dividends (reduced retention rates) at the expense of maintaining long-term target payout ratios. Earnings performance was perceived to be the most significant influence upon dividend changes, even at the limit of strategic planning. Whilst this conflicts with the shareholders' preference as rationalised by Gordon, that an increased retention ratio (dividend reduction) results in a rise in the discount rate and a fall in the value of a firm, the conclusion is the same. Management believe that dividend policy affects share price, the difference being that it is not the dividend *per se* but the extent to which it compromises their investment policy that is important.

Whilst much of the traditional financial literature of the period anecdotally reflected a shareholder preference for high payout ratios, the empirical data on long-run industry payout ratios confirmed the conservative managerial attitude to dividend distributions found by Lintner. Mature companies with stable earnings exhibited high payout ratios. Growth companies distributed a small proportion of earnings.

This is not to say that, given imperfect markets, particularly uncertain knowledge of the future on the part of risk-averse shareholders, investors are not indifferent between dividends now and capital gains later (i.e. current dividends are capitalised at a lower rate reflecting lower financial risk). Rather, that equity capitalisation rates might also be determined by the business risk of the cash-flows which stem from investments and that the uncertainty derived from future profits might not imply any greater preference for dividends *vis á vis* retentions on the part of shareholders. In other words, it may well be that the quality of earnings determined by the riskiness of managerial investments, as well as how the earnings are packaged for the shareholders' benefit, determines equity value. So, do dividends have a positive, neutral or negative effect upon share price?

8 EARLY STATISTICAL PROBLEMS

Nearly thirty years prior to Gordon the results of a least squares regression of price on dividends, earnings, book value, working capital and transaction volume during a year for 502 shares was reported by Meader. The first study (1935) revealed a multiple correlation coefficient of 0.93, but repetition for other years resulted in radically different coefficients for the independent variables. This led him to conclude (1940) that the model was not satisfactory for predicting the variation in price with a change in one independent variable. High correlation among the independent variables was the fundamental problem (i.e. multicollinearity).

With other studies too, the multiple correlation was invariably high. As a consequence, models of share price determination were good predictors of the variation in price with a given percentage change in all the variables. However, companies typically cannot raise all the variables, so that for specific decisions facing management concerning dividend and investment policy the models were of limited value. Further work related stock prices to current dividends and retained earnings and reported higher dividend payouts associated with higher price/earnings ratios. Other studies found the dividend capitalisation rate was also very much higher than the retained earnings capitalisation rate. The overall conclusion was that variations in dividend per share explained a considerable variation in share prices between companies.

The usual cross-section equation for the regression analysis was (and still is):

(24) $\qquad P_{it} = a + bD_{it} + cR_{it} + e_{it}$

where:

P_{it} = price per share
D_{it} = aggregate dividends paid out
R_{it} = retained earnings
e_{it} = error term.

The problem with Equation (24), however, should now be familiar to the reader. Dividends are a question of fact and can be measured without any error whatsoever but retained earnings (the difference between the accrual accounting profit and cash dividends paid) are only an estimate of the true economic earnings upon which value is based. Thus, retained earnings possess a great deal of measurement error. Consequently, the estimates of the effect of retained earnings on the price per share is biased downwards, a result obtained by Johnson, Shapiro and O'Meara (1951). This led subsequent researchers to incorrectly conclude that dividends had a greater effect on price per share than retained earnings.

The problem was encountered as late as 1961 in a UK study by G.R. Fisher, using variants to Equation (14) which identify:

(25) $\qquad P = f(d, u, v)$

where:

P = price of the share
d = last declared dividend per share
u = last declared undistributed profit per share
v = a residual term summarising the effects of all other variables.

However, Fisher not only questioned the applicability of his statistical techniques, but also admitted that it was not possible to draw any precise conclusion from his analysis. When dividends alone were used to explain share prices (as opposed to retentions) the estimates still revealed large percentage errors. Moreover, the past rate of growth in dividends per share, which figures so prominently in the Gordon model, represented a dubious indicator of future prospects. Its effect on share prices was both small and uncertain (a conclusion previously noted in the US by Durand (1955 and 1957)).

Fisher's doubts about the validity of his own analysis are understandable today, since there is always some measurement error which results in bias when taking sample statistics. Yet, there exists a study of historical significance by Friend and Puckett (1964) which is worth recounting in some detail, because the precise importance of measurement error and investor risk was revealed when trying to estimate the relative effects of dividends and retained earnings on the price of ordinary shares.

They used cross-section data in the form of a regression model based on five American industry samples (chemicals, electronics, electric utilities, foods and steel) in each of two years to test the effect of dividend payout on share value. The industries were selected to permit a distinction to be made between the results for growth and non-growth industries, and to provide a basis for comparison with results by other authors for earlier years who used Equation (24):

(24) $\qquad P_{it} = a + bD_{it} + cR_{it} + e_{it}$

Friend and Puckett criticise this earlier work on three major points.

(**a**) Equation (24) is mis-specified because it assumes that the riskiness of a company is uncorrelated with dividend payout and price/earnings ratios. However, observable data suggests that riskier companies have both lower dividend payout and lower price/earnings ratios. Consequently, the omission of a risk variable may cause an upward bias in the dividend coefficient in Equation (24).

(**b**) There is almost no measurement error in dividends but a well-known measurement error associated with accounting measures of retained earnings. This error will cause the earnings coefficient to be biased downward.

(**c**) Even if dividends and earnings do have a differential impact on share price one should expect their coefficients in Equation (24) to be equal. In equilibrium, companies would change their dividend payout until the marginal effects of dividends are equal to the marginal effects of retained earnings. This will provide the optimum effect on their price per share.

No theory had been fully developed to allow for the pricing of risk when they wrote their paper (a subject which will be addressed in full in Part 5 and specifically in Chapter 12) but Friend and Puckett were able still to eliminate the measurement error on retained earnings. Instead of using accounting measures of earnings, they derived time series regressions for each company in the relevant industry group using a *normalised* earnings variable (a time series estimate of predicted earnings) based on the following equation:

(26) $$\frac{(E/P)_{it}}{(E/P)_{jt}} = a_i + b_{it} + e_{it}$$

where:

$(E/P)_{it}$ = earnings price ratio for the firm
$(E/P)_{jt}$ = average earnings price ratio for the industry
t = a time index
e_{it} = error term.

Normalised retained earnings were obtained by deducting dividends from normalised earnings and then substituted for cR_{it} in Equation (24). The results of their analysis revealed a considerable reduction in the difference between the dividend and retained earnings coefficients in comparison to previous studies. Thus, Friend and Puckett concluded 'that there is little basis for the customary view that in the stock market generally, except for unusual growth stocks, a dollar of dividends has several times the impact on price as a dollar of earnings.'

9 DIVIDENDS AS A PASSIVE RESIDUAL: WALTER'S LEGACY

Friend and Puckett were not the first to assert that the price of a company's shares might be independent of its dividend payout ratio. For example, Walter (1956) formulated a theoretical model which depicts an optimal dividend policy determined solely by the profitability of investments which created the mind-set for subsequent research, notably that of Modigliani and Miller. If a company has an abundance of investment opportunities more profitable than the shareholders' desired rate of return, he argued that there should be no dividend payout. Earnings should be used to finance investments. Conversely, if the equity capitalisation rate exceeds the marginal return on incremental investment the optimal payout ratio should be 100 per cent. Thus, dividends are a passive residual.

Admittedly, Walter restricts his attention to the ordinary shares of large public companies because of the imperfect market for the securities of small companies (institutional neglect) and the close identification of small firms with their principal shareholders. Moreover his fundamental premise is that, over long periods (i.e. long enough to remove distortions caused by short-run speculative considerations), share prices reflect the present values of expected dividends. Granted this premise, retained earnings influence share prices principally through their effect upon future dividends. The fact that some stocks may have substantial value, even though little or no dividends are anticipated in the foreseeable future, need not (he maintains) contradict this proposition.

Undistributed earnings are immediately realisable to the shareholder through the capital market provided prospective investors can be found who are willing to wait and to assume the required risk (although this obviously implies marketability).

Walter isolates for consideration three groups of share, namely: *growth* stocks, *intermediate* stocks, and *creditor* stocks. One of the principal features by which these types of stocks are often differentiated is diversity of dividend policy. Thus:

(*i*)   Growth stocks are customarily characterised by low dividend payout ratios.

(*ii*) Intermediate stocks by medium to high ratios.

(*iii*) Creditor stocks by fixed dividend rates irrespective of short-run earnings.

Walter maintains, however, that with the possible exception of (*iii*), the relationship between dividends and earnings is neither a necessary nor a sufficient condition for assigning stocks to any given category. The crucial condition is, he maintains, the rate of return on additional investment.

The concept of a growth stock refers in general terms to ordinary shares, which possess superior prospects for long-term appreciation. The surface characteristics include:

(*i*)   low dividend pay-out ratios

(*ii*) high market multipliers (i.e. low dividend capitalisation rates)

(*iii*) prices which increase through time with relative rapidity.

However, according to Walter, the basic criterion is marginal profitability. The rate of return on additional investment determines the magnitude of future dividends obtainable from given amounts of retained earnings or external financing.

The anticipated level of future dividends, when discounted at the appropriate capitalisation rate, in turn yields the present value for a given stock. If the rate of return on added investment is sufficiently great it follows that low dividend payout ratios may add to, rather than subtract from, stock values.

Walter makes certain further observations on the distinction between growth stocks and intermediate stocks. He says that the crucial point of distinction is whether or not the capitalised values of future dividends attributable to the retention of earnings exceeds the money magnitudes of retained earnings. If so, i.e. where rates of return on additional investment exceed market capitalisation rates, the ordinary shares in question belong to the growth stock category. In the case of growth stocks low dividend payout ratios can be expected to enhance stock values.

He adds the further point that for most large industrials, rates of return on additional investment are presumed to exceed zero but to be less than corresponding market capitalisation rates. This condition leads to the commonly observed direct relationship between divided payout ratios and ordinary share prices. Moreover, although earnings retention occasions appreciation in share prices over time, shareholders benefit from the distribution of the maximum feasible amount of earnings.

To illustrate Walter's proposition that dividend policy is a passive residual determined by the financial requirements of profitable investment opportunities consider his formula:

$$(27) \qquad P = \frac{D + \dfrac{r}{k_e}(E - D)}{k_e}$$

where:

P = market price per share of ordinary shares
D = dividends per share
E = earnings per share
r = return on investment
k_e = equity capitalisation rate.

Assume that:

$E = £10.00$
$D = £5.00$
$r = 10\%$
$k_e = 5\%$

The market price per share would be:

$$P = \frac{5 + (0.10/0.05)(10 - 5)}{0.05} = £300$$

The optimal payout ratio is determined by varying D until share price is maximised. However, as stated earlier the optimal dividend payout ratio should be zero if $r > k_e$. Thus:

$$P = \frac{0 + (0.10/0.05)(10 - 0)}{0.05} = £400$$

and share price is maximised. Similarly, if $r < k_e$ the optimal payout ratio should be 100 per cent.

Suppose $r = 5\%$ and $k_e = 10\%$ with the original values for E and D. Then:

$$P = \frac{5 + (0.05/0.10)(10 - 5)}{0.10} = £75$$

169

However, with a dividend payout ratio of 100 per cent

$$P = \frac{10 + (0.05/0.10)(10 - 10)}{0.10} = £100$$

If $r = k_e$ it can also be shown that market price per share is insensitive to the dividend payout ratio.

Following the publications of Gordon (1962 and 1963), Walter (1964) posed the question of whether dividends are in some sense weighted differently from retained earnings to the margin in the minds of marginal investors. As revealed by the literature at the time, he concluded that the answer was not self-evident.

He explained two conditions under which changes in dividend payout have minimal influence upon stock values. These are where:

(**a**) The level of future cashflows from operations (i.e. the growth rate) is independent of the dividend payout policy. This essentially implies that the impact of a change in dividend payout upon operating cashflows will be exactly offset (or negated) by a corresponding and opposite change in supplemental (or external) financing.

(**b**) The weights employed are independent of the dividend payout policy. In other words, the discount factors or weights, i.e. the ratios of indifference values between one period and the next, are invariant with respect to changes in dividend payout.

A further requirement which Gordon (1963) specifies is that the weights employed must also be constant between periods, but Walter states that this is unlikely to be the case under uncertainty. In the light of condition (**a**) above, Walter refutes Gordon's argument claiming that if the level of total operating cashflows is unaffected by the policy revision (dividend policy), a change in current cash dividends will alter the shareholders' stake in future cashflows. The gain or loss in current dividends will just equal the gain or loss in the present value of future cashflows (or dividends, if you wish) provided the system of weights remains unchanged. Gordon's point is thus unacceptable because the firm has to go into the market for funds to replace those paid out in dividends and, in so doing, has to pay the market rate.

On the question of statistical testing, Walter makes the point that the correlation between dividend payout and growth (i.e. the level of future cashflows), which seems likely to exist in many instances, contributes to the difficulty of interpreting results obtained from regression analyses. He adds that, at the extreme, there may be no way to distinguish between the effect of dividend policy and investment policy. On the one hand, uncertainties exist as to precisely what is being measured. On the other, the closer the linkage between dividend policy and the dimensions of the total cash stream, the less meaningful are the coefficients attached to each independent variable.

10   MILLER–MODIGLIANI AND THE IRRELEVANCY OF DIVIDENDS HYPOTHESIS

By 1964, Walter, to whom subsequent academics owe an immense debt, was not alone in advocating dividends as a passive residual. A year before Gordon's work, Miller and Modigliani (1961) (MM henceforth) argued on theoretical grounds that dividend policy was not one of the determinants of share price. In one of their classic articles they assert under a number of assumptions, including certainty, that, given a firm's investment policy, 'the dividend payout policy it chooses to follow will affect neither the current price of its shares nor the total return to its shareholders'. They maintain that like many other propositions in economics, the irrelevance of dividend policy given investment policy is 'obvious when you think of it'. They go on to say that in a rational and perfect economic environment values are determined solely by 'real' considerations, in their view the earnings power of the firm's assets and its investment policy, and not by how the fruits of the earnings are packaged for distribution.

Specifically the MM hypothesis states that the effect of dividend payments on shareholder wealth is offset exactly by any other means of financing, debt as well as equity. It is based on the following assumptions:

(*i*)   Perfect capital markets in which all investors are rational but no investor is large enough to affect share price. Information is available to all at no cost. Transactions are costless and instantaneous. Shares are infinitely divisible on new issues.

(*ii*)   An absence of flotation costs.

(*iii*)   Transaction costs are zero.

(*iv*)   A neutral tax system.

(*v*)   A given investment policy for the company.

(*vi*)   Absolute certainty by every investor as to future investment and profits of the company (although MM relax this assumption later).

According to MM, when an all-equity firm has made a decision to invest it must decide whether to pay for new projects by retaining earnings or to pay dividends and sell new shares to the amount of these dividends to finance the investment (or a combination of the two). MM's suggestion is that the effect on shareholders' wealth and, therefore, managerial behaviour is neutral. The sum of the discounted value per share, after the dividend has been paid and external financing has been carried out, is the same as the discounted value before payment of the dividend. In other words, they demonstrate that the *ex div* price at the end of the period would fall by exactly the same amount as the increase in dividend (or *vice versa*). Since their summation is unchanged, its present value is unchanged for a given discount rate.

The market price of a share at time zero is defined as equal to the present value of the dividend paid at the end of the year plus the *ex div* price of the share at the end of the year. Based upon the *single-period valuation model* explained in Chapter 5:

$$(28) \qquad P_0 = \frac{1}{1+k_e}(D_1 + P_1)$$

where

D_1 = dividend at the end of the year.

P_1 = *ex div* share price at the end of the year.

k_e = discount rate for capitalisation of that firm's risk class, constant over time.

P_0 = market price per share at the beginning of the year.

MM assume that n is the number of shares issued at time period zero, and m is the number of additional new shares sold at time period one for P_1. The present value of the original shares is then given by:

$$(29) \qquad nP_0 = \frac{1}{1+k_e}(nD_1 + nP_1)$$

This may be re-written in terms of the total value of all shares outstanding at the end of the year if new shares are issued:

$$(30) \qquad nP_0 = \frac{1}{1+k_e}[nD_1 + (n+m)P_1 - mP_1]$$

which is the present value of total dividends paid at time one on the original shares, plus the total value of all shares outstanding at time one, less the total value of new shares issued. The revision is necessary to isolate the effect of an increased number of claims upon earnings and hence the value of the original shares.

Now assume that a firm has the opportunity to undertake new investment at the year end. The total amount of new equity is given by the general formula:

$$(31) \qquad mP_1 = I_1 - (E_1 - nD_1)$$

where:

I_1 = total new investments during period

E_1 = total earnings during the period.

The total amount of financing by the issue of new shares, mP_1, is determined by the amount of investments not financed by retained earnings, $(E_1 - nD_1)$. Substituting mP_1 from Equation (31) into Equation (30), MM find that the nD_1 term cancels out:

$$(32) \qquad nP_0 = \frac{1}{1 + k_e} [nD_1 + (n + m)P_1 - I_1 + E_1 - nD_1]$$

$$= \frac{1}{1 + k_e} [(n + m)P_1 - I_1 + E_1]$$

Since D_1 does not appear in Equation (32) and since I, E, $(n + m)P_1$ and k_e are assumed to be independent of D_1 by MM, they conclude that the current value of the firm is independent of either its current distributions or retentions. In other words, they are perfect substitutes.

Mathematically, the whole process can be simplified if it is assumed that the investment policy for the company has not changed. Rearranging Equation (31):

$$(33) \qquad mP_1 = (I_1 - E_1) + nD_1$$

Because there is no *new* investment during the period and, therefore, no need to retain earnings to finance that investment, the first term on the right-hand side of Equation (33) equals zero. It therefore simplifies to:

$$(33A) \qquad mP_1 = nD_1$$

Substituting for mP_1 in Equation (30) the present value of all the shares outstanding at time period one after the dividend has been paid equals the present value of the original shares, i.e. Equation (29):

$$(34) \qquad nP_0 = \frac{1}{1 + k_e} (n + m)P_1$$

which is equivalent to:

$$(29) \qquad nP_0 = \frac{1}{1 + k_e} (nD_1 + nP_1)$$

Now assume that the firm chooses not to issue new equity to finance new investment but to increase its retained earnings, R_1. This necessitates a corresponding reduction in dividends. Using the MM basic valuation model:

$$(28) \qquad P_0 = \frac{1}{1 + k_e} (D_1 + P_1)$$

let:

R_1 = increased retained earnings per share at the end of the year such that:

$$D'_1 = D_1 - R_1 \qquad \text{revised dividend per share at the end of the year}$$
$$P'_1 = P_1 + R_1 \qquad \text{revised } ex \ div \text{ price at the end of the year.}$$

Note that the *ex div* price has risen at the end of the period by exactly the same amount as the reduction in the dividend per share, i.e. R_1. This is because the perpetual capitalised value of the increased retention per share which determines P'_1 has also been reinvested at k_e (MM's constant equity capitalisation rate for that firm's risk class), such that:

$$(35) \qquad R_{e1} = \frac{R_1 k_e}{(1 + k_e)^2} + \frac{R_1 k_e}{(1 + k_e)^3} + \frac{R_1 k_e}{(1 + k_e)^4} + \cdots$$

Note also, that this value is dated at period one because the first annual return on reinvestment does not arise until time period two, i.e. the year following the time of the investment. It must, therefore, be discounted back one year if it is to be incorporated into the revised current share price at time period zero. This revision is given by:

$$(36) \qquad P'_0 = \frac{D_1 - R_1}{1 + k_e} + \frac{P_1 + R_1}{1 + k_e}$$

But, of course, this equation simplifies to:

$$(37) \qquad P'_0 = \frac{1}{1 + k_e}(D_1 + P_1) = P_0$$

Since P'_0 equals P_0 which is the original valuation model of Equation (28), MM are able to conclude that shareholders can be indifferent between dividends now and retention financed capital gains later. In other words, their wealth is unaffected.

Such a conclusion appears to confirm Walter's notion that dividends are a passive residual but to contradict Gordon's proposition that shareholders express a *positive* preference for current dividends. However, the MM proof of dividend *neutrality* suggests that shareholders can create their own dividends (*home-made*, if you will) at any time, if they so desire. They can sell part of their holdings at an enhanced price, P'_1, which reflects the capital gain consequential upon a higher EPS. For its part too, the firm can afford to be indifferent between dividends and retentions, since it can resort to new issues of equity in order to finance any shortfall in its investment plans.

Following MM's initial assumptions, in a world of certainty and perfect capital markets, which exhibit neither transaction costs nor taxation, the chronologically earlier conclusion drawn by Walter (op. cit.) subsequently confirmed by the 1964 analysis of Friend and Puckett (op. cit.) would appear to be vindicated.

Dollar for dollar (or pound for pound) dividend values should equate to the present value of funds which are retained for investment. Thus, it appears impossible to support Gordon's contention that the substitution of dividends for retained earnings (or *vice versa*) can affect the market value of equity; a dictum which is now regarded as part of the MM *law of one price*.

To illustrate, consider a company with a nil distribution policy but a dedicated investment policy, whose shares are valued as follows:

$$(28) \qquad P_0 = \frac{D_1 + P_1}{1 + k_e} = \frac{0 + £1.10}{1.10} = £1.00$$

The firm now decides to distribute a dividend of 10 pence per share on 100,000 shares currently in issue. If investment projects are still to be implemented, the company must raise new equity finance equal to the proportion of investment which is no longer funded by retained earnings. From the earlier discussion:

$$(33) \qquad mP_1 = nD_1 = £10,000$$

so that the substitution of this figure into the equation for the total market value of the original shares based on all the shares outstanding at time period one:

$$(30) \qquad nP_0 = \frac{1}{1 + k_e} [nD_1 + (n + m)P_1 - mP_1]$$

simplifies to:

$$£100,000 = \frac{1}{1.10} £10,000 + nP_1$$

Since there is only one unknown in the equation, P_1, then dividing throughout by the number of shares in issue (n equal to 100,000):

$$£1.00 = \frac{£0.10 + P_1}{1.10}$$

and solving for P_1:

$$P_1 = £1.00$$

Thus, as MM hypothesise, the *ex div* share price at the end of the period has fallen from £1.10 to £1.00, which is exactly the same as the 10 pence rise in dividend per share.

11 THE MM–GORDON CONTROVERSY

For a firm's investment policy not to change and shareholder wealth to be maximised MM reveal that the payment of a dividend must be substituted by a corresponding issue of equity. Failure to do this will erode the earnings capability of the company. As a corollary, if not a direct consequence, the further assumption of absolute certainty by every investor as to future investments and profits of the company also becomes invalid.

It will be recalled that Gordon does not disagree with the conclusion of MM's proof under conditions of certainty and perfect markets, believing also that movements in share price relate to the profitability of investment opportunities arising from retentions, rather than changes in dividend policy. However, under conditions of uncertainty, he subscribes to a *bird in the hand* philosophy by asserting that:

(*i*)   Rational (risk-averse) investors might prefer the expectation of early dividends rather than future capital appreciation.

(*ii*)   The expectation of a share issue may have a depressing influence on share price because subsequent earnings will have to divide among a larger number of investors, reducing EPS and hence dividends per share.

Thus, the price of shares may change when dividends change and new shares are issued. All that earnings advocates may logically assert is that the financial risk confronting investors relating to the distribution of earnings between dividends and retentions is irrelevant to the price of a share. However, for this to be true it is necessary that the rate at which the dividend expectation is discounted be independent of the expected rate of growth in the dividend.

On the question of dividend discount rates, Gordon argues that because of increasing uncertainty associated with financial risk, the rate applied by an investor to a future dividend payment will rise with the time interval between the payment and the date of discounting. Thus, if all financing is assumed to be internal, the weighted average discount factor $\overline{k}_e$ will be an increasing function of the rate of retention of b (as the balance of dividend payments arises in the distant as opposed to the near future). The conclusion, therefore, is that the relationship between k_e the investor return and rb the expected rate of growth in dividend, where r equals the rate of return on reinvestment, is a question of fact. The question cannot be resolved by deductive argument. It therefore follows that there is no *a priori* basis for rejecting the hypothesis. On the contrary, the analysis suggests the value of a share is dependent upon a company's dividend rate.

MM criticise Gordon's argument by saying that it is a tautology to suggest that an investor can arrive at the value of a share by estimating its future dividends and discounting the series at a rate appropriate to its uncertainty. To predict the current level of a share's price, the profitability of all future invest-ments must be known, since future dividends depend on future investments. But logically this is impossible.

MM also allege that in the determination of k_e Gordon confuses dividend policy with investment policy, a point cogently argued by Brennan (1971). A change in dividend policy, given investment policy, implies only a change in the distribution of the total earnings in any period as between dividends and capital gains. Once investors agree upon a company's business risk, i.e. the periodic variability of total earnings associated with a firm's declared invest-ments and profitability, k_e is determined and will not change.

This argument is, of course, very persuasive. Precisely because the Gordon model assumes that a company will engage in no outside financing, the use of changes in dividend policy to explain changes in the capitalisation rate must change investment policy as an inevitable consequence. And under these cir-cumstances MM themselves are the first to concede that their k_e might change, thereby affecting share price.

The fundamental point of disagreement, therefore, is whether the investors' rate of return k_e is a function of the quality of earnings associated with a com-pany's investment policies (business risk) or how those earnings are packaged for distribution (financial risk). Suffice it to say that, whilst empirically incon-clusive (see MM 1958, 1966 and 1967; Gordon 1967), the MM proposition is at least unambiguous. In contrast, Gordon himself acknowledges that:

$$(22) \qquad P_0 = \frac{D_1}{\overline{k}_e - g} \qquad \text{from} \quad \frac{(1 - b)E_1}{\overline{k}_e - rb}$$

represents both a dividend share valuation and investment model, since share price is maximised by establishing an optimum retention rate using:

$$(23) \qquad \frac{\Delta P_0}{\Delta b} = \frac{E_1}{(\overline{k}_e - rb)^2} (r - \overline{k}_e)$$

MM would not disagree with Gordon's conclusions drawn from Equation (23) namely that:

(ii)   Price is independent of the retention rate when $r = k_e$
(ii)   Price increases with the retention rate when $r > k_e$
(iii) Price falls as the retention increases when $r < k_e$.

Because of the problems of specifying all future investments, however, MM could only state what effect a single investment would have on a one-period share price. Nevertheless, their conclusion was that share price will rise, fall or remain unchanged, depending on whether the investment's rate of profit is above, below or equal to k_e and this is quite consistent with their share valuation model, since any change in the earning power of a firm's assets that changes k_e must obviously change share price given by:

$$(28) \quad P_0 = \frac{1}{1 + k_e}(D_1 + P_1)$$

where $(D_1 + P_1)$ are constant

As stated earlier, it is the isolation of the independent variables which comprise a model that determines its utility as a predictor of variations in share price.

To understand the problems encountered by Gordon, consider the two situations, A and B, presented in Table 7.1. The first represents a dividend policy of full distribution. The second reflects a rational managerial decision to retain funds, since their return on reinvestment exceeds the shareholders' overall capitalisation rate. The figures are either money values or proportions.

The data conforms to the basic requirements of the dividend growth model under conditions of uncertainty:

(i) The equity capitalisation rate, k_{e_t}, applied by investors to a future dividend payment will rise with the time interval between the payment and the date of discounting.

(ii) k_{e_t} is an inverse function of the dividend payout $(1 - b)$. Thus, the average equity capitalisation rate, $\bar{k}_e$, in Table 7.1 is an increasing function of the retention rate b and, as a consequence, the rate of growth in dividends, $rb = g$.

All this is very good if k_{e_t} and hence k_e are known. It will be recalled that values for r and b and their relationship is obtainable from a companys' internal data. However, not only is there a real world problem of observing k_{e_t} but because it may possibly vary with b this function must also be specified before value can be established. Consequently, Gordon's hypothesis that the equity capitalisation rate increases with the expected rate of growth in dividends has been accepted. So has share price fallen as the Gordon model predicts?

Table 7.1 Dividend policy and growth

	Forecast EPS	Retention rate	Dividend payout	Return on investment	Growth rate	Overall shareholder returns
	E_1	(b)	$(1 - b)$	r	$rb = g$	$\bar{k}_e$
A	£1.00	0	1.0	—	—	0.10
B	£1.00	0.5	0.5	0.2	0.1	0.15

Applying Equation (17) to the data:

	Dividend policy A	Dividend policy B

(17) $\quad P_0 = \dfrac{D_1}{k_e - g} = \dfrac{£1.00}{0.1} = £10.00 \qquad\qquad P_0 = \dfrac{£0.50}{0.15 - 0.10} = £10.00$

The answer is no. A justifiable reduction in the dividend payout has elicited an increase in both the growth rate and the average rate of equity capitalisation. Unfortunately (for Gordon) the net effect of the relationships between the variables which constitute the revised share price is zero. Halving the dividend payout, consequential upon a return on reinvestment which is twice the original equity capitalisation rate, which in turn rises by 50 per cent, neutralises the impact of a change in dividend policy on share price. By adjusting the variables provided in Table 7.1 the reader might care to confirm that it would be just as easy to demonstrate a positive effect of a reduction in dividends (for example, if r exceeded 20 per cent), as well as the negative impact which Gordon originally suggested.

Now assume that the equity capitalisation rate for the full distribution in Table 7.1 reflects what MM define as the shareholders' return for that firm's risk class, and investment policy. The current price of a share is then determined by their basic valuation model. Since D_1 equals E_1, however, this simplifies to the capitalisation of a constant dividend stream in perpetuity:

$$P_0 = \frac{1}{1 + k_e}(D_1 + P_1) = \frac{D_1}{k_e} = \frac{£1.00}{0.1} = £10.00$$

Substituting the values for P_0, k_e and D_1 into the MM formulation, Equation (28):

$$£10.00 = \frac{£1.00 + P_1}{1.1}$$

and solving for the *ex div* price at time period one gives:

$$P_1 = £10.00$$

To illustrate MM's proposition that a change in dividend policy (ultimately dividends per share) elicits a compensatory change in the *ex div* price which leaves the current price unaffected, consider next the partial distribution provided in Table 7.1.

At time period one the firm has reduced the dividend per share by 50 pence. This implies that for the level of risk associated with its initial investment policy, it can at least earn a return on retentions, r, commensurate to k_e, the shareholders'original capitalisation rate (10 per cent). The decision to retain earnings also means that, in the absence of any subsequent equity issues, the same number of shareholders can expect an enhanced future EPS. and a corresponding increase in dividends per share through subsequent capital gains. Returning to the MM model:

$$(28) \qquad P_0 = \frac{1}{1 + k_e}(D_1 + P_1) = \frac{1}{1.1}(£0.50 + £10.50) = £10.00$$

The *ex div* price at the year end has risen by 50 pence, which is precisely the fall in the dividend per share, therefore leaving the shareholders' original wealth unchanged. If funds were retained for reinvestment at 20 per cent, as Table 7.1 suggests, MM would be the first to admit that this could alter the share price at the beginning of the period. Specifically, P_0 will rise or fall depending upon whether $r \gtrless k_e$. But this is because the firm has been presented with new risk-adjusted capital projects which were not incorporated into their original investment plans. By isolating the effects of a change in investment policy from dividend policy, MM are able to assert that for the purposes of equity valuation the former is the relevant variable.

12 REAL WORLD CONSIDERATIONS AND DIVIDEND POLICY

MM (1961) prove the theoretical irrelevance of dividend policy in a taxless world, with no transaction costs where all investors are fully informed about the distribution of future cashflows. They assert that if $r > k_e$ dividend policy is a passive residual determined solely by the availability of investment proposals. If the investment rate $r < k_e$, dividends become a means of returning unused funds. The question now arises as to what occurs in reality where MM's assumptions are relaxed?

MM's argument should extend into a world of uniform corporate taxation but not of personal taxation, since historically capital gains tax is less than marginal rates of income tax on dividends. Moreover, capital gains do not arise until shareholders sell their shares. For shareholders with a marginal tax rate in excess of their capital gains liability the preferred dividend payment is zero. This suggests a *clientele* effect with tax efficient investors choosing a company according to dividend payout ratio. For high tax payers, clientele theory also suggests that some companies (but obviously not all) can maximise the value of shareholders wealth *via* share price by paying no dividends.

MM actually suggested this phenomena in their 1961 paper. Numerous empirical studies, such as Farrar and Selwyn (1967), Brennan (1970) and Ang and Peterson (1985) subsequently confirmed it, although Miller and Scholes (1978) developed a sophisticated model based upon Miller (1977) to show that, in America at least, individuals need not pay more than capital gains tax on dividend payments by using sophisticated methods of avoidance. This phenomenon will be explained in Chapter 10.

On the subject of transaction costs and financing, Rozeff (1981) suggests that even in a taxless world an optimal dividend policy may exist because of the differential transaction costs of external financing. Shareholders may well prefer companies with high retention rates. Consider also two companies with the same average cashflows across time but different variability. The one with greater volatility will borrow in bad years and repay in good. It will need to finance externally more often. Consequently, it too will prefer a lower dividend payout ratio.

Although greater dividend payouts imply greater costs of taxation and finance there are benefits if shareholders believe that firms which pay high dividends are more confident about their prospects and will exhibit permanently higher future earnings. They will bid up the price of shares with high dividend payout ratios. Ross (1977) proved that an increase in the use of debt in a company's capital structure will represent an unambiguous *signal* to the capital market that trading prospects have improved. As a consequence, Bhattachary (1979) developed a similar model to explain why firms may pay dividends despite the tax disadvantage of doing so (followed up by Hakansson (1982)).

The application of signalling theory to imperfect markets implies that dividends convey information about the value of a company which cannot be communicated through less reliable channels, such as the Balance Sheet. Thus, the dilemma facing management is that by failing to produce little more than historical cost data in their accounts, a dividend cut may be interpreted by the market as desperation rather than financial prudence. This goes some way to explaining observable cross-sectional irregularities in dividend payout ratios and share price between companies. In an attempt to maintain market capitalisation a number of less successful (but more unscrupulous) companies are undoubtedly mimicking the dividend signal by declaring excessive distributions, which are then externally financed at exorbitant cost.

Using the terminology of MM, by changing their dividend payout (and capital structure) such companies have altered their perceived risk class but not their actual risk class because it cannot be substantiated by future earnings. As such it can only represent a temporary strategy, since investors will eventually be able to see whether the informational content of dividends is justified.

13 AN OVERVIEW OF EMPIRICAL EVIDENCE

The MM theory of share valuation clearly demonstrates why in the absence of taxes dividend policy has no effect on share price. Yet, if taxes are introduced, in an otherwise perfect capital market, then a company can obviously maximise shareholders' wealth by paying no dividends if the personal tax rate on dividends exceeds that on capital gains. However, this is not true for all share-holders. Hence there exists the possibility of a clientele effect which explains variations in dividend policy between companies. The further admission of transaction costs associated with external financing would reinforce this trend.

On the other hand, the extent to which changes in dividend policy are inter-preted by the market as new information about long-run profitability suggests that a company would strive to maintain a constant-dividend payout ratio which is increased only when management is relatively certain that the high dividend payout can be maintained indefinitely. This in turn implies that management has a target dividend payout ratio, a policy originally substantiated by Lintner (1956) (op. cit.) and confirmed in an extensive study by Fama and Babiak (1968).

Subsequent empirical studies have concentrated primarily on the tax effect and informational content of dividends. The evidence with respect to the former, however, is conflicting. It ranges from a negative effect, i.e. investors who hold shares with high dividend yields are in low tax brackets, and vice versa, Elton and Gruber (1970), Pettit (1977); to dividend neutrality, Lewellen, Stanley, Lease and Schlarbaum (1978) and Miller and Scholes (1978). In con-trast, there is strong evidence to support a dividend signalling effect. The first study to look at this issue was that of Fama, Fisher, Jensen and Roll (1969). They found that where share splits were accompanied by dividend announce-ments there was an increase in adjusted share prices for the group which announced dividend increases and a decline in share prices for the dividend decrease group. More recent studies also indicate unequivocally that dividend changes do convey some unanticipated information to the market. See Aharony and Swary (1980), Kwan (1981), Randall Woolridge (1983), Miller and Rock (1985) and Healy and Palepu (1988).

What then are the implications of this conflicting evidence, in relation to the original theories? One way to assess this is to look directly at the relationship between dividend payout and the price per share. And here the preponderance of studies do support the MM conclusion, namely that foreseeable dividend yields have little impact on the value of equity which Miller (1986) confirmed by a review of the research. See, for example, Friend and Puckett (op. cit.), Black and Scholes (1974), Piper and Fruhan (1981), Miller and Scholes (1983), as well as the more recent evidence of Rappaport (1986) and Hill (1994). The notable exceptions are Gordon's ambiguous work (op. cit.), the Litzenberger and Ramaswamy (1979) study, which found dividends to be undesirable, i.e. higher dividend yields required higher rates of return to compensate investors for the disadvantage of dividend payout, and the work by Long (1978) which found the reverse to be true.

And this leads to a final point. Whilst empirical work tends to support the MM irrelevancy hypotheses it cannot be emphasised too strongly that this applies for *individual* companies only. It does not rule out the possibility that there may exist an *aggregate* equilibrium supply of dividend (or debt) which will change as a result of macro-economic factors, such as a decrease in the difference between personal tax on dividends and capital gains in relation to corporation tax. Indeed, the studies by Khoury and Smith (1977) and Morgan (1980) support this thesis. They observed that Canadian corporations significantly increased their dividend payout ratio after a capital gains tax was introduced and dividend tax rates were reduced for the first time in 1982. This also corroborated Miller's prior suggestion (1977), to be considered in the next section, that for individual economies in a taxed world there may not only be an aggregate, optimal supply of dividends but also an aggregate, optimal capital structure.

14 SUMMARY AND CONCLUSIONS

Assuming that a company's normative objective is the maximisation of shareholder wealth, new capital projects of equivalent business risk, financed by increased retentions, can only be defended if their marginal return at least equals that which shareholders would receive if new investment was not undertaken.

According to Fisher's Separation Theorem (op. cit.) the equity capitalisation rate should also equal the incremental return which shareholders could obtain by investing their funds for commensurate risk elsewhere. A firm's discount rate and the shareholder return, therefore, stems from an appropriate opportunity cost of capital rate. In a neo-classical world of complete certainty, where borrowing and lending rates are equal, this would be the market rate of interest.

According to Miller and Modigliani (1961), under conditions of equilibrium and certainty with perfect capital markets, exhibiting no taxes or transaction costs, a company with new investment opportunities of equivalent risk which are more profitable than the shareholders' desired rate of return should not pay dividends. If the reverse holds, the optimal dividend payout ratio would be 100 per cent. Funds should be returned to the shareholders for reinvestment. If the two risk-adjusted returns are equal, distribution policy is immaterial. Current dividends foregone will be compensated precisely, by either increased future dividends or home made dividends through a capital gain if the shares are sold. Thus, shareholder wealth is maintained.

Under conditions of uncertainty and imperfect capital markets, Gordon (1959, 1962 and 1963), developed an alternative 'bird in the hand' philosophy. He explains how a rational investor can reduce the financial risk associated with their investment if the return is received in the form of dividends earlier, rather than capital gains or higher dividends later. The equity capitalisation rate is an increasing function of the dividend payment's futurity and the size of the retention ratio. These combine to precipitate a reduction in the discounted value of a share.

Leaving aside its relevance to overall capital structure and cost, the MM–Gordon controversy precipitated by Walter (1956), therefore, centres upon whether a division of earnings between dividends and retentions in the real world can affect equity capitalisation rates, the price of a company's shares and shareholder wealth. Conflicting evidence concerning the incidence of taxation, tax differentials and transaction costs was presented, particularly whether tax clienteles can influence share price. The informational content of dividends and corporate attitudes to dividend policy suggested that, in an imperfect market for information, dividends can signal changes in equity values. Set against this, a preponderance of empirical studies which focus directly upon the relationship between dividend yields and dividend payout ratios to share price suggest that they are independent. Several plausible reasons were offered, statistical and otherwise, as to why this should be, even under tax regimes where dividends and capital gains are treated differently.

The conclusion to be drawn is that corporate management should realistically adjust dividend levels to the attainable in sympathy with their investment plans and forecast levels of earnings, ideally in cash terms. Moreover, the firm should communicate this information to all its stakeholders, rather than operate secretively behind ex-post published records of stewardship on some notion of dividend pressure, which may be misguided and cause permanent damage. If the preference of various shareholder clienteles for speedy returns, through either capital gains or dividends, was tempered by an awareness of corporate investment strategies, management would then be in a position to reappraise the validity of target dividend payout ratios, based on short-termism rather than long-run earnings. A further *quid pro quo* would be direct feedback on its investment policy, once this emerged as a significant factor which prompts shareholders either to buy, sell or hold equity. As a corollary, the company might not feel obliged to deplete its cash reserves *via* dividend distributions that exceed those of its competitors.

Within the European Community (EC), most notably Germany and Italy, dividend payout ratios are extremely flexible. Throughout the Tiger economies historical dividend levels have been far lower than those of the US and UK, with no adverse effects on share price, until their recent melt-down. As a consequence, the MM dividend irrelevancy hypothesis should be viewed as more real than apparent for the mutual benefit of the firm and its investors in an increasingly global market for information. Suffice it to say that more detailed consideration of their hypothesis will have to wait until the statistical models which were subsequently developed, relating to the pricing of risk (business, financial and otherwise), are considered in Part 5.

References

(1) Aharony, J. and Swary, I., 'Quarterly dividend and earnings announcements and stockholder's returns: an empirical analysis', *Journal of Finance*, Vol. 35, No. 1, March 1980.

(2) Ang, J.S. and Peterson, D.R., 'Return, risk and yield: evidence from ex ante data', *Journal of Finance*, Vol. 40, No. 3, June 1985.

(3) Bhattacharya, S., 'Imperfect information, dividend policy and "the bird in the hand" fallacy', *Bell Journal of Economics*, Vol. 10, Spring 1979.

(4) Black, F. and Scholes, M., 'The effect of dividend yield and dividend policy on common stock prices and returns', *Journal of Financial Economics*, Vol. 1, No. 1, May 1974.

(5) Brennan, M., 'Taxes, market valuation and corporate financial policy', *National Tax Journal*, Vol. 23, No. 4, December 1970.

(6) Durand, D., 'Bank stocks and the analysis of covariance', *Econometrica*, Vol. 23, 1955.

(7) Durand, D., *Bank Stock Prices and the Bank Capital Problem*, National Bureau of Economic Research, 1957.

(8) Elton, E.J. and Gruber, M.J.,'Marginal stockholders tax rates and the clientele effect', *Review of Economics and Statistics*, Vol. 52, No. 1, February 1970.

(9) Fama, E.F. and Babiak, H., 'Dividend policy: an empirical analysis', *Journal of the American Statistical Association*, Vol. 63, December 1968.

(10) Fama, E., Fisher, L., Jensen, M. and Roll, R., 'The adjustment of stock prices to new information', *International Economic Review*, February 1969.

(11) Farrar, D. and Selwyn, L., 'Taxes, corporate financial policy and return to investors', *National Tax Journal*. Vol. 20, No. 4, December 1967.

(12) Fisher, I., *The Theory of Interest,* Macmillan 1930.

(13) Fisher, G.R., 'Some factors influencing share prices', *Economic Journal*, Vol. 71, 1961.

(14) Friend, I. and Puckett, M., 'Dividends and stock prices', *American Economic Review*, Vol. 54, September 1964.

(15) Gordon, M.J., *The Investment, Financing and Valuation of a Corporation*, Irwin 1962.

(16) Gordon, M.J., 'Optimal investment and financing policy", *The Journal of Finance*, Vol. 18, No. 2, May 1963.

(17) Gordon, M.J., 'Some estimates of the cost of capital to the electric utility industry: 1954–1957', *American Economic Review*, Vol. 56, No. 3., June 1966.

(18) Graham, B., and Dodd, D.L., *Security Analysis: Principles and Techniques*, McGraw-Hill 1951.

(19) Graham, B., Dodd, D.L. and Cottle, S., *Security Analysis: Principles and Techniques*, McGraw-Hill 1962.

(20) Hakansson, N., 'To pay or not to pay dividends', *Journal of Finance*, Vol. 37, No.2, May 1982.

(21) Healy and Palepu, K., 'Earnings information conveyed by dividend initiations and omissions', *Journal of Financial Economics*, Vol. 21, 1988.

(22) Hill, R.A., 'Insurance institutions and fund management: a UK perspective', *Journal of Applied Accounting Research*, Vol. 1, Issue No.2, 1994.

(23) Johnson, L.R., Shapiro, E. and O'Meara, J., 'Valuation of closely held stock for federal tax purposes: approach to an objective method', *University of Pennsylvania Law Review*, Vol. 100, 1951.

(24) Khoury, N. and Smith, K., 'Dividend policy and the capital gains tax in Canada', *Journal of Business Administration*, Spring 1977.

(25) Kwan, C., 'Efficient market tests of the informational content of dividend announcements: critique and extension', *Journal of Financial and Quantitative Analysis*, June 1981.

(26) Lewellen, W., Stanley K., Lease, R. and Schlarbaum, G., 'Some direct evidence on the dividend clientele phenomena', *Journal of Finance*, Vol. 33, No. 2, December 1978.

(27) Lintner, J., 'Distribution of income and dividends among corporations, retained earnings and taxes', *American Economic Review*, Vol. 46, No. 2, May 1956.

(28) Litzenberger, R. and Ramswamy, K., 'The effect of personal taxes and dividends on capital asset prices: theory and empirical evidence', *Journal of Financial Economics*, Vol. 7, June 1979.

(29) Long, J. Jr., 'The market valuation of cash dividend: a case to consider', *Journal of Financial Economics*, June/September 1978.

(30) Meader, J.W., *The Analyst*, 1935.

(31) Meader, J.W., *The Analyst*, 1940.

(32) Miller, M.H., and Modigliani, F., 'Dividend policy growth and the valuation of shares', *Journal of Business of the University of Chicago*, Vol. XXXIV, No. 4, October 1961).

(33) Miller, M.H. and Modigliani, F., 'Some estimates of the cost of capital to the electric utility industry: 1954–57', *American Economic Review*, Vol. 56, No. 3, June 1966.

(34) Miller, M.H., 'Behavioural rationality in finance: the case of dividends', *Journal of Business*, Vol. 59, October 1966.

(35) Miller, M.H. and Modigliani, F., 'Some estimates of the cost of capital to the electric utility industry: 1954–1957, Reply, *American Economic Review*, Vol. 57, No. 5, December 1967.

(36) Miller, M.H., 'Debt and taxes', *Journal of Finance*, Vol. 32, No. 2, May 1977.

(37) Miller, M. and Scholes, M., 'Dividends and taxes', *Journal of Financial Economics*, December 1978.

(38) Miller, M. and Scholes, M., 'Dividend and taxes: some empirical evidence', *Journal of Political Economy*, Vol. 90, 1983.

(39) Miller, M.H. and Rock, K., 'Dividend policy under asymmetric information', *Journal of Finance*, Vol. 40, No. 4, September 1985.

(40) Modigliani, F. and Miller, M.H., 'The cost of capital, corporation finance and the theory of investment', *American Economic Review*, Vol. XLVII, No. 3, June 1958.

(41) Morgan, I.S., 'Dividends and stock price behaviour in Canada', *Journal of Business Administration*, Fall 1990.

(42) Pettitt, R., 'Taxes, transaction costs and clientele effects of dividends', *Journal of Financial Economics*, December 1977.

(43) Piper, T.R. and Fruhan, W.E., 'Is your stock worth its market price?', *Harvard Business Review*, May/June 1981.

(44) Porterfield, J.T., *Investment Decisions and Capital Costs*, Prentice Hall 1965.

(45) Randall Woolridge, J., 'Stock dividends as signals', *Journal of Financial Research*, Spring 1983.

(46) Rappaport, A., *Creating Shareholder Value*, The Free Press 1986.

(47) Ross, S.A., 'The determination of financial structure: the incentive – signalling approach' *Bell Journal of Economics*, Vol. 8, Spring 1977.

(48) Rozeff, M., 'Growth, beta and agency costs as determinants of dividend payout ratios', *Working Paper No 81–11*, University of Iowa, June 1981.

(49) Walter, J.E., 'Dividend policy and common stocks', *Journal of Finance*, Vol. 11, March 1956.

(50) Walter, J.E., 'Dividend policy: its influence on the value of the enterprise', *Journal of Finance*, Vol. 19, May 1964.

PART FOUR

The finance decision

8

The anatomy of capital costs

Chapter profile

Previous chapters referred obliquely to the 'cost of capital' as a cut-off rate or discount rate applied to investment decision models. These are designed to maximise shareholders' wealth, based upon Fisher's Separation Theorem. Part 3 concluded by considering whether dividend policy affects the shareholders' desired rate of return and, hence, wealth (the MM debate). This chapter integrates the various approaches to the cost of equity into a detailed study of the component costs which comprise a company's cost of capital.

The principles of security valuation which determine the cost of redeemable debentures, as well as preference shares, which incorporate taxation and transaction costs is explained. The exposition is analogous to that for equity contained in Chapter 5.

A general formula for the weighted average cost of capital (WACC) is given and applied. *Inter alia* explicit and implicit component costs are explained. A distinction is also drawn between the weighted average cost of capital and the marginal cost of capital.

Finally, a more sophisticated WACC is defined as a summation of the basic cost of money (which includes the explicit and implicit cost of shares and debentures), the costs of unallocated expenditure and the cost of non-profit-making investment. A cut-off rate is then computed which can be applied to the type of corporate investment decision considered in Part 2.

1 INTRODUCTION

In Parts 1 and 2, it was explained how either a predetermined cost of capital or a desired rate of return could be employed as the discount rate in NPV calculations, or as a cut-off rate for investment in conjunction with an IRR, so that the value of a firm and hence shareholders' wealth would at least be maintained, when selecting investment proposals. Using the investment–consumption model (Fisher's Separation Theorem), under conditions of equilibrium, certainty, and perfect capital markets (where borrowing and lending rates are equal), the correct discount rate was defined as a uniform market rate of interest.

In Part 3, under the same conditions, the minimum return required by shareholders (variously defined) was identified as a company's minimum cost of capital if all its investments were funded from ordinary shares alone. The marginal equity yield constitutes the shareholders' opportunity cost of capital, i.e. their return foregone by not investing externally, irrespective of whether the internal project is financed by new issues, existing equity or retained earnings (which have no explicit cost). For example, assuming equilibrium and a perfect capital market with zero transaction costs in a taxless world, Miller and Modigliani (MM 1961) hypothesised that instead of paying dividends, a firm could retain earnings to finance new investments, without compromising equity value, provided a project's return matched the incremental yield to shareholders obtainable from alternative investments of equivalent business risk outside the firm. Since the shareholders are a company's legal owners, management should only deploy such funds if its investment proposals are to recoup the ownership claims which retentions imply. If an all-equity company undertakes a project using the marginal cost of equity as its discount rate, the total market value of shares should, therefore, increase by the project's NPV.

Retaining the assumption of perfect capital markets but introducing uncertainty, the debate on dividend relevancy in the preceding chapter (the MM–Gordon controversy) introduced the possibility of not a single equity capitalisation rate but the existence of a selection of expected rates to compensate for financial risk. According to Gordon (1959, 1962 and 1963) these are positively related to the futurity of shareholder returns and the level of retained earnings. The discount rate becomes an average equity yield which incorporates a market rate of interest commensurate with the project's anticipated level of business risk. Since investors are assumed to be rational (i.e. risk averse), the greater the financial risk, the greater their expected return and *vice versa*. The company's cost of capital must, therefore, reflect this.

The question now arises as to what discount rates should be applied if equity is no longer the only source of funds, and capital investments are financed from a miscellany of sources, such as preference shares, debentures and bank loans.

2 THE COSTS OF CAPITAL

Fortunately, the investment decision with a capital mix still comprises two distinct yet inter-related aspects, which remain amenable to a normative exposition of shareholders' wealth maximisation:

(a) The *external finance function* now identifies all funds sources (as opposed to one), evaluates the investors' opportunity return expected by each and selects the optimal mix, which minimises their combined cost.

(b) The *internal control function* then allocates these funds between products, service and markets by selecting those investment opportunities which maximise NPV and thereby share price.

In other words, the financing decision and the investment decision are now inter-related via an overall cost of capital which incorporates debt as well as equity.

Within the context of corporate discount rates or cut-off rates, it is important to realise that an investment still determines its finance and not the reverse. *Gregentei* From a financial viewpoint, the figure represents the costs incurred by employing funds in one use rather than another. Nor is it restricted to the explicit returns to shareholders and interest on borrowings.

The company might only desire to satisfy the ordinary shareholders' immediate dividend expectations (ignoring capital gains) and the contractual obligations of preference shares, debt interest, plus any impending capital redemption payments. However, there are also implicit or opportunity costs to consider, apart from those associated with retained earnings, which must be incorporated into the overall cost of capital equation. These now include the financial risks confronting each provider of capital, all of which impinge upon the shareholders' original return.

Companies may also finance their operations by utilising funds from a variety of other sources, both long and short term, which do not even manifest an explicit cost. But these too possess an implicit, opportunity cost. They should be identified and included in the overall cost of capital calculation because they represent money which firms have at their disposal to generate *equity* output. Like retained earnings, such funds include trade credit granted by suppliers and deferred taxation, without which a company would have to raise finance from elsewhere at the market rate. In addition, there are implicit costs associated with deprecation and other non-cash expenses. These represent retentions which are available for reinvestment. There also exists corporate expenditure which does not necessarily produce demonstrative results, most notably R and D and unallocated overheads.

Moreover, if the assumptions of general equilibrium and perfect markets are relaxed, further factors emerge. The current market price of securities and their respective yields may not reflect their longer-term values, due to short-run extraneous market conditions which produce disequilibrium. In the presence of economies of scale, transaction costs may be prohibitively expensive if small numbers of securities are issued or traded, thereby increasing their component cost. In a taxed world, the system may also be biased.

Where debt interest is tax deductible, companies can minimise their overall cost of capital by issuing debt, rather than equity. With regard to equity, there is the differential fiscal treatment of dividends *vis a vis* capital gains. Under a *classical* tax system, raising the dividend also increases the corporate tax liability making debt issues even more attractive. Conversely, if the system of Corporation Tax confers a tax credit to the shareholder, such as Advanced Corporation Tax (ACT) under the UK's imputation system, this relative tax advantage will be lower.

All these points will be considered throughout this chapter, whilst the implications of debt's beneficial effects in relation to capital structure and cost will be specifically addressed in the next. For the time being, it is important to appreciate that in terms of the managerial control function (the investment decision) the overall *cost* of capital represents a *return* criterion which justifies the deployment of funds. To reiterate, a company wishing to maximise money profits and hence shareholders' wealth would not wish to employ finance, unless its marginal yield was in excess of a measurable alternative investment rate. In the presence of market imperfections, the computations may be more problematical but the procedure is the same. If projects are funded from a variety of sources (explicit or implicit) an overall cost of capital must be calculated by deriving a weighted average which comprises each of its constituents. This weighted average cost of capital will be termed WACC henceforth and denoted by K with appropriate subscripts for its component parts. Thus, the shareholder's capitalisation rate k_e becomes K_e. This revised notation will serve as a reminder that an entity's perception of an income stream may well differ from the multiplicity of views held by its proprietors, other providers of capital, as well as all the potential investors who determine stock market sentiment.

3 THE COST OF DEBENTURE CAPITAL

In order to explain the derivation of a WACC a convenient starting point is an examination of the major alternative to equity as a source of long-term funds: debenture capital. Not only are the principles of valuation which determine its cost analogous to those for preference shares and bank finance (except that preference dividends do not qualify for corporate tax relief) but as shown in Chapter 9 the choice between issuing debt or equity is pivotal to company valuation, as well as investment appraisal.

A debenture is a marketable security in the form of a secured loan with a contractually fixed interest rate, invariably a fixed redemption date and a precedence over equity to the income of a company, as well as its assets in the event of liquidation. Although debenture holders are creditors and not owners of a company, because of these special rights their investment is perceived as less risky, so their required rate of return will typically be less than that which ordinary shareholders expect.

A debenture's nominal yield or face rate of interest is termed the *coupon rate*. This is determined by the company according to prevailing market rates of return for similar securities in that risk class. It should be noted, however, that like ordinary shares, a debenture's return still comprises three elements:

(*i*) The risk-free rate, as measured by the minimum yield on government securities.

(*ii*) The business risk premium, which reflects an increase in the required rate of return due to the uncertainty associated with a company's future business prospects. The more profits vary, the greater the business risk and the higher the premium.

(*iii*) The financial risk premium arising out of the contractual deduction of interest payments to holders of debt capital.

In the presence of business risk, higher debt levels (high gearing) exacerbate financial risk if corporate income is volatile.

As a consequence, the extent to which the second and third factors are unique to an individual company means that the debenture's return may also be unique.

Debentures are issued at par or nominal value, usually in blocks of £100. If a debenture is *redeemable* at some future date, it is normally redeemed at par (£100) but sometimes specifically above, as an inducement to purchase. If debentures are *irredeemable* the investor is buying a perpetual annuity, i.e. there will be no future capital repayment by the company. In both cases, however, debentures may be traded on the stock exchange like any other marketable security, such as ordinary shares. Depending on supply and demand, price may be above or below par value and redemption may occur at a premium or a discount.

The principles of debenture valuation are similar to those already encountered for equity in Part 3. However, estimating the cost of debentures, like all securities with a fixed return (such as preference shares), is less problematical than estimating the cost of ordinary shares, since the return is guaranteed by contract and the investment term is invariably finite.

Ignoring taxation and transaction costs for the moment, the market value of a debenture is determined by a summation of the expected future interest flow, plus the redemption price (if applicable) discounted to a present value. The cost of debentures is the rate of interest which equates the current market price with these expected future cash flows.

In the case of irredeemable debentures, the value and cost at issue are the issue price and coupon rate respectively. Thereafter, since debentures can be bought and sold on the stock exchange and current market price may differ from par value, according to supply and demand and prevailing economic conditions:

(1) $\quad P_0 = \dfrac{I}{1+K_d} + \dfrac{I}{(1+K_d)^2} + \dfrac{I}{(1+K_d)^3} + \cdots$

where:

P_0 = current market price of debentures after payment of the current interest (*ex-interest*)

I = constant level of interest received per annum in perpetuity

K_d = cost of debenture capital.

Since the annual market rate of interest is fixed in perpetuity Equation (1) simplifies to:

(2) $\quad P_0 = \dfrac{I}{K_d}$

so that the current yield or cost of debentures K_d is the coupon rate expressed in pounds per annum I divided by the current market price P_0:

(3) $\quad K_d = \dfrac{I}{P_0}$

If debentures are redeemable then because the nominal interest in the year of redemption will be enhanced by the redemption payable, the current yield must be found by solving for K_d in the following equation:

(4) $\quad P_0 = \dfrac{I}{1+K_d} + \dfrac{I}{(1+K_d)^2} + \cdots + \dfrac{I+P_n}{(1+K_d)^n}$

which is equivalent to:

(5) $\quad P_0 = \displaystyle\sum_{t=1}^{n} \dfrac{I}{(1+K_d)^t} + \dfrac{P_n}{(1+K_d)^n}$

where:

n = number of periods under observation.

Irrespective of whether the debentures are redeemable or irredeemable, already in issue or currently on offer, the solution for the cost of capital K_d is *always* the internal rate of return (IRR). This equates the current price with the discounted sum of future cash receipts which they will produce. However, only if the current price and redemption value (if any) equals the issue price will the IRR equal the coupon rate. If a debenture has a coupon rate which is below the prevailing market rate of interest (IRR), then its market value will be below its £100 par value and vice versa.

To illustrate, consider a £100 issue of irredeemable 10 per cent debentures.

The ex-interest market price is £90 (conventionally termed £90 per cent). Using Equation (3), the current cost of debt is:

$$\frac{£10}{£90} = 11.1\%$$

If the debt were redeemable ten years hence, even at par, the current yield would now have to be found by trial and error solving for the IRR in Equation (5):

$$£90 = \sum_{t=1}^{n=10} \frac{£10}{(1 + K_d)^t} + \frac{£100}{(1 + K_d)^{10}}$$

The cost of debentures K_d is approximately 11.8 per cent per annum.

It must also be emphasised that there is no difference between the conceptual meaning of these formulae and the valuation models for equity presented in Part 3. Even though interest is fixed and the redemption date specified, debentures can be traded at either a premium or a discount. Like equity yields, the current rate of interest is only a guide to the *true* return on investment which can only be determined under conditions of uncertainty by incorporating the capital gain or loss retrospectively, once a security is sold. In the case of redeemable debentures, this ex-post return calculation is termed the *yield to maturity* or *redemption yield*.

This introduces a further important point. The current yield on debentures represents the return from holding the investment rather than selling at its current market price. It is, therefore, an opportunity cost of capital, because it is the minimum return below which debenture holders could transfer their funds elsewhere at commensurate risk (Fisher's Separation Theorem). If the company were to make a current issue of debentures in the same risk class, presumably it would need to match this yield. In an untaxed economy, the market rate of interest K_d represents the company's *marginal* cost of capital for this fund source. As such, it is the relevant measure for assessing the viability of any new investment project financed by debentures. Using the previous example, if debentures redeemable in ten years were issued, the discount rate applied to a net present value (NPV) calculation should be the current yield of 11.8 per cent and not the original 10 per cent coupon rate. Explained simply, the latter might elicit a positive NPV, but if the former produces a negative value and the firm proceeds with the project, its future cashflows will be diminished. Consequently, shareholder wealth will be compromised.

Investment decisions should therefore be evaluated using a marginal cost of capital. However, it must be noted that only if the return required by new investors equals the current yield to existing investors will the marginal cost of raising additional finance as defined equal the current cost of capital in issue.

Even then, the formulae only apply to perfect capital markets, since they all assume zero transaction and issue costs in a taxless world.

4 THE IMPACT OF TAXATION AND TRANSACTION COSTS

From the company's viewpoint, the marginal cost of debenture capital for investment purposes is an allowable tax deduction which must be identified in DCF computations. One approach, explained in Part 2, is to include tax savings arising from interest payments in every project's cashflows. A simpler alternative is to calculate a company's after-tax cost of debentures.

The cost of irredeemable debt after tax is:

$$(6) \qquad K_{dt} = \frac{I(1-t)}{P_0}$$

where:

K_{dt} = after-tax cost of debt
I = annual interest payment
P_0 = current market price of debt (ex-interest)
t = rate of corporation tax (assumed to be constant)

such that:

$$(6A) \qquad K_{dt} = K_d(1-t)$$

where:

K_d = pre-tax cost of debt

Therefore, if a company pays £100,000 a year interest on irredeemable debentures with a market price of £1 million and the rate of corporation tax is 25 per cent, the effective cost of debentures is:

$$\frac{£100,000 \, (1-0.25)}{£1 \text{ million}} = 7.5\%$$

For redeemable debentures, the redemption payment is not allowable for tax. To calculate the cost of capital it is necessary to calculate an IRR which incorporates tax relief on the interest alone. Assuming that the tax relief is not delayed, the after-tax cost of debentures is established by solving for K_{dt} in the following equation:

$$(7) \qquad P_0 = \sum_{t=1}^{n} \frac{I(1-t)}{(1+K_{dt})^t} + \frac{P_n}{(1+K_{dt})^n}$$

Consider redeemable debentures issued at £100 par with a current market price of £90 (i.e. 90 per cent). The debentures will be redeemed at par with a coupon

198

rate of 15 per cent. The rate of corporation tax is 33 per cent. By trial and error, from Equation (7) in £ terms:

$$90 = \sum_{t=1}^{n=5} \frac{15(1-0.33)}{(1+K_{dt})^t} + \frac{100}{(1+K_{dt})^5}$$

$$K_{dt} \simeq 13\%$$

Now assume a one-year time lag between the payment of annual interest and the receipt of the tax benefit. For redeemable debentures, K_{dt} can be found by solving the IRR in the following equation:

$$(8) \qquad P_0 = \sum_{t=1}^{n} \frac{I}{(1+K_{dt})^t} + \frac{P_n}{(1+K_{dt})^n} - \sum_{t=2}^{n+1} \frac{It}{(1+K_{dt})^t}$$

The value of debentures is equal to the pre-tax discounted cashflows on the right-hand side of Equation (6), less the discounted sum of tax benefits from the second year of issue to the year after redemption.

Introducing greater realism, consider next corporate issue or transaction costs which are tax deductible one year after issue. Substituted into Equation (8):

$$(9) \qquad P_0 = C - \frac{C(1-t)}{1+K_{dt}} = \sum_{t=1}^{n} \frac{I}{(1+K_{dt})^t} + \frac{P_n}{(1+K_{dt})^n} - \sum_{t=2}^{n+1} \frac{It}{(1+K_{dt})^t}$$

where:

C = transaction costs.

Therefore, if a company issues a new fifteen-year debenture with a redemption premium of 20 per cent and transaction costs of £3.00 per cent under a 50 per cent corporate tax regime:

$$100 - \left(3 - \frac{1.5}{1+K_{dt}}\right) = \sum_{t=1}^{n=15} \frac{12}{(1+K_{dt})^t} + \frac{120}{(1+K_{dt})^{15}} - \sum_{t=2}^{n=16} \frac{6}{(1+K_{dt})^t}$$

By trial and error, the after-tax cost of debentures is approximately 7.4 per cent per annum.

Certain facts now emerge. For the company and investor respectively, the presence of market imperfections, such as issue costs and transaction costs, increases their marginal cost of capital. This is best understood by substituting the costs of issue into the cost of irredeemable debt in a taxless world. The denominator of Equation (3) is now reduced by issue costs as follows:

$$(10) \qquad K_d = \frac{I}{P_0(1-C)}$$

Assuming debenture interest is tax deductible with no time lag, the cost of debt given by Equation (6) is similarly enhanced:

$$(11) \qquad K_{dt} = \frac{I(1-t)}{P_0(1-C)}$$

The analysis can also be extended to *new issues* of equity capital. Assuming a constant dividend stream D in perpetuity, and introducing upper case notation for the cost of equity, the marginal cost of ordinary shares is:

$$(12) \qquad K_e = \frac{D}{P_0(1-C)}$$

It is also worth noting that this differs from the cost of retained earnings which do not incur any explicit costs, including those of issue. Under the conditions stated, the cost of retained earnings is correctly measured by the current dividend yield foregone by existing shareholders, namely their opportunity cost of capital:

$$(13) \qquad K_e = \frac{D}{P_0}$$

With regard to taxation, the higher the rate of corporation tax, the greater the tax benefits conferred on the company by issuing debt rather than equity finance. It will be recalled from Part 3 that the cost of equity capital is calculated on the basis of net dividends as opposed to gross. Given the imputation system of corporate taxation operable in the United Kingdom, a firm need only have sufficient post-tax profits to pay shareholders dividends net of personal taxation at their base rate, i.e. Advance Corporation Tax (ACT).

Different shareholders may have different tax positions, which affect their real yields, a well as different preferences concerning dividends *vis a vis* capital gains. Since their personal tax liability is deemed to be satisfied by ACT, however, these rarely enter into a firm's WACC calculation for the purposes of evaluating investment projects. For the moment, suffice it to say that the company must not only generate sufficient tax liability to claim the tax relief on debenture interest, but also to satisfy the ACT payment on behalf of shareholders (which has the effect of raising its cost of equity slightly). It should also be aware that the marginal costs of issuing debentures not only includes the explicit contractual interest and redemption payments but also the implicit costs associated with the financial risks to ordinary shareholders, which arise because of a reduced equity base in a revised capital structure. Both may combine to produce a change in the existing weighted average cost.

5 A GENERAL FORMULA FOR THE WEIGHTED AVERAGE COST OF CAPITAL (WACC)

Having established the opportunity costs of ordinary shares and debentures, how can a firm derive a weighted average of its component costs as a discount rate in DCF calculations? The question is important because investments which offer a return in excess of their WACC can increase the market value of equity by enhancing returns to shareholders in the long run.

A generalised formula for the WACC in a taxless world is:

$$(14) \qquad K = K_e\left(\frac{V_E}{V_E + V_D}\right) + K_d\left(\frac{V_D}{V_E + V_D}\right)$$

where:

K = WACC
K_e = cost of equity
K_d = cost of debt
V_E = market value of equity
V_D = market value of debt.

Incorporating taxation, the after-tax cost of debt K_{dt} should be substituted into the preceding equation using the appropriate equations explained earlier in the chapter, so that:

$$(15) \qquad K = K_e\left(\frac{V_E}{V_E + V_D}\right) + K_{dt}\left(\frac{V_D}{V_E + V_D}\right)$$

For example, in the case of redeemable debt:

$$(16) \qquad K = K_e\left(\frac{V_E}{V_E + V_D}\right) + K_d(1 - t)\left(\frac{V_D}{V_E + V_D}\right)$$

which may be rewritten as:

$$(17) \qquad K = K_e(W_E) + K_{dt}(W_D)$$

where:

W_E = weighting applied to equity
W_D = weighting applied to debt.

Thus, a firm financed equally by debt and equity, which yields 10 per cent and 5 per cent respectively, would calculate its WACC as follows:

$$K = 10\% \ (0.5) + 5\% \ (0.5) = 7.5\%$$

Consider next a company evaluating a new investment project which will cost £100,000 and yields £11,500 in perpetuity. Management requires a WACC applicable to the proposal using NPV criteria, subject to the proviso that the investment decision is financed in the same proportion as the existing assets, i.e. the capital structure remains stable.

The following information is available:

(i) Existing capital structure (at cost)

	£000
Issued Ordinary shares – 12,000,000	12,000
Retained earnings	4,000
6% Preference shares	2,000
9% Debentures	6,000
	24,000

(ii) Ordinary shares
(a) The market price of an ordinary share is £7.00.
(b) £6 million in dividends are to be paid which represent 75% of earnings.
(c) Earnings are expected to grow at an annual rate of 5%.
(d) If new ordinary shares were issued now, costs incurred would represent 25 pence per share and a reduction below market value of 50 pence per share would also be required.

(iii) 6% Preference shares
(a) Preference shares have a par value of £1 and were originally issued at 92 pence per share.
(b) Current price is 43 pence.
(c) A similar issue if made now would require to be at 40 pence per share.

(iv) 9% Debentures
(a) Issued in 1988 at a par value of £100.
(b) Current price is £92.
(c) A similar issue if made now would require to be made at £90.

(v) Corporation tax
The tax rate can be assumed to be 50%.

In its simplest form, using perpetual capitalisation formulae under growth and non-growth conditions, a dividend based *marginal*, weighted-average, cost of capital (WACC), i.e. incorporating issue costs, might be calculated as follows:

(vi) Component costs (£s)

(a) Issue of Ordinary shares

Marginal cost = Dividend per share/Net proceeds of issue + Growth rate

$$= (0.50/6.25) + 0.05$$

$$= 13\%$$

(b) Retained earnings = Dividend yield + Growth rate

$$= (0.50/7.00) + 0.05$$

$$= 12.1\%$$

(c) Preference shares

Marginal cost = Dividend per share/Proceeds of current issues

$$= 6/40 \text{ (in pence)}$$

$$= 15\%$$

(d) Debentures

Marginal cost after tax

$$= \text{Post tax interest per debenture/Proceeds of current issue}$$
$$= 9(1 - 0.5)/90$$
$$= 5.0\%$$

(vii) Weighted average, marginal cost of capital

	Capital structure (£ million)	Weight	Component cost (%)	Weighted cost (%)
Ordinary shares	12	0.50	13.0	6.50
Retained earnings	4	0.17	12.1	2.06
Preference shares	2	0.08	15.0	1.20
Debentures	6	0.25	5.0	1.25
	24	1.00		11.01

Of course, the above calculation is derived using the Gordon growth model which represents a fundamental point of disagreement for many academics, most notably proponents of Modigliani and Miller, explained in Chapter 7. It is not simply a question of whether share price or cost of equity capital is a function of dividends or earnings, but also whether the WACC is a function of capital structure. However, it is not intended to debate the issue here; for that, see Chapter 9. Suffice it to say for the moment that, if earnings are an appropriate basis of calculation, the cut-off rate for investment for any firm in a particular class of business risk, irrespective of its gearing, would simplify to the earnings yield for an equity firm in that class, which would be different to the WACC above.

Of more immediate interest is the operational validity of the preceding calculation, which depends upon the rather naïve assumptions that the future capital structure, dividend payout ratio and each security's return will remain constant. As a corollary, book values have been used to represent the balance of the structure, whereas fluctuating market values, which themselves may be consequential upon revisions to capital, are clearly more appropriate, affecting as they do WACC calculations considerably.

For example, the substitution of market values for book values *ex div* and *ex interest* in the preceding table raises the WACC from approximately 11.0 per cent to 12.5 per cent as follows:

(viii) *Weighted average, marginal cost of capital*

	Capital structure (£ million)	Weight	Component cost (%)	Weighted cost (%)
Ordinary shares	84.0	0.89	13.0	11.57
Retained earnings	4	0.04	12.1	0.48
Preference shares	0.8	0.01	15.0	0.15
Debentures	5.4	0.06	5.0	0.30
	94.2	1.00		12.50

The implication is obvious. Returning to the project under consideration, the present value of £11,500 in perpetuity using a WACC of 11.1 per cent based on book values is:

$$PV = \frac{£11,500}{0.111} = £103,603$$

The NPV of the £100,000 investment is, therefore:

$$NPV = £103,603 - £100,000 = £3,603$$

Compare this with the NPV from the project using the market-based WACC of 12.5 per cent:

$$PV = \frac{£11,500}{0.125} = £88,000$$

$$NPV = £88,000 - £100,000 = (£12,000)$$

Applying the NPV decision rule with book values, the project would be accepted. Using a market-based WACC, it would be rejected. So, which is correct?

As stated earlier, investments must be evaluated *at the margin* in terms of current investment opportunities foregone. Hence, market valuation of securities, like current rates of return, are the correct factors to determine a discount rate or cut-off rate for investment. Only if a company is unlisted are book values likely to be less subjective than market valuations.

To prove the point, an alternative way of looking at the investment proposal demonstrates that the application of a marginal WACC as a discount rate ensures that the shareholders' wealth is not diminished.

From the previous example, first calculate the proportion of equity applied to the investment:

£100,000 (0.89) = £89,000

Now calculate the net annual cashflow available to the new ordinary shareholders:

	Capital investment (£)	Capital cost (%)	Investor return (£)
Annual cashflow			11,500
Retained earnings £100,000 (0.04)	4,000	12.1	484
Preference shares £100,000 (0.01)	1,000	15.0	150
Debentures £100,000 (0.06)	6,000	5.0	300
	11,000		
Distributable cashflow			10,566

Finally, define the return on shareholders funds:

$$\text{Return to equity} = \frac{£10,566}{89,000} = 11.87\%$$

Since this is less than the marginal cost of new issues (13 per cent), the investment proposal should be rejected. The reader may confirm that, if retained earnings were incorporated into the return calculation, the equity return would still only be 11.88 per cent which is also lower than the yield on shares in issue. Again, the project should not be undertaken.

6 WACC ASSUMPTIONS

It must be emphasised that, even under the assumption of perfect markets, the WACC computation is still only an approximation which depends for its validity upon a number of assumptions. Apart from the question of whether the market value of equity can be divided between the ordinary share capital and reserves, which are based upon historical cost accounting conventions, many companies raise *floating rate* as opposed to fixed rate debt capital, as well as debentures and preference shares which are convertible into ordinary shares. Because of their variable components – the rate of interest, the date of conversion, the proportion of investors converting to ordinary shares and the subsequent dividend stream received – these securities are more difficult (but not impossible) to incorporate into a WACC calculation.

With regard to the assumptions, the use of K as defined implies that:

- Investments selected are homogenous with respect to the overall level of business risk which already confronts the firm. Otherwise, investors will react by buying or selling (as opposed to holding) their securities, thereby affecting the respective yields which comprise the WACC.
- The capital structure will remain stable, or if it changes at all will do so imperceptibly, so as not to invalidate the weightings applied to the WACC components.
- As a corollary to the above, acceptable investment projects must, therefore, be marginal to a firm's existing operations.

Fundamental criticisms of the WACC for investment appraisal purposes relate to these assumptions:

- New capital investments might exhibit different business risk characteristics from a company's existing activities, thereby precipitating a change in investor returns.
- The funds raised to finance incremental investments might alter the capital structure radically and therefore the investors' perception of corporate financial risk. This is particularly important if a company with a mixed capital structure finances projects by debt or equity capital alone.

An obvious response to these criticisms is that in many instances it will be difficult, if not impossible, to assign a particular project to a particular source of finance. A company's funds should be viewed collectively, inasmuch as finance is withdrawn from a stock of funds to invest in new projects and is replenished as new finance is raised or profits are retained. In the short term, certain funds, i.e. debt or equity, might also be secured at advantageous rates depending upon prevailing market conditions, which necessarily implies a brief departure from its long-run capital structure. Under such circumstances, a WACC is entirely appropriate as a discount rate for long-term investment, provided the projects undertaken display a commensurate level of business risk.

Even if funds are raised explicitly from one source to finance an incremental investment, there are sound reasons for using the WACC as a discount rate, particularly if the change in the capital structure represents a short-run deviation from the desired capital mix. First, a rational choice of funds is a financing decision taken not in relation to the investment decision but in relation to the long-term capital structure. Second, there are substantial economies of scale to be gained in terms of reduced issue costs by raising large amounts of capital from one source and then another.

Under the assumptions of homogenous business risk, a stable long-term capital structure and marginal investments, and ignoring the possible effects of market imperfections (such as stock market disequilibrium, inflation and other economic factors), a single estimate of the marginal WACC is, therefore, a suitable proxy for a company's theoretical opportunity cost of capital. As such, it can be applied by management throughout the life of an investment project under evaluation.

7 CAPITAL BUDGETING AND THE CUT-OFF RATE FOR INVESTMENT

As mentioned earlier, there exists a wide variety of funds available for capital investment, other than debt and equity, some without any explicit cost but all with an implicit or opportunity cost which should be incorporated into any realistic WACC calculation. This chapter's final section, therefore, seeks to establish a discount or cut-off rate for investment which expands upon the generalised WACC model already presented.

Recalling Equation (17), the general WACC formula in a taxed world:

(17) $K = K_e(W_E) + K_{dt}(W_D)$

First define K as the *basic cost of money*, denoted by K_B, which represents the weighted average cost of equity and the after-tax cost of debt capital.

The overall cut-off rate can be expressed:

(18) $K = K_B + K_U + K_N$

where:
K_B = basic cost of money which is the weighted average cost of equity K_e and the cost of debt capital K_d
K_U = cost of unallocated expenditure
K_N = cost of non-profit-making investment.

This rate should be set as the minimum rate of return expected from a company's overall capital investment. When it becomes necessary to set individual cut-off returns for various sectors of a group, each sector must be examined separately to ascertain its unallocated expenses K_U and non-profit-making investments K_N. The basic costs K_B to the group remains the same for all sectors of the group.

For simplicity, the discussion makes no specific allowance for inflation, although an allowance could be made where applicable. On the other hand it can be argued that due to the uncertainty associated with future rates of inflation and the extent to which current market rates of return already incorporate an expectation about the future, inflation can be ignored, irrespective of whether future profits increase at approximately the same rate. Moreover, the analysis does not get enmeshed in the niceties of different tax regimes. Issue costs are also ignored.

8 THE BASIC COST OF MONEY

The weighted average cost of equity and loan capital may be expressed:

$$(19) \qquad K_B = (W_E)K_e + (1 - W_E)K_d(1 - t_C)$$

where the terms:

K_e = cost of equity as determined by management

W_E = proportion of equity to total capitalisation

t_C = rate of corporation tax

$K_d(1 - t_C)$ = marginal cost of debt, net of corporation tax (if a deductible expense).

Sources of finance for which there are no explicit costs, but implicit or opportunity costs such as retained earnings and trade credit received, would also be included in the calculation. The former are included in the weighted K_e since they represent a proxy for future dividends. The latter is measured by the alternative funds source that would have been used by the company in its absence.

The cost of equity capital can be derived by at least three methods.

K_e: method 1

The annual cost of equity capital is found by dividing profits after tax available to the equity holders by the average market value of the equity in that year, expressed as a percentage figure.

This cost is then averaged over a number of years (preferably more than 10) taking care to avoid distortions which might arise in exceptional years. A suggested formula is:

$$(20) \qquad K_e = \frac{\pi - \{T_C + Dt_I + [\pi - (T_C + D)]t_g\}}{V_E}$$

where:

π = profits available to equity holders before all taxes

T_C = total corporation tax payable

t_I = base rate of income tax

Dt_I = income tax payable on dividend (where appropriate)

D = gross dividend payable

t_g = rate of capital gains tax (where appropriate)

V_E = average capitalisation of equity.

Under an imputation system of corporation tax, like that of the United Kingdom, Dt_I can be ignored. Likewise, in the absence of capital gains tax $[\pi - (T_C + D)]t_g$ can be deleted so that Equation (20) simplifies to:

$$(21) \qquad K_e = \frac{\pi - T_C}{V_E}$$

In essence, the numerators of the two equations (20) and (21) represent net cash after all taxes which the shareholder receives in dividends, plus net retained earnings of the company (the growth element), less a notional capital gains tax on them.

By way of illustration, consider a company with an equity market valuation of £9.9 million. The profits available to shareholders before all taxes is £1.5 million. Management's intention is to pay a gross dividend of £638,300. The rate of capital gains and corporation tax is a uniform 30 per cent, with income tax payable on dividends equal to £263,300.

Equation (20) becomes (£000s):

$$K_e = \frac{1500 - 450 + 263.3 + [1500 - (450 + 638.3)]0.3}{9900} = 6.7\%$$

Now using the following records of percentage earnings yields for the past 10 years:

1988	(1)	7.1	1993	(6)	10.0
1989	(2)	7.9	1994	(7)	5.0
1990	(3)	9.7	1995	(8)	5.9
1991	(4)	16.6	1996	(9)	7.2
1992	(5)	16.4	1997	(10)	9.3

If these are summated and added to the latest cost of equity, the average return since 1988 is given by:

$$\overline{K}_e = \frac{95.1 + 6.7}{11} = 9.25\%$$

It is also interesting to note that, if the tax regime ignored capital gains and dividend taxes, Equation (21) becomes (£000s):

$$K_e = \frac{1500 - 450}{9900} = 10.6\%$$

i.e. the fiscal system makes a difference to the annual cost of equity capital and hence its periodic average.

K_e: method 2

To an investor, the profitability of a share can be determined by net after-tax dividends received over a period of years, plus the realisation of shares by sale at the end of a period, and less any tax debit for capital gains or tax credit for a capital loss, which can be used to offset capital gains elsewhere. The calculation is thus similar to a DCF internal rate of return (IRR) on any investment proposal.

The cost of equity is the solution rate K_e in the familiar equation:

$$(22) \qquad P_0 = \frac{D_1}{1 + K_e} + \frac{D_2}{(1 + K_e)^2} + \frac{D_3}{(1 + K_e)^3} + \cdots + \frac{D_n}{(1 + K_e)^n} + \frac{P_n}{(1 + K_e)^n}$$

or

$$(23) \qquad P_0 = \sum_{t=1}^{t=n} \frac{D_t}{(1 + K_e)^t} + \frac{P_n}{(1 + K_e)^n}$$

where:

P_0 = purchase price of equity, or average market price in Year 0

$\dfrac{D_t}{(1 + K_e)^t}$ = present value in year 0 of net after-tax dividends received by shareholders in years 1, 2 ... n.

$\dfrac{P_n}{(1 + K_e)^n}$ = present value in year 0 of selling (or average market price) of shares in year n, after taking into account capital gains tax payable (if any) or taking credit for capital gains tax relief on any losses which should be set off against capital gains.

It should also be noted that where n tends to infinity and dividends are constant, Equation (23) simplifies to:

$$(24) \qquad P_0 = D_1/K_e$$

so that rearranging terms:

$$(25) \qquad K_e = D_1/P_0$$

With a finite period of observation, care is required so that the first and final years (0 and n) do not distort the calculation. If year 0 is a bad year then year n should be a bad year and *vice versa*. Equation (25) is only applicable where dividends are constant.

Moreover, it must be assumed in this method that all stock dividends and splits have been retained throughout the period of the investment. If there are any rights issued during the period, then either the price paid for these rights (R) should be added to the cost of the original investment (P_0) in present value terms and the dividend received should be increased accordingly, or the premium realised from the sale of these rights should be discounted to year 0 and deducted from the original cost of investment P_0.

By way of illustration and returning to the original example, assume shares were acquired in 1988 at an all-time low. The purchase price is therefore taken as an average of the years 1988–1990 which equals £1.82. The 1998 selling price of £35.2 is taken as an average of 1996, 1997 and 1998, since 1997 appears to be above trend. Adjustments for rights and bonus issues have also been incorporated into the investment cost and dividends received.

Table 8.1 below sets out the resultant information and solves for the IRR which is close to 10%, using present value (PV) techniques.

Table 8.1

Year	Investment £	Dividends £	Sale £	DCF factor £	10% PV £
1988	(1.82)			1.00	(1.82)
1989		0.054		0.909	0.049
1990		0.054		0.826	0.045
1991		0.060		0.751	0.045
1992		0.060		0.683	0.041
1993		0.080		0.621	0.050
1994		0.090		0.565	0.051
1995		0.090		0.513	0.046
1996		0.100		0.467	0.047
1997		0.120		0.424	0.051
1998		0.138	3.52	0.386	1.411
					1.836

K_e: method 3

If a company has adopted a policy of a fixed payout ratio of dividends to earnings it is possible to use the following equation:

(26) $K_e = \dfrac{D(1 - t_C)}{P} + br$

where:

$\dfrac{D(1 - t_C)}{P}$ = average annual after-tax dividend yield over years 1 to n taking average market price of the shares in each year

b = fraction of income the company is expected to retain in every period

r = return on investment the company is expected to earn in every period

br = the annual rate of increase in absolute amount of net after-tax dividend per share over years 1 to n, i.e. the growth rate.

The equation is derived from the Gordon growth valuation model (1962) but in a taxed world:

(27) $P_0 = \dfrac{D_1(1 - t_C)}{K_e - br}$

This, too, represents a fundamental point of disagreement for many academics, yet again Modigliani and Miller (1961 onwards), as to whether share price or cost of equity capital is a function of dividends. Suffice it to say that if the methodology is considered appropriate, distortion to the right-hand term br of Equation (26) can arise by selecting starting and final years displaying faster or slow rates of growth than the intervening period. In the case of the example, it is assumed that net after-tax dividends have fluctuated between 3.25% and 3.8% (with a figure of 3.8% for 1998) but an average say of 3.5% per annum. The dividend has been covered approximately twice (i.e. the dividend payout ratio is 50%) yet dividends have increased over the period from £0.054 per share in 1988 to £0.138 per share in 1998, which represents an annual increase of about 10% compound.

The basic cost of money : a summary

As defined earlier, the basic cost of money is the weighted average costs of equity and loan capital, namely:

(19) $K_B = (W_E)K_e + (1 - W_E)K_d(1 - t_C)$

Assume, therefore, that the company under analysis has loans of £1 million, £2 million and trade credit of £1 million at 5%, 6% and 7% respectively. Recalling the £9.9 million market valuation of equity, management consider it prudent to retain the gearing ratio in the proportion 30% debt and 70% equity. The marginal cost of debt is also assumed to be 7.5% gross. Hence the future cost of loan capital is 5.25% given the corporate tax rate of 30%.

Thus, given $K_e = 10\%$ from method 2, the basic cost of money is:

$$K_B = (0.7 \times 10\%) + (0.3 \times 5.25\%) = 8.57\%$$

9 THE COST OF UNALLOCATED EXPENDITURE

Unallocated expenditure relates typically to speculative research and development, administrative overheads and certain technical services. Its annual cost should be calculated net of tax in a similar way to the cost of equity. This should then be divided by total market capitalisation, plus the book value of loan capital. It may be formulated as follows:

$$(28) \qquad K_U = \frac{U - \{T_C + D't_i + [U - (T_C + D')]t_g\}}{V_E + V_D}$$

where the new terms are:

U = total unallocated costs which equals profits foregone

D' = gross dividends which would have been paid

$D't_i$ = income tax payable if dividends had been distributed on additional profits in accordance with company policy

V_D = total book value of loan capital in that year.

The above equation is, of course, similar to Equation (20) but substitutes U for π and adds V_D to the denominator. The effect is to calculate an implicit or opportunity cost for unrecouped expenditure. It is, therefore, equivalent to incorporating within the basic cost of capital an additional element to cover costs which cannot be recovered in the selling price.

Given all the previous data, assume that the unrealised profit equal to unallocated expenditure is estimated at 10% of the current profit level of £1.5 million and that the additional dividend that would have been paid accords with current management policy, i.e. 10% of £638,300. Then given corporation tax and capital gains tax of 30%, a market valuation of equity of £9.9 million and £4 million loan capital, Equation (28) in terms of £000s becomes:

$$K = \frac{150 - 45 + 26.33 + [150 - (45 + 63.83)]0.3}{9900 + 4000} = 0.5\%$$

However, under an imputation system and in the absence of capital gains, Equation (28) simplifies in a manner analogous to Equation (21) such that:

$$(29) \qquad K_U = \frac{U - T_C}{V_E + V_D}$$

Using the data given, the reader may care, therefore, to recalculate the capital cost.

10 NON-PROFIT-MAKING CAPITAL EXPENDITURE

Certain capital expenditure does not produce and, moreover, is not expected to produce measurable returns. Such examples are office accommodation, welfare facilities and capital expenditure on research and training. However, these can be calculated as a proportion of total capital spent over a period of years (and also of forecast years) and then related to the cost of capital. An equation is given by:

(30) $K_N = \dfrac{N_n}{N_t} K_B$

where the new terms:

N_n = total cost of non-profit-making investments in any period of time
N_t = total new profit-making investments in the same period of time.

Thus, if it is assumed that since 1988 the company has spent 10% of total capital on non-profit-making investments:

$K_N = 0.1 \times 8.57\% = 0.857\%$

It can be argued that the incorporation of K_N, along with K_U, adds a premium to K_B the basic cost of finance, analogous to criticism relating to the addition of risk premiums. In other words, if the cost of finance to a company is believed to be 8.57 per cent this is because the market has already categorised the company within a particular risk class which presumably has some regard for the past and anticipates an earnings stream, net of items such as research and development and unabsorbed overhead. Therefore, the setting of a higher cut-off rate in these circumstances not only disregards the time-preferences of the market and lowers the potential of investments in terms of their net present values but also introduces a bias towards projects with higher returns which, because of their associated risk, may well be those that management wishes to avoid.

In the absence of perfect market information only management can resolve the dilemma. The extent to which the market can assess indirect inputs into the investment process, as opposed to the risks associated with the investment itself, suggests that overhead and non-profit-making capital expenditure should appear in the cost equation. If nothing else, the amounts involved, like the retained earnings incorporated into the cost of equity, have an implicit or opportunity cost, in the sense that there may always be profitable investment opportunities foregone. This is obvious, once one accepts that money capital is not simply the controlling factor but frequently the contracting factor for many companies and therefore necessitates a cut-off rate for investment opportunities in the first place!

11 THE CUT-OFF RATE

It will be recalled that the overall cut-off rate or WACC is expressed:

(18) $\quad K = K_B + K_U + K_N$

In the example, a possible calculation would be equivalent to:

$\quad K = 8.57\% + 0.5\% + 0.857\% = 9.9\%$

Armed with this information, assuming homogeneity of risk, marginal investment and a stable capital structure, a company should only accept new investment proposals if the IRR at least equals 9.9 per cent or preferably if the project's NPV discounted at $K = 9.9$ per cent is equal to or greater than zero. Stated simply, the weighted average cost of capital represents the minimum rate of return, rather than a capital cost (which is a misnomer) that the company should expect to recoup from its overall capital investment. Correctly applied, according to Fisher's Separation Theorem, shareholders' wealth will not be compromised.

12 SUMMARY AND CONCLUSIONS

This chapter's introduction to the finance decision has shifted the emphasis from the shareholders' desired rate of return to that of the company. In an era where ownership is divorced from control, it is management's responsibility to secure a flexible inflow of funds which can be applied to their investment decisions at minimum cost. Such fund sources may extend beyond equity.

In a leveraged situation, management is, therefore, charged with the additional responsibility of ensuring that the returns from its investments not only maximise shareholders' wealth but also satisfy other providers of capital. The appropriate acceptance criterion to be incorporated into project appraisal was defined as a company's weighted average cost of capital (WACC) rather than the cost of equity. It will be recalled that, provided numerous conditions are satisfied, projects are then selected which produce a positive NPV when discounted by what is effectively the firm's *marginal* opportunity rate of return.

The question arises, therefore, as to whether management can establish an optimal mix of fund sources which minimises WACC and maximises the NPV of all its projects. If so, the firm's overall value can be maximised by its financial decisions. Unfortunately, the answer is not that simple. If it were, firms would choose exclusively to finance their investments by debt.

On the one hand, revisions to capital structure will obviously revise the weightings which are incorporated into the WACC calculation. On the other, because the returns to the various providers of capital are interdependent, to the extent that they emerge from common investment decisions, the impact of financial risk associated with leverage upon the investor's costs of capital must enter into the equation. Moreover, changing economic conditions which are beyond the firm's control might also elicit a change in constituent capitalisation rates, irrespective of the corporate financial mix. All these issues, therefore, will be addressed in the next chapter and thereafter.

References

A guide to further reading is provided at the end of Chapter 9.

9

Cost of capital and leverage

Chapter profile

This chapter provides the reader with further opportunities for reflection concerning the behaviour of the costs of debt and equity within a *changing* capital structure, before considering the Modigliani–Miller (MM) *law of one price* within the context of financial policy.

The operational validity of a weighted average cost of capital (WACC) calculation which depends upon the naive assumptions that a company's future capital structure and anticipated level of earnings will remain constant is questioned. These assumptions are relaxed using arithmetic, graphical and algebraic analyses. The differential impact of capital gearing upon corporate values and capital costs, including the effects upon the shareholders' desired rate of return (beneficial or otherwise), is illustrated by the seminal work of David Durand.

The conclusion drawn is that if the market value of a share is independent of a company's distribution policy, as MM hypothesise (Chapter 7), then it should be impossible to conclude that a company's overall cost of capital and total corporate value is a function of leverage.

1 INTRODUCTION

For the purposes of exposition, the previous chapter's derivation of a weighted average cost of capital (WACC) as a cut-off or discount rate for investment initially assumed that the firm's capital structure and component costs were stable. However, it was suggested that because capital costs are dynamic, the WACC might not be static and its corporate financial structure could not be institutionalised. WACC constituents, the commonest of which are conveniently summarised in Table 9.1, might require continual revision if project discount rates are to be kept at a minimum and the company's overall NPV is to be maximised, as normative financial theory prescribes.

However, a company should not only alter its capital structure to take advantage of changes in the explicit and implicit costs of various sources of finance,

Table 9.1 Various sources of finance and capital costs

Source	Cost
1 Share issues: Ordinary	EPS
Preference	Fixed dividend
2 Loan issues: Secured ⎫ Unsecured ⎬	Interest payable plus any premium payable on repayment.
Convertible	Present interest plus future EPS (with normal conversion price typically above current market price)
3 Retained earnings	Shareholder's return
4 Depreciation	Opportunity cost
5 Short-term borrowings	Market rate of interest
6 Deferred taxation	Opportunity cost
7 Deferred payments to creditors	Opportunity cost plus any loss of goodwill and administrative costs
8 Reduction in stocks ⎫ 9 Reduction in debtors ⎬	Opportunity cost plus any loss of goodwill and loss of sales
10 Debt factoring	Above base rate
11 Sale of excess or idle assets	Alternative yield
12 Sale of property and lease back	Leasing cost plus any capital appreciation

but also two other inter-related factors: maximum control and capital gearing (leverage).

Maximum control is achieved through a division of voting capital and loan capital, which favours ownership. From a Balance Sheet viewpoint, the total amount borrowed should not exceed a reasonable proportion of the fixed assets. For example, if debentures represent a majority of the fixed assets, the higher the probability of shareholders losing control to creditors. With regard to the Income Statement, earnings before interest and tax (EBIT) must be sufficient to cover all types of fixed charges, whether interest or preference dividends. Otherwise, the firm can be forced into liquidation.

The derivation of an optimum level of gearing or leverage is more vexatious. Represented by the percentage of debt capital and preference shares in a firm's total capital structure, the *gearing ratio* determines the proportion of fixed interest and fixed dividend claims upon income and assets. High gearing can mean that ordinary shareholders cannot be paid an adequate return and that at the margin a new issue of debt capital or preference shares might also represent a more speculative investment. Low gearing can have the opposite effect.

Much depends upon the forecast level of earnings, EBIT and economic conditions. Nevertheless, if prospective investors are rational, leverage can have a significant impact upon their respective incremental yields, which then impacts upon existing investor attitudes. All this combines to redefine the company's overall cost of capital and value. Thus, it is reasonable to assume that firms should attempt to apply a least cost combination of financing sources to their new asset investments if WACC is to be minimised, their overall NPV is to be maximised and all stakeholder expectations are to be met.

It should come as no surprise to the reader that yet again this implies a series of conflicting models where Modigliani–Miller (MM) figure prominently. Fortunately, theories of capital structure are entirely consistent with their equity counterparts explained in Part 3. To simplify the exposition still further and without compromising the analyses, it will be assumed that companies have access to a capital market which only offers two sources of finance, namely ordinary shares and irredeemable debentures (equity and debt henceforth). Thus, the gearing ratio simplifies to the debt/equity ratio. Finally, the corporate and personal tax regimes will be kept simple, if only because they are under continual review by government.

2 GEARING: AN OVERVIEW

Conventional wisdom implies that a company's WACC and total value is determined by its overall profitability, as well as the *total risk* associated with investment policies. However, it will be recalled that risk is a function of two inter-related variables. First, *business risk* which arises from the variability of an asset investment's innate profitability in relation to industrial and general economic conditions. Second, the *financial risk* which stems from the manner in which the firm actually finances investment and subsequently distributes their returns to the providers of capital.

As explained in Chapter 7, if ordinary dividends and retentions are not perfect substitutes, an increase in the retention rate (a reduction in the dividend payout ratio) to finance new projects of equivalent business risk can sharpen the shareholders' perception of the financial risk associated with their stake in the firm. In a world of uncertainty, they might prefer dividends now rather than dividends or capital gains later. As a consequence, an increase (decrease) in the retention rate can elicit an increase (decrease) in the equity capitalisation rate which, by definition equals, the WACC for an all-equity firm. Thus, without any revisions to the level of forecast earnings, there is one school of thought which subscribes to the view that changes in the capitalisation rate, share price and corporate value are a concomitant of the firm's distribution policy.

219

Without yet wishing to resurrect the alternative dividend irrelevancy hypothesis which relates to the Modigliani–Miller 'law of one price', the impact of financial risk becomes even more complex with the introduction of debt into the firm's capital structure. One is not simply considering the pattern of returns to shareholders but their inter-relationship with distributions to other providers of capital. Business risk and financial risk still articulate with one another but the shareholders' total return, irrespective of whether it is preferred in the form of dividends or retention financed capital gains, is now determined by the gearing ratio as well as business risk.

When a firm is financed by equity alone, the shareholders' return must in some way equal a forecast of post-tax profits (ideally cash-based) determined solely by the business risk which confronts it. However, when a firm borrows, this return in the form of an EPS to each shareholder can be enhanced, provided the effective cost of debt is less than the current earnings yield on shares.

In an efficient capital market, such an assumption is not unrealistic. Holders of corporate debt not only have a prior claim on income *vis á vis* shareholders for a going concern but also an initial capital repayment from the realisation of assets in the event of liquidation. A contractual obligation to pay regular interest further encourages debt holders to accept a lower return than shareholders, whose dividends can be waived periodically. From the company's viewpoint, an issue of debt, rather than equity, therefore represents an attractive proposition, since it can lower its WACC and increase corporate value. If tax is introduced there is also an added benefit. Under a system like that in the UK, where interest is still a tax-deductible expense and dividends are an appropriation of profits which do not qualify for tax relief, the company's *true* cost of debt is further reduced by a corporate tax saving. The higher the gearing and the higher the rate of corporate taxation, the larger the saving.

For the purposes of illustration, consider two firms with the same profits before interest, which arise from identical investments with uniform business risk. The companies only differ with regard to their methods of financing. One is sourced exclusively by equity, the other with 25 per cent debt in its capital structure. The cost of equity and debt are 10 per cent and 5 per cent respectively.

In a taxless world, the formula for the WACC is given by:

(1) $K = K_e(W_E) + K_d(W_D)$

where:

K = WACC
K_e = cost of equity
K_d = cost of debt
W_E = proportion of equity in the total capital structure
W_D = proportion of debt in the total capital structure (the gearing ratio).

For the geared firm:

$$K_G = 10\% \ (0.75) + 5\% \ (0.25) = 8.75\%$$

which is lower than the 10 per cent cut-off rate for investment (K_e) in the all-equity firm. Applying the appropriate rate to a uniform earnings figure (E) it now becomes apparent that the total capitalised value (V) will be higher for the geared firm than its equity counterpart:

(2) $\quad V_U = E/K_e < E/K_G$ $\qquad Ungeard - Geard$

given:

$$K_e > K_G = f(K_e > K_d)$$

For example, if earnings are £1 million in perpetuity for both companies:

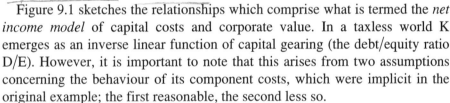

Company 1 (Ungeared) $\qquad$ *Company 2 (Geared)*

$vol\ve$ $V = \dfrac{£1 \ \text{million}}{0.10 \ _{Ke}} = £10 \ \text{million} < \dfrac{£1 \ \text{million}}{0.0875 \ _{Kd}} = £11.453 \ \text{million}$

Generalising, the conclusion to be drawn is that firms should maximise their leverage. By increasing the gearing ratio (W_D), the WACC (K) is minimised and corporate value (V) is maximised.

Figure 9.1 sketches the relationships which comprise what is termed the *net income model* of capital costs and corporate value. In a taxless world K emerges as an inverse linear function of capital gearing (the debt/equity ratio D/E). However, it is important to note that this arises from two assumptions concerning the behaviour of its component costs, which were implicit in the original example; the first reasonable, the second less so.

(i) The cost of equity (K_e) is higher than the cost of debt (K_d).
(ii) K_e and K_d are constant irrespective of the gearing ratio (W_D).

For the moment, suffice it to say that, if the return to shareholders is to assume the characteristics of fixed interest securities, any enhancement in EPS caused by gearing explained earlier must create a demand for leveraged equity which elicits a directly proportional increase in share price and leaves its capitalisation rate unchanged.

3 GEARING AND TAXATION

Turning to a world of taxation, let it be assumed in the previous example that the uniform EBIT figure is £1 million and the rate of corporation tax is 25 per cent.

Clearly, the geared company's shareholders remain in a preferential position. By debt-financing 25 per cent of its investments at half the cost of equity

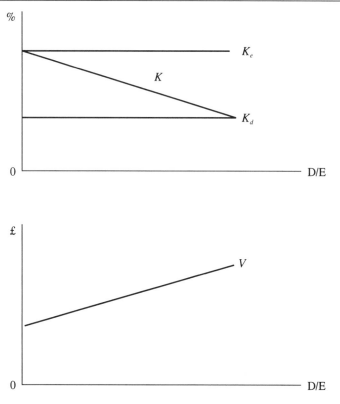

Fig 9.1   The net income model of capital costs and corporate value (constant costs of debt and equity)

(5 per cent *vis á vis* 10 per cent) only 12.5 per cent of the firm's total earnings (EBIT) are attributable to debenture holders, whereas the same proportion of shareholders would require 25 per cent. However, the debt issue now produces a tax saving. The firm will only pay tax on its earnings after interest (EAT) which are 87.5 per cent of the £1 million EBIT figure. Given a 25 per cent rate of tax, the geared company will therefore pay £218,750 compared with the £250,000 tax bill which confronts the all-equity firm. A combination of cheaper financing and the tax saving produces a proportionally higher EPS for the leveraged shareholders. Post-tax earnings might only be 65.6 per cent of EBIT (i.e. £1 million minus interest and tax), compared with 75 per cent for the all-equity firm but the former only relates to 75 per cent of investors and not 100 per cent. It should also be noted that this has been achieved without divorcing ownership from control. Figure 9.2 provides a schematic view of the beneficial impact of gearing on EPS.

From the company's viewpoint, the dual benefits of cheaper financing and

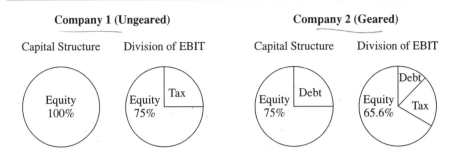

Company 1 (Ungeared)

Capital Structure   Division of EBIT

Company 2 (Geared)

Capital Structure   Division of EBIT

The EPS Proportion

$$\frac{\text{Shareholder income}}{\text{Shareholders}} = \frac{75\%}{100\%} = 0.75$$

$$\frac{\text{Shareholder income}}{\text{Shareholders}} = \frac{65.6\%}{75.0\%} = 0.87$$

Fig 9.2 Beneficial gearing and shareholder return (EPS) in a taxed world

the tax saving are manifest in a lower WACC with leverage relative to its all equity counterpart.

It will be recalled from Chapter 8 that, after tax, the cost of irredeemable debt is:

(3) $\quad K_{dt} = \dfrac{I(1-t)}{P_0}$

where:

K_{dt} = after-tax cost of debt
I = annual interest payment
P_0 = current market price of debt (ex-interest)
t = rate of corporation tax (assumed to be constant)

such that:

$\quad K_{dt} = K_d(1-t)$

where:

(4) $\quad K_d$ = pre-tax cost of debt

The formula for the WACC in a taxed world is given by:

(5) $\quad K_t = K_e(W_E) + K_{dt}(W_D)$

so that in terms of the example:

$\quad K_t = 10\% \ (0.75) + 5\% \ (1 - 0.25)(0.25) = 8.44\%$

which is not only lower than the 10 per cent cut-off rate for investments of equivalent business risk in the all-equity firm but also below the WACC of 8.75 per cent calculated earlier in the absence of corporate taxation.

Now applying the appropriate rate (K) to the distributable earnings for each company, i.e. the post-tax earnings (E_t) which are attributable to the share-holders, plus interest (I) (if any), the capitalised value (V_t) of each company is determined as follows:

(6) $V_t = \dfrac{E_t + I}{K_t}$

such that:

Company 1 (Ungeared)   *Company 2 (Geared)*

$V_t = \dfrac{£750,000}{0.10} = £7.5$ million $\dfrac{£781,250}{0.844} = £9.26$ million

Distributable income for the all-equity firm simply equals:

(7) $E_t = E(1 - t)$

where:

$E = \text{EBIT}$
$t\ =$ rate of corporation tax

The corresponding figure for the geared company is more problematical but is defined as follows:

(*i*) Subtract interest of £125,000 from the EBIT of £1 million.
(*ii*) Deduct from the balance (£875,000), tax at 25 per cent (£21,8750) to yield a post-tax profit of £656,250.
(*iii*) Add back the debenture interest of £125,000 to post-tax profits to deter-mine the total amount distributable to the equity and debt-holders (£781,250).

Expressed mathematically:

(8) $E_t + I = (E - I)(1 - t) + I$

Thus, substituting Equation (8) into Equation (6) the total capitalised value of a company, irrespective of its financial mix or the rate of corporate taxation, is given by the expanded *generalised valuation formula:*

(9) $V_t = \dfrac{(E - I)(1 - t) + I}{K_t}$

$\qquad = \dfrac{E_t + I}{K_t}$

For an all-equity company, this contracts to:

(10) $V_t = E_t / K_e$

The conclusion to be drawn is that given two firms exhibiting identical total earnings (EBIT) with equal business risk, the one which introduces an increment of debt at lower cost into its capital structure will not only experience a reduction in its overall cost of capital (WACC) which incorporates a tax saving, but will also exhibit a higher corporate value. As a corollary, the higher the rate of corporate taxation, the greater the saving. Even leveraged companies should continue to gear up to prove themselves more attractive to prospective investors, to be able to access the capital market more easily and to protect themselves from takeover.

4 CAPITAL GEARING : THE TRADITIONAL VIEW

When a firm is financed by equity alone, the shareholders' total return (dividends plus capital gains) stems from a stream of post-tax profits which are determined by business risk. However, if a firm has borrowed at a fixed rate of interest to fund part of the investment's earnings a smaller number of shareholders will receive a higher EPS, provided the true cost of borrowing is lower than the original equity yield. In an efficient capital market, even ignoring the tax deductibility of debt, such an assumption is not unrealistic.

Notice that the productivity of the firm's resources is unchanged. There is the same overall return on assets characterised by the same level of business risk, irrespective of the financing source. What has changed is the mode of financing which increases the shareholders' income but reduces the financial risk of their investment. As a consequence of capital gearing, the demand for leveraged equity should therefore be higher and command a higher price than its unleveraged counterpart. Moreover, if this is directly proportionate to the enhanced EPS the equity capitalisation rate will remain unchanged. From the company's viewpoint, however, if the cost of equity, as well as the cost of debt, remains constant, its overall cost of capital will fall and the capitalised market value of total earnings (debt plus leveraged equity) will rise as the firm gears up.

Although the equity capitalisation rate remains in equilibrium, given the dual benefits of capital gearing to the company, the question arises as to why extreme leverage is an exceptional observable phenomenon rather than the rule in the real world.

One answer is that, even without the tax breaks, when a firm introduces more debt into its capital structure, equity holders feel exposed to greater financial risk. Thus, the demand for equity tails off and the market value of shares, which initially rose, ultimately declines, so much so that the equity capitalisation rate increases, even if the cost of debt is constant and EPS is not being compromised. Beyond a judicious level of gearing commensurate with business risk, the company's declining overall cost of capital will therefore rise and, as a corollary, its total value (debt plus equity) will fall.

Figure 9.3 depicts the functional relationships which underpin a U-shaped average cost curve in a taxless world. These comprise what is now termed the *traditional model* of capital costs and corporate value. This suggests that companies should still determine an optimal capital structure, which reflects a least-cost combination of financing sources and maximises the capitalised value of total corporate earnings, as normative financial theory prescribes. However, such a structure is highly unlikely to conform to a position of extreme leverage.

The increased financial risk of higher gearing arises because the returns to debt and equity holders are interdependent stemming from the same investments. Because of the contractual obligation to pay interest, any variability in overall profitability caused by business risk is therefore passed on to the shareholders who must bear the inconsistency of returns. This variability is greater as the gearing ratio rises. To compensate for a higher level of financial risk shareholders require a higher yield on their investment, thereby producing a lower capitalised value of earnings available for distribution. At extremely high levels of gearing the situation may be further aggravated by debt holders. They too may require increased returns commensurate with risk as their investment no longer represents a prior claim on either the assets or income and debt takes on the characteristics of equity.

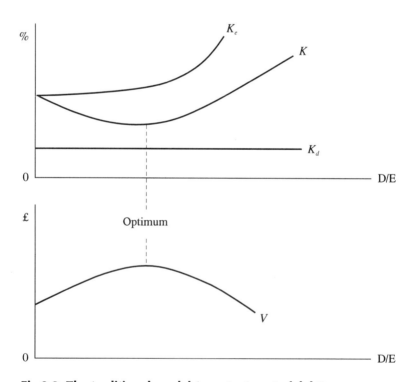

Fig 9.3 The traditional model (constant cost of debt)

The implications of this rising cost of debt is the subject of conflicting theories of capital structure which will be examined later. As a prerequisite to their comprehension, however, an appreciation of what shareholders consider optimal and to whom the firm is ultimately responsible is crucial.

5 CAPITAL GEARING AND SHAREHOLDERS' WELFARE

Suppose an all-equity firm is financed by 500,000 £1 shares (nominal). Earnings before tax are £88,000. The corporate tax rate is 25 per cent and the current P/E ratio is 16. The company wishes to raise £600,000 in order to finance new investment, either through an equity issue, or the sale of 6 per cent irredeemable debentures.

Of prime concern to management must be the conditions under which either would be more beneficial to the shareholders, irrespective of the dividend payout ratio. Accordingly, the data might be reformulated as follows:

Current position

Earnings before tax	£88,000	Given
Earnings after tax	£66,000	75% of the above
P/E ratio	16	Post-tax
Earnings yield	6.25%	Post-tax (i.e. the reciprocal of the P/E ratio)
Market value of equity	£1,056,000	Capitalisation of post-tax earnings
Current price per share	£2.11	Market value/Number of shares

Future positions

Equity issue

Market value of equity	£1,656,000	Existing equity plus new issues

Debenture issue

Market value of equity	£1,056,000	Existing equity
Market value of debt	£600,000	Debenture issue
Debenture interest	£36,000	6% of £600,000

Two questions now arise. First, if the shareholders' current yield of 6.25 per cent is to be maintained does an issue of equity or debt produce any disparity between the higher levels of future total earnings (EBIT) which will be required to satisfy the revised claims on income? If not, shareholders would presumably be indifferent to the firm's financing policy.

Second, if future profits vary as a result of business risk, would this change the shareholders' perception of the two alternatives? If so, the current market price of equity (£2.11) would no longer prevail and total market value of £1,656,000 would change.

Answers to both of these questions can be approached in a variety of ways.

(a) Arithmetic analysis

Table 9.2 compares the relationship between the requisite level of EBIT required to sustain different earnings yields, depending upon whether the firm chooses to issue debt or equity. For example, if the former option was chosen and the equity yield was 1 per cent, the shareholder would receive £10,560 (1 per cent of £1,056,000). Grossed up to allow for tax at 25 per cent, pre-tax profits would be £14,080 so that with interest of £36,000 the EBIT figure equals £50,080. This can be compared with the same yield following an equity issue (1 per cent of £1,656,000) grossed up to produce an equivalent pre-tax figure of £22,080.

What the table reveals is that if the earnings yield is to be maintained at 6.25 per cent, shareholders would not be indifferent between the two financing options. If yields are to be maintained at 5 per cent or above, a debenture issue is advantageous, since a lower level of EBIT will sustain them. Below 5 per cent and an equity issue is favoured.

(b) Graphical analysis

If the two sets of data contained in Table 9.2 are plotted on a graph, the relationship between EBIT and earnings yield proves to be linear. For an all-equity firm, a shareholder's return of zero corresponds to an EBIT figure of zero and passes through the origin (see Figure 9.4). For a geared company, the EBIT figure which equates to a zero earnings yield intersects the horizontal axis at the value of the interest payable; £36,000 for a 6 per cent debenture issue.

Table 9.2 Capital gearing and the relationship between EBIT and earnings

Shareholder return (%) Earnings yield	Debenture issue (£000s) 6%				Equity issue (£000s)	
	EAT	EBIT	interest	EBIT	EAT	EBIT
0	–	–	36.00	36.00	–	–
1.00	10.56	14.08	36.00	50.08	16.56	22.08
2.00	21.12	28.16	36.00	64.16	33.12	44.16
3.00	31.68	42.24	36.00	78.24	49.68	66.24
4.00	42.24	56.32	36.00	92.32	66.24	88.32
5.00	52.80	70.40	36.00	106.40	82.80	110.04
6.00	63.36	84.48	36.00	120.48	99.36	132.48
6.25	66.00	88.00	36.00	124.00	103.50	138.00

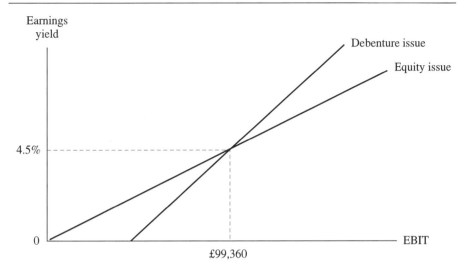

Fig 9.4 Capital gearing and the relationship between EBIT and earnings yield

Armed with this information, any yield in excess of zero (say 4 per cent) can then be chosen to plot infinite straight lines for any equity issue and debenture issue, respectively.

Their intersection represents a point of shareholder indifference between the two issues. Using the example, an equivalent earnings yield of 4.5 per cent corresponds to an equivalent EBIT of £99,360. To the left of this point, shareholders would prefer an equity issue because it provides a better return at a lower profit. To the right, a debt issue is superior.

Explained simply, leverage, which here means the introduction of 6 per cent debentures into the capital structure, increases shareholders' sensitivity to changes in EBIT. In other words, the financial risk associated with equity investment is enhanced.

As a general rule, if economic conditions deteriorate, ordinary shares represent a more speculative investment in a leveraged company. This situation is exacerbated if overall earnings fluctuate (i.e. business risk increases), since there is still a contractual obligation on the part of the company to pay periodic interest on debt, which itself may have risen as the firm geared up.

(c) Algebraic analysis

On closer scrutiny, Table 9.2 and Figure 9.4 suggest equations of a line for the debenture issue and the equity issue. Let:

EBIT	$= E_1$	for a debenture issue
	$= E_2$	for an equity issue
Earnings yield	$= K_{e_1}$	for a debenture issue
	$= K_{e_2}$	for an equity issue
Market value	$= V_1$	for a debenture issue
of equity	$= V_2$	for an equity issue
Debenture interest $= I$		
Tax rate	$= t$	

Method 1

The solution for any level of EBIT corresponding to any shareholders post-tax return can now be written as follows for a debenture issue and equity issue respectively:

(11) $E_1 = K_{e_1} V_1/(1 - t) + I$

(12) $E_2 = K_{e_2} V_2/(1 - t)$

Thus:

$$E_1 = K_{e_1} \frac{\pounds 1,056,000}{0.75} + \pounds 36,000$$

$$E_2 = K_{e_2} \frac{\pounds 1,656,000}{0.75}$$

Since $E_1 = E_2 = E$ and $K_{e_1} = K_{e_2} = K_e$ at the point of shareholders' indifference, subtracting the two equations produces:

$$\pounds 36,000 = K_e \frac{\pounds 600,000}{0.75}$$

so that:

$$K_e = \frac{\pounds 36,000 \times 0.75}{\pounds 600,000}$$

and

$$K_{e_1} = K_{e_2} = 4.5\%$$

Substituting K_e into Equation (11) and Equation (12) now reveals that:

$$E_1 = E_2 = \pounds 99,360$$

Method 2
From Method 1 it follows that:

(13) $K_{e_1} = \dfrac{(E_1 - I)(1 - t)}{V_1}$

(14) $K_{e_2} = \dfrac{E_2(1 - t)}{V_2}$

And at the point of indifference:

(15) $K_e = \dfrac{(E - I)(1 - t)}{V_1} = \dfrac{E(1 - t)}{V_2}$

such that:

$$K_e = \frac{E - £36,000(0.75)}{£1,056,000} = \frac{E \times 0.75}{£1,656,000}$$

Hence:

$E_1 = E_2 = £99,360$

and

$K_{e_1} = K_{e_2} = 4.5\%$

Finally, it is worth noting that the incorporation of the tax term $(1 - t)$ into the preceding equations does not alter the level of earnings at which shareholders are indifferent between an issue of debt and an issue of equity. Ignoring tax, Equation (15) reduces to:

(16) $K_e = (E - I)/V_1 = E/V_2$

such that:

$K_e = (E - £36,000)/£1,056,000 = E/£1,656,000$

and solving for E:

$E = E_1 = E_2 = £99,360$

However, the reader may wish to confirm that if Equation (15) is used rather than Equation (14) the common equivalent earnings figure (E) produces an equity capitalisation rate of 6 per cent and not 4.5 per cent. In other words, K_e now represents an earnings yield gross of tax at 25 per cent.

6 CAPITAL GEARING : THE NET OPERATING INCOME MODEL

The preceding sequence of analyses demonstrates why investors should be attracted to highly geared ordinary shares when economic conditions are good or improving and business profits rise. Conversely, it explains why they switch to lower geared equities when conditions deteriorate. Both strategies represent a rational trade-off between financial risk and financial return. As a general rule, the higher the gearing and more uncertain a firm's profits before interest (net operating income) the greater the fluctuation in dividends plus reserves and, therefore, share price. Because of the interdependency of financial returns, a larger proportion of business risk is being transferred from debt to equity. This situation is aggravated further if debenture holders require higher interest rates as the firm gears up.

For the company it will also be recalled that the determination of a minimum WACC which maximises total value would appear to be a function of an optimum capital structure which minimises the variance of returns from its investments (business risk) to both the holders of debt and equity. The control of financial risk, rather than business risk, relates to factors which are more susceptible to managerial manipulation, such as the investment-related financing decision to issue debt, equity or to retain earnings Thus, management would be well advised to finance its operations so that the owners (to whom they are ultimately responsible) receive the highest return in the form of either dividends or a capital appreciation of ordinary shares for a given level of profitability and business risk.

Unfortunately, as long ago as 1952, Durand demonstrated that if a company requires unequivocal guidance on such matters, there could be three hypotheses, with respect to the impact of gearing upon share price, even in a taxless world where the cost of debt is constant:

1 The *net income* model, explained earlier, where the equity capitalisation rate is constant irrespective of the debt/equity ratio because share price increases linearly with earnings per share as the firm gears up.

2 The *traditional* model (also explained) where the equity capitalisation rate is initially constant and then rises because share price first conforms to the net income model but reaches an optimum and ultimately declines as the firm becomes too heavily indebted (a more plausible hypothesis favoured by Durand).

3 The *net operating income* (NOI) model (a new proposition) where the equity capitalisation rate begins to rise linearly as soon as the firm introduces debt into its capital structure and continues to do so, due to increased financial risk. Applied to increasing EPS this leaves their capitalised value (share price) unchanged as the firm borrows more.

Table 9.3 compares the NOI hypothesis to the net income and traditional approaches using assumed values for EPS at different levels of gearing and an unlevered equity capitalisation rate of 10 per cent. What the figures confirm

Table 9.3 Capital gearing hypotheses and the behaviour of equity

	All-equity Company 1	Leverage Company 2 (low geared)	Leverage Company 3 (high geared)
EPS	£0.10	£0.15	£0.20
The net income model			
Price (rising)	£1.00	£1.50	£2.00
Yield (constant)	10.0%	10.0%	10.0%
The traditional model			
Price (optimum)	£1.00	£1.50	£1.20
Yield (rising)	10.0%	15.0%	16.7%
The net operating income model			
Price (constant)	£1.00	£1.00	£1.00
Yield (rising)	10.0%	15.0%	20.0%

is that the behaviour of equity yields and prices in response to shareholder preference, aversion and indifference to leverage must be an important determinant of a company's choice of capital structure and hence WACC and value.

As previously noted, if the equity capitalisation rate remains constant firms would adopt a position of extreme leverage, provided debt is available at a lower cost. Through borrowing more, its WACC declines and market value increases. However, this is an absurd proposition, since it assumes that debt-holders would bear all the firm's business risk at a lower return than the original shareholders in an all-equity firm. If the equity capitalisation rate eventually rises, as Durand and the traditionalists believe, WACC first declines and then rises. Its minimum position reflects an optimal capital structure, which maximises corporate value. It has also been shown that if interest rates were to rise as debt-holders assume some of the firm's business risk, this conclusion would still hold. So what are the financial implications if the behaviour of share price is entirely neutral and the cost of equity rises with leverage, as the NOI model prescribes?

The key can be found in Durand's choice of accounting terminology. The *net income* model is so termed because it focuses upon the *equity* capitalisation of profits *after* interest at the same rate of return, irrespective of leverage. The *NOI* model values *debt and equity* by capitalising operating income, i.e. earnings *before* interest at a uniform WACC. The WACC is unaffected by the level of gearing because the increase in shareholders' return as more debt is assumed exactly offsets cheaper financing. Consequently, corporate value is no longer a function of capital structure and financing decisions become an irrelevance as Figure 9.5 reveals.

To illustrate this startling conclusion, consider two companies in a taxless world with an identical NOI of £100,000 of equivalent business risk. Only one firm is geared with debentures worth £200,000. The unlevered cost of equity is 10 per cent and the cost of debt is a constant 5 per cent.

Using the following notation Equations (17) and (18) define the weighted average cost for both companies:

Total market value (ungeared) = V_U
Total market value (geared)　　= V_G
Cost of equity　　　　　　　= K_e, K_{e_G}
Cost of debt (interest rate)　　= K_d
Market value of equity　　　　= V_E, V_{EG}

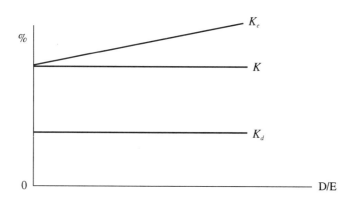

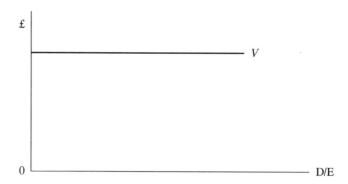

Fig 9.5　The NOI model (constant cost of debt)

Market value of debt	$= V_D$
Net operating income	$= I$
Interest	$= K_d V_D$
Net income	$= I - K_d V_D$

(17)   WACC (ungeared) $= K_U = K_e$

(18)   WACC (geared) $= K_G = V_{EG}/V_G(K_{e_G}) + V_D/V_G(K_d)$

Because the net income model assumes that the equity capitalisation rate is constant irrespective of the gearing ratio ($K_e = K_{e_G}$), the proposition that the geared firm will exhibit a higher value can be proven by capitalising investor returns at the appropriate rate. This reveals:

(19) $V_U = V_E = \dfrac{£100,000}{0.1} = £1 \text{ million} < V_G$

since:

(20) $V_G = V_{EG} + V_D = \dfrac{£90,000}{0.1} + \dfrac{£10,000}{0.05} = £1.1 \text{ million}$

The corresponding WACC's are:

(17) $K_U = K_e = 10\% \text{ (given)} > K_G$

since:

(18) $K_G = 0.9/1.1(10\%) + 0.2/1.1(5\%) = 9.09\%$

Thus, WACC and overall value are a function of the debt/equity ratio. With cheaper financing, the former declines and the latter rises.

In contrast, the NOI model assumes that because K_e increases with gearing there is no optimal capital structure. Both WACC and value are independent of the debt/equity ratio. Using the example:

(21) $V_U = V_E = £1 \text{ million (from above)} = V_G$

Since $V_G = £1$ million and $V_D = £200,000$ it follows that:

$V_{EG} = £800,000$

Because shareholders in the geared firm are entitled to net income of £90,000 the equity capitalisation rate conforms to the NOI hypothesis. It rises as follows:

$K_{e_G} = \dfrac{£90,000}{£800,000} = 11.25\% > K_e = 10\%$

Turning to the WACC calculations, it can now be shown that irrespective of gearing the two figures are identical:

(17) $K_U = 10\%$ (given) $= K_G$

since:

(18) $K_G = 0.8\ (11.25\%) + 0.2\ (5\%) = 10\%$

Using the example, Table 9.4 provides a summary of the various claims on earnings, market values and capital costs under regimes of net income and NOI in a taxless world, where the cost of debt is constant.

Table 9.4   Theories of capital structure in a taxless world (constant cost of debt) (£000s)

	The Net Income Model		The NOI Model	
	Company 1 (ungeared)	Company 2 (geared)	Company 1 (ungeared)	Company 2 (geared)
Income:				
NOI	100	100	100	100
Interest	–	10	–	10
Net income	100	90	100	90
Value:				
Market value	1,000	1,100	1,000	1,000
Value of debt	–	200	–	200
Value of equity	1,000	900	1,000	800
Capital costs:				
WACC	10%	9.09%	10%	10%
K_e	10%	10%	10%	11.25%
K_d	–	5%	–	5%
Conclusions:	Value and WACC are dependent on capital structure		Value and WACC are independent of capital structure	

7 SUMMARY AND CONCLUSIONS

This chapter began by analysing the effects of financial risk, which arises from introducing debt into a firm's capital structure, upon shareholders' welfare. For a given level of business risk, which reflects the variability of returns from an asset investment, it seemed reasonable to assume that, if companies can borrow at an interest rate lower than their return on investment, increasing the debt/equity ratio may be expected to increase earnings per share (EPS) and thus their capitalised value, i.e. share price. This suggested that financial policy decisions matter and firms should aspire to an optimum level of gearing which minimises their weighted average cost of capital (WACC) and maximises total corporate value.

However, Durand (1952) has shown that there are in fact three hypotheses with respect to the impact of gearing upon share price, WACC and corporate value:

(*i*) The *net income* model where the shareholders' capitalisation rate remains unchanged irrespective of the debt/equity ratio, with the result that price will increase proportionately with EPS. As a consequence, WACC declines and corporate value rises with leverage, although few would support this.

(*ii*) The *traditional* view where the equity capitalisation rate is initially constant and then rises, so that share price first rises and then after reaching a maximum falls with increased gearing. Thus, WACC can be minimised and corporate value maximised. Durand, along with many contemporary financial analysts, believes this to be true.

(*iii*) The *net operating income model* where the capitalisation rate may rise due to increased gearing, so as to leave share price, WACC and corporate value all unchanged.

The NOI model therefore turns the conventional wisdom of the net income and traditional views of optimal of capital structure on its head. Because ordinary share prices are unaffected by gearing, financial managers who agonise over whether to issue debt or equity in the presence of uniform business risk are actually wasting their time. Specifically, under certain assumptions, including a taxless world, and a constant cost of debt, the NOI model states that:

- Capital structure is irrelevant as long as the investment decisions of the firm are known.
- Value is independent of capital structure. The firm's assets are not affected by the division of an income stream between debt and equity claims.
- WACC is independent of capital structure. The expected return on assets is not affected by borrowing.
- The argument that EPS increases with leverage does not affect the value of the firm. EPS may rise, but share price does not.
- The expected returns on equity for a geared firm increases proportionately to the increase in the debt/equity ratio.

If all this seems vaguely familiar to the reader it is because the NOI model underpins the Miller–Modigliani 1961 dividend irrelevancy hypothesis explained in Chapter 7. Based upon the law of one price, it will be recalled that this states that identical assets (such as companies or shares) should cost the same irrespective of how their earnings are packaged for distribution. Financial risk may transfer from one investor clientele to another, but overall business risk is unaffected. So, just as the retention versus dividend decision proves to be irrelevant to the equity capitalisation rate and price of an ordinary share, so too, they argue, is the division of the total return between equity holders and other providers of capital when determining either WACC as a cut-off rate for investment or overall corporate value.

The MM capital structure hypothesis (which actually predates their dividend irrelevancy model by three years) and the debate it subsequently inspired are the subject of Chapter 10. As a precursor, however, consider an all-equity company in a tax-free world financed by 100,000 £1 shares (nominal). Total earnings (NOI) are £100,000 and the market price per share is £10.00. Hence:

Earnings (NOI)		E_1	= £100,000
Equity:			
	Market value	V_{E1}	= £1,000,000
	Capitalisation rate	$K_{e_1} = E_1/V_{E1}$	= 10%
	Corporate value	$V_U = V_{E1}$	= £1,000,000

Now consider an identical firm in terms of business risk with the same level of earnings, which differs only in the manner by which it finances its operations. Assume that 50 per cent of the market value of capital is represented by debentures yielding 5 per cent. According to MM (1958 and 1961) because identical assets cannot sell at different prices in the same market, i.e. total corporate value and the price per share remain the same, it follows that:

Earnings (NOI)		E_2	= £100,000
Debentures:			
	Market value	V_D	= £500,000
	Interest (%)	$K_d = I/V_D$	= 5%
	Interest (£)	$K_d V_D$	= £25,000
Equity:			
	Market value	V_{E2}	= £500,000
	Capitalisation rate	$K_{e_2} = \dfrac{E_2 - K_d V_d}{V_{E2}}$	$= \dfrac{£75,000}{£500,000} = 15\%$
	Corporate value	$V_G = V_{E2} + V_D$	= £1,000,000

The WACC for the all-equity firm can now be written in a manner equivalent to Equations (17) and (18):

$$(22) \qquad K_U = \frac{E_1}{V_{E1}} \cdot \frac{V_{E1}}{V_U} = 10\%$$

whilst for the gearing company:

$$(23) \qquad K_G = \left(\frac{E_2 - K_d V_D}{V_{E2}} \cdot \frac{V_{E2}}{V_G}\right) + \left(\frac{K_d V_D}{V_D} \cdot \frac{V_D}{V_G}\right)$$

or alternatively:

$$(24) \qquad K_G = \left(K_{e_2} \cdot \frac{V_{E2}}{V_G}\right) + \left(K_d \cdot \frac{V_D}{V_G}\right)$$

so that:

$$K_G = (15\% \times 0.5) + (5\% \times 0.5) = 10\%$$

Thus, irrespective of gearing, the weighted average cost of capital for the two companies is identical. It is also worth noting, *inter alia*, that in the presence of uniform share price, the earnings yield (K_e) is 10 per cent for the all-equity firm and 15 per cent for the geared company. As a corollary, the P/E ratio falls from 10 to 6.66. Notice too that the EPS rises from £1.0 to £1.50 with leverage.

This all follows logically from Durand's third proposition that the equity capitalisation rate rises with gearing. A precise mathematical relationship between the two is also incorporated in the 1958 *arbitrage* proof of MM presented in Chapter 10 which explains why two assets (shares and corporate value in the example) cannot exhibit different prices. As a direct consequence, the WACC or cut-off rate for investment for any firm in a particular class of business risk equals the equity capitalisation rate for an all-equity firm in that class. In general terms:

$$(25) \qquad V_{E_U} = V_U = V_G$$

and

$$(26) \qquad K_{e_U} = K_U = K_G$$

Thus, given the MM hypothesis that the market value of a share is independent of a company's distribution policy, it should be impossible to conclude that a company's overall cost of capital or corporate value is a function of gearing.

References

(1) Durand, D., 'Cost of debt and equity funds for business: trends and problems of measurement', *Conference on Research on Business Finance*, New York: National Bureau of Economic Research, 1952.

(2) Miller, M.H., and Modigliani, F., 'Dividend policy, growth and the valuation of shares', *The Journal of Business of the University of Chicago*, Vol. XXXIV, No. 4, October 1961.

(3) Modigliani, F. and Miller, M.H., 'The cost of capital, corporation finance and the theory of investment', *American Economic Review*, Vol. XLVIII, No. 3, June 1958.

240

10

Capital structure and the law of one price

Chapter profile

No financial article has been more controversial than the one published in 1958 entitled 'The Cost of Capital, Corporation Finance and the Theory of Investment' by Franco Modigliani and Merton Miller.

As this chapter reveals, not only did it reinvent the theory of finance but it also determined the mind-set for both an academic and practical consideration of what drives capital markets, financial institutions, companies and individual investors alike under real world conditions. Not surprisingly, therefore the authors were awarded the Nobel Prize in 1985 and 1990, for this, their seminal work, as well as subsequent contributions to the debate which they fomented and which continues to this day.

1 INTRODUCTION

The influential article on debt and equity funds published by Durand in 1952 confirmed the *traditional view* of most academics and financial analysts presented in the previous chapter: that a company is confronted by a perplexing phenomenon when financing its investments in an efficient capital market.

Because investors are exposed to lower financial risk when purchasing debt, its interest rate is lower than the long-run returns to shareholders. The acquisition of debt finance is, therefore, less costly. This implies that if a firm incorporates debt into its capital structure it will lower its weighted average cost of capital (WACC) and increase its overall corporate value.

However, at some level of gearing investors will perceive the firm to be too heavily indebted and shareholders and debt-holders alike will require higher returns to compensate for increased financial risk, even if the variability of the profitability of resources (business risk) is unaffected. As a consequence, the WACC will rise and value will fall. So between the polar extremes of all-equity finance and total gearing (leverage) there must exist, or so the argument goes, an optimal debt/equity ratio which elicits a least-cost combination of financial resources that minimises the firm's WACC and maximises its total value.

In 1958, Modigliani and Miller (MM) discredited this view by developing an alternate hypothesis rejected by Durand six years previously. Their seminal article abandoned conventional wisdom (all too often based upon anecdote) in favour of what Durand termed the *net operating income (NOI) model*. Underpinned by mathematical rigour, it paved the way for subsequent economic models and burgeoning econometric tests which continue to this day.

Specifically, under certain conditions MM explained why:

- Financial assets, such as ordinary shares or companies, which are close financial substitutes must exhibit a uniform value (the rehabilitation of the economic *law of one price*).
- Corporate value and the overall cost of capital (WACC) are *independent* of the debt/equity ratio.

2 THE MODIGLIANI–MILLER COST OF CAPITAL HYPOTHESIS

By subscribing to the net operating income (NOI) model outlined by Durand, MM sought to prove (albeit under restrictive assumptions) that the total value of a firm, which comprises the net present value of an income stream, discounted at a rate appropriate to its risk class, should be unaffected by shifts in financial structure. As a corollary, any rational debt/equity ratio also induces the same weighted average cost of capital (WACC, algebraically defined as $\overline{K}$).

Their basic theorem, which is a *partial equilibrium model*, assumes that:

(**a**) Average NOI, i.e. earnings before interest and tax (EBIT), is represented by a subjective random variable and all investors agree upon the expected value of its probability distribution.

(**b**) Firms can be placed in an equivalent class of business risk so that all firms are homogeneous. The average expected NOI and its variability (business risk) are identical for all firms in a given class.

(**c**) Capital markets are perfect, where information is freely available, investors act rationally and there are no transaction costs.

(**d**) The tax system is neutral (i.e. the tax deductibility of debt is ignored) and the cost of borrowing is constant at all levels of gearing. However, these assumptions are later dropped with important consequences.

There are in fact three propositions advanced by MM, namely:

- *Proposition I*   Market value (*V*) is independent of the debt/equity ratio (D/E),

- *Proposition II*   The equity capitalisation rate (K_e) increases as D/E rises, with the corollaries:

  (a) $\overline{K}$ is unaffected by D/E

  (b) $\overline{K} = K_e$ for an unlevered firm.

- *Proposition III*   Shareholders' wealth is maximised by employing $\overline{K}$ as the cut-off rate for investment in a levered firm which equals K_e, the equity capitalisation rate, in an unlevered firm.

MM then show how:

(*i*)   Proposition I can be proved by *arbitrage*.

(*ii*)   Proposition I can be used to prove that $\overline{K}$ is unaffected by D/E. In other words, Proposition I can be used to prove Proposition II.

(*iii*)   Given (*i*) and (*ii*) above, Proposition III follows logically, since market value equals equity value $(V = V_E)$ and $\overline{K} = K_e$ in an unlevered firm.

3 PROPOSITION I: THE ARBITRAGE PROCESS

MM maintain that rational (risk-averse) investors in a perfect market will use arbitrage to prevent the existence of two firms with identical business risk and the same total income (EBIT) from selling at different prices.

Behaviourally, shareholders in an overvalued company (what the traditionalists would call highly geared) will act so as to change its total value by selling shares in that company and buying shares in an undervalued (i.e. ungeared) company. In the process shareholders will also undertake personal borrowing to invest in the geared company until their personal portfolios of investment have the same gearing ratio as the overvalued firm.

As a result of what MM termed *home-made leverage* (personal borrowing), investor income is increased at no greater risk. Eventually, through supply and demand forces, the price of shares in the overvalued company will fall, while those in the undervalued company will rise until no further financial advantage is gained from arbitrage. At this equilibrium point the cost of capital of the two companies will then be equal; so too will value.

This can be proved following even the most restrictive assumptions of a traditional view, namely the *net income* model in a tax-free world where the costs of debt and equity remain constant at all levels of gearing. Under such conditions, capital value maximises at extreme leverage. Given two firms in the same class of business risk that differ only with respect to their gearing, the following relationships would hold:

	Company 1 (ungeared)		Company 2 (geared)
Corporate value (V):	$V_1 = V_{E1}$	$<$	$V_2 = V_{E2} + V_D$ where V_D = the value of debt.
Net operating income ($\bar{I}$):	$\bar{I} = Y_1$	$=$	$\bar{I} = Y_2 + K_d V_D$ where K_d = the cost of debt
Shareholders' income (Y):	$Y_1 = \bar{I}$	$>$	$Y_2 = \bar{I} - K_d V_D$
WACC ($\bar{K}$):	$\bar{K}_1 = K_{e_1} = Y_1/V_1$	$>$	$\bar{K}_2 = \bar{I}/V_2$ $= \bar{I}/V_{E2} + V_D$
Cost of equity (K_e):	$K_{e_1} = Y_1/V_1 = \bar{I}/V_1$	$=$	$K_{e_2} = \dfrac{\bar{I} - K_d V_D}{V_{E2}}$
		$>$	$K_d = K_d V_D / V_D$

Of particular interest, however, are the following less obvious relationships, which are implicit in MM's analysis:

(1) $Y_1/V_1 > Y_2/V_2$

and as a corollary:

(2) $Y_1/Y_2 \simeq V_2/V_1$

Specifically they demonstrate that if an equity investor holds a proportional investment (A) in the geared firm, company 2, such that:

(3) $AY_2 = A(\bar{I} - K_d V_D)$

the investor can sell shares in that company for $A(V_{E2})$ and borrow at the margin if necessary to invest in the ungeared company at the same level, namely:

$A(V_{E1})$

Thus investor income becomes,

(4) $AY_1 = A(\bar{I})$

Multiplying both sides of Equation (2) by AY_2, Equation (4) may be rewritten as follows:

(5) $AY_1 \simeq V_2/V_1 . A(Y_2)$

and if, as the traditionalist advocates, $V_1 < V_2$ it now becomes clear that $AY_1 > AY_2$.

Thus, investor income may be increased by arbitrage. Undertaking personal borrowing and switching investment from the overvalued company to the ungeared firm will depress the equity value of the former while raising the price of the latter until they are in equilibrium with $V_2 = V_1$. Moreover, the proportional difference in investor income will be inversely related to the proportional difference in original corporate values. Only when, or if, as MM suggest $V_2 = V_1$ will $Y_1 = Y_2$.

Then shareholders will be indifferent to levels of gearing and the arbitrage process will achieve nothing.

4 THE TRADITIONAL AND NOI MODELS COMPARED AND CONTRASTED

The elegance of the MM proof is that if value increases as debt is introduced into a firm's capital structure (i.e. K_d lowers the overall capitalisation rate $\overline{K}$), as the traditional income model suggests, arbitrage will eventually force the two firms back into equilibrium. If however, as MM hypothesise, two firms in the same risk class are valued equally, the arbitrage process is unnecessary. Moreover, it can be seen that as the NOI for both companies is identical, when $V_1 = V_2$, the overall cost of capital for both companies is also the same, whereas before arbitrage $V_2 > V_1$, $\overline{K}_2 < \overline{K}_1$. So in equilibrium, changes in capital structure affect neither corporate values nor capital costs.

Consider a situation which extrapolates the £000 values from the previous chapter's numerical example. Using the *traditional income* model where:

Company 1 (ungeared):£   *Company 2 (geared)*:£
$V_1 = V_E = 1000$ $V_2 = V_{E2} + V_D = 900 + 200 = 1100$
$\overline{I} = 100$ $\overline{I} = Y_2 + K_d V_D = 90 + 10 = 100$
$Y_1 = 100$ $Y_2 = I_2 - K_d V_D = 100 - 10 = 90$

Assume there is only one investor who holds the proportion A equal to 100 per cent of the equity in company 2.

Using Equation (3):

$$Y_2 = A(\overline{I} - K_d V_D) = £90$$

Now assume that the investor sells all the shares $A(V_{E2})$ for £900 and personally borrows £100 at the market rate of interest for debt (K_d), which is equal to 5 per cent, in order to invest in the ungeared company in the same proportion: $A(V_{E2}) = £1000$.

Using Equation (4) investor income becomes:

$$Y_1 = A(\bar{I}) = £100$$

or by substituting Equation (3) into Equation (5):

$$Y_1 = V_2/V_1 \cdot A(\bar{I} - K_d V_D)$$

so that:

$$\frac{£1100}{£1000} \cdot £90 = £99$$

The investor's increase in income after interest on borrowing may now be measured as follows:

Y_1	=	£100
Y_2	=	90
ΔY	=	10
100 K_d(5%) =		5
Net gain		5

Note that the portfolio of investment, £900 cash and £100 debt, has the same gearing as the income I_2, i.e. £90 dividend and £10 interest. Note also that the investor could continue to borrow a further £100 at 5 per cent such that the leverage of the *home-made* portfolio (£900 and £200 debt) would be identical to the original gearing of company 2 (£900 equity and £200 debt). Yet the investor would still be in no worse a position than when proportional funds resided in company 2. Income would still be £90, calculated as follows:

Y_1	=	100
Y_2	=	90
ΔY	=	10
200 K_d(5%) =		10
Net gain		0

Consider now the impact of arbitrage using the *net operating income* model favoured by MM. Explained algebraically, the following relationships would hold for two firms in the same class of business risk that again only differ with respect to their gearing:

	Company 1 (ungeared)		Company 2 (geared)
Value	$V_1 = V_{E1}$	=	$V_2 = V_{E2} + V_D$
NOI	$\bar{I} = Y_1$	=	$\bar{I} = Y_2 + K_d V_D$
Shareholders' income	$Y_1 = \bar{I}$	>	$Y_2 = \bar{I} - K_d V_D$
Cost of capital	$\bar{K}_1 = K_{e_1} = Y_1/V_1$	=	$\bar{K}_2 = \bar{I}/V_2$
		=	$\bar{I}/V_{E2} + V_D$

Cost of equity
$$K_{e_1} = Y_1/V_1 = \bar{I}/V_1 \quad < \quad K_{e_2} = \frac{\bar{I} - K_d V_D}{V_{E2}}$$

$$> \quad K_d = K_d V_D/V_D$$

In other words, increased equity yields exactly offset cheaper debt financing, with the result that cost of capital and corporate value are unaffected by gearing (the independency propositions)

As with the traditional model, the above relationships together with the arbitrage process can be simply illustrated arithmetically. Again assume that there is only one investor who holds a 100 per cent proportion (A) of the equity in the geared firm below:

Company 1 (ungeared): £
$V_1 = V_{E1} = 1000$
$\bar{I} = 100$
$Y_1 = 100$

Company 2 (geared): £
$V_2 = V_{E2} + V_D = 800 + 200 = 1000$
$\bar{I} = Y_2 + K_d V_D = 90 + 10 = 100$
$Y_2 = \bar{I} - K_d V_D = 100 - 10 = 90$

Using Equation (3) and a proportion (A) of 100 per cent, equity investor income in company 2 may be defined as:

$$Y_2 = A(\bar{I} - K_d V_D) = £90$$

Now assume that the investor sells all the shares $A(V_{E2})$ for £800 and borrows £200 at the market rate of interest for debt K_d (5 per cent) in order to invest in the ungeared company in the same 100 per cent proportion (A).

Then using Equation (4) investor income becomes:

$$Y_1 = A(\bar{I}) = £100$$

but substituting Equation (3) into Equation (5)

$$Y_1 = V_2/V_1 \cdot A(\bar{I} - K_d V_D)$$
$$= £1000/£1000 \cdot £90$$
$$= £90$$

What has happened? The two values for Y_1 may be reconciled arithmetically as follows:

Y_1	$= 100$
Y_2	$= \underline{90}$
ΔY	$= 10$
$200\ K_d(\%)$	$= \underline{10}$
Net gain	0

In other words, investor income has not changed by shifting investment

247

from company 2 to company 1 once the interest on personal borrowing is included.

$$Y_2 = Y_1 - £200\,K_d$$
$$= £100 - £10$$
$$= £90$$

Note also that the investors home-made portfolio of new investment has the same gearing as company 2 (£800 cash plus £200 debt corresponding to £800 equity plus £200 debt).

5 PROPOSITION II

Proposition I, namely that the market value of a company is independent of its debt equity (D/E) ratio, can be used to prove the second MM proposition that WACC ($\bar{K}$) is similarly unaffected because the equity capitalisation rate (K_e) rises with leverage.

Given:

(6) $\bar{K}_1 = \bar{I}/V_1$

where $\bar{K}_1 = K_{e_1}, \bar{I} = Y_1, V_1 = V_{E1}$.

(7) $K_2 = \bar{I}/V_2$

where $\bar{I} = Y_2 + K_d V_D, V_2 = V_{E2} + V_D$.

(8) $K_{e_2} = \dfrac{\bar{I} - K_d V_D}{V_{E2}}$

and recalling Proposition I, based upon Equations (3) and (5), namely:

(9) $AY_1 = V_2/V_1 \cdot \bar{A}(I - K_d V_D)$

such that if V_2 equals V_1 then Y_1 equals Y_2, Proposition I can be rewritten so that the identical annual income of two firms $\bar{Y}$ can be derived by multiplying V_2 by K_{e_1}:

(10) $\bar{Y} = V_2 K_{e_1} = (V_{E2} + V_D)K_{e_1} = \bar{I}$

Substituting Equation (10) into Equation (8):

(11) $K_{e_2} = \dfrac{(V_{E2} + V_D)K_{e_1} - K_d V_D}{V_{E2}}$

which simplifies to:

(12) $K_{e_2} = K_{e_1} + V_D/V_{E2} \cdot (K_{e_1} - K_d)$

In other words K_{e_2} is equivalent to K_{e_1}, the appropriate capitalisation rate for an all-equity stream of the same class of business risk, plus a premium related to financial risk which is equal to the debt/equity ratio times the spread between K_e and K_d. This premium causes equity yields to rise at a constant rate as compensation for the financial risk which confronts shareholders as more debt is introduced into the firm's capital structure, thereby offsetting cheaper financing. As Figure 10.1 reveals, neither an optimal capital structure nor value exists, since the financial mix of a company (D/E) does not change $\overline{K}$.

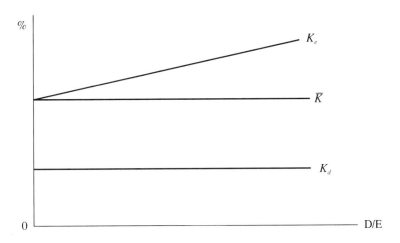

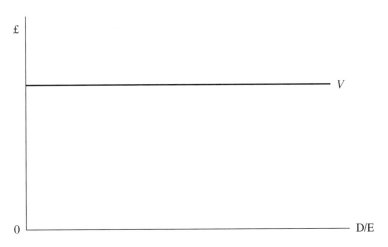

Fig 10.1 The MM model (constant cost of debt)

As an example, consider the now familiar values:

$$\bar{I} = £100, K_{e_1} = 10\%, K_d = 5\%, V_D = £200$$

where K_{e_1} is the appropriate capitalisation rate for a pure equity stream in the same class of business risk. This implies that $V = £1000$ and $V_{E2} = £800$.

Then recalling Equation (8):

$$(8) \qquad K_{e_2} = \frac{\bar{I} - K_d V_D}{V_{E2}} = \frac{100 - 10}{800}$$

or from Equation (12):

$$K_{e_2} = 0.10 + \frac{200}{800}(0.10 - 0.05)$$

$$= 11.25\%$$

The weighted average cost of capital may then be determined in a familiar manner based upon the WACC formula:

$$(13) \qquad \overline{K}_2 = \frac{V_{E2}}{V_2} K_{e_2} + \frac{V_D}{V_2} K_d$$

$$= 0.8(0.1125) + 0.2(0.05)$$

$$= 10\%$$

6 PROPOSITION III

Although MM's third proposition is generally believed to follow logically from their first two, it is worthwhile illustrating why shareholders' wealth is maximised by employing the return of a pure equity stream for any geared firm, such that $K_{e_1} = \overline{K}$. This cut-off rate for investment, rather than any other rate, including an equity capitalisation in the presence of leverage should be applied to an ungeared firm, even if NOI is not kept constant.

Consider again the leveraged company which exhibits the following values:

$$V_{E2} = £800, V_D = £200, \bar{I} = £100,$$
$$\overline{K} = K_{e_1} = 10\%, K_{e_2} = 11.25\%, K_d = 5\%$$

where V_{E2} represents 800 ordinary shares with a current market value of £1.00.

Now assume that management is considering (quite correctly) an incremental capital project which maximises wealth *via* an investment of £100 with an anticipated yield of 11 per cent. Original net operating income (NOI) rises from £100 to £111. The preferred mode of funding is equity.

Accounting logic dictates that financing the marginal investment by issuing 100 additional shares to new investors at £1.00 per share would dilute the earnings of existing shareholders (EPS), since the incremental yield of 11 per cent is 0.25 per cent below the current equity yield (11.25 per cent).

However, the third MM proposition effectively states that the cut-off rate of return for new investment for any firm in a particular class of business risk need only be equal to the WACC of an unlevered firm, which by definition corresponds to its cost of equity. Given that changes in a firm's capital structure cannot affect its cost of capital, the WACC must be constant. A constant WACC means that in the numerical example the marginal investment, irrespective of finance, need only achieve a target rate of return which equals $K_{e_1} = \overline{K}_2 = 10$ per cent (Propositions I and II).

Since income rises from £100 to £111 (denoted as I_2):

$$V_2 = \frac{I_2}{K_{e_1}} = \frac{I_2}{\overline{K}_2} = \frac{£111}{0.10} = £1110$$

What has happened? The value of debt is still £200 and there are no further fixed charges against profits. So shareholder wealth is maximised. From a capital viewpoint, equity is now valued at £910 (£1110 minus £200) and even though there are 900 shares, each would be worth £1.01. Income-wise, EPS may be diluted by 0.03 pence (from £90/£800 =11.25 pence down to £101/£900 = 11.22 pence). But this is still more than offset by the beneficial impact of debt at 5 per cent (albeit at a lower level of gearing,) which produces a capital appreciation of one pence per ordinary share.

The reader may now wish to ascertain what would occur if the incremental investment had yielded 10 per cent.

7 THE RISING COST OF DEBT IN A TAXLESS WORLD

Given the assumptions of their partial equilibrium model, the MM conclusions appear logically correct. Corporate value and the weighted average cost of capital are independent of financial structure. However, a deeper insight into their approach to capital structure is provided by an explicit consideration of the financial risk of debt and the effect this has on changing equity yields as the firm gears up.

Solomon (1963) contradicts MM's original formulation by stating that there does exist a clearly definable optimum capital structure, namely the point or range at which the marginal cost of debt (mK_d) is equal to, or greater than, a company's weighted average cost of capital $(\overline{K})$.

If investors act rationally in reasonably perfect markets, as MM assume, then Solomon argues that interest rates should increase with leverage because of greater financial risk. At the extreme, the inconsistency of returns borne by the suppliers of debt capital would be identical to that borne by equity investors, with the result that K_d will be at least equal to $\overline{K}$. Given the more cautious attitude of debt holders, however, it is also likely that this point will be reached quite rapidly and that at extreme leverage K_d will actually rise above $\overline{K}$.

As a result, the MM thesis becomes invalid, since no rational company will use debt finance exclusively when $mK_d \geqslant \overline{K}$, it being possible to finance incremental investment more cheaply by using a mixture of debt and equity similar to that in its existing capital structure. Thus, the conclusions to be drawn are very similar to those embraced by traditional theory. There may exist an optimal debt/equity ratio which minimises capital cost and maximises corporate value.

As Figure 10.2 reveals, $\overline{K}$ declines at low levels of gearing but when the introduction of further debt becomes unacceptable its marginal cost mK_d rises rapidly. When $mK_d > \overline{K}$ further injections of debt capital will bring about a rise in $\overline{K}$. As a consequence corporate value also exhibits a curvilinear relationship.

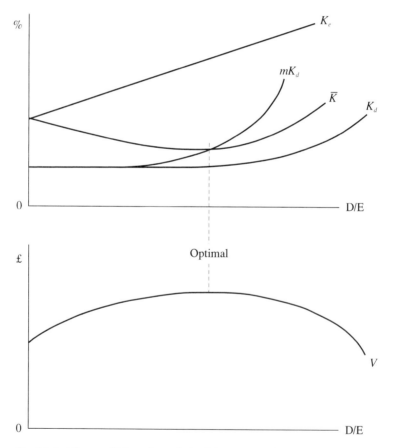

Fig 10.2 The traditional model (rising cost of debt)

Debenture issues increase value up to a point or range beyond which higher interest rates (greater financial risk) cause value to fall.

When MM considered the rising cost of debt they chose to reject this conclusion, preferring to argue that K_e must start to decline as gearing increases through the use of increments of debt which cost more. The trade-off between debt and equity yields leaves WACC and overall value unaffected by leverage, as outlined in Figure 10.3. The behavioural explanation which MM offered in support of a K_e curve that falls is that at higher levels of gearing equity investors will capitalise a less certain income stream at a lower K_e than a more certain one. They become *risk seekers*, attracted by the possibility of a relatively high level of dividend per share, in what has become a limited market for equity.

Whilst this is an interesting suggestion, suffice it to say that it represents the

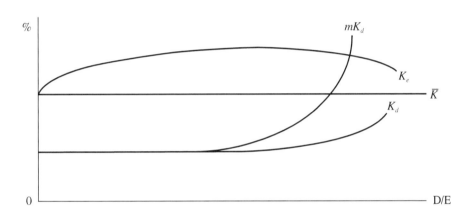

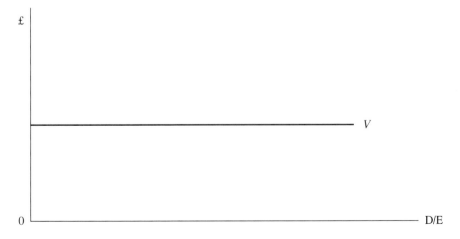

Fig 10.3 The MM model (rising cost of debt)

253

weakest aspect of their argument. For example, interest on debt has periodically exceeded equity returns in the UK and elsewhere (the reverse gap yield phenomenon). However, this appears to have been influenced more by a combination of dividend restraint and fiscal policy, including the tax deductibility of debt, rather than the gearing effect alone (see Hill 1985). Even in the perfect and tax-free world initially envisaged by MM where all investors behave rationally (i.e. are risk-averse) the suggestion that a company's cost of capital and hence value is independent of its financial structure, particularly at high levels of gearing, must therefore be treated with scepticism.

8 THE EFFECT OF CORPORATE TAXATION

Although MM initially ignored all taxes in their original paper followed by a reply (1958) they noted that the American system of corporate taxation (like that of the UK and others) favours the issue of debt rather than equity. A company can deduct interest from profit before paying tax but not dividend payments or the capital appreciation of shares. In their 1963 article they quantified this *tax shield*, conceding that if the tax deductibility of debt is taken into account $\overline{K}$ will decline with increased gearing, unlike their original model. This fall in the cost of capital increases the capitalisation ratio $1/\overline{K}$, thereby increasing corporate value.

Consider two firms identical in terms of size, riskiness and expected annual pre-tax cash flow, except that one firm is geared. The post-tax cashflow Y_t of each company where t is the annual rate of corporation tax may be represented as follows:

Company 1 (ungeared)   *Company 2 (geared)*

$\overline{I}(1-t)$

$(\overline{I} - K_d V_D)(1-t) + K_d V_D$

$= \overline{I}(1-t) - K_d V_D(1-t) + K_d V_D$

$= \overline{I}(1-t) + K_d V_D t$

The geared firm has a higher post-tax annual cashflow since it pays less tax, the saving being equal to its annual debt charge multiplied by the tax rate, $K_d V_D t$.

The value of the all-equity company is given by:

$$(14) \qquad V_1 = \frac{Y_t}{K_{e_{1t}}} = \frac{I(1-t)}{\overline{K}_t}$$

The total value of the geared company is given by:

$$(15) \qquad V_2 = \frac{\overline{I}(1-t) + K_d V_D t}{\overline{K}_{2t}}$$

where the subscript t denotes the after-tax yield.

The value of the geared company, however, may be rewritten in terms of two separable elements, namely the value of the ungeared company, plus the discounted tax saving. Since the tax relief on interest payments has the same lower level of risk as the debt itself this should be capitalised using the constant cost of debt. Thus, Equation (15) can be expressed as:

$$(16) \qquad V_2 = \frac{\bar{I}(1-t)}{K_{e_{1t}}} + \frac{K_d V_D t}{K_d} = \frac{\bar{I}(1-t)}{K_{1t}} + V_D t$$

which simplifies to:

$$(17) \qquad V_2 = V_1 + V_D t$$

Thus, the total value of a geared firm equals the value of an ungeared firm plus a premium equivalent to the debt in the former's capital structure multiplied by the tax rate. It therefore follows that a firm can maximise its market value by maximising the amount of debt in its capital structure.

Turning to cost of capital, the post-tax average cost may be represented as follows:

Company 1 (ungeared)   *Company 2 (geared)*

$$\bar{K}_{1t} = \frac{\bar{I}(1-t)}{V_1} \qquad\qquad \bar{K}_{2t} = \frac{\bar{I} - K_d V_D(1-t) + K_d V_D}{V_2}$$

$$= K_{e_{1t}} = \frac{Y_t}{V_{E1}}$$

For the geared firm the average cost of capital simplifies to:

$$(18) \qquad \bar{K}_{2t} = \frac{\bar{I}(1-t) + K_d V_D t}{V_2}$$

which can be expressed in the form:

$$(19) \qquad \bar{K}_{2t} = K_{e_{1t}} - t\,(K_{e_{1t}} - K_d)\,V_D/V_2$$

where $K_{e_{1t}}$ is the after-tax capitalisation rate for an all-equity firm. Thus, when interest is tax deductible the average cost of capital is not independent of a firm's capital structure. It now becomes a function of the tax rate and the level of gearing.

The derivation of Equation (19) may be explained as follows. It will be recalled that the value of a geared firm is given by:

$$(16) \qquad V_2 = \frac{\bar{I}(1-t)}{K_{e_{1t}}} + \frac{K_d V_D t}{K_d}$$

Rearranging terms:

$$K_{e_{1t}}\left(V_2 - \frac{K_d V_D t}{K_d}\right) = \bar{I}(1 - t)$$

so that:

(20) $$K_{e_{1t}}\left(1 - t\frac{V_D}{V_2}\right) = \frac{\bar{I}(1 - t)}{V_2}$$

Equation (20) is important since the right-hand term represents an after-tax return which is lower than that for a pure equity stream in the same risk class. This follows logically from the inequality:

$$\frac{\bar{I}(1 - t)}{V_1} > \frac{\bar{I}(1 - t)}{V_2}$$

because it has already been established that the value of the levered firm exceeds that of the unlevered firm by the capitalised value of the tax relief on debenture interest:

(17) $$V_2 = V_1 + V_D t$$

As the left-hand term of Equation (20) also reveals, the decline in the cost of capital is a function of the tax rate (t) and the *target* level of borrowing V_D/V_2. Thus, it would appear that a firm can lower its cost of capital with increased gearing.

Substituting the left-hand term of Equation (20) into Equation (18) produces Equation (19):

$$\overline{K}_{2t} = K_{e_{1t}}\left(1 - t\frac{V_D}{V_2}\right) + \frac{K_d V_D t}{V_2}$$

$$= K_{e_{1t}} - (K_{e_{1t}} t)\frac{V_D}{V_2} + K_d t\frac{V_D}{V_2}$$

(19) $$= K_{e_{1t}} - t(K_{e_{1t}} - K_d) V_D/V_2$$

Instead of the cost of capital being constant (according to MM's original formulation), it now declines as a function of the tax rate and gearing.

Turning to the cost of equity capital, it will be recalled that in a tax-free world Proposition II states that the expected equity yield for a geared firm K_{e_2} is equal to the appropriate capitalisation rate K_{e_1} for an all-equity stream in the same class of business risk, plus a premium, related to financial risk, equal to the debt/equity ratio, times the spread between K_{e_1} and K_d:

(12) $$K_{e_2} = K_{e_1} + V_D/V_{E2} \cdot (K_{e_1} - K_d)$$

Table 10.1 Company values and capital costs in an MM world of corporate taxation (constant cost of debt)

	Company 1 (ungeared) £	Company 2 (geared) £	Company 3 (geared) £
INCOME			
Net operating income: $\bar{I}$	100	100	100
Interest: $K_d V_D$	–	10	20
$I - K_d V_D$	$\overline{100}$	$\overline{90}$	$\overline{80}$
Taxation	50	45	40
Net income: $I - K_d V_D (1 - t)$	$\overline{50}$	$\overline{45}$	$\overline{40}$

VALUE

Market value: $V = \dfrac{\bar{I}(1 - t)}{K_{e_{1t}}} + V_D t$

V	$V_1 = 50/0.10$ $= 500$	$V_2 = 500 + 200(0.5)$ $= 600$	$V_3 = 500 + 400(0.5)$ $= 700$
Debt: V_D	–	200	400
Equity: $V_E = V - V_D$	500	400	300

CAPITAL COSTS

Average cost: $K_t = \bar{K}_{e_{1t}} - t(K_{e_{1t}} - K_d) V_D/V$

$\bar{K}_{1t}$	$\bar{K}_{2t} = 0.10 - 0.5(0.05)\dfrac{200}{600}$	$\bar{K}_{3t} = 0.10 - 0.5(0.05)\dfrac{400}{700}$
$= 10\%$	$= 9.16\%$	$= 8.57\%$

Cost of debt: K_d

–	5.0%	5.0%

Cost of equity: $K_{e_t} = K_{e_{1t}} + (1 - t)(K_{e_{1t}} - K_d)V_D/V_E$

$K_{e_{1t}}$	$K_{e_{2t}} = 0.10 + 0.5(0.05)\dfrac{200}{400}$	$K_{e_{3t}} = 0.10 + 0.5(0.05)\dfrac{400}{300}$
$= 10\%$	$= 11.25\%$	$= 13.33\%$

With the introduction of tax deductibility, however, the after-tax yield on equity capital changes and becomes:

$$(21) \qquad K_{e_{2t}} = K_{e_{1t}} + (1 - t)(K_{e_{1t}} - K_d)V_D/V_{E2}$$

The implications of this change are important since the cost of equity now increases with increased gearing by a lower amount than the difference between the overall cost of a pure equity stream and the cost of debt. The reduction in the increase is by a factor of $(1 - t)$. As gearing rises the tax-adjusted component of $K_{e_{2t}}$ becomes an increasingly large and important element of Equation (21). Hence, $K_{e_{2t}}$ does not rise as rapidly as it otherwise would do in the absence of tax, which confirms that a firm can lower its average cost of capital and increase its value continually with increased gearing. As a consequence, the firm should strive for the maximum level of gearing in order to achieve an optimal capital structure.

To illustrate the impact of corporate tax shields on MM's basic propositions consider three companies in the same risk class with identical annual earnings $\bar{I} = £100$ before interest and tax. Let $K_{e_{1t}} = \bar{K}_{1t} = 10\%$, $K_d = 5\%$ and the rate of tax $t = 50\%$. The values of debt are zero, £200 and £400 respectively. Table 10.1 computes the various capital costs and market values for each firm assuming that the cost of debt is constant. Figure 10.4 then sketches the implications, including the capitalised value of tax relief on debenture interest.

9 THE RISING COST OF DEBT AND BANKRUPTCY IN A TAXED WORLD

The preceding analysis leads one to ask why firms do not finance themselves entirely by debt once the realities of the corporate tax system are accepted.

An obvious answer is that, as with their basic propositions, the MM conclusions which incorporate the tax-deductibility of interest still suffer from the assumption that the cost of debt remains constant at all levels of gearing. Since debt would ultimately fail to represent a prior claim on the profits or assets of a company at high levels of gearing, it is illogical that the suppliers of debt capital would be satisfied with a lower yield than that on a pure equity stream of the same degree of business risk. If debt does take on the characteristics of equity the point of controversy is the impact which a rising value for K_d has on $\bar{K}_t$.

The previous analysis in a world of corporate taxation illustrated how increased gearing tends to pull down $\bar{K}_t$ because of the tax deductibility of debt. If investors behave rationally, however, as MM hypothesise, $\bar{K}_t$ should equal a pure equity capitalisation rate at extreme leverage. If $\bar{K}_t$ is to fall below the appropriate all-equity K_{e_t} one must therefore assume that it will be a U-shaped function since it must return to this level at full gearing. Once this is accepted,

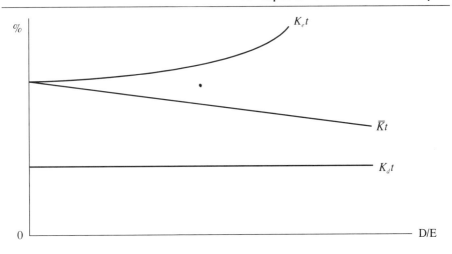

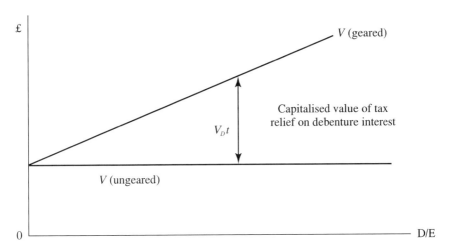

Fig 10.4 The MM model in a taxed world (constant cost of debt)

optimal capital structures with minimal capital costs also enter into MM's tax system and corporate values will be maximised. The precise shape of $\overline{K}_t$ will depend, of course, upon the rate of increase of K_d as gearing rises, any constraints upon this rise, as well as the rate of corporation tax. $\overline{K}_t$ may also vary from company to company or temporally for each one. However, the important point is that far from enhancing corporate value by increased gearing, as MM predict, optimal investment decisions may well require optimal financing decisions concerning alternative capital structures which will minimise a company's weighted average cost of capital just as the traditionalists predict.

259

For much of the 1960s, academics argued that the tax-deductibility of debt was offset by the increasing financial risk associated with payments to creditors as the firm gears up, the rising interest rate phenomenon explained by Solomon (op. cit.). Moreover, at higher leverage the benefits of debt/equity-induced tax savings must be weighed against the increasing probability of future financial distress and eventual bankruptcy, since the firm is more likely to default on capital, as well as interest repayments.

In the event of default, secured creditors may appoint *receivers* to protect their interests, either by trading under restrictive conditions or by selling the company's assets: (unsecured creditors appoint *liquidators*). Apart from the significant legal and administrative costs of receivership which may be solely attributable to geared firms, operating cashflows may be reduced, the realised value of assets may be lower than their going concern value, or that of an orderly disposition on a piecemeal basis. Since debt-holders have a prior claim on both income and assets, shareholders could well experience a traumatic diminution in their wealth.

With rising gearing, the expected costs of bankruptcy can be defined as the increasing probability of bankruptcy multiplied by the anticipated costs if financial distress occurs. Hence, the MM expression for the total market value of a levered firm, namely that of an unlevered firm of equivalent business risk, plus the discounted value of the tax relief, Equation (17), is reduced by the present value of the expected costs of financial distress:

(22) $V_G = V_U + V_D t - E(B)$

where:

V_G = market value of the geared firm
V_U = market value of the ungeared firm
$V_D t$ = capitalised value of the tax saving
$E(B)$ = present value of the expected costs of financial distress or bankruptcy.

The curvilinear effects of bankruptcy costs and the corporate tax advantages of debt upon capital structure and value are illustrated in Figure 10.5. For an all-equity firm, market value already incorporates a small adjustment to anticipated returns which reflects the possibility of financial distress. With moderate debt/equity ratios, tax benefits enhance value and the probability of financial distress remains insignificant. As more debt is used, the probability rapidly increases and the costs of bankruptcy measurably detract from the tax shield component of corporate value. Furthermore, the tax benefit is worth less to some firms than to others if they have less profit to set against interest. If a firm secures no fiscal advantage from issuing debt the tax shield will completely disappear, a phenomenon known as *tax exhaustion*. Between the polar extremes of

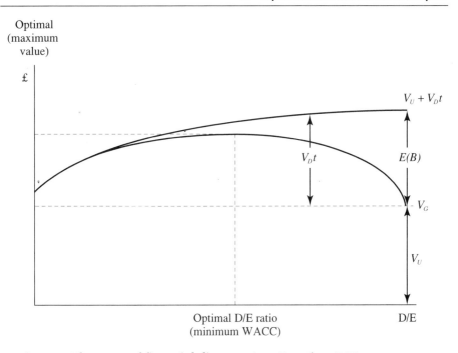

Fig 10.5 The costs of financial distress: (see Equation (22))

all-equity and complete leverage a theoretical optimum debt/equity ratio occurs. The weighted average cost of capital is minimised and overall value is maximised when the capitalised value of tax savings from incremental borrowings is exactly offset by the present value of the anticipated costs of financial distress.

10 PERSONAL TAXATION AND THE MILLER MODEL OF GENERAL EQUILIBRIUM

The preceding analysis suggests that, despite the advantages of issuing debt in MM's taxed world, once the realities of bankruptcy are accepted there is still a corporate incentive to determine a constrained optimal D/E ratio which minimises capital costs and maximises value in line with changing economic circumstances, as the traditionalists originally predicted.

However, in a 1977 article, based upon a presidential address to the American Finance Association, Miller scorned this view, pointing to the stability of debt equity/ratios over time and arguing that for most firms the threat of bankruptcy was insignificant. Citing recent empirical evidence, notably Warner (1976), he explained that the costs of financial distress represented little more than one per cent of corporate value for the previous seven years, where bankruptcy petitions were actually filed.

Miller also reminded his audience that it is not just the company which pays tax but also the shareholders and debenture holders. When the personal tax positions of marginal investors are taken into account the corporate tax advantages of issuing debt are eliminated through the sale and purchase of securities by individuals with their own agenda: a tax *clientele* effect. The value of the firm is, therefore, independent of its capital structure because a position of *general equilibrium* in the economy is achieved when the corporate tax rate equals the marginal rate of personal taxation for the marginal debt-holder.

Without delving too deeply into the peculiarities of different tax systems (i.e. classical *vis a vis* imputational), Miller's argument is best understood by considering American fiscal policies which prevailed at the time.

Individuals had to pay up to 50 per cent tax on dividends and interest income. They had to satisfy any capital gains tax liability by paying at most only 20 per cent. Thus, personal income tax could be radically reduced by opting for growth, rather than income-bearing securities. Furthermore, the bulk of capital gains could be deferred quite legally. The corporate tax rate was 46 per cent.

Miller noted that:

- The one per cent cost of bankruptcy found by Warner could hardly threaten a 46 per cent tax saving associated with the issue of debt.
- Companies could issue debt to investors who paid little or no income tax and equity to those with high marginal tax rates.
- Firms could fund their investments through equity, rather than debt, if the personal tax saving exceeded the increase in corporate tax liability.

To illustrate, consider the valuation relationship between, a geared and ungeared firm which is defined by Miller's *general equilibrium* equation:

$$(23) \qquad V_G = V_U + V_D\left(\frac{(1 - t_D) - (1 - t)(1 - t_E)}{1 - t_D}\right)$$

where:

t = corporate tax rate
t_D = debenture-holders personal tax rate
t_E = shareholders personal tax rate

which simplifies to:

$$(24) \qquad V_G = V_U + V_D t$$

if the marginal tax rates of shareholders and debt-holders are identical, i.e. $t_D = t_E$.

According to Miller, leverage secures a corporate tax advantage if the personal tax system discriminates between the two types of investors. The final term of Equation (23) is positive if:

(25) $(1 - t_D) > (1 - t)(1 - t_E)$

or

(26) $t_D < 1 - (1 - t)(1 - t_E)$

Assume that the shareholders' personal tax liability is eliminated by taking a deferred capital gain, rather than a dividend. By setting t_E equal to zero, there is a corporate gearing benefit if the personal debenture-holders' tax rate is lower than the firm's tax rate:

(27) $t_D < t$

This incentive to issue corporate debt to marginal tax-paying investors prevails until their tax rate equals that of the company in general equilibrium (46 per cent in 1977). This can be proved by substituting $t_D = t = 46$ per cent and $t_E = 0$ into Equation (23) to yield:

(28) $V_G = V_U$

Therefore, in general equilibrium the potential tax advantages of issuing debt to higher-rate tax payers evaporates, so that at the margin the company cannot alter its total value by changing its capital structure.

Miller concludes that there may well be an equilibrium level of aggregate corporate debt in the economy, just as there is with the supply of dividends (see Chapter 7). Thus, an equilibrium debt/equity ratio prescribes the whole private sector. But for individual companies no such optima (either debt or dividends) exist.

11 A RECONCILIATION OF DEBT AND TAXES

Miller not only crystallised why companies issue both debt and equity in a world of personal and corporate taxation but also why debt/equity ratios had not risen through time. Capital structure was a function of personal and corporate tax differentials which in America, hitherto, had been fairly stable. Yet anomalies remained. Just as MM's original hypotheses assumed the perfect substitution of personal leverage for corporate leverage (1958) and capital gains for dividends (1961), so too Miller's (1977) argument assumes the perfect substitution of one tax clientele for another. However, these assumptions seem implausible once one acknowledges the existence of the differential costs of transacting securities, borrowing and acquiring market information as between financial institutions, companies and individuals. Why else do tax-exempt institutions purchase equity and individual top-rate tax payers acquire debt? Moreover, can Miller's general model be applied to economies with different fiscal systems or tax differentials such as the prospective UK regime? Certainly, a position of equilibrium seemed untenable after 1986 when American and personal tax rates were unified at 28 per cent with a reduction in corporate liability to the higher rate of 34 per cent.

However, in their long-established text, Brealy and Myers (1996) still maintain that a form of equilibrium is possible, even if personal tax rates fall short of corporate tax rates, because the anticipated tax shield might be less than 34 per cent, let alone 46 per cent. Recall Miller argued that a company will issue debt up to a point when the recipients' personal tax liability matches that of the company. They suggest that if a levered firm's profits are uncertain and the interest cannot be offset against tax, *tax exhaustion* (alluded to earlier) would set in, and the expected tax benefit tail off and eventually disappear, preventing a new lower equilibrium.

The various possibilities are shown in Figure 10.6 which charts the corporate tax advantage of issuing debt (line C_D) relative to the investors fiscal benefit of purchasing equity (line I_E) and their equilibrium position (intersection E).

The first diagram illustrates Miller's 1977 general equilibrium model where the corporate tax saving (46 per cent) equals the incremental personal tax paid by investors. Beyond this point, extra personal tax continues to rise as the debt/equity ratio increases, to the highest rate (50 per cent).

After 1986, the corporate and maximum personal tax rates were reduced. But at 34 per cent and 28 per cent respectively, the benefit of issuing debt now exceeded that of purchasing equity, seemingly prohibiting an equilibrium position, as revealed in the second diagram.

Finally, Brealy and Myers' reconciliation is sketched, where the corporate tax shield falls away from 34 per cent as the firm gears up because of tax exhaustion. This re-establishes an equilibrium position (again point E as C_D and I_E cross). Note, however, that this is lower than Miller's optimum in the first diagram. Moreover, it is not independent of the firm's debt/equity ratio. According to Brealy and Myers, both WACC and corporate value are function-

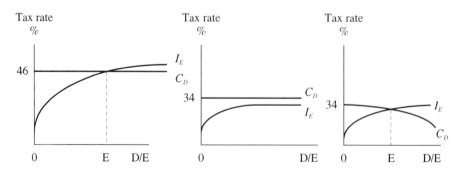

Fig 10.6 Debt and tax equilibria

ally related to managerial financial decisions determined by the anticipated corporate tax shield. Unlike Miller's proposition, the optimum debt/equity ratio may be unique to each company, rather than reflect an aggregate supply of creditor-based finance in the economy.

12 INFORMATION SIGNALLING AND AGENCY THEORY

So far, the sequence of arguments presented in this chapter has ebbed and flowed from the restricted mathematical logic of the MM partial equilibrium hypothesis in favour of models which incorporate the economic realities of a rising cost of debt, bankruptcy costs and the discriminating tax regimes of Miller in general equilibrium. Once the existence of the differential costs which also arise from transacting securities and acquiring market information is acknowledged, the case against MM would appear complete. According to their detractors, the utility of both the partial and general equilibrium models is limited by their assumptions, and serves only to support a traditional view of the dependency between capital structure, cost and value.

Further questions arise concerning uncertainty, imperfect capital markets and investor rationality within the context of behavioural theory. It will be recalled from Chapter 7 how numerous academics developed the pioneering work of Ross (1977) to explain the managerial use of dividend policies to communicate information concerning future profits to the investment community at large (dividend *signalling*). Specifically, Ross had proposed that if managers as insiders are better informed than investors, i.e. the imperfect market for information is asymmetric, they can utilise the debt/equity ratio as a financial performance indicator.

Thus, if business conditions are good or improving, the higher the proportion of debt in its capital structure, the more confident the company should be concerning its investment plans. As explained in Chapter 9, rational (i.e. risk averse) stock market participants will interpret this by seeking higher-geared firms and avoiding lower-geared firms, so that their values rise and fall respectively. Of course, during a recession the logic of this argument is reversed.

A complex phenomena, particularly if it is combined with dividend signalling to communicate overall financial policy, it also presents individual companies with a complex decision, well explained by Myers and Majluf (1984). First, the possibility of bankruptcy must be set against depressed corporate values. Second, it is not only investors who are affected by an appropriate choice of debt/equity ratios under changing economic circumstances. As employees, management too might suffer a loss of remuneration; at one extreme redundancy and at the other reduced performance-related pay and share options.

Nor should the gravity of these problems be underestimated. Whilst Miller (op. cit.) dismissed the costs of financial distress based upon Warner's findings, which were subsequently confirmed by Haugen and Senbet (1978), a more recent American study by Weiss (1990) reveals that whilst bankruptcy costs only averaged 3 per cent of the book value of total assets they comprised 20 per cent of the market value of equity in the year prior to filing a petition.

On this evidence, firms would still issue debt until the probable costs of financial distress offset the benefits of increasing corporate value. Prior to this point, capital investment can be financed at a lower cost given the tax deductibility of debt, especially during periods of inflation, thereby enhancing EPS and equity values (subject to the proviso that the owners do not lose control to creditors by the addition of non-voting capital). However, depending upon their risk-return attitude, management's preferred degree of leverage, and *inter alia* that of the shareholders to whom they are ultimately responsible, might be even more constrained and certainly lower than Miller believed. Moreover, random differences in gearing among firms, even with the same debt/equity ratio, can occur as they adjust to their new optimum associated with a revised cost-value trade-off.

A year before Miller's paper, Jensen and Meckling (1976) provided a further behavioural explanation of why managers decide to seek a target debt/equity ratio, rather than the position of extreme leverage suggested by MM in 1963. They may pursue optimising or satisficing goals which actually conflict with the normative objective of shareholder wealth maximisation, as explained in Chapters 1 and 6. This produces *agency costs,* so called because they define the contractual relationship between any supplier of external finance who may require a higher rate of return to compensate for the incremental costs of monitoring management who act on their behalf.

Jensen and Meckling argued that management as shareholders would spend money on personal fringe benefits in inverse relationship to their stake in the company. Thus, the larger the proportion of managerial equity, the more the company will be worth to outside suppliers of capital and *vice versa.* Conversely, successive debenture issues increase agency costs. As the firm gears up, suppliers of debt capital may be confronted by a situation where owner-managers seek to transfer wealth to equity holders, either by an equalisation of business risk or by the receipt of executive perks.

Highly levered companies are predisposed to undertake increasingly risky investments. If the strategy is successful owner-managers partake of the profits. If it fails, debenture-holders will share the losses. So rational creditors will require rising interest rates and impose other condition of security which raise the total cost of the incremental supply of debt. In this way, a watching brief on unscrupulous companies by investors constrains managerial ability to exploit debt equity/ratios because agency costs rise and corporate values fall.

13 PECKING ORDER THEORY

A further piece in what Myers terms the *capital structure puzzle* was introduced in his 1984 paper to explain why the most profitable firms within an industry frequently have the most conservative debt/equity ratio, rather than gear up to take advantage of Miller's potential tax trade-off.

Termed *pecking order* theory it ranks firms' preferences on the basis of their risk aversion associated with prudent financial decision making:

- Short-term funds should be applied to working capital investment.
- Retained earnings, which have no explicit cost, should be used to finance working capital, fixed asset replacement, new fixed asset formation and the redemption of debt, whenever they are available.
- Capital issues of debt or equity, if required, should only be used to fund new capital investment where the risks are commensurate with their return (value).

Thus, a firm would first choose to finance a capital project via retained earnings, then debt, then equity to avoid either issuing shares at a price they consider to be currently undervalued or rejecting an investment with a positive NPV. If managers are assumed to be better informed than investors, information signalling also comes into play. Stock market participants will interpret an equity issue as bad news because they assume it is only countenanced by management when other funds sources are exhausted or bankruptcy threatens. There is also evidence to support this (see Baskin 1989). Equity prices usually fall when a new issue is announced. Periodically, companies have successfully approached the market in order to finance working capital deficits and additional provisions for depreciation, exacerbated by inflation; even to reduce intolerable levels of short-term indebtedness which retained earnings could not meet.

However, it would be erroneous to conclude from pecking order theory that equity issues represent a minor source of funds associated only with financial distress in an asymmetric market for information. As the author concluded from an analysis of the UK capital market (Hill op. cit.), the primacy of reserves as a source of total finance and debenture issues as a source of external funding is unassailable. But within the context of the *use* to which they are put, equity issues represent a substantial source of funds for new fixed asset formation. And rightly so. For the various reasons mentioned throughout this chapter, many companies who are reluctant or unable to increase their long-term borrowings are compelled to either issue further equity capital or to cut back their investment plans.

14 SUMMARY AND CONCLUSIONS

The pivotal issue in Part 4 considered whether a company can implement financial policies concerning capital structure which minimise its weighted average cost of capital (WACC) and maximise its total corporate value. Using equity valuation models presented in Part 3 and calculations of the cost of debt and WACC in Chapters 8 and 9, the focus of attention centred upon the vexed question of whether an optimal financial structure exists independently from the capital investment decision modelled in Part 2.

The traditional view states that, if a firm trades lower-cost debt for equity, WACC will fall and value rise to a point of indebtedness where both classes of investor will require higher returns to compensate for increasing financial risk. Thereafter, WACC rises and value falls, suggesting an optimum capital structure.

In 1958, Modigliani and Miller (MM) discredited this view under the assumptions of a perfect capital market by proving that WACC and total value are independent of financial structure. Based on the economic law of one price, they used arbitrage to demonstrate that close financial substitutes, such as two firms in the same class of business risk with identical net operating income (NOI), cannot sell at different prices, thereby negating financial risk.

The MM proof galvanized the academic community. The consequences of relaxing their assumptions posed numerous questions which this chapter has also addressed:

- Does corporate taxation affect capital structure?
- Are the costs of financial distress and bankruptcy important?
- What happens if personal tax rates differ between individuals and different classes of investor?
- Are management better informed than stock market participants?
- Do managerial utility functions conflict with the interest of investors?
- Does management reveal a preference for different sources of finance?

Unfortunately, the capital structure puzzle remains more intractable than the dividend one subsequently presented by MM in their 1961 paper which was considered in Part 3. For example, Modigliani (1982) conceded that in a world of uncertainty differential rates of personal taxation *will* result in different equity portfolios, even for individuals with the same risk tolerance. It will be recalled from Chapter 7 that rational investors with high marginal tax rates prefer shares which elicit capital gains, rather than dividends, and *vice versa* (the clientele effect). All one can say about capital structure is that, in the face of the market imperfections enumerated above, some level of gearing associated with the marginal issue of fixed interest bearing securities *should* benefit the firm, particularly during a period of inflation. For recent reviews of the theory and evidence see Harris and Raviv (1991) and Myers (1993).

To complicate matters further, given the degree of sophistication which characterises to-day's global capital markets and the extent to which individual vicariously invest *via* multi-national financial institutions (who diversify their investment portfolios through borrowing to beat the market), the gearing effect on WACC and value may not conform to either the traditional or MM prediction, as Part 5 will reveal.

For the moment, however, it is worth remembering that MM's partial and general equilibrium positions on financial policy, viewed in their entirety, are at least consistent with regard to the perfect substitution of:

- personal (home-made) leverage for corporate leverage (1958)
- capital gains (home-made dividends) for corporate dividends (1961)
- personal taxation for corporate taxation (1977).

If their 1961 dividend hypothesis is accepted (for which there is considerable empirical support), namely that a value placed upon a company's shares is dependent upon investor agreement on the level of earnings (NOI) and the degree of business risk attached to these, rather than the proportion distributed, it still seems reasonable to conclude that K_e, the equity capitalisation rate, is a function of two variables:

- the shareholders' rate of return, based on dividends plus retentions (net income)
- the risk factor.

Taking the argument further:

(a) The return on shareholders' funds is itself determined by:
  - (*i*) the return on asset investments based on EBIT (net operating income)
  - (*ii*) the debt/equity ratio of the company.

(b) The risk element is a function of:
  - (*i*) the variance of the rate of return on investment
  - (*ii*) the level of gearing.

(c) The variance of return on investment depends on two factors:
  - (*i*) business risk, arising out of the characteristics of the industry concerned
  - (*ii*) the utility function of corporate management.

The level of gearing determines the degree of financial risk which confronts the shareholders, since they must suffer any inconsistency of returns arising out of the contractual nature of debt in the presence of business risk.

In the absence of any discernible hypothesis concerning managerial utility in an asymmetric market for information, the equity capitalisation rate for the ith company in the jth industry may now be defined as follows:

(29) $K_{e_{ij}} = \mathrm{f}(r_i, G_i, \delta_j, \delta_i)$

where

   $K_{e_{ij}}$ = investors' rate of return
   r_i = return on investment
   G_i = gearing ratio
   δ_j = cyclical variance of r_j, about its mean where r_j is the average return on investment for the industry
   δ_i = variance of r_i about the industry mean.

The author's equation is of course crude. However, its definition implies that, when valuing a company's shares, earnings rather than dividends are the relevant measure. Where only a proportion of earnings are distributed, it is assumed that this is based upon management's investment strategy and hence the company's long-run rate of return, net of tax and depreciation. Thus, if tax and depreciation policies are relatively stable, the dividend rate is simply an informational signal for the long-run expected return on investment, given the debt/equity ratio, as first suggested by Ross (op. cit.).

Moreover, Equation (29) reaffirms two distinct, but nevertheless related aspects of a company's operations which will have a bearing upon $K_{e_{ij}}$, namely:

(**a**) Business efficiency which results from the company making the best use if its resources in producing and marketing its products.

(**b**) Financial efficiency which results from the company financing its operations in such a way that the shareholders receive the highest return from a given level of business efficiency and risk.

Quite correctly, however, Equation (29) also implies that financial efficiency should be subsumed under business efficiency, rather than the reverse, since the substitution of earnings between shareholders and creditors in the form of dividends, retentions and interest can only be a reality after a company makes the initial decision to invest. When a firm purchases a new capital asset, the return it expects r_i is, therefore, a summary measure of the productivity of capital. As such, the corporate investment decision, rather than the financing decision, must represent a prime determinant of its equity capitalisation rate, $K_{e_{ij}}$.

This is not to deny the traditional importance of financial efficiency. Returning to theories of capital structure, because companies can typically borrow at an interest rate lower than their return on investment, a judicious increase in the debt ratio may be expected to enhance earnings per share (or at least not to dilute it). But what if the equity capitalisation rate also increases? It will be recalled that this conforms to Durand's third (NOI) proposition, which underpins MM's arbitrage method of proof concerning the irrelevancy of capital structure. The point is that, given their hypothesis that the market value of equity is independent of a company's dividend policy, it should be impossible to conclude that a company's overall cost of capital or total corporate value is a function of gearing. So how do investors (institutional or otherwise) beat the market in the presence of imperfections?

References

(1) Baskin, J., 'An empirical investigation of the pecking order hypothesis', *Financial Management*, Vol. 18, Spring 1989.

(2) Brealy, R.A., and Myers, S.C., *Principles of Corporate Finance*, McGraw-Hill, 1996.

(3) Durand, D., 'Cost of debt and equity funds for business: trends and problems of measurement', *Conference on Research on Business Finance*, New York: National Bureau of Economic Research, 1952.

(4) Harris, M. and Raviv, A., 'The theory of optimal capital structure', *Journal of Finance*, Vol. 48, No.1, March 1991.

(5) Haugen, R.A. and Senbet, L.W. 'The insignificance of bankruptcy costs to the theory of optimal capital structure', *Journal of Finance*, Vol. 33, No. 2, May 1978.

(6) Hill, R. A., 'The UK capital market: a reassessment', *The Business Economist,* Vol. 16, No. 3, Summer 1985.

(7) Jensen, M.C. and Meckling, W.H., 'Theory of the firm: managerial behaviour, agency costs and ownership structure', *Journal of Financial Economics*, Vol. 3, October 1976.

(8) Miller, M.H., 'Debt and taxes', *The Journal of Finance*, Vol. 32, No. 2, May 1977.

(9) Modigliani, F. and Miller, M. H., 'The cost of capital, corporation finance and the theory of investment', *American Economic Review,* Vol., XLVIII, No. 3, June 1958.

(10) Modigliani, F. and Miller, M. H., 'The cost of capital, corporation finance and the theory of investment – reply', *American Economic Review*, Vol., XLVIII, No. 4, September 1958.

(11) Modigliani, F. and Miller, M. H., 'Corporate income taxes and the cost of capital: a correction', *American Economic Review,* Vol. LIII, No. 3, June 1963.

(12) Modigliani, F., 'Debt, dividend policy, taxes, inflation and market valuation', *The Journal of Finance,* Vol. 37, No. 2, May 1982.

(13) Myers, S.C. and Majluf, N.S., 'Corporate financing and investment decisions when firms have information investors do not have', *Journal of Financial Economics*, Vol. 13, June 1984.

(14) Myers, S.C., 'The capital structure puzzle', *The Journal of Finance*, Vol. 39, No. 3, July 1984.

(15) Myers, S.C., 'Still searching for optimal capital structure', *Journal of Applied Corporate Finance*, Vol. 6, Spring 1993.

(16) Ross, S.A., 'The determination of financial structure: the incentive–signalling approach', *Bell Journal of Economics and Management Science*, Vol. 8, Spring 1977.

(17) Solomon, E., 'Leverage and the cost of capital', *The Journal of Finance,* Vol. XVIII, No. 2, May 1963.

(18) Warner, J., 'Bankruptcy costs, absolute priority and the pricing of risky debt claims', *Research Paper* (University of Chicago), 1976.

(19) Weiss, L.A., 'Bankruptcy resolution: direct costs and violation of priority of claims', *Journal of Financial Economics*, Vol. 27, October 1990.

PART FIVE

The portfolio decision

11

Risk and portfolio selection

Chapter profile

The previous chapters all indicate that optimum investment, dividend and financing decisions require knowledge of the investors' (ultimately the shareholders') attitudes towards risk which is not easily identified. This chapter addresses the problem directly by extending Chapter 4's analysis of the risk–return trade-off and the concept of utility within the context of capital budgeting to a consideration of risk minimisation associated with a portfolio of financial securities. The reader unfamiliar with this material is, therefore, redirected to Part 2 of the text.

Based upon the pioneering work of Markowitz, it is explained how a rational investor in an efficient capital market, requiring an optimal portfolio of investments, can maximise utility, having regard to the relationship between expected returns and the risk associated with their covariablity of returns, within the portfolio. The problems of variance–covariance matrix calculations associated with portfolio diversification and the fact that *total* risk reduces to *market* risk as the number of portfolio constituents rise are also described as a precursor to the more mathematically elegant Capital Asset Pricing Model (CAPM), which is explained in the following chapter.

1 INTRODUCTION

A recurrent theme throughout this text is that investment, dividend and financing decisions implemented by management on behalf of the shareholders (whose creature the firm is) all assume a knowledge of the external investors' attitudes toward risk which is not readily identifiable. As a consequence, a fundamental assumption of conventional capital market theory, which was introduced in Chapter 3, is the Separation Theorem of Fisher (1930).

This states that in a perfect capital market a firm's investment decisions are independent of its shareholders' financial preferences, because the latter can choose either to buy, to sell, or to hold securities consistent with their expected future consumption patterns (a clientele effect). Provided an incremental project's return on investment is measured by an opportunity cost of capital rate, which at least matches the return shareholders can earn on comparable investments elsewhere, their wealth will not be jeopardised.

It will be recalled that a perfect capital market is a prerequisite of the Separation Theorem because it is assumed that:

(a) Investors are at liberty, either to borrow or lend or to buy and sell securities, in order to transfer cash from one period to another.

(b) Transaction costs are negligible and the tax system is neutral, so as not to prohibit the above.

(c) Information concerning a firm's investment strategy is universally available and costless.

(d) Investors can transfer funds to other companies to earn their desired rate of return without further risk.

(e) The required rate of return is determined by a market which is characterised by a large number of buyers and sellers who act rationally (they are risk-averse), none of whom are large enough to distort prices by their singular actions.

The question therefore arises as to how investors, including the corporate management and financial institutions which act on their behalf, incorporate the *relative* risk–return trade-off between a prospective investment and their existing asset portfolios into a quantitative model which still maximises wealth.

2 PORTFOLIO ANALYSIS

To answer this question first requires a rudimentary knowledge of the problems of investment in securities.

Normative financial theory proclaims that the objective of rational investors or the management who act on their behalf is the selection of a portfolio of financial assets including cash which maximises their holder's utility by maximising the discounted net present value (NPV) expected to be generated by that portfolio, commensurate with an acceptable level of risk.

With regard to each security selected for inclusion in the portfolio, the basic variables to consider when determining their value are:

(*i*)   the purchase price of the investment
(*ii*) prospective yields or interest payments
(*iii*) transaction costs associated with purchase and sale
(*iv*) the tax and regulatory implications of all the above.

However, as explained in Parts 3 and 4 each item still represents a fundamental point of disagreement among academics and practitioners alike, most notably in relation to proponents of Modigliani and Miller (MM) who maintain that because similar assets cannot sell at different prices:

(a) Share price and the cost of equity are a function of the variability of earnings before interest and tax (investment policy), rather than dividend distributions (financial policy); in other words, business risk, rather than financial risk. (MM 1961)

(b) As an entirely consistent prerequisite, corporate value and overall cost of capital are independent of the corporate capital structure, and if they are not, this can be frustrated by the arbitrage process. (MM 1958)

(c) The tax implications of the above with regard to any differential treatment of dividends *vis a vis* capital gains may be irrelevant. (Miller 1977)

Fortunately, none of this need concern us here, because irrespective of whether management and investors (institutional or otherwise) attribute different weightings to distributable income and retained earnings (i.e. dividends and capital gains) or prefer equity as opposed to fixed interest and other securities, they should still aim to maximise the expected NPV from their portfolios, irrespective of how their constituents are valued. Thus, it is pertinent to consider quite separately, not only what securities to transact, but also when transactions should take place, so as to take full advantage of market opportunities.

As long ago as 1952, H.M. Markowitz explained how, in an efficient market, a rational investor requiring an optimal portfolio of investments could maximise utility with complete security and liquidity, having regard to the trade-off between expected returns and risk associated with the covariability of returns. A portfolio will not diversify risk if returns are highly correlated. If correlation is low, the portfolio will be highly diversified and the risk much less. An *efficient portfolio* is one which satisfies two conditions relative to any other combination of financial assets, namely:

(*i*)   maximum expected return for its given risk
(*ii*) minimum risk for its given expected return

where the expected return and risk are measured by the arithmetic mean and standard deviation of the portfolio.

At any point in time there will be a number of portfolios which satisfy these conditions.

If all this seems vaguely familiar to the reader it is because the statistical methodology of portfolio theory is simply an extension of the mean-variance analysis of capital budgeting decisions, explained in Chapter 4, where the standard deviation (square root of the variance) of a project's return is employed as a probabilistic estimate of risk. Portfolio analysis is, therefore, based upon the same set of assumptions, which explains why it applies equally to corporate management considering a new project in relation to their existing investments or individuals wishing to incorporate additional securities into their existing asset portfolios:

- A risky project or security is one where there is at least a plurality of cashflows.
- The expected returns are assumed to be normally distributed (i.e. random variables), so that their probability density function is defined by the mean and variance of the distribution.
- An *efficient choice* between individual projects or securities maximises the mean NPV of anticipated cashflows, discounted at the risk-free rate of interest, and minimises the standard deviation of the NPV.

3 PORTFOLIO MEAN, VARIANCE AND STANDARD DEVIATION

Within the context of portfolio theory, the selection of a single investment project (or security) explained in Chapter 4 is termed the *single asset case*.

The mean of a normally distributed (random) return r_i is defined as:

(1) $$\overline{R} = \sum_{i=1}^{n} r_i p_i$$

where p_i is the probability of a return occurring.

The variance of r_i around its mean is given by:

(2) $$\text{VAR}(r_i) = \sum_{i=1}^{n} \{(r_i - \overline{R})^2 p_i\}$$

and the standard deviation (square root of the variance);

(3) $$\delta(r_i) = \sqrt{\text{VAR}(r_i)}$$

The optimum decision rules are:

(4)   Max: $\overline{R}$, given δ

(5)   Min: δ, given $\overline{R}$.

It will also be recalled from Chapter 4 that the measure of variability used to reflect risk (the variance or standard deviation) is a matter of convenience. When considering the *proportion* of risk due to some factor, the variance will suffice. However, because the standard deviation is measured in the same units as the return, whether expressed as a percentage or in absolute terms (unlike the variance where the deviations around the mean are squared), it is possible to find the *percentage* probability that a random (normal) variable lies within one standard deviation *above* the mean.

Using the z statistic from Appendix 4, this equals:

$$z = (x - \bar{x})/\delta = 34.13\% \text{ probability}$$

Because a normal distribution is symmetrical, the percentage probability that a random variable lies one standard deviation above or below the mean equals 68.26 per cent. Generalising, the percentage probability that an expected return, r_i, will lie one, two or three standard deviations, $\delta(r_i)$, *around* the mean, $\bar{R}$, is based upon the table of z statistics which produces the following confidence limits:

Number of standard deviations $(n\delta)$	*Probability of* $r_i = \bar{R} \pm n\delta(r_i)$
$n = 1$	68.26%
$n = 2$	95.44%
$n = 3$	99.74%

Armed with this information, individual investors can either select or reject investment projects with identical expected values and standard deviations with equanimity. According to the degree of confidence which they wish to attach to the likelihood of a subjective desired rate of return occurring, no investor would compromise the optimum decision rules given by Equations (4) and (5).

These rules do not change if the analysis is extended to a consideration of the risk–return trade-off from a combination of securities, although the statistical measures become more sophisticated. The expected return on a portfolio proper is a weighted average of the return of its constituents. In its simplest form, the *two asset case*, with investments of equal proportion (*A* and *B*) the portfolio return is given by:

(6) $\quad \bar{R}(A + B) = [\bar{R}(A) + \bar{R}(B)]/2$

Consider next the variability of returns associated with the same combination of investments. The variance of a single random return r_i about its mean is the standard deviation squared. From Equation (3):

(7) $\quad \delta^2 = \text{VAR } (r_i)$

So, if r_i equals the sum of two random returns (r_iA and r_iB) from two investments, *A* and *B*, which are substituted into Equation (7):

$$\delta^2(A + B) = \text{VAR } (A + B) = \sum_{i=1}^{n} \{(r_iA + r_iB - \bar{R}A - \bar{R}B)^2 p_i\}$$

$$= \sum_{i=1}^{n} \{(r_iA - \bar{R}A + r_iB - \bar{R}B)^2 p_i\}$$

$$= \sum_{i=1}^{n} (r_iA - \bar{R}A)^2 p_i + \sum_{i=1}^{n} (r_iB - \bar{R}B)^2 p_i$$

$$+ 2 \sum_{i=1}^{n} (r_iA - \bar{R}A)(r_iB - \bar{R}B) p_i$$

279

(8) $\text{VAR}(A + B) = \text{VAR}(A) + \text{VAR}(B) + 2\,\text{COV}(A, B)$

Unlike the variance of a single random variable, the variance of $(A + B)$ comprises three terms. The first two terms are the variances of A and B respectively. The third term is twice the *covariance* of A and B. (Covariance measures the correspondence between the movement of two random variables.) Thus, the standard deviation of $(A + B)$ is:

(9) $\delta(A + B) = \sqrt{\{(\text{VAR}(A) + \text{VAR}(B) + 2\,\text{COV}(A, B)\}}$

where the covariance for each observation (i) is calculated by multiplying three terms together: the deviation of r_iA from its mean, the deviation of r_iB from its mean and the probability of occurrence. The results for each event are then added together.

Thus, the essence of risk reduction is captured by *diversification*, statistically measured by the covariance which calibrates the variability of the combined returns of two or more investments (which now constitute a portfolio) around their mean in absolute terms. So, if A and B represent two random investments, the degree to which their returns (r_iA and r_iB) vary together is measured by the separable element:

(10) $\text{COV}(A, B) = \displaystyle\sum_{i=1}^{n} \{(r_iA - \overline{R}A)(r_iB - \overline{R}B)p_i\}$

The logic of the covariance is that if the returns on two assets are *independent*, i.e. there is no statistical relationship between the variability of the returns on the individual investments, the covariance will be zero. Therefore, the variance of the two investments combined will equal the sum of the individual variances. Total risk can still be reduced by diversification without affecting the overall return, which suggests that management or investors should not be concerned with the risk of individual projects or securities, but rather with the overall portfolio – more of this later.

If returns are *dependent*, i.e. a relationship exists between the two assets, diversification is not always possible:

(i)   If each of the paired deviations around the mean is negative their product is positive and so too is the covariance.

(ii)   If each of the paired deviations is positive, the covariance is still positive.

(iii)   If large paired deviations move in sympathy, the covariance will be positive and large.

(iv)   If one of the paired deviations is negative, their product is negative and their covariance is negative.

(v)   If dissonant paired deviations are large, the covariance will be negative and large.

If returns are dependent, *efficient* diversification (maximum risk reduction) is achievable under condition (*iv*) and by implication (*v*) above. Note, however, that not all paired deviations need be negative for diversification to secure an element of risk reduction. Conversely, if two investments move in sympathy their variance in combination (Equation 8) will exceed the sum of the variances of the individual investments by twice the covariance.

To demonstrate the use of the covariance consider two securities A and B with the following probabilistic paired returns;

p_i	A	B
	%	%
0.3	10	5
0.4	12	20
0.3	20	12

Let it be assumed that the investors' objective is to minimise the standard deviation of return (risk) for a given expected return. For simplicity and symmetry of treatment this decision rule will be retained throughout the remainder of the chapter.

From Equation (1) the expected return on each investment is calculated as follows:

$$\overline{R}(A) = (0.3 \times 10) + (0.4 \times 12) + (0.3 \times 20) = 13.8\%$$
$$\overline{R}(B) = (0.3 \times 5) + (0.4 \times 20) + (0.3 \times 12) = 13.1\%$$

In Table 11.1, the variance of A, the variance of B and the covariance of A and B are calculated. If these values are substituted into Equation (8) the portfolio variance is given by:

$$\delta^2(A + B) = 0.001716 + 0.003090 + 2(0.000222)$$
$$= 0.00525$$

Because the covariance is positive (albeit small) the two investments modestly move in sympathy. As a consequence, their variance in combination exceeds

Table 11.1 The variances of two investments and their covariance

Probability	Deviations		VAR (A)	VAR (B)	COV (A + B)
p_i	$(r_iA - \overline{R}A)(r_iB - \overline{R}B)$		$(r_iA - \overline{R}A)^2 p_i$	$(r_iB - \overline{R}B)^2 p_i$	$(r_iA - \overline{R}A)(r_iB - \overline{R}B)p_i$
0.3	(0.038)	(0.081)	0.0004332	0.0019683	0.0009234
0.4	(0.018)	0.069	0.0001296	0.0019044	(0.0004968)
0.3	0.062	(0.011)	0.0011532	0.0000363	(0.0002046)
1.0			0.0017160	0.0039090	0.0002220

the sum of the variances of the individual investments. Given the portfolio return

$$\overline{R}(A + B) = \frac{13.8\% + 13.1\%}{2} = 13.45\%$$

it would seem reasonable to conclude at this point that rational (risk averse) investors should place all their funds in Security A, since this corroborates the mean-variance decision rules specified earlier:

$$\overline{R}(A + B) < \overline{R}(A) = 13.8\%$$

$$\delta(A + B) > \delta(A) = \sqrt{0.0017} = 0.04\%$$

4 THE CORRELATION COEFFICIENT

Because the covariance is an *absolute* measure of variability which can assume large positive and negative values if paired deviations are large its interpretation is difficult. Fortunately, the covariance is similar to the linear correlation coefficient, COR, which is a *relative* measure calculated by taking the covariance of securities and dividing by the product of the standard deviations of all securities which comprise the portfolio. For two assets, A and B:

(11) $$COR\,(A,B) = \frac{COV\,(A,B)}{\delta(A)\,\delta(B)}$$

Using the previous example:

$$COV\,(A, B) = 0.000222$$
$$\delta(A) = \sqrt{0.001716} = 0.04142\%$$
$$\delta(B) = \sqrt{0.003909} = 0.06252\%$$

so:

$$COR\,(A,B) = \frac{0.000222}{(0.04142)(0.06252)} = 0.0857$$

which confirms that the two securities exhibit a marginal positive relationship.

The attractiveness of the correlation coefficient is that as a relative measure of covariability it has limits of +1 and −1. In the example it measures how much two investments vary together as a proportion of their combined individual variations as measured by their respective standard deviations. Thus, if two investments are perfectly related in a linear way they deviate by constant proportionality. The correlation coefficient is also favoured by textbook writers, question setters and students of finance, because if a correlation value is assumed the problem of covariance calculations can be avoided. It disappears from the formula for portfolio risk. Reformulating the variance of the combination of two projects; from Equation (11):

(12) $COV(A,B) = COR(A,B)$

and substituting into Equation (8):

(13) $VAR(A+B) = VAR(A) + VAR(B) + 2 COR(A,B)$

The variance of two investments still comprises three terms where the first two are the variances of the individual investments. However, the third term is the substitution of twice the linear correlation coefficient for twice the covariance which distinguishes it from Equation (8).

The logic of the correlation coefficient is that:

(*i*)   If returns are independent, i.e. there is no relationship between the variability of returns, COR will be zero but risk can be reduced by diversification.
(*ii*) If returns exhibit a perfect positive relationship (COR = +1), risk reduction is not possible.
(*iii*) If returns are perfectly negative (COR = −1) an *efficient* portfolio can be constructed which is risk-free with zero variance.
(*iv*) Between + 1 and -1 the value of COR is determined by the closeness of the direct and inverse relationships between investments and even a low positive correlation can be beneficial to the investor in terms of risk reduction.

As long as the correlation coefficient between investments is less than + 1, then the risk of the portfolio as measured by Equation (13) will be less than the weighted average standard deviation of its portfolio constituents.

5 THE ALGEBRA OF A TWO-ASSET PORTFOLIO

Using the previous notation for a simple two-asset portfolio, where a proportion x is invested in security A and $(1 − x)$ is invested in B, the general expressions for the expected return $R(P)$ and risk $VAR(P)$ of the portfolio are equal to:

(14) $R(P) = x\overline{R}(A) + (1 − x)\overline{R}(B)$

(15) $VAR(P) = x^2 VAR(A) + (1 − x)^2 VAR(B) + 2x(1 − x) COR(A,B)$

However, because

(11) $COR(A,B) = \dfrac{COV(A,B)}{\delta(A)\,\delta(B)}$

and Equation (10) for the covariance is equivalent to:

$$(16) \quad \text{COV}(A,B) = \frac{\text{COV}(A,B)}{\delta(A)\,\delta(B)} \cdot \delta(A)\,\delta(B)$$

the covariance can be redefined as follows:

$$(17) \quad \text{COV}(A,B) = \text{COR}(A,B) \cdot \delta(A)\,\delta(B)$$

so that the portfolio variance, Equation (15), may be rewritten:

$$(18) \quad \begin{aligned} \text{VAR}(P) &= x^2 \text{VAR}(A) + (1-x)^2 \text{VAR}(B) \\ &\quad + 2x(1-x)\,\text{COR}(A,B)\,\delta(A)\,\delta(B) \end{aligned}$$

This equation has a convenient property in relation to Equation (15). If two investments exhibit *perfect positive* correlation (COR $(A,B) = +1$), it may be rewritten:

$$\text{VAR}(P) = x^2 \text{VAR}(A) + (1-x)^2 \text{VAR}(B) + 2x(1-x)\,\delta(A)\,\delta(B)$$

which equals:

$$(19) \quad \text{VAR}(P) = \{x\,\delta(A) + (1-x)\,\delta(B)\}^2$$

and since this is a perfect square, the probabilistic estimate of portfolio risk, based upon the statistical properties of the standard deviation explained in Chapter 4, is given by:

$$(20) \quad \delta(P) = x\,\delta(A) + (1-x)\,\delta(B)$$

In other words, if the relationship between two investments is perfectly positive the portfolio variance and its square root simplify to the weighted average of the respective statistics for the individual investments (a calculation analogous to the portfolio return).

With *perfect inverse* correlation, COR $(A, B) = -1$, Equation (15) can also be simplified:

$$\text{VAR}(P) = x^2 \text{VAR}(A) + (1-x)^2 \text{VAR}(B) - 2x(1-x)\,\delta(A)\,\delta(B)$$

which equals:

$$(21) \quad \text{VAR}(P) = \{x\,\delta(A) - (1-x)\,\delta(B)\}^2$$

so that the portfolio standard deviation is:

$$(22) \quad \delta(P) = x\,\delta(A) - (1-x)\,\delta(B)$$

Similarly, if the two investments are independent and exhibit *neutral* correlation, COR $(A, B) = 0$, Equation (15) reduces to:

$$(23) \quad \text{VAR}(P) = x^2 \text{VAR}(A) + (1-x)^2 \text{VAR}(B)$$

with a portfolio standard deviation:

(24) $\delta(P) = \sqrt{VAR(P)}$

Finally, in a *risk-free* portfolio (zero variance), the portfolio variance is eliminated completely and satisfies the following equality:

(25) $VAR(P) = x^2 VAR(A) + (1-x)^2 VAR(B) = 0$

such that the probabilistic estimate of risk measured by the portfolio's standard deviation also equals zero:

(26) $\delta(P) = x\,\delta A - (1-x)\,\delta(B) = 0$

To demonstrate the application of the general statistical formulae for a two-asset portfolio, consider an equal investment in two securities with an equal probability of paired cash returns as follows:

p_i	A	B
	%	%
0.5	8	14
0.5	8	12

The objective is to minimise risk.

From Equation (1) the expected return on each investment is calculated as follows:

$\overline{R}(A) = (0.5 \times 8) + (0.5 \times 12) = 10\%$

$\overline{R}(B) = (0.5 \times 14) + (0.5 \times 6) = 10\%$

In Table 11.2, the variance of A, the variance of B and the covariance of A and B are derived.

Armed with this information the portfolio return is given by:

(14) $R(P) = (0.5 \times 10) + (0.5 \times 10) = 10\%$

This matches the expected returns on each investment A and B. So what about the objective function: minimising the variance (risk)? With a negative

Table 11.2 The variances of two investments and their covariance

Probability	Deviations		VAR (A)	VAR (B)	COV (A + B)
p_i	$(r_iA - \overline{R}A)$	$(r_iB - \overline{R}B)$	$(r_iA - \overline{R}A)^2 p_i$	$(r_iB - \overline{R}B)^2 p_i$	$(r_iA - \overline{R}A)(r_iB - \overline{R}B)p_i$
0.5	(2)	4	4	16	(8)
0.5	2	(4)	4	16	(8)
1.0			8	32	(16)

value for the covariance, COV $(A, B) = -16$, risk can obviously be reduced by combining the investments in equal proportions. The question is by how much?

The answer is provided by the correlation coefficient:

(11) $COR\ (A, B) = \dfrac{COV\ (A, B)}{\delta(A)\ \delta(B)} = \dfrac{16}{\sqrt{8}.\sqrt{32}} = -1$

The variability of expected returns exhibits a perfect inverse negative relationship. So it is possible to eliminate risk completely by creating a portfolio with zero variance. How then does the portfolio as currently constructed compare?

Using Equation (21) for a portfolio variance which is a perfect square:

(21) $VAR\ (P) = \{x\ \delta(A) - (1 - x)\ \delta(B)\}^2$

$$= \{(0.5\sqrt{8}) - (0.5\sqrt{32})\}^2$$

$$= 1.4142^2 = 2.0$$

The portfolio's risk can be measured by its standard deviation:

(24) $\delta(P) = \sqrt{2.0} = 1.4142\%$

So the portfolio is definitely not risk free, but given the mean-variance decision rule:

(5)   Min: δ, given R

the decision to place funds in both investments in equal proportions, rather than A or B exclusively, is vindicated.

This can be confirmed if one compares the expected returns from the portfolio $(A + B)$, investment A and investment B with their respective standard deviations.

Investments	$\bar{R}$	δ
	%	%
P	10	$\sqrt{2} = 1.4142$
A	10	$\sqrt{8} = 2.8284$
B	10	$\sqrt{32} = 5.6568$

The following relationships emerge

(5) $\delta(P) < \delta(A) < \delta(B)$ given $R(P) = \bar{R}(A) = \bar{R}(B)$

6 MINIMUM VARIANCE: THE TWO-ASSET CASE

Where a proportion of funds x is invested in security A and $(1 - x)$ is invested in

B, the general expression for the variance of a portfolio is given by:

$$(18) \qquad VAR\ (P) = x^2\ VAR\ (A) + (1-x)^2\ VAR\ (B) \\ + 2x(1-x)\ COR\ (A,B)\ \delta(A)\ \delta(B)$$

The value of x, the proportion of funds invested in security A, for which the portfolio variance is at a minimum is given by differentiating VAR (P) with respect to x and setting $dVAR\ (P)/dx = 0$ to yield:

$$(27) \qquad x = \frac{VAR\ (A) - COR\ (A,B)\ \delta(A)\ \delta(B)}{VAR\ (A) - VAR\ (B) - 2COR\ (A,B)\ \delta(A)\ \delta(B)}$$

Using the previous example, where the correlation coefficient of A and B is -1 and the following data was calculated:

$$\overline{R}(A) = 10\%,\ VAR\ (A) = 8,\ \delta(A) = 2.8284\%$$

$$\overline{R}(B) = 10\%,\ VAR\ (B) = 32,\ \delta(B) = 5.6568\%$$

The minimum variance is found according to Equation (27) when a proportion x is invested security A such that:

$$x = \frac{32 - \{-1(2.8284 \times 5.6568)\}}{8 + 32 - 2\{-1(2.8284 \times 5.6568)\}}$$

$$= 2/3$$

Next, substituting $x = 2/3$ into Equation (21) for a portfolio variance which is a perfect square (i.e. COR $(A, B) = -1$):

$$VAR\ (P) = \{(\tfrac{2}{3} \times 2.8284) - (\tfrac{1}{3} \times 5.6568)\}^2 = 0$$

and obviously:

$$\delta(P) = 0$$

So, if securities A and B are perfectly and negatively correlated, rather than invest funds in equal proportions which earlier produced a portfolio variance of 2.0 and a corresponding standard deviation of 1.4142, an investor can place two-thirds and one-third in securities A and B respectively to create a *risk-free* portfolio which completely eliminates the variance. It is also worth noting that the expected return on the original portfolio has not been compromised since:

$$R(P) = (\tfrac{2}{3} \times 10) + (\tfrac{1}{3} \times 10) = 10\%$$

7 THE MULTI-ASSET PORTFOLIO

According to Markowitz if individual returns, standard deviations and covariances for each pair of returns are known the portfolio return $R(P)$, portfolio variance VAR (P) and a probabilistic estimate of risk as measured by its square root, the standard deviation of the portfolio $\delta(P)$, can be calculated. The covariance COV_{ij} enters into the variance expression to determine the degree to which variations in the return to one investment, i, can serve to offset the variability of another, j. For a multi-asset portfolio where x_i represents the proportion invested in each security:

(28) $\qquad R(P) = \sum_{i=1}^{n} x_i R_i$

(29) $\qquad \text{VAR } (P) = \sum_{i=1}^{n} x_i^2 \, \text{VAR}_i + \sum_{i \neq j}^{n} x_i x_j \, \text{COV}_{ij}$

(30) $\qquad \delta(P) = \sqrt{\text{VAR } (P)}$

where the sum of the proportion of funds invested in each security satisfies the following requirements:

$$\sum_{i=1}^{n} x_i = 1, x_i \geqslant 0$$

The portfolio objective consists of Equation (29) which is to be minimised subject to a constraint obtained by setting Equation (28) equal to a constant:

(31) $\qquad$ Min: VAR (P), given $R(P) = K$ (constant)

i.e. minimise risk for any given return.

For the mathematically minded a number of observations can be made. First, both the constraints are linear functions of the n variables x_i, whilst the objective function is an equation of the second degree in these variables. Consequently, methods of quadratic programming, rather than a simple linear programming calculation, must be employed in order to minimise VAR (P) for various values of $R(P) = K$.

Secondly, if the analysis of portfolios is extended beyond the two-asset case the data requirements become formidable if the covariance is used as a measure of the variability of returns. It requires estimates for the expected return and the variance for each security in the portfolio and estimates for the correlation matrix between the returns on all securities. For example, if funds are invested equally in three securities, A, B and C, each deviation from the expected return of the portfolio is

$$\tfrac{1}{3}(r_i A - \bar{R}A) + \tfrac{1}{3}(r_i B - \bar{R}B) + \tfrac{1}{3}(R_i C - \bar{R}C)$$

If the deviations are now squared to calculate the variance, the proportion 1/3 becomes $(1/3)^2$ and:

$$\text{VAR} (P) = \text{VAR} (A + B + C)$$

$$= (1/3)^2 \quad \text{(sum of three variance terms plus the sum of six covariance terms)}$$

For a twenty-asset portfolio:

$$\text{VAR} (P) = (1/20)^2 \quad \text{(sum of twenty variance terms plus the sum of 380 covariance terms)}$$

As a general rule if there are $\sum x_i = n$ securities, the number of terms in the portfolio variance calculation is:

$$(32) \qquad \text{VAR} (P) = (1/n)^2 \quad \text{(sum of } n \text{ variance terms plus the sum of } n(n-1) \text{ covariance terms)}$$

In the covariance matrix, $x_i \dots x_n, x_i$ is paired in turn with each of the other securities $x_2 \dots x_n$ making $(n-1)$ pairs in total. Similarly, $(n-1)$ pairs can be formed involving x_2 with each other x_i and so forth, through to x_n making $n(n-1)$ permutations in total. Of course, half of these pairs will be duplicates (the set x_1, x_2 is identical with x_2, x_1). The n product case therefore requires only $\frac{1}{2}(n^2 - n)$ distinct covariance figures altogether, which is a substantial data saving in relation to Equation (32). Nevertheless, the decision-makers task is still daunting, as the number of securities considered for inclusion in a portfolio increases. It also explains why a number of academics began a search for a less onerous measure of risk even as the Markowitz model was being developed, as the next chapter will reveal.

8 THE GEOMETRY OF PORTFOLIO RISK AND INVESTOR UTILITY

Markowitz explained how in an efficient capital market, where the returns are normally distributed (symmetrical), a rational (risk-averse) investor requiring an optimal portfolio could maximise utility by diversification. A combination of securities produces a trade-off between the two statistical variables which define a symmetrical normal distribution: the expected return and standard deviation (risk) associated with the covariability of individual returns. An efficient diversified portfolio is one which minimises its standard deviation without compromising the investor's desired rate of return or *vice versa*.

Figure 11.1 illustrates normal distributions of possible returns from two paired investment opportunities, X and Y. The first pair, A and B, have equal expected returns but different standard deviations (risk), because the variability of returns associated with B is greater. The second pair, C and D, exhibit equal

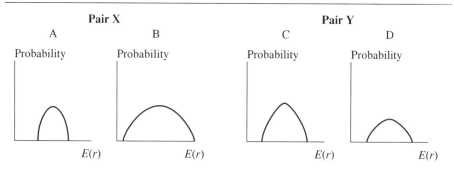

Fig 11.1 The probabilistic normal distribution of expected returns

standard deviations (spread) but different returns (*C* high and *D* low). Analysed separately, in terms of what portfolio theorists call the *single-asset case*, risk-averse investors required to make a choice would either prefer *A* to *B*, or *C* to *D*. This conforms to the capital budgeting decision rule based upon the maximisation of expected net present value explained in Chapter 4:

Max: $E(r)$, given δ,

Min: δ, given $E(r)$.

Consider next an investor who wishes to deploy funds in two securities; the *two-asset case*. Figure 11.2 plots the relationship between possible portfolio returns, $R(P)$, and portfolio risk, $\delta(P)$, of different combinations of investment in a more complex but typical situation where the expected returns and standard deviations of both securities (*E* and *F*) differ. So which asset combination should the investor choose?

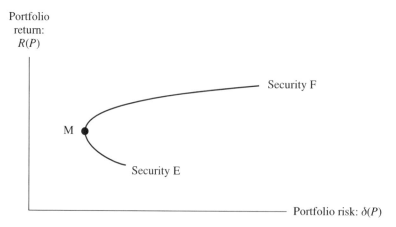

Fig 11.2 The risk–return trade-off: the two-asset case

The decision again depends upon the investor's personal attitude toward risk. Inveterate speculators would place all their funds in security F, hoping to maximise their return (completely oblivious to risk). Moving to the left and downwards along the curve F–E, when it turns in on itself below point M, the combination of securities becomes *inefficient*. A higher expected return for the same degree of risk can be achieved through portfolios to the right and upwards of M. Thus, the most risk-averse individual would invest funds proportionately in securities E and F which corresponds to point M on the curve. The line F–M therefore defines the *efficiency frontier* of portfolios which comprises two investments. By diversifying, rather than putting all your eggs in one basket, these combinations of securities can reduce risk commensurate with a desired rate of return.

Moving on to the *multi-asset case*, which offers a larger choice between risk and expected return, the efficiency frontier is plotted in Figure 11.3. Again, at any point in time there will be a number of risky portfolio returns which are efficient in terms of their trade-off. The points below the curve F–F′ represent the expected returns and corresponding standard deviations from investing in a single financial security. Within the confines of the area below F–F′, possible combinations of the expected return and the standard deviation of multi-asset portfolios are captured.

The efficiency frontier F–F′ of risky portfolios reveals that, to the right and below, alternative investments yield inferior results. To the left, no possibilities exist. Thus, an optimum portfolio for any investor can still be determined at a point on the efficiency frontier once the individual's attitude toward risk is known. So how is this calibrated?

It has been shown how the derivation of an efficient set of portfolios can be

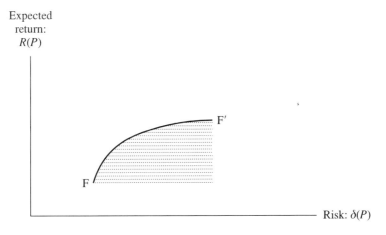

Fig 11.3 The efficiency frontier of portfolios: the multi-asset case

obtained using quadratic programming techniques based upon estimates of the expected return and standard deviation for each security, plus the correlation between each pair of securities. It was also explained how this methodology is an extension of the linear programming model employed in Chapter 4 to select projects which maximise expected net present value under conditions of uncertainty. However, it will also be recalled from Chapter 4 that the *calculation* of means and standard deviations is a separate procedure to their *interpretation*.

For example, a rational investor would not be indifferent between £1000 to be received with absolute certainty juxtaposed against a lottery with either a 50 per cent chance of receiving nothing or a 50 per cent chance of receiving £2000. Yet, if the choice is translated into an actuarial certainty equivalent, the investor should be indifferent between the two because:

$$\text{Certainty Equivalent:} \quad 1.0 \ (\pounds) = p_i(\pounds) + p_i(\pounds)$$

$$1.0 \ (1000) = 0.5(0) + 0.5(2000)$$

$$= \pounds 1000$$

Thus, a selection technique which corresponds to different investor risk preferences is required, whether it be a lottery, an optimum project or an efficient portfolio.

Within the context of portfolio analysis, one possibility is for the investor to consider a value for the portfolio's expected return $R(P)$, say $R(p_i)$, depicted schematically in Figure 11.4. All $R(p_i),\delta(p_i)$ combinations for different portfolio mixes are then represented by points along the horizontal line $R(p_i) - R(p_i)'$ for which $R(P) = R(p_i)$. F, the leftmost point on this line, yields the portfolio investment mix which satisfies the objective function:

(33)   Min: $\delta(p_i)$ for an expected value $R(p_i) = K$ constant

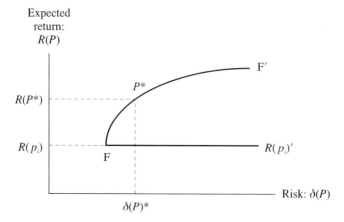

Fig 11.4 The multi-asset efficiency locus and investor choice

By repeating the calculations for all other possible values of $R(P)$ and obtaining every corresponding value of $R(p_i)$ the entire opportunity locus F – F′ may be traced. The investor then subjectively selects the investment combination yielding a maximum return subject to a constraint imposed by the degree of risk the individual is willing to assume, say P^* corresponding to $R(P^*)$ and $\delta(P^*)$ in the diagram. This conforms to the use of the z statistic and confidence limits for the single-asset case explained earlier.

Unfortunately, even with modern quadratic computer programming techniques, which were not universally available to contemporaries of Markowitz, the optimisation procedure is still an iterative process based on trial and error. So how did academics during the 1950s circumvent the problem?

9 INVESTOR UTILITY AND THE SEPARATION THEOREM

It was explained in Chapter 4 that if a company's objective is to minimise the standard deviation of an investment's expected return this can be determined by reference to a managerial utility indifference curve, which calibrates their attitude towards risk and return. With regard to portfolio analysis, the equation of any curve of indifference between portfolio risk and portfolio return for an individual can therefore be written:

(34) $\text{VAR}\,(P) = \alpha + \lambda R(P)$

where graphically the value of λ indicates the steepness of the curve and α indicates the horizontal intercept. Thus, the ultimate objective of the Markowitz portfolio model is to minimise α. Rewriting Equation (34), for any indifference curve which relates to a portfolio containing n securities, the objective function is given by:

(35)   Min: $\alpha = \text{VAR}\,(P) - \lambda R(P)$

for all possible values of $\lambda \geqslant 0$, where $R(P) = \text{K}$ (constant), subject to the non-negativity constraints mentioned earlier:

$\alpha_i \geqslant 0,\ i = 1, 2, 3 \ldots n$

and the essential requirement that sources of funds equals uses and x_i be proportions expressed mathematically as:

$$\sum_{i=1}^{n} x_i = 1$$

The portfolio which satisfies Equation (35) is efficient because no other combination of securities will have a lower degree of risk for the requisite expected return.

The optimum portfolio for an individual investor is plotted in Figure 11.5.

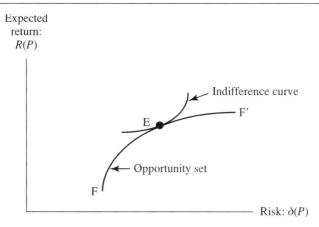

Fig 11.5 **The determination of an optimal portfolio: the multi-asset case**

The efficiency frontier F – F' of risky portfolios still reveals that, to the right and below, alternative investments yield inferior results. To the left, no possibilities exist. Thus, an optimum portfolio for the investor can be determined at the point where the equation for the individual's utility indifference curve (compositing an attitude towards risk and expected return) is tangential to the efficiency frontier (point E in Figure 11.5).

Of course, the analysis hitherto has only considered a wholly risky portfolio. But what if investors are either totally risk-averse or desire liquidity? They may opt for:

(a) A risk-free selection of short to medium term government securities, provided that their expected return is secondary and inflation rates are ignored (highly unlikely).

(b) A mixed portfolio which comprises any combination of risk and risk-free investments, including cash (reasonable).

These possibilities, first explored by Tobin (1958), which expand upon Fisher's Separation Theorem explained in Chapter 3, are portrayed in Figure 11.6, where E still represents an optimal 100 per cent risky portfolio, A denotes the risk-free portfolio and the line (A–B) (which can be infinitely extended) represents the *capital market line* (CML) showing the boundary of efficient mixed portfolios.

Since E denotes a 100 per cent risky portfolio, the line (A–E) represents increasing proportions of portfolio E combined with a reducing balance of lending at the risk-free rate. The line beyond E can only represent opportunities for borrowing at the risk-free rate in order to increase the size, but not the composition, of the optimal portfolio. By 'leveraging' (borrowing against) the investment, the investor's risk would rise but so would the return. Thus, in an

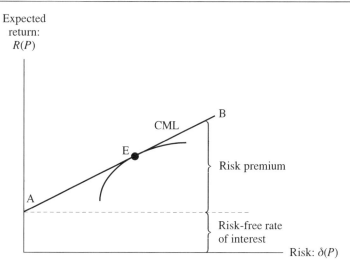

Fig 11.6 The capital market line: Tobin's separation theorem

efficient capital market where all investors can borrow or lend at the same rate of interest, Tobin's Separation Theorem concluded that they all ought to choose the same optimal portfolio, irrespective of their attitude to risk, by first finding the point of tangency E, along the CML line (A–B), and then borrowing or lending to adjust the balance between risk and return.

10 SUMMARY AND CONCLUSIONS

The linear relationship between risk and expected returns shown in Figure 11.6 applies to all efficient portfolios. Unfortunately, it does not hold for individual risky investments, since securities with higher standard deviations may have lower returns and *vice versa*. As stated at the beginning of this chapter, the objective of portfolio diversification is to achieve an overall standard deviation lower than that of its component parts.

To recapitulate, suppose that there was a perfect positive correlation between two securities (A and B) that comprise the market. In other words, high and low returns always move in sympathy. It would pay the investor to place all funds in whichever security yields the higher return at the time. However, if there was perfect inverse correlation, i.e. a high rate of return on A was always associated with a low return on B and *vice versa*, or there was random (zero) correlation between the returns, then it can be shown statistically that overall risk reduction can be achieved by diversification.

As long as the correlation coefficient between any number of investments is less than unity (perfect positive), then the total risk of the portfolio as measured

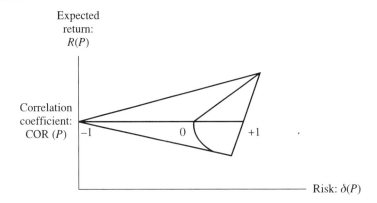

Fig 11.7 Risk return profiles for differing correlation coefficients: the two-asset case

by the standard deviation would be lower than the weighted average of its constituent elements, with the greatest reduction reserved for a correlation coefficient of −1 (perfect inverse). This is plotted in Figure 11.7 for the two-asset case.

Ceteris paribus, if the standard deviation of an individual security is higher than that for a portfolio in which it is held, then part of the standard deviation must have been diversified away through correlation with other constituents, leaving only that portion of risk which is correlated with the economy as a whole. Measured by the covariances of each security with the market portfolio, the latter is inescapable (undiversifiable). Consequently, the contribution of an individual investment to the variance of a well diversified portfolio (its covariance) is the only risk which investors will pay a premium to avoid.

So finally, what definitions can be applied to these two elements of portfolio risk?

Total risk is split between:

- *Unique risk,* sometimes termed specific, residual, diversifiable or more commonly *unsystematic* risk. It relates to economic factors which relate specifically to the individual company or financial security and can be eliminated completely through efficient diversification.
- *Market risk,* undiversifiable or *systematic* risk, so called because it is endemic throughout the system. It relates to general economic factors which affect all firms or securities and explains why share prices tend to move in sympathy.

Thus, all the risk in a fully diversified portfolio is market or systematic risk. However, market risk can also be subdivided into *business risk* and *financial risk*.

It will be recalled from previous chapters that business risk reflects the variance of asset returns and the innate nature of the industry concerned (investment policy). This may or may not reflect financial risk, which arises from either the proportion of debt to equity in a firm's capital structure or the amount of dividends paid in relation to the level of retained earnings (financial policy). Irrespective of whether financial policies matter (the Modigliani–Miller controversy), for an-all equity firm which pursues a policy of full distribution there is an academic consensus that market or systematic risk, which is undiversifiable, will comprise business risk. To clarify the position further, Figure 11.8 summarises the relationships between each of the different types of risk.

Under conditions of Markowitz efficiency, the conclusion to be drawn is that individuals are capable of diversifying away unsystematic risk by expanding their investment portfolios. Thus, they should be rewarded only for taking on systematic or market risk. Unfortunately, it has been explained that such a proposition poses formidable data and statistical requirements associated with the covariance calculations necessary to determine an optimal portfolio as the number of constituents increases. Not surprising, therefore, that in the absence of modern computer technology this precipitated the development of much simpler models of asset selection during the 1960s, as the following chapter will reveal.

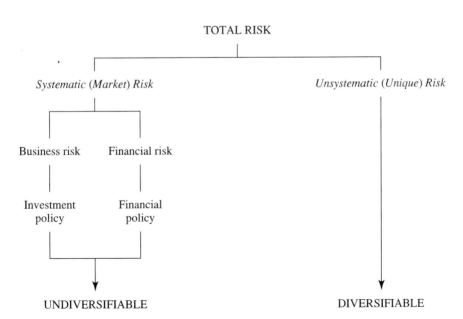

Fig 11.8 The interrelationship of risk concepts

References

(1) Fisher, I., *The Theory of Interest,* Macmillan 1930.
(2) Markowitz, H.M., 'Portfolio selection', *The Journal of Finance,* Vol. 13, No. 1, March 1952.
(3) Miller, M.H. and Modigliani, F., 'Dividend policy, growth and the valuation of shares', *Journal of Business of the University of Chicago,* Vol. 34, No. 4, October 1961.
(4) Miller, M.H., 'Debt and taxes', *Journal of Finance,* Vol. 32, No. 2, May 1977.
(5) Modigliani, F. and Miller, M.H., 'The cost of capital, corporation finance and the theory of investment', *American Economic Review,* Vol., XLVIII, No. 3, June 1958.
(6) Tobin, J., 'Liquidity preferences as behaviour towards risk', *Review of Economic Studies,* February 1958.

12

Models of capital asset pricing

Chapter profile

The previous chapter explained how the problems of variance–covariance matrix calculations associated with Markowitz portfolio selection in an efficient capital market precipitated a search for a computationally simpler model of asset diversification and security price behaviour.

This chapter begins with the observation that total risk reduces to market risk as the number of portfolio constituents rises. A relative measure of a portfolio constituent's systematic risk is defined as its beta coefficient, which determines the Security Market Line. The single-index one-period capital asset pricing model (CAPM), based upon Markowitz efficiency, and the Modigliani–Miller law of one price are presented. Unlike portfolio theory, the CAPM is shown to apply to portfolios, as well as individual securities.

An appreciation of the assumptions which underpin the CAPM is provided before considering its operational veracity and theoretical limitations. The influence of indexation models in relation to the development of the UK stock exchange is outlined. Finally, an entirely consistent model of capital asset pricing based upon Arbitrage Pricing Theory, which subdivides systematic risk into any number of macro-economic factors, is explained and reviewed.

1 INTRODUCTION

According to Markowitz (1952), the objective of portfolio diversification is the selection of a negatively correlated combination of asset investments which reduce the total risk of the portfolio as measured by its standard deviation. If the standard deviation of an individual security is higher than that for a portfolio in which it is held, then part of the standard deviation must have been diversified away through correlation with other constituents, leaving only that element of risk which is correlated with the portfolio as a whole. Measured by the covariances of each security with the portfolio, such risk is undiversifiable and represents the portion of total risk which rational investors will pay a premium to avoid.

Undiversifiable risk is termed systematic or market risk, since it measures the way in which the returns on the security move systematically with the totality of financial securities which comprise the market portfolio. It describes a particular portfolio's inherent sensitivity to global political and macro-economic volatility. A particularly good example at the time of writing (early 1998) is the currency devaluations and stock market implosions of the overgeared Tiger economies. 1987 and 1929 provide earlier graphic analogies. Since individual investors have no control over such events, they require a rate of return commensurate with their relative systematic risk. The greater this risk, the higher the rate of return required by investors, whose widely diversified portfolios reflect movements in the market.

In contrast, diversifiable or unsystematic risk relates to an individual security's price which is independent of market risk. Specific to individual companies, it is caused by micro-economic factors such as profitability, product innovation and the quality of management. Because it is escapable, unsystematic risk carries no price in the market.

Although neither element of risk can be observed directly, Figure 12.1 highlights the empirical fact that up to 95 per cent of unsystematic risk can be diversified away by randomly increasing the number of securities in a portfolio to about thirty. With one security, portfolio risk is represented by the sum of unsystematic and systematic risk, i.e. the security's total risk as measured by its standard deviation. When the portfolio approaches the composition of the market virtually all the risk associated with holding that portfolio becomes

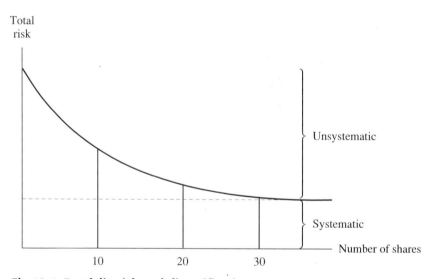

Fig 12.1 Portfolio risk and diversification

systematic or market risk. See Fisher and Lorie (1970) for one of the best explanations of this phenomenon.

Unfortunately, using the Markowitz approach to portfolio diversification, the introduction of an additional security contributes additional covariance terms to the total risk of the portfolio. The variance of the portfolio (and its square root, the standard deviation) is quickly dominated by covariance calculations. In general terms, it was explained in the previous chapter that for an n asset portfolio:

$$\text{VAR } (P)_n = (1/n)^2 \quad \text{(sum of } n \text{ variance terms plus the sum of}$$
$$n(n-1) \text{ covariance terms)}$$

so that for thirty securities:

$$\text{VAR } (P)_{30} = (1/30)^2 \quad \text{(sum of 30 variance terms plus the sum of}$$
$$870 \text{ covariance terms)}$$

Not surprisingly, therefore, in the absence of todays computer technology, academic and financial analysts of the 1950s requiring a far simpler model than that offered by Markowitz to enable them to diversify efficiently, as they invested across innumerable securities, sectors and countries, were quick to appreciate the utility of the relationship between the systematic risk of either a stock or a portfolio and their returns. But how to measure relative risk and how to choose the market portfolio?

2 BETA VALUES AND SYSTEMATIC RISK

If the price of a selected security increases when the market rises, then statistical measurements are still needed to identify how much of the security price increase occurred because of systematic (market) and unsystematic (specific) risk respectively.

In the UK, prior to the introduction of the FT-SE 100 (more of which later), the obvious procedure was to compare movements in an individual share price with movements in the market using the FT All Share Index.

A scatter diagram was plotted over a *single* time period correlating percentage movements in:

(*i*)   market prices as measured by the index (on the horizontal axis)
(*ii*) the selected share price (on the vertical axis)

The line of 'best fit' for the observations could then be determined by regressing stock prices against the overall market over time using the statistical method of least squares. This linear regression line is known as the share's *characteristic line*.

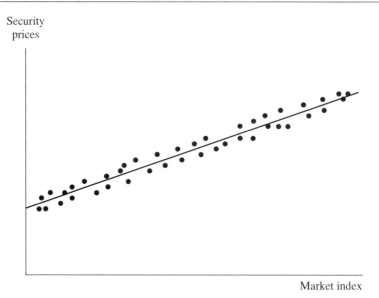

Fig 12.2 The relationship between security price and market movements: the characteristic line

As Figure 12.2 reveals, the intercept of the line measures the average percentage movement in the share price occurring if there is no movement in the market and is called the *alpha* of the stock. A positive alpha over the period of observation indicates a share which has outperformed the market.

The slope of the regression line in relation to the horizontal axis is the *beta factor*. It reveals the volatility of share price to market movements in terms of the ratio of expected change in the price of the stock to the market itself. Measured by the share's covariance with the market (rather than individual securities), divided by the variance of the market, it is a computationally simple proxy for covariance or relative risk in the Markowitz portfolio.

Instead of generating numerous new covariance terms all that is required is the covariance of the rate of return on the additional security with the overall rate of return on the efficient market portfolio. Suppose an investor places funds in all the assets which comprise the capital market in proportion to their individual values in relation to the markets' total value. The market portfolio has a variance of VAR (M) and the covariance of an individual asset A with the market average is COV (A, M). So the relative risk, *beta*, denoted by β_A, is given by:

(1) $$\beta_A = \frac{\text{COV (A, M)}}{\text{VAR (M)}}$$

Although the investor has no control over beta factors, as a measure of systematic risk they are now known to exhibit other convenient properties.

First, although alpha risk varies considerably over time, numerous studies have long since shown that beta values are more stable, displaying a near straight line relationship with their returns; see Black, Jensen and Scholes (1972). Thus, the latter are invaluable for portfolio selection. Investors can tailor a portfolio to their specific risk return (utility) requirements, aiming to hold securities with beta factors in excess of unity while the market is rising, and less than unity when the market is falling. A beta of 1.15, for example, implies that if the underlying market with a beta factor of one were to rise by 10% then the stock may be expected to rise by 11.5%. Conversely, a security with a beta of less than one would not be as responsive to market movements. In this situation, smaller systematic risk would mean that investors would be satisfied with a return which is below the market average. The market portfolio has a beta of one because the covariance of the market portfolio with itself is identical to the variance of the market portfolio. Needless to say, a risk-free investment has a beta of zero because its covariance with the market is zero.

Secondly, whereas the linear relationship between total portfolio risk and expected returns (the capital market line, CML, in the Markowitz model) does not hold for individual risky investments, all the characteristics of systematic beta risk apply to portfolios, as well as individual securities. The beta of a portfolio is simply the weighted average of the beta factors of its constituents. The attraction of this relationship becomes clear if the CML is, therefore, reconstructed to form what is termed the *security market line* (SML) by substituting systematic (market) risk for total risk on the horizontal axis.

Once beta factors are calculated, the SML provides a usable measure of risk. By retaining the efficiency criteria of Markowitz, namely:

(*i*) maximise expected return for a given level of risk
(*ii*) minimise risk for a given expected return

it also implies that the optimum portfolio is the market portfolio. Because the return on a share depends on whether it follows market prices as a whole, the closer the correlation between a share and the market index, the greater will be its expected return. Finally, the SML predicts that shares with higher beta values will have higher returns.

As Figure 12.3 confirms, the expected risk rate return of $\bar{r}_m$ from a balanced market portfolio (M) will correspond to a beta value of one, since the portfolio cannot be more or less risky than the market as a whole. The expected return on risk-free investment (r_f) remains unchanged with a beta value of zero.

Portfolio A (or anywhere on the line r_f–M) is still termed a lending portfolio and consists of a mixture of risk and risk-free securities. Portfolio B is a

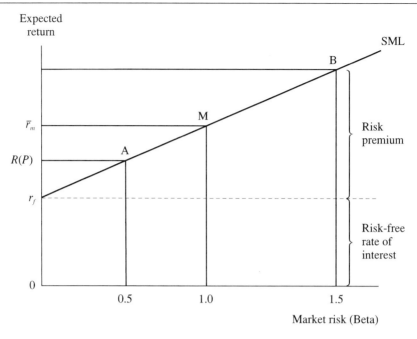

Fig 12.3 The security market line

borrowing or leveraged portfolio, because beyond (M) additional securities are purchased by borrowing at the risk-free rate of interest.

Proceeding one stage further, the SML can now be utilised in order to establish whether individual securities are under or over-priced (hence its name), since their expected rates of return and beta factors can be compared with the SML.

3 THE TRADITIONAL CAPITAL ASSET PRICING MODEL (CAPM)

It was explained in Chapter 4 how a company could rank its investment projects by reference to their expected returns and standard deviations. In the previous chapter it was shown how Markowitz used the same efficiency criteria to derive an optimum portfolio of investments which can reduce risk (standard deviation) without impairing return. But if one project or portfolio has a higher expected return and a higher standard deviation than another it is necessary to calibrate the individual's attitude towards risk if a choice is to be made between the two.

The SML, which incorporates beta factors as a measure of relative (systematic) risk, explains how rational investors with different utility (risk–return) requirements can make such a choice. By using the capital market to determine the price of risk, a number of academics, Sharpe (1963), Lintner (1965), Treynor (1965) and Mossin (1966), were, therefore, able to develop independently the Capital Asset Pricing Model (CAPM) which explains how rational investors should behave when selecting a portfolio of financial assets.

The model assumes that investors have three possible options when managing a portfolio:

(*i*)   to trade
(*ii*) to hold
(*iii*) to substitute (i.e. securities for property, property for gilts, etc.).

A profitable trade is, accomplished by buying (selling) undervalued (overvalued) securities relative to an appropriate measure of systematic risk, such as a stock market index.

To derive the traditional CAPM it is also assumed that Markowitz criteria still hold:

- Asset values are determined by random variables which are normally distributed, characterised by mean expected returns (and covariances) upon which all investors agree.
- Mean-variance efficiency criteria determines the optimum portfolio (P):

    Max: $R(P)$, given $\delta(P)$

    Min: $\delta(P)$, given $R(P)$.

- All assets are infinitely divisible.
- Transaction costs are zero and the tax system is neutral.
- There is a perfect capital market where all information is available and costless.
- All investors are *price takers*, since no individual, firm or financial institution is large enough to distort prevailing market values.

Armed with this information, now assume that an investor who initially places nearly all their funds in a portfolio which reflects the composition of the market subsequently invests the balance in security j. From Chapter 11 it follows that the expected rate on the revised portfolio, defined as the weighted average of the expected returns of the individual components, is given by:

(2) $R(P) = x\, \bar{r}_j + (1 - x)\, \bar{r}_m$

where:

x = an extremely small proportion

r_j = expected rate of return on security j

r_m = expected rate of return on the market portfolio

and the variance of the portfolio is given by:

(3) $\text{VAR}\,(P) = x^2\,\text{VAR}\,(r_j) + (1 - x)^2\,\text{VAR}\,(r_m) + 2x(1 - x)\,\text{COV}\,(r_j, r_m)$

subject to the common non-negativity constraints and the essential requirements that sources of funds equals uses. This portfolio will be efficient if it has the lowest degree of risk for the highest expected return, given by the objective functions:

(4)   Max: $R(P)$, given VAR $(P) = K$ (constant)

(5)   Min: VAR (P), given $R(P) = K$ (constant)

However, by introducing security j into the market portfolio the investor has altered the risk–return characteristics of their original portfolio. According to Sharpe (op. cit.) the marginal return per unit of risk is derived by:

(a)   Differentiating the portfolio return with respect to the amount invested in security j: $\Delta R(P)/\Delta x$.

(b)   Differentiating the portfolio variance with respect to the amount invested in security j: $\Delta \text{VAR}\,(P)/\Delta x$.

(c)   Solving for $\dfrac{\Delta R(P)/\Delta x}{\Delta \text{VAR}\,(P)/\Delta x}$ as $x \to 0$

Since (c) above simplifies to $\Delta R(P)/\Delta VAR\,(P)$ as x tends to zero, the incremental return per unit of risk is therefore given by:

(6) $\dfrac{\Delta R(P)}{\Delta \text{VAR}\,(P)} = \dfrac{\bar{r}_m - \bar{r}_j}{2(1 - \beta_j)\,\text{VAR}\,(r_m)}$ for $x \to 0$

However, it will be recalled from the explanation of the SML that an investor can either borrow or lend at the risk-free rate of interest, r_f with a beta value of zero. So by incorporating a risk-free investment or a liability (if x is negative) the incremental rate of return, given by Equation (6), is established by substituting $\bar{r}_j = r_f$ and $\beta_j = 0$ into the equation such that:

(7) $\dfrac{\Delta R(P)}{\Delta \text{VAR}\,(P)} = \dfrac{r_m - r_f}{2\,\text{VAR}\,(r_m)}$

In a perfectly competitive capital market, the incremental risk–return trade-off must be the same for all investors, so Equations (6) and (7) are identical:

(8) $\dfrac{\bar{r}_m - \bar{r}_j}{2(1 - \beta_j)\,\text{VAR}\,(r_m)} = \dfrac{\bar{r}_m - \bar{r}_f}{2\,\text{VAR}\,(r_m)}$

Now, multiplying both sides of this equation by the denominator on the left-hand side and rearranging terms, Sharpe's *one*-period *single*-factor Capital Asset Pricing Model (CAPM) is defined:

(9) $\bar{r}_j = r_f + (\bar{r}_m - r_f)\beta_j$

It is a one-period model because the independent variables, r_f, $\bar{r}_m$ and β_j are assumed to be constant. It is single-factor because systematic risk is prescribed entirely by beta.

The equation represents the expected rate of return on security j which comprises a risk-free return plus a premium for accepting market risk (the market rate minus the risk-free rate), assuming that all correctly priced securities will lie on the SML. The market portfolio offers a premium $(\bar{r}_m - r_f)\beta_j$ over the risk-free rate, r_f, which may differ from the jth security's risk premium measured by the beta factor β_j.

Thus, the Sharpe single-index CAPM enables an investor to establish whether individual securities (or portfolios) are under or over-priced, since the linear relationship between their expected rates of return and beta factors (systematic risk) can be compared with the SML (the market index).

For example, stock X might have an expected return of 8 per cent and a beta coefficient of 0.5. Superimposed on Figure 12.3, this would reveal that the return was too low for the risk involved and that the share was overpriced, since X is located below the SML. Consequently, rational shareholders would sell their holdings, eliciting a fall in price, whilst potential investors would delay purchase until price had fallen and the increased yield (A), impinged upon the SML.

Given a market return of 16 per cent from a balanced portfolio and a risk-free rate of 6 per cent, Figure 12.4 illustrates why the required rate of return with a

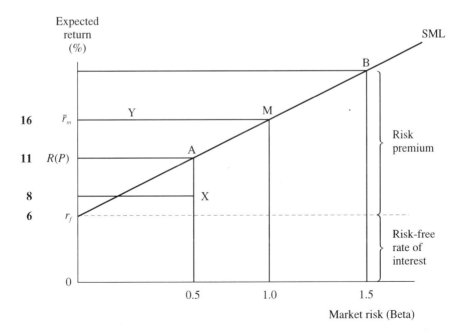

Fig 12.4 The capital asset pricing model

beta value of 0.5 should be 11 per cent. This may be confirmed by Sharpe's formula for the expected return of a portfolio or individual security. This comprises a risk-free return, plus a premium for accepting market risk assuming that all correctly priced securities will lie on the SML. Thus, from Equation (9):

Expected return = Risk-free rate plus beta multiplied by market rate minus risk-free rate

In this instance:

$$11\% = 6\% + 0.5(16\% - 6\%)$$

It is also clear from Figure 12.4 why investment in security Y is beneficial. Stocks above the line will be in great demand; they will rise in price.

Thus, it seems reasonable to conclude that, in theoretical equilibrium in an efficient capital market which assimilates all information concerning a security into its price, all securities or portfolios will lie on the SML. Individual investors need not conform to the market portfolio. They need only determine how much systematic risk they wish to assume, leaving market forces to ensure that any security can be expected to yield the appropriate return for its beta.

4 CRITICISMS OF THE CAPM

Although there is recent controversial evidence by Black (1993) to suggest that portfolios with high betas can underperform relative to predictions and zero beta portfolios have higher returns than risk-free portfolios (suggesting compensation for unsystematic risk), most early tests corroborated the CAPM. The beta-return characteristics of individual securities also held for portfolios. In fact, the beta of a portfolio was assumed to be more stable because fluctuations among its constituents tend to cancel each other out, as Black, Jensen and Scholes (op. cit.) first discovered.

The New York Stock Exchange was analysed over a 35-year period by dividing the listing into 10 portfolios, the first comprising constituents with the lowest beta factors and so on. Based on time series tests and cross-sectional analysis they found that the intercept term was not equal to the risk-free rate of interest, r_f, which they approximated by 30-day Treasury Bills. However, their study revealed an almost straight-line relatiohship between a portfolio's beta and its average return.

As an alternative to the CAPM, Black (1972) tested a two-factor model which assumed that investors cannot borrow at a risk-free rate but at a rate, r_z, which is the return on a portfolio with a beta value of zero. This is equivalent to a portfolio whose covariance with the market portfolio's rate of return is zero.

The Black two-factor model:

(10) $\bar{r}_j = \bar{r}_z + (\bar{r}_m - \bar{r}_z)\beta_j$

confirmed the Black, Jensen and Scholes study and that a zero beta portfolio with an expected return, $\bar{r}_z$, exceeds the risk-free rate of interest, r_f.

Despite further modifications to the original model still to be discussed (multi-factors, multi-periods), the CAPM in its traditional guise was not without detractors, particularly in relation to its fundamental assumptions. Accepting that all investors could borrow or lend at the risk-free rate it is a *non-sequitor* to assume that r_f describes a Treasury Bill in real terms given inflation which can neither be predetermined nor affect individuals equally. Marginal adjustments to a portfolio's constituents may also be prohibited by substantial transaction costs which negate future benefits. The tax system too is biased so that different investors will construct or subscribe to portfolios which minimise their tax liability, the clientele effect. Even the stock market must be inefficient, otherwise investors could not profit from legitimate, new information, and events such as the 1987 crash could not have occurred. Equally, the market has not always responded to significant changes in information, ranging from patterns of dividend distribution to major political events. Why else do even professionally managed funds periodically underperform relative to the market index? The only way to beat the market, so the argument goes, is through either pure speculation or insider information, a complex subject which will be given detailed consideration in the next chapter.

Yet other forces are at work. The CAPM implies that the optimum portfolio is the market portfolio, which lies on the Security Market Line (SML) with a beta factor of one. Individual securities and portfolios with different levels of risk (betas) can be priced, since their expected rate of return and beta can be compared with the SML. In equilibrium, all securities will lie on the line, because those above or below are either under or over-priced in relation to their expected return. Thus, market demand, or the lack of it, will elicit either a rise or fall on price, until the return matches that of the market.

However, a problem arises as to how to define the market. It is frequently forgotten that the CAPM subscribes to the Modigliani–Miller law of one price. Based on their arbitrage process (1958) this states that two similar assets must be valued equally. In other words, two portfolio constituents which contribute the same amount of risk to that portfolio are in effect close substitutes and should, therefore, exhibit the same return. But what if an asset has no close substitute, such as the market itself? How can one establish whether it is under or overvalued?

According to Roll (1977), most CAPM tests are invalid because stock exchange indices are only a partial measure of the true market portfolio which, by definition, should include every security world-wide. He demonstrated that a change in the American market surrogate from the Standard and Poor 500 to the Wilshire 5000 can radically alter a security's expected return as predicted by the CAPM.

Furthermore, if betas and returns derived from a stock market listing were unrelated, the securities might still be correctly priced in relation to the global market portfolio. Conversely, even if the listing was efficient (i.e. shares with high betas did exhibit high returns) there is no *à priori* reason for assuming that each constituent's return is only affected by global systematic risk.

A further criticism of the CAPM is that, however one defines the market, movements up and down are dominated by price changes in the shares of larger companies and it is to these companies that institutional investors are more attracted, even though they have regularly underperformed relative to smaller companies since the 1960s; see Fama and French (1992). Moreover, in dealing with rising systematic risk, fund managers with portfolios consisting of fully paid equities and interest-bearing securities acquired for cash have only two main strategies.

First, they can liquidate all or part of a portfolio. However, if the whole portfolio were sold it could be difficult to dispose of a large fund quickly and efficiently without affecting the market. Unlike a private investor, total disposal may also be against the fund's trust deed. If only part of the portfolio was liquidated there is the further vexed question of which securities to sell.

The second option is to reduce all holdings, to be followed by subsequent reinvestment when the market bottoms out. However, the fall in prices may have to be in excess of 2 per cent to cover transaction and commission costs (see Hill and Meredith 1994).

Clearly, these alternatives may be untenable and they impose significant constraints upon the opportunities to control risk. Indeed, those sceptical of portfolio management maintain that successful investment is still a matter of luck rather than judgement, insider information or unlikely economic circumstances where all prices move in unison. A more considered view is that while it certainly depends upon the following combination of factors:

(*i*)   legitimate financial instruments with which to short the market
(*ii*) extremely low transaction costs
(*iii*) negotiable commissions
(*iv*) speed and simplicity of dealing
(*v*)   the segregation of systematic and unsystematic risk

the CAPM still has much to offer the investor, institutional or otherwise.

It is for these reasons that the UK stock exchange, with its vital time zone spanning the closure and opening of the Eastern and American markets, has introduced numerous new financial products since the 1970s. And if proof of their popularity and the veracity of the CAPM were needed, it is best exemplified by the dramatic growth in exchange-traded financial futures and options on a wide underlying market and, more recently, products related to their own index, the FT-SE 100, which on its own terms now fulfils a vital role as a means of managing risk.

5 THE OPTIONS AND FUTURES MARKETS

A traded 'call' or 'put' option is a speculative device in the form of a contract that provides its holder (the buyer) with the right but not the obligation to purchase or to sell an underlying financial instrument at an agreed price on or before a given date up to one year hence. Following their successful introduction to the US capital market during the early 1970s the London Stock Exchange, now the International Stock Exchange (ISE), created the London Traded Options Market (LTOM) in 1978 to introduce traded options on a wide range of products, which now include leading equities, exchange rates and the FT-SE 100.

In 1981, the Bank of England sponsored the complementary idea of an organised financial futures exchange market in the UK. The London International Financial Futures Exchange (LIFFE) opened in 1982 to trade a range of financial futures and options products which now embrace international money markets, government bond and exchange rate instruments, in addition to FT-SE 100 based futures.

Unlike an option, a futures contract is a legally binding agreement between two parties, the buyer (or 'long') and the seller (or 'short') of the underlying instrument. The contract has to be fulfilled by a specified date, three months hence, or used for reference purposes in the case of early settlement. The contract can also be offset prior to maturity by an equal and opposite transaction.

The necessity for both an options and futures market is obvious in a climate of financial volatility, where knowledge of a security's historical price movements may be an inappropriate guide to its subsequent performance. Buying shares in a portfolio of companies can create a dividend flow, whereas there are no dividends on an options or futures contract. On the other hand, the extension of an equity portfolio involves a significant cash outlay and risk. Opening an options or futures contract only requires a deposit of around 5 per cent of its underlying value and involves extremely low commission and transaction costs. As a consequence, the balance of funds may be placed on risk-free deposit, such as UK Treasury Bills until the contract matures (the substitution effect).

Of course, whenever an option is exercised or a futures contract is struck the buyer or seller may be what is termed 'in the money', 'out of money' or at parity. For a buyer, the first instance is where the initially agreed (exercise or strike) price is below the eventual market price of the underlying instrument.

'Out of money' is where the exercise or strike price is higher than market price, an obvious situation with exchange rate futures following the UK currency devaluation of 16 September 1992. For sellers, the reverse held. They were 'in the money', since exercise or strike prices fell below the price of the underlying instrument, and fortunes were made.

The mathematics of option-pricing lie beyond the scope of this text. However, it is worth noting that the basic model developed by Black and Scholes (1973) sits well with the CAPM, being entirely consistent with the M–M view that close substitutes cost the same.

The Black–Scholes option-pricing model shows that a traded 'call' or 'put' can be mirrored by:

(*i*)   owning or borrowing a proportion of the security
(*ii*) lending or borrowing money.

The price of this synthetic option equals the price of the real option.

Whilst options and futures should be used judiciously, their introduction on a broad underlying market has provided alternative strategies for managing systematic portfolio risk. Traded in isolation, or in conjunction with UK Treasury Bills, Certificates of Deposit or Floating Rate Notes, they are a speedy, cost effective way for investors to adopt a position in the market, adjust portfolio liquidity or gearing, whilst protecting against or taking advantage of short-term movements in the asset value of their portfolio.

However, just as academics developed simplified alternatives to the treatment of systematic portfolio risk through the development of single index models, such as the CAPM, so too LTOM and LIFFE soon appreciated the merits of options and futures contracts, based not on individually traded securities, but priced on the movement of an index of the UK equity market as a whole. The question was which index to use?

6 THE FT-SE 100

By 1983, research indicated a latent demand for centrally administered, index-related options and futures. They could facilitate the management of systematic risk related to movements in the UK equity market. Investors could back their view on the market, rather than make value judgements on individual shares. The resultant instrument would also act as a surrogate portfolio of the index constituents, involving significantly lower cash outlay, commission and transaction costs.

The two indices available at the time were *The Financial Times* 30 Share Index (FT 30) and *The Financial Times* Actuaries' All Share Index (FT All Share)

The FT 30 was introduced in 1935 in response to investor demand for a performance measure of the UK equity market. It was based originally on thirty blue chip industrial stocks, although this has changed significantly as other new sectors have emerged.

The index was initially calculated and published each hour (now at each change in the price of a constituent). However, it only comprises 30 per cent of the total market capitalisation of UK equity, making it unrepresentative for fund managers with diversified portfolios. It functions primarily as a short-term indicator of industrial sector direction. The fact that it is an unweighted geometric average also means that the FT 30 consistently underperforms relative to the market as a whole. Moreover, if the price of any one of its shares should fall to zero, the index would also be zero.

The FT All Share Index was introduced in 1962 based on 710 individual share issues to provide a more sensitive measure of the whole market. It represents over 90 per cent of UK equity capitalisation, divided into six main categories, typically covering 35 market sectors.

The FT All Share is an arithmetically weighted average, which means that the higher the market capitalisation of a constituent company, the more influence it has on the index. Because of the large number of companies which comprise the index, it is only practical to recalculate and publish at the end of each day. Whilst it functions as a measure of portfolio performance, it is used as a long-term, rather than short-term, equity market indicator.

Because of their limitations, neither of the two indices were deemed appropriate for options and futures contracts based on the UK equity market. As a result, a new index was created (administered by a steering committee comprising members of the Stock Exchange and representatives of *The Financial Times*), the FT-SE 100.

The objective of the FT-SE 100 is to represent the 100 largest UK registered companies in terms of market capitalisation and so provide a surrogate for the whole UK equity market. It is a real-time index recalculated by computer every minute from 09.00 to 17.00.

It was introduced in January 1984, having been thoroughly back-tested by the London Business School to 1978. The base date for the index is 31 December 1983 and at that time its level was set at 1000. Options and Futures were priced at £10 and £25 per index point (i.e. contract values of £37,500 and £15,000 respectively, when the FT-SE 100 stood at 1500). The index is weighted arithmetically according to the market capitalisation of its components, which account for 65 per cent of the UK equity market, Thus, a change of 10 per cent in the highest capitalised constituent would have a significantly greater effect on the index than a 10 per cent adjustment to the lowest capitalised shares, which hover around the £1000m mark.

Because the FT-SE 100 is a subset of the FT All Share Index (generally only the latter are included in the former), there has been a high correlation between the two over time. However, because of differences in their composition and rules of inclusion, the indices have diverged occasionally. But this is not surprising, if one recalls the observations by Roll (op. cit.).

Three factors account for most of this differential:

(*i*)   sectoral effects
(*ii*) the small companies effect
(*iii*) privatisation new issues.

Sectorally, the FT-SE 100 attaches greater weight to its larger constituents, the banking and oil sectors. Smaller companies included in the FT All Share Index can experience faster growth and share price performance than larger participants in both indices (a point returned to later). The new issue pricing effect is best exemplified by British Telecom. In 1984, BT's market capitalisation (4 per cent of the UK equity market) first entered the FT All Share at its issue price of 130 pence, whilst the FT-SE 100 incorporated the closing price of 173p. This effect has diminished over time, but it was the reason for the first significant divergence between the two indices.

Despite such anomalies, the FT-SE 100's statistical qualities and coverage are now universally acknowledged. Originally designed to satisfy the practical requirements of an index upon which to develop options and futures contracts, its criteria, namely:

(*i*)   a broad, liquid, underlying market with instantly available prices
(*ii*) an accessible index suitable for a variety of market participants

means that it now fulfils a comprehensive role.

Unlike the FT 30 and the FT All Share, the FT-SE 100 operates as an indicator of both long and short-term movements in the UK equity market. As a subset of the FT All Share it can provide a reliable surrogate for measuring overall portfolio performance, yet offer a more cost-effective basis for managing short-term risk. All of which leads one to ask why even significant, professionally managed funds have periodically underperformed relative to the market, since the introduction of the FT-SE 100 a decade ago.

7 ARBITRAGE PRICING THEORY

An obvious explanation of the variable performance of institutional portfolios is provided by Roll's critique of the CAPM (op. cit.). Not only is it impossible for the most discerning investor to establish the composition of the true market portfolio, but there is also no assumed reason that a security's expected return is affected by systematic risk alone. Firth (1977) further observes that if the stock market is so efficient that it assimilates all relevant information into security prices it is a tautology to claim that it is either efficient or inefficient, since there is no way of telling. This conundrum will be investigated in Chapter 13.

Such criticisms are also important not because they invalidate the CAPM (most tests refute this) but because they give credibility to the contemporaneous development of an alternative approach to asset price determination based on stock market efficiency: the Arbitrage Pricing Theory (APT) presented by Ross (1977).

Unlike the CAPM, the APT possesses the advantage of explaining the pricing of securities in relation to each other, rather than in relation to an unidentifiable market portfolio. Whereas the CAPM focuses upon an assumed *specific* linear relationship between beta factors and expected returns plotted by the SML, the APT is a *general* model which subdivides systematic risk into smaller components which need not be specified in advance. These define the Arbitrage Pricing Plane (APP). Any macro-economic factors, including market sentiment, which impact upon investor returns may be incorporated into the APP (or ignored if believed to be of little consequence). For example, an unexpected change in the rate of inflation (purchasing power risk) might affect the price of securities generally. The advantage of the APT, however, is that it can be used to eliminate this risk specifically, as in the need for a pension fund portfolio's immunity to inflation.

Statistical tests on the model, including those of Roll and Ross (1980), established that a four-factor linear version of the APT is a more accurate predictor of security and portfolio returns than the CAPM. Specifically, this APT states that the expected return is directly proportional to its sensitivity to:

(*i*)   inflation
(*ii*) interest rates
(*iii*) industrial productivity
(*iv*) investor attitude towards risk.

The return equation for a four-factor APP conforms to the following simple linear relationship for the expected return on the *j*th security in a portfolio:

(11) $\bar{r}_j = a + b_1(\bar{r}_1) + b_2(\bar{r}_2) + b_3(\bar{r}_3) + b_4(\bar{r}_4)$

where:
   $\bar{r}_j$ = expected rate of return on security j
   $\bar{r}_i$ = expected return on factor i ($i = 1, 2, 3, 4$)
   a = intercept
   b_i = slope of $\bar{r}_i$.

The expected risk premium on the *j*th security is defined as the difference

315

between its expected return, $\bar{r}_j$, and the risk-free rate of interest, r_f, associated with each factor's return, r_i, and the security's sensitivity to each of these factors, b_i. The four-factor equation is given by:

$$(12) \qquad (\bar{r}_j - r_f) = b_1(r_1 - r_f) + b_2(r_2 - r_f) + b_3(r_3 - r_f) + b_4(r_4 - r_f)$$

Like the CAPM, the general APT is, therefore, a linear model, although it has embraced non-linear events with mixed results (as the following chapter will reveal). It also assumes that unsystematic (unique) risk can be eliminated in a well diversified portfolio, leaving only the portfolio's sensitivity to unexpected changes in macro-economic factors. Subsequent research has, therefore, focused upon identifying further significant factors, such as the study by Chen, Roll and Ross (1986). In this respect, however, the work of Dhrymes, Friend and Gultekin (1984) had already created controversy, since their study concluded that as the number of portfolio constituents increase, the greater the number of factors which must be incorporated into the model. Thus, at the limit, the APT might equate with the CAPM which defines risk in terms of a single over-arching micro-economic factor relative to the return on the market portfolio. For a lucid comprehensive explanation of APT, given its current unrefined state, the reader is therefore directed to Elton, Gruber and Mei (1994).

8 SUMMARY AND CONCLUSIONS

The body of research which comprises Markowitz portfolio theory (1952), the Sharpe CAPM (1964), the Ross APT (1977) and the subsequent vast literature on the subject combine to form what is now termed Modern Portfolio Theory (MPT). Whilst the APT differs in detail from the CAPM, its operation is still a linear simplification which also builds upon Markowitz portfolio theory. Unfortunately, it yields conflicting results. Conversely, despite a number of common simplifying assumptions, most notably that capital markets are efficient, most tests of the CAPM have shown that it works, i.e. high betas tend to elicit high returns which can be predicted in the long-run.

It will be recalled that Markowitz explains how diversification reduces risk. The CAPM explains how investors would behave if they are rational, that is risk-averse with a preference for the highest expected return for a given level of risk. Instead of analysing covariances among a portfolio's constituents, the CAPM ingeniously divides a security's risk into systematic and unsystematic. Systematic or market risk is the extent to which the share price is correlated with the market as a whole and is measured by the beta factor. Unsystematic risks are the remaining variations specific to individual companies which cancel each other out in a well diversified portfolio. Since investors cannot eliminate systematic risk merely by diversifying, the CAPM concentrates upon the relationship between systematic risk, the beta of a security or a portfolio, and returns.

The CAPM states that the return on a security, whether it be gilts, debt, equity, an option or a portfolio, depends on whether their prices follow prices in the market as a whole by reference to a suitable index, such as the FT-SE 100. The closer the correlation between the price of either an individual security or a portfolio and the price of this market proxy (the beta factor), the greater will be their expected returns. Securities and portfolios with high beta factors should yield high returns and *vice versa*. Thus, if an investor knows the beta factor (relative risk) of a share or portfolio, their returns can be predicted with accuracy. Profitable trading of portfolios which outperform the market index is then accomplished by buying (selling) undervalued (overvalued) securities relative to their systematic or market risk.

The CAPM also states that all investors would choose to hold a portfolio which comprises the stock market as a whole. By definition, the market portfolio has a beta of one and is 'efficient' in the sense that no other combination of securities would give a higher return for the same risk. It is, therefore, a benchmark by which the CAPM establishes the Security Market Line (SML), in order to compare other beta factors and returns. From this, rational investors can ascertain whether individual shares are underpriced or overpriced and determine other efficient portfolios which balance their personal preference for risk and return.

Finally, on an historical note, whilst Modern Portfolio Theory (of which the CAPM is a part) has been developed within living memory its historical antecedent is Dow Theory. Named after Charles H. Dow, the first editor of the *Wall Street Journal*, who started to compile daily averages of share prices in 1897 it is still manifest in the world's best known barometer of stock market performance, the Dow Jones Index.

Today Dow theorists are termed *technical* analysts whose investment decisions are premised on the belief that capital markets are efficient by assimilating all relevant available information concerning a security into its price. Stock exchange indices, therefore, reflect all that is known about business in general and companies in particular whose securities comprise the index.

Unlike *fundamental* analysts, who make investment decisions on the historical records of individual companies (dividend trends, current state of profits, competitive position and so on) in relation to the state of the economy, technical analysts believe that stock market movements are a more accurate criterion. Patterns of performance are a combination of macro-economic factors, such as political events, economic growth, inflation, interests rates and market sentiment, which can all be found to repeat themselves cyclically. As a consequence future changes in the index can be predicted *via* past trends and portfolio investors can expect to earn a return above the risk-free rate commensurate with the degree of risk which has not been eliminated by diversification.

If the capital market is so predictable it, therefore, remains to ask two questions:

(*i*) Is it actually possible to beat the market using technical analysis?

(*ii*) What do single-period portfolio models such as the CAPM have to offer individuals and companies within the context of their multi-period investment, dividend and financing decisions which alternative models previously considered in this text fail to deliver?

The first issue will be addressed in the next chapter and the second thereafter.

References

(1) Black, F., 'Beta and return', *Journal of Portfolio Management*, Vol. 20, Fall 1933.

(2) Black, F., Jensen, M.L. and Scholes, M., 'The capital asset pricing model: some empirical tests', reprinted in Jensen, M.L. (Ed) *Studies in the Theory of Capital Markets*, Praeger 1972.

(3) Black, F., 'Capital market equilibrium with restricted borrowing', *Journal of Business*, Vol. 45, July 1972.

(4) Black, F. and Scholes, M., 'The pricing of options and corporate liabilites', *Journal of Political Economy*, Vol. 81, May–June 1973.

(5) Chen, N.F., Roll, R. and Ross, S.A., 'Economic forces and the stock market', *Journal of Business*, Vol. 59, July 1986.

(6) Dhrymes, P.J., Friend, I. and Gultekin, N.B., 'A critical re-examination of the empirical evidence on the arbitrage pricing theory', *Journal of Finance*, Vol. 39, No. 3, June 1984.

(7) Elton, E.J., Gruber, M.J. and Mei, J., 'Cost of capital using arbitrage pricing theory: a case study of nine New York utilities', *Financial Markets, Institutions and Instruments*, Vol. 3, August 1994.

(8) Fama, E.F. and French, K.R., 'The cross-section of expected stock returns', *Journal of Finance*, Vol. 47, No. 3, June 1992.

(9) Firth, M., *The Valuation of Shares and the Efficient Markets Theory*, Macmillan 1977.

(10) Fisher, L. and Lorie, J., 'Some studies of variability of returns on investment in common stocks', *Journal of Business*, April 1970.

(11) Hill, R.A., and Meredith, S., 'Insurance institutions and fund management: a UK perspective', *Journal of Applied Accounting Research*, Vol. 1, No. 2, 1994.

(12) Lintner, J., 'The valuation of risk assets and the selection of risk investments in stock portfolios and capital budgets', *Review of Economic Statistics*, Vol. 47, No. 1, December 1965.

(13) Markowitz, H.M., 'Portfolio selection', *The Journal of Finance*, Vol. 13, No.1, March 1952.

(14) Modigliani, F. and Miller, M.H., 'The cost of capital, corporation finance and the

theory of investment', *American Economic Review*, Vol. XLVIII, No. 4, September 1958.

(15) Mossin, J., 'Equilibrium in a capital asset market', *Econometrica*, Vol. 34, 1966.

(16) Roll, R., 'A critique of the asset pricing theory's tests', *Journal of Financial Economics*, Vol. 4, March 1977.

(17) Roll, R. and Ross, S.A., 'An empirical investigation of the arbitrage pricing theory', *Journal of Finance*, Vol. 35, No. 5, December 1980.

(18) Ross, S.A., 'Arbitrage theory of capital asset pricing', *Journal of Economic Theory*, Vol. 13, December 1976.

(19) Sharpe, W., 'A simplified model for portfolio analysis', *Management Science*, Vol. 9, No. 2, January 1963.

(20) Treynor, J.L., 'How to rate management of investment funds', *Harvard Business Review*, January–February 1965.

13

Efficient markets, volatility and investor behaviour

Chapter profile

This chapter reviews the normative stance of corporate finance concerning investment decisions, with particular reference to portfolio risk in all its guises and stock market volatility.

Given recurring erratic movements of security prices, worldwide, the conventional objective of shareholders' wealth maximisation, which embraces the Efficient Market Hypothesis based upon investor rationality, the case for *random walks* and Gaussian mean-variance analysis, is explained and seriously challenged. Arguments for newer, alternative models of investor behaviour which incorporate stock market volatility, with particular reference to the 1987 crash, are presented. *Inter alia*, the rationale for managerial policies of short-termism in a multi-billion dollar financial services industry now characterised by a *bonus culture* is also considered.

By accident and not design the material presented in this chapter is also particularly apposite at the time of writing (1997–98). The currency devaluations and stock market implosions of the Tiger economies, whose highly geared companies are withdrawing their investments worldwide, all provide grist to the mill.

1 INTRODUCTION

Previous chapters have subscribed to a basic tenet of financial theory, namely that the stock market represents a profitable long-term investment commensurate with risk. Historical evidence is said to reveal that over any five-year period security prices invariably rise. However, one legacy of the 1987 crash, given the erratic movements in markets since, is the realisation by a growing number of analysts and academics that many of the traditional assumptions concerning investor behaviour which underpin their various approaches to financial management require a fundamental re-examination.

The theoretical constructions of Modern Portfolio Theory (MPT), which comprise Markowitz Efficiency and its derivatives, most notably the Capital Asset Pricing Model (CAPM) and Arbitrage Pricing Theory (APT), are being challenged. Their operational veracity under a common assumption of efficient markets, which also underpins the Modigliani–Miller (MM) law of one price and Fisher's Separation Theorem, is also under threat. The purpose of this chapter is to provide a critical review, to expand upon the debate and to explain:

(*i*)   The rationale for newer alternative models of market behaviour which incorporate stock market volatility, with particular reference to 1987.

(*ii*)   Why financial policies of *short termism* represent an attractive and pragmatic option for many investors (institutional or otherwise) but not necessarily the only one, given recent developments in capital market theory.

2 STOCK MARKET EFFICIENCY

Conventional capital market theory is based on three key concepts:

(*i*)   Rational investors
(*ii*)   Efficient markets
(*iii*) Random walks.

Rational investors assess anticipated returns by a probabilistic weighting that generates expected returns based on a normal distribution, the familiar bell-shaped curve. Risk is measured as the standard deviation of returns (the square root of the variance), which is a measure of the probability that an observation will be a certain distance from the average observation. Using the criterion of *mean-variance efficiency*, investors require either a maximum return for a given level of risk or a given level of return for minimum risk. They are risk-averse.

Investors have three possible options when managing a portfolio of financial assets:

(*i*)   to trade
(*ii*)   to hold
(*iii*) to substitute (shares for property, property for gilts, etc.).

Markowitz (1952) reveals how efficient portfolio diversification can reduce risk without impairing return. Models of asset pricing such as the option-pricing model of Black and Scholes (1973), the general APT developed by Ross (1976) or its earlier, special case, the CAPM independently formulated by Sharpe (1963), Lintner (1965), Treynor (1965) and Mossin (1966) explain how investors should behave if they are rational, i.e. risk-averse. A profitable trade is accomplished by buying (selling) undervalued (overvalued) securities relative to appropriate measures of market or *systematic risk*.

These quantitative ('Quants') models assume that capital markets are efficient, so that security prices also behave rationally. However, this concept of *efficiency* is multi-faceted. Applied to share price, one can first identify *business efficiency* associated with variations in overall operating cash profitability of a firm's projects. This conforms to the normative objective of business finance, namely the maximisation of net present value (NPV). If a company undertakes an investment with a positive NPV, then an efficient stock market will find out and the market price of its shares will rise. Conversely, a poor investment will precipitate a fall in the share's price. Subsumed under business efficiency there is *financial efficiency* which relates to the returns to all providers of money capital (i.e. how the profits are divided). Exacerbated by increasing the proportion of debt in the firm's capital structure, i.e. the degree of leverage, if interest rates rise, shareholders will also require a higher return from their investment, so market price will fall. Finally, one can identify purchasing power efficiency, whereby 'real' rates of return for each class of investor should be maintained relative to changes in the rate of inflation.

Different types of efficiency can also be distinguished in the stock market itself. *Allocative efficiency* exists if funds are directed towards companies which make the optimum use of them. There is *operational efficiency* if transaction costs are minimised by open competition among market participants. *Information processing efficiency* occurs if the market prices all the securities traded on it fairly, speedily and on the basis of all the available information.

Formalised as the Efficient Market Hypothesis (EMH) by Fama (1965), information processing efficiency has come to mean that the price of a share incorporates all 'public' information, both 'fundamental' and 'technical', about that share. It will be recalled that *fundamental* analysts determine a share's price by discounting expected future dividends to a present value, based upon the shareholder's cost of capital. *Technical* analysts (or chartists) base their expectations upon an analysis of past price patterns in order to identify future trends, particularly trend reversals. A combination of the two ensures that securities are fairly priced at their *intrinsic* value and will only change when new information enters the market place. This can cause investors to reassess the size of future cashflows or the future discount rates at which they are to be capitalised. Because of investor rationality and the EMH, however, prices follow a *random walk* to the extent that new information will be independent of the last piece of information which has already been incorporated into share price. In other words, markets have no memory, or only a limited memory, of the past. Neither individual buyers nor sellers have a comparative advantage, and investment is a *martingale* or fair game which requires a diversified portfolio to achieve a maximum return for a level of risk. There is no possibility of either *speculative bubbles* on which share prices move to unrealistically high or low levels in response to speculative pressure or *noise* trading which follows the dictates of fashion.

The EMH evolved from the notion of a perfect market which assumes that:

(*i*)   Information is freely and instantly available.

(*ii*) The products or services traded are homogeneous.

(*iii*) There is perfect competition among large numbers of buyers and sellers.

(*iv*) Investors act rationally.

(*v*)   There are no transaction costs.

(*vi*) There are no taxes.

Under these conditions, exogenous factors, such as new information, may perturb the market in a linear fashion but they will be absorbed so quickly into price that a new equilibrium will be achieved instantaneously.

But this introduces a number of anomalies. If stock markets are so efficient:

(**a**) Why have markets, institutions and individuals not always responded to significant changes in information ranging from patterns of dividend distribution to major political events?

(**b**) How can investors earn excess returns from changing fundamentals, technical analysis or a Quants analysis of either market trends (based on the CAPM), or individual factors such as inflation, interest rates, industrial performance and risk attitudes (using the APT)?

(**c**) Conversely, if not a direct consequence, why do even professionally managed institutional portfolios periodically under-perform relative to the market as a whole?

To explain why, the EMH has been propounded in three forms:

(**a**) The *weak form* states that only knowledge of past share prices is fully absorbed into today's price. The next price change is random in relation to currently available information concerning past prices, thereby debarring technical analysts from making excess returns. Fundamentalists, who make investment decisions on the expectations of individual firms, may still profit to the extent that such information is not assimilated into share price (a phenomenon particularly applicable to less publicised companies, shares which are infrequently traded, the 'low P/E effect' and the 'January syndrome').

(**b**) The *semi-strong form* postulates that randomness occurs because current prices reflect, not simply price history, but all publicly available information. Thus, fundamental analysts with access to such information would not be able to beat the market, long term.

(c) The *strong form* declares that current prices fully reflect all information, including 'private' insider information. The fundamental market price of a share must, therefore, be the best approximation to its intrinsic or 'true' value based on anticipated cashflows. As a consequence, even the most privileged professional analyst is unlikely to achieve higher returns from a portfolio of securities in the longer term than the most naïve investor with an indiscriminate selection of shares.

So, as the theory strengthens, speculative opportunities weaken. Competition among large numbers of well-informed market participants drives financial asset prices to a consensus value which reflects the best possible forecast of their future payment stream. And since the late 1940s, particularly the decade prior to the 1987 stock market crash, academic support for the EMH has been impressive. Studies in the US and UK comprising several hundred papers suggest that the semi-strong form best reflects the behaviour of share prices, thereby leaving investors with some room for manoeuvre.

Of course, the EMH is still an abstraction of the real world, a model with questionable assumptions. Investors do not always behave rationally – consider any national lottery. Capital markets are not perfectly competitive. Fiscal obstacles and barriers to trade do exist. But instead of asking whether the EMH is too divorced from reality, the relevant question is whether it works.

Certainly, market economies and financial markets believe that it does, if the impact of the EMH on both public policy and corporate management worldwide is considered.

(a) Policies of stock market deregulation, the lowering of fiscal barriers and computerised dealing have been designed to facilitate a speedier adjustment of share prices to new intrinsic values, in response to global information.

(b) Merger and takeover activity has been encouraged as a means of promoting managerial efficiency. According to the EMH, companies become vulnerable to takeover when their share prices are depressed relative to those of other companies whose prospects are rated more highly under better management.

(c) With the threat of takeover imposed by a more efficient market, the rationale for conglomerates has been gradually eroded. By incorporating all information about a company into a share's price, stock markets are thought to reflect its future prospects more accurately than remote corporate management with their reliance on historical accounting conventions and creative accounting techniques.

(d) Deregulation, allied to a weakened case for conglomerates, has sponsored the view that market forces can also impose a more effective discipline upon the management of public utilities; hence the UK policy of privatisation.

(e) With the advent of privatisation, small private investors have been encouraged to buy listed securities on the stock market. According to the EMH, any additional information that professional analysts possess is likely to be reflected in share prices. Thus, over a period of time investment is a fair game for all, i.e. a martingale.

3 THE EFFICIENT MARKET HYPOTHESIS (EMH) AND THE 1987 CRASH

So, what can the EMH theorist offer by way of explanation for the crash of 19 October 1987 as an insight into more recent stock market volatility?

Certainly, it is now widely agreed that the EMH with its emphasis on fundamental new information failed to explain why on one day in 1987 the Dow Jones Industrials Index plunged 509 points from 2247 to 1738 in just a few hours (an index drop of 23 per cent compared with 15 per cent in the 19 October 1929 crash). Nor is it clear why reactions to the collapse of the US market, which was transmitted instantaneously to other financial centres via global satellite links, were so varied. With the exception of Tokyo, where the government suspended trading (despite only a modest fall), the strongest responses (in descending order) were seen in Sydney, Hong Kong, Singapore and the European markets with the London FT-SE 100 on a par with the US.

With the benefit of hindsight, reasons for the crash are varied. In terms of the US economy:

(*i*)   Disappointing trade deficit figures announced a week previously.

(*ii*) Reports of impending tax legislation that would affect mergers and takeovers adversely.

(*iii*) A likely increase in lending rates to defend a falling dollar and ward off inflation in response to a persistent West German policy of increasing interest rates.

(*iv*) The prospects of reduced domestic industrial and consumer spending and hence little economic growth in response to a deflationary monetary policy.

(*v*)   The possible introduction of barriers to international trade designed to lessen the impact of world recession in response to deflation.

In terms of financial markets, the collapse of share prices also appears to have been triggered by a combination of factors:

(*i*)   A realisation that equities were overpriced in relation to their intrinsic value following a prolonged period of optimism (a 'bull' market).

(*ii*) Increased bond yields associated with increased leverage.

(*iii*) A consequential fall in demand for securities worldwide, accompanied by an increase of liquidity in trading systems.

(*iv*) Investor concern because of the increased costs of unexpected time lags associated with the sale of securities in a slack market.

(*v*) The inability of recently introduced computerised trading techniques to cope with significant adverse information in an overpriced market (the transition from a 'bull' to a pessimistic or 'bear' market).

The evidence suggests, therefore, that the US market was fuelled by conflicting uncertainties and speculation, rather than fundamental values. In order for the crash to have occurred the EMH predicts that, given the inter-relationship between corporate management, investors and the capital market, American companies should have assimilated all the available information and issued warnings indicating a 23 per cent reduction in their future earnings (i.e. the intrinsic value of their shares), thereby vindicating the amount by which Wall Street fell.

Since this did not happen, it suggests that the EMH, and hence the market, is at its most efficient when conditions are stable. This presents minimum opportunities for speculation because the rational expectation is for prices to remain constant, leaving values to be determined by the consensus of a large number of fundamentalist traders. Unfortunately, for advocates of the EMH this is usually in the middle of a bull or bear phase, which can only be ascertained with the benefit of hindsight. Thus, a significant proportion of the market may be driven for a significant period of time by irrationality.

As a consequence, critics claim today that, after more than a decade of international financial scandals, the EMH, if it operates at all, does so in only the weakest of forms; or investors have come to believe in the use of insider information by the privileged few. Many have lost the incentive to take advantage of known market information. Hence, the market has become even more inefficient and, therefore, more volatile.

Of course, this hypothesis can never be tested fully, since true insider information is illegal and remains outside the public domain. Besides, an alternative but equally disturbing explanation may well be that major players on what is now a global electronic market reject the EMH and are either short-termist or indulge in periodic bouts of speculation. Thus, a security's price can be bid above its intrinsic value (based on expected future cashflows) because speculative market participants believe that others will be naïve enough to pay still more for it tomorrow. For a while, this belief is self-sustaining and the market booms, but eventually the more astute participants sell and the market crashes. To compound the irony, it may well be that, in the long-term, the consequences for even the most adept speculators still conform to the EMH prediction: sometimes you win, sometimes you lose. The question is when?

Unfortunately, the EMH cannot provide an answer. Based on investor rationality, it takes a linear view of society. Investors, who are risk-averse, receive information and adjust to it immediately. In the case of models based upon the EMH, such as the CAPM, securities and portfolios do so through their betas, which are the slope of a linear regression between a stock or a portfolio and the market portfolio's excess returns (the SML). They do not react in a cumulative fashion to a series of events. The linear paradigm is incorporated into the rational investor concept because past information has already been discounted in security prices. The market, therefore, follows a random walk, because each day's price movement is unrelated to the previous day's activity.

But what if the behaviour of investors is non-linear, as the 1987 crash suggests? Unlike assuming away transaction costs or taxes, assuming that people are irrational changes the nature of the whole system. Individuals are no longer risk-averse at all times. Rationality is also limited. Investors may not know how to interpret all known information, let alone recognise it. They may be over-confident with forecasts. Investors may not react to information as it is received. Instead, they may respond after the event, particularly if it confirms a change in recent trends. These are all non-linear reactions. There is ample evidence to support the belief that investors in aggregate are no more rational than individuals. Historical precedents for the stock market crash of 1929 let alone 1987 are legion, as Mackay's treatise on the 'theory of crowds' (1841) reveals.

If the linear assumption that stock prices follow a random walk is invalid and the market has a memory, albeit short-term, the case for the EMH as presented is seriously weakened. And because the EMH is a justification for the CAPM, Modern Portfolio Theory (MPT), including specific models of asset pricing which assume investor rationality, is also called into question. Admittedly, the APT, which states that price changes occur from unexpected changes in factors, can handle non-linear relationships. But invariably in practice, standard econometrics using linear relationships still tend to be used in order to simplify its implementation. See Elton, Gruber and Mei (1994) for a review of the evidence.

4 THE EMH AS 'BAD SCIENCE'

Such quantitative expediency explains why the EMH itself is flawed. It is often forgotten that efficient markets do *not* necessarily imply a random walk but a random walk *does* imply market efficiency. The assumption that stock market returns follow a random walk, initially arose from empirical observations and a 'standard' statistical analysis of these observations, prior to any acceptable hypothesis concerning efficiency.

The EMH was developed subsequently but not independently. Its function was to provide explanations of rational investor behaviour, eventually embracing fundamentalism, technical analysis and Quants, all designed to validate the simple statistical tests previously employed.

If returns are independent, identically distributed (IID) variables they are random variables and they follow a random walk. According to the law of large numbers, as the observations collected approach infinity, the probability distribution becomes a normal or log-normal distribution with finite mean and variance (the Central Limit Theorem of Calculus). The assumption of normality justifies the use of 'Gaussian' techniques. Probability calculus, standard statistical tests, and models of investment behaviour which reduce the mathematics to simple linear differential equations can be used to create optimal solutions for decision-makers.

A body of early twentieth century literature collated by Cootner (1964), which presents the rationale for the EMH, reveals that researchers were well aware of the limitations of the normality assumption which underpinned their statistical analyses. Thus, it was postulated that because capital markets are huge systems characterised by large numbers of investors they must value securities according to the probability weighted average of possible returns, if it is assumed that they are unbiased and act rationally. Current prices, therefore, reflect all the information in their possession and changes in price are independent of previous prices, since they arise from new unexpected information. Consequently, the EMH, as first formalised by Fama (1965), concluded that investment on the stock market is a fair game for all, a martingale based on the randomness of historical returns.

If security returns are commensurate to their degree of risk, how then to beat the market? Lorie and Hamilton (1973), in their excellent survey, noted that the assumption of efficient markets is stronger than the assumption that historical changes in share prices are independent, i.e. the weak-form EMH. This confounded fundamental analysts, as well as technical analysts. Lorrie and Hamilton asserted that efficient markets must impound all that is knowable about companies whose shares are being traded, thereby acknowledging the fruitlessness of any effort to earn excess returns by the analysis of public information. A dialectic between proponents of the weak-form EMH and this new strong-form emerged. As a compromise, a flurry of academic papers articulated semi-strong market efficiency (see Fama 1970).

Naturally, this proved attractive to professional investment communities, not least because it justified their very existence. Semi-strong prices are determined independently by an extremely large number of fundamental analysts who utilise public information which produces a 'fair' value, based on consensus, i.e. market 'sentiment'. Hence, markets are efficient because of analysis, not in spite of it. Worldwide, through the 1970s to date the EMH in its semi-strong form has been taught as fact.

Yet, despite these self-serving developments a number of empirical studies designed to test the dependence of market efficiency on normally distributed returns continued to produce results to the contrary. Unfortunately, the dual alternative assumptions, that investors are not rational and that markets or securities are inter-dependent, i.e. not random, have been largely ignored.

5 THE CAPITAL ASSET PRICING MODEL

Having begun to question the evidence for efficient markets, based upon the random walk hypothesis, what are the implications for Quants, i.e. mathematical models of investor behaviour which assume rationality? As stated earlier, the acceptance of market characteristics under the EMH explains the parallel development of Modern Portfolio Theory (MPT) and the standard by which it is still judged, the CAPM.

Like the EMH, the CAPM is an abstraction of the real world, a construct with dubious, simplifying assumptions. It requires efficient markets and normally or log-normally distributed returns because variances are assumed to be finite. So again, instead of asking whether the model is too divorced from reality to guide investor decisions, the relevant question is whether it works.

It will be recalled that the CAPM explains how investors would behave in an efficient market if they are rational, that is risk-averse, with a preference for the highest expected return for a given level of risk, as measured by the standard deviation of returns.

The CAPM states that the return on a share or a portfolio depends on whether their prices follow prices in the market as a whole by reference to a suitable index, such as the FT-SE 100. The closer the correlation between the price of either an individual share or a portfolio and the price of this market proxy (the beta factor), the greater will be their expected returns. Securities and portfolios with high beta factors should yield high returns and *vice versa*. Thus, if an investor knows the beta factor of a share or portfolio, their returns can be predicted with accuracy. Profitable trading of portfolios is then accomplished by buying (selling) undervalued (overvalued) securities relative to their systematic or market risk.

Although there is evidence to suggest that shares with high betas may underperform relative to predictions (Black 1993) and zero beta shares have higher returns than risk-free securities (suggesting compensation for 'unsystematic' risk), numerous tests corroborate the CAPM. The beta-return characteristics of individual securities also hold for portfolios. In fact, the beta of a portfolio is often more stable because fluctuations among its constituents tend to cancel each other out, as Black, Jensen and Scholes (1972) first discovered. The New York Stock Exchange was analysed over a 35-year period by dividing the listing into 10 portfolios, the first comprising constituents with the lowest beta factors and so on. Their findings revealed, *inter alia*, an almost straight-line relationship between a portfolio's beta and its average return, and set a standard for tests of capital market theory.

The only real critique of the CAPM came from Roll (1977). It will be recalled that the CAPM concludes that all investors would choose to hold a portfolio which comprises the stock market as a whole. By definition, the market portfolio has a beta of one and is 'efficient' in the sense that no other combination of securities would give a higher return for the same risk. It is, therefore, a benchmark which establishes the Security Market Line (SML), in order to compare other beta factors and returns.

The SML, remember, is the line which plots the beta of a security against its expected return that intercepts the risk-free rate of interest and passes through the market portfolio. From this, rational investors can ascertain whether individual securities, which do not lie on the SML, are either underpriced or overpriced. They can also determine other efficient portfolios which balance risk and return. But how do you measure the market portfolio?

The CAPM subscribes to the still controversial Modigliani–Miller (MM) law of one price (1958). Based on the arbitrage process, this states that two similar assets cannot sell at different prices in equilibrium. In other words, two portfolio constituents which contribute the same amount of risk to that portfolio are in effect close substitutes and should, therefore, exhibit the same return. But what if an asset has no close substitute, such as the market itself? How can one establish whether it is under or over-valued?

According to Roll (op. cit), most CAPM tests are invalid because they depend upon a proxy, such as a stock exchange index, for the market portfolio. In the formal statement of the CAPM, the market portfolio is the portfolio of all risky investments, not just shares, which by definition must include every security worldwide. He demonstrated that a change in the American market surrogate from the Standard and Poor 500 to the Wilshire 5000 can radically alter a security's expected return as predicted by the CAPM. Roll also proved that the return on an asset is always a linear function of beta if the proxy chosen is any efficient portfolio. Hence, any test of the CAPM will support the CAPM. All one is testing is whether the proxy for the market portfolio is efficient.

Roll went on to say that if betas and returns derived from a stock market listing were unrelated, the securities might still be correctly priced in relation to the global market portfolio. Conversely, even if the listing was efficient (i.e. shares with high betas did exhibit high returns) there is no *a priori* reason for assuming that each constituent's return is only affected by global systematic risk.

Rolls' work does not contradict the CAPM or the assumptions which underpin the EMH. It is a critique of CAPM tests, not the CAPM itself. So where does that leave the investor?

6 PORTFOLIO MANAGEMENT AND THE EMH

To reiterate, all investors, institutional or otherwise, have three available options when managing their portfolios:

(*i*)   to trade
(*ii*) to hold
(*iii*) to substitute.

MPT explains how a particular portfolio can be managed profitably relative to appropriate measures of systematic risk. If the EMH is accepted, however, this must be viewed collectively as a zero-sum strategy, since one investor's gain is another's loss. Individually, the only way to outperform the market is by short-term speculation or privileged information, neither of which represents a realistic basis for risk–return management.

Yet, portfolios are actively traded and the growth of a multi-billion dollar investment industry implies that the financial institutions who manage them can evidently do better than either the personal investor, or the professional fund manager who prefers to adopt a passive policy of 'buy and hold', designed to match the long-run return of the market.

In order to trade profitably, fund managers, active or otherwise, require a strategy which:

- Incorporates a financial objective in terms of the portfolio's expected return over time.
- Eliminates unsystematic risk by efficient diversification.
- Establishes a tolerance to systematic risk which determines where to position the portfolio on the Capital Market Line (CML), the Security Market Line (SML) or the Arbitrage Pricing Plane (APP), depending on the asset pricing model (Markowitz, CAPM and APT, respectively).
- Selects an asset mix which is designed to achieve that position.
- Minimises transaction costs and is tax efficient.
- Reviews the position periodically.

The selection of an appropriate asset mix itself, is a product of three independent decisions:

(**a**) Strategic asset allocation, relating to the long-term policy to create a portfolio which balances the desired levels of risk and expected return along the SML, CML or APP.

(**b**) Tactical asset allocation, which reflects opportunistic decisions to enhance return by moving away from the 'normal' mix.

(**c**) Operational asset allocation, which may be both temporary and perhaps more dynamic; an obvious example being risk reduction in a falling market, paying for that protection through lower returns when conditions improve by adjusting position along the SML, CML or APP.

The balance of allocatory decisions taken by fund managers over time determines a portfolio's classification as either *passive* or *active*. Advocates of the former adopt a policy of strategic allocation and then hold securities, citing the benefits of indexed funds through lower management charges, dealing, research and analysts' costs in a situation where profitable trading is not possible in the presence of market efficiency. Activists maintain that a portfolio should be reviewed on a regular basis and securities bought and sold, depending on the prospects of individual companies and economies as a whole. Otherwise, it can become inefficient in terms of strategic objectives as the levels of risk and return periodically change (see Hill and Meredith 1994).

Whilst the zero-sum qualities of traded portfolios provides a powerful reason to adopt a passive approach, the empirical evidence is inconclusive. Studies have shown that active managers have failed consistently to beat the market. Proponents of the EMH use this fact as proof that markets are efficient. Critics of the EMH say that the results merely prove the incompetence of fund managers, particularly short-termists. Fuelling the debate is an observation that fundamental analysis sometimes works, but so does technical analysis.

Institutional investors who believe that a passive policy hinders investment performance can cite the work of Sharpe (1989) which explains how the use of tactical allocations enhances portfolio return without a corresponding increase in risk. However, this is to ignore its behavioural implications. For tactical allocation to succeed, fund managers may have to take decisions with which they feel uncomfortable, an obvious example being the acquisition of equity following the crash of 1987.

Prior to this, Brinson, Hood and Beebower (1986) analysed the results of two opposing active strategies. Using the Zerox pension fund, 5 per cent of the assets in the most successful market sector were transferred to the worst and vice versa (based upon their previous two year's performance). Obviously, the second policy option held more psychological appeal, as it possessed the logic of a proven track record. Yet, the study found that the first strategy outperformed the whole fund by 0.8 per cent, which was not inconsiderable given its size and the competitive nature of pension fund management. Unfortunately, they were unable to confirm that active asset allocation enhances portfolio value generally. Their study also analysed the performance of the 91 largest US pension funds over 10 years and found that those with an active investment policy were, on average, 0.66 per cent worse off annually (6.8 per cent over the whole period) than those who consistently adhered to the normal mix.

Findings of this nature, which are not unique (see Wood 1989), naturally lend support to strategic allocation, so much so that after the 1987 crash, a number of leading American fund managers acknowledged that actively traded portfolios were ineffectual. For example, Taylor (1990) reported how the administrators of New York City's $540bn pension fund earmarked 75 per cent to be governed by an indexation strategy of 'buy and hold', designed to match the return on the market, leaving only the balance to be individually traded.

In the UK, a 1989 report, issued by the Combined Actuarial Performance Services (CAPS), which surveyed over 2000 pension funds between 1980 and 1988, found no significant correlation between trading and performance, as measured by the FT All Share. In fact, actively managed funds under-performed relative to the market by 1.6 per cent, suggesting that investment performance is inversely related to asset turnover. As if to seal the case, Campbell (1988) further revealed that between 1983 and 1988 only one third of all equity fund managers outperformed the FT All Share. Presumably, this is why post-1987, the Rover Group (conforming to American practice) decided to transfer £960m of its pension fund from individual active trading to an indexed fund with lower management charges.

Perhaps the CAPM only works in the long-run, but performs short random walks. As Malkiel (1985) reports, the returns of American mutual funds bore no relation to their betas during the early 1980s. In fact there was a tendency for high beta funds to underperform relative to low beta ones.

The author's own survey of equity fund managers within the UK insurance industry (Hill and Meredith 1994) reveals that, despite a significant variation in management style and methods of analysis, 77 per cent of sample respondents set themselves, short-term, the collectively impossible target of beating the UK equity market. Moreover, 22 per cent wished to outperform an upper subset, the FT-SE 100, based upon the belief that more than 50 per cent of a share's price is determined within five years. Asked how the EMH affected their trading decisions, 64 per cent therefore claimed to ignore it completely. Yet, when questioned on future trends in portfolio management, respondents revealed a belief that the stock market is actually more efficient than short-termism sug-gests. Whilst 82 per cent managed a negligible proportion of funds under index-ation, half of those surveyed anticipated a growth of indexed portfolios allied to the use of liquid financial instruments (more hedging via options and futures) and an extension of programmed computer trading.

These results are interesting, not simply because they confound prior empir-ical evidence, such as that by Piper and Fruhan (1981) and Rappaport (1986), which suggests that an equation of share price is a long-term function, but also reveals capital markets to be efficient in the long-run (Malkiel 1985). Moreover, the responses sit uncomfortably with the pioneering work of Ross (1976), which revealed the superiority of APT techniques in relation to index models such as the CAPM. There is also Roll's critique (1977) concerning the difficulties of defining an efficient index against which to measure portfolio performance. Yet, a comparatively recent stock market development can explain the anomaly.

7 INDEX TRACKER FUNDS

Fashionable unit trusts came into the market nearly a decade ago, termed *index trackers*. They are passive portfolio funds which buy and hold all the securities used to calculate a particular market index, according to their weightings within it. Based on Markowitz efficiency, a tracker assumes that no combination of investments, other than the market portfolio, can provide a higher return for the same risk. The fund manager is no longer judgmental, but is essentially a computer program fed with data to allow for rights issues or sales when a share is dropped from the index. Tracker advocates claim superior performance over a three to five year period than the most actively managed portfolios, because their investment clientele is independent of human ingenuity when selecting appropriate stocks to hold.

Their rationale is that tracker funds perform well when their chosen market rises. If the market collapses, the fund can only fall as far as its index. Proponents of actively traded portfolios may cite impressive gains, based on the fund manager's perception of rising world markets, but an actively traded portfolio can also plumb the depths. During periods of uncertainty, so the argument goes, an index tracker fund offers downside protection whilst also retaining exposure to any potential recovery.

For example, an active fund with a majority of Japanese constituents would have benefited from sharply rising share prices and property values in 1990. But, in the absence of perfect foresight or a timely readjustment, when the market collapsed the portfolio would have followed suit. In contrast, a world tracker fund would have been cushioned from this effect. At the time of writing (late 1997), the Morgan Stanley Capital International's World Index (MSCI), which allocates global weightings precisely to its tracker portfolio, comprises 47 per cent of American assets with only 14.7 per cent invested in Japan (which is the world's second largest market) followed by the UK at 10.2 per cent.

Of course, a tracker fund's performance still depends upon the choice of an appropriate index, which astute active managers may assiduously avoid. During the early 1990s, and the 1997 collapse of the Tiger economies, Japanese tracker funds produced impoverished returns because necessarily they incorporate the components of their market. In Japan's case, these included banking stocks which performed abysmally as a consequence of recurrent financial crises. Conversely, the top ten international index-tracker unit trusts, based on the various American Standard and Poor and UK Financial Times indices, produced an annual increase in performance of at least 30 per cent toward the end of 1997 (according to Micropal).

To hedge one's bets, there are also other more sophisticated tracker funds which permit the investor to access individual markets at a lower cost. These use futures and options or derivatives based on the option pricing model of Black and Scholes (1973). They may also track an index in reverse, moving up each time the market falls and *vice versa*. However, five years after their introduction, derivative tracker funds claimed the bottom four places out of 1330 unit trusts in Micropal's ranking of one year performance to April 1994, with the worst (Fidelity Europe Reverse Index) displaying a loss of 25.5 per cent. Subsequent annual performance has still proved variable depending upon the choice of index.

In their defence, investors who buy derivatives are moving large amounts of money in and out of their portfolios on a real-time basis as downside protection, using the most sophisticated and up to the minute information. Certainly, they would not normally hold a position for twelve months. But returning to the original proposition, if the EMH is accepted surely they, too, must still aspire to an impossible collective goal.

To circumvent the problem, why then agonise over active management or a policy of buying and holding a passively indexed fund? One solution, increasingly favoured by professional analysts, is to adopt a *core-satellite* portfolio strategy.

The policy is to invest a major proportion of funds in a large, mature market (i.e. efficient) using trackers, since an actively traded portfolio will be unlikely to outperform the index. The balance of funds (say 30 per cent) is then actively managed in risky but potentially high return markets, which may be emerging or less efficient. Much will be unknown, because, contrary to the EMH, information is no longer universally available to all market participants and will not be assimilated into security prices. But, with an ear to the ground, the newly focussed fund manager's prospects for incremental returns should be enhanced, or so the argument goes.

Yet, what if the most efficient markets do not behave efficiently (circa 1987 *et al*) and by moving beyond the main index the portfolio enters the realms of uncertainty?

8 MARKET INFORMATION AND INSTITUTIONAL NEGLECT

Whilst the martingale effect on traded portfolios justifies the adoption of passive holding strategies based on indexation, other factors are important.

MPT only assumes that the stock market is efficient, not the market for information, which is imperfectly competitive and costly. It will be recalled that the optimum portfolio is the market portfolio, which lies on the Security Market Line (SML) with a beta factor of one. Individual securities and portfolios with different levels of risk (betas) can be priced, since their expected rate of return and beta can be compared with the SML. In equilibrium all securities will lie on the line, because those above or below are either under or overpriced in relation to their expected return. Thus, market demand, or the lack of it, will elicit either a rise or fall in price until the return matches that of the market. Hence, fundamental traders, as well as speculators, with selective access to news can earn excess returns, particularly in the short-term, without invalidating the EMH (and MPT) because they have the ability to purchase information ahead of competitors. Real time, they recognise that prices are out of line and make abnormal profits by driving them back to an equilibrium which is consistent with available information, the MM rule.

Cornell and Roll (1981) proved the reasonableness of efficient financial markets where investors earn different gross rates of return. However, they also noted that these corresponded to the incurrence of differing acquisition costs for information. Consequently, net of costs, their long-term risk-adjusted rates were all equal to a net present value of zero. Altman (1988), among others since, has also cited excessive transaction costs associated with sophisticated trading operations and research departments designed to acquire price-sensitive information ahead of competitors, as a significant determinant of mediocre net performance among actively managed portfolios.

Equally pernicious is the extent to which financial institutions now dominate the capital market, thereby imposing severe constraints upon their behaviour. To compensate for rising systematic risk, the author's research (1994) reveals, *inter alia*, two strategies mentioned by UK equity fund managers.

First, they could liquidate all or part of a portfolio. However, if the whole portfolio were sold it would be impossible to dispose of a large fund quickly and efficiently without affecting the market. Unlike a private investor, total disposal might also be against the fund's trust deed. If only part of the portfolio was liquidated there was the further vexed question of which securities to sell.

The second option would be to reduce all holdings, to be followed by subsequent reinvestment when the market bottoms out. However, the fall in prices could be in excess of 2 per cent to cover transaction and commission costs. Moreover, as investment in individual companies increases, selling their shares may precipitate lower prices. If the upper quartile is involved, it might also depress the market, thereby becoming self-defeating, as noted by Drucker (1991).

Clearly, these alternatives are untenable, imposing further significant constraints upon the opportunities to control risk. Indeed, those sceptical of portfolio management maintain that successful investment is still a matter of luck rather than judgement, insider information or unlikely economic circumstances where all prices move in unison. A more considered view is that while it certainly depends upon the following combination of factors:

(*i*)   legitimate financial instruments with which to short the market
(*ii*) extremely low transaction costs
(*iii*) negotiable commissions
(*iv*) speed and simplicity of dealing
(*v*)   the segregation of systematic and unsystematic risk

there is a further option.

If the active or passive trading of major companies, indexed or otherwise, is not a viable policy for institutional investors to pursue, then an alternative strategy is to diversify selectively across smaller firms. Research has long since established that they produce higher returns than the larger ones. For example, Arbel, Carvell and Strebel (1983) revealed that between 1926–1981 the average annual rate of return on the New York Stock Exchange was 9.1 per cent, but constituents with a market capitalisation in the smallest 20 per cent averaged 12.1 per cent. Moreover, between 1971–1980 the return on what they termed 'institutionally neglected' stocks was 16.4 per cent against 9.4 per cent for the larger, more actively traded companies. A more recent study by Fama and French (1992) also confirms that since the mid-1960s larger companies have regularly underperformed relative to smaller companies.

This is not surprising, if one accepts that firms with a small market capitalisation may be overlooked by investment analysis. Infrequently traded, their shares operate within the weak form of the EMH displaying a more inaccurate fundamental valuation relative to the much publicised upper end of the market. Why then do institutional investors ignore this opportunity for higher returns?

First, institutional requirements for a considered policy of liquidity, diversity and flexibility of investment still necessitates an ability to transact large numbers of shares without destroying their underlying market. As a portfolio's funds increase, the number of companies which are eligible for inclusion, therefore, falls. Consider a fund manager with £1000m to invest, research analyst cover for 100 securities and a maximum holding policy of 5 per cent in any one company. The average to be invested is £10m (£1000m/100). As a consequence, only those shares with a market capitalisation in excess of £200m (£10m/0.05) would be available for acquisition.

Even if an institution is in a position to increase the number of stocks in its portfolio, they will still tend to be those of major companies as the author's research reveals (1994). Unlike an investor whose interpretation of performance fails to discriminate between whether a higher return on lower capital employed is preferable to a lower return on higher capital, one would not expect fund managers to be so naïve but merely constrained, particularly in a bonus climate which cultivates short-termism. The absolute profit, as opposed to the percentage return from investments in 'neglected' companies, may not be sufficient to cover the necessary trading and research costs, as outlined by Altman (1988) and the author (1994).

Given the degree of market concentration within financial institutions world-wide, the gravity of these problems should not be underestimated. Paradoxically, a number of major players may have little choice but to opt for a policy of acquiring still larger blocks of shares but trading them much less frequently despite movements in markets; hence the belief in indexation. As a corollary, the performance of the largest institutional funds may tend towards underperformance, relative to the competition and the market as a whole.

9 NON-LINEAR SYSTEMS

With the constraints placed upon institutional fund management, the analytical framework of MPT and the EMH prediction that collective investment is a martingale are seriously weakened.

Conversely, if the EMH operates in its semi-strong form, the only way for investors (institutional or otherwise) to beat the market is by successful specu-lation, insider dealing, or access to monopolistic information. One is illegal, all may be costly, and none represents a rational long-term strategy for profitable risk–return management.

Alternatively, even if individuals do not behave rationally, according to the EMH, so many investors still react to information in a cause and effect manner that a common consciousness or unbiased 'sentiment' is reflected in a fair equilibrium price by the market. Because new information is independent of past information, price changes follow a random walk and a security's returns are normally distributed.

But what if capital markets are non-linear and reaction to information is constrained or occurs in clusters once trends are established? The past and future would now be interdependent and share prices would not be random. There is ample evidence to support such a *feedback* system.

The first comprehensive analysis of daily stock market returns was under-taken by Fama (1965), who revealed their non-normal distribution. The fre-quency of observation was not the familiar bell-shaped curve but negatively skewed displaying *leptokurtosis*: the condition of higher peaked means and 'fat' tails associated with significant 'outlier' observations more than three standard deviations away from the mean. Like the founders of the EMH (Cootner 1964), CAPM's advocates were also aware of these conditions which are characteristic of a Pareto distribution. So much so that Sharpe (1970) and Miller (1972), among others, published texts modifying MPT for non-normality, to include the Stable Paretian Hypothesis of Mandelbrot (1963) which suggests that returns are characterised by undefined or infinite variance.

More recently, the extensive study by Turner and Weigal (1990), who utilised 1928 through 1990 daily Standard and Poor 500 Index returns and the Dow Jones, reconfirmed negative skewedness and leptokurtosis. This immediately invited the criticism that any frequency distribution incorporating the October 1987 crash, that of 1929, a World War, Korea and the oil crises of the 1970s will be negatively skewed with a fat lower tail. But as Friedman and Laibson (1989) observed, these were only five of a sequence of unusual events. On a quarterly basis they also noted that, utilising Standard and Poor 500 returns from 1946 to 1988, outlier price movements more than three standard deviations away from the mean are associated with crashes rather than rallies, irrespective of the time period chosen.

Technically, this does not imply that capital markets are inefficient, but are they normal? The EMH, the Gaussian methodology of mean-variance analyses, correlation coefficients and tests of significance upon which the CAPM depends are seriously weakened. In the absence of alternative predictive models this also sponsors the theoretical case for short-termism, which at a practical level now appears so pervasive.

Such a view has long been popular with financial institutions who actively trade their portfolios based on qualitative judgements and appear to reject the EMH, as confirmed by the author's survey of equity fund managers operating within the UK insurance sector. With hindsight, it also accommodates the behaviour of the US stock market in 1987 which was fuelled by adaptive expectations, rather than changing intrinsic values in response to fundamental news. The EMH works best (if at all) on the few occasions when markets are stable and values are determined by rational behaviour, leaving little room for speculation. Between times, in the presence of volatility, it cannot predict what proportion of traders operate on fundamental news, as opposed to rumour.

Since October 1987 several crises have been witnessed in stock markets worldwide which appear to have no association with economic circumstances (although the 1997 meltdown of the Tiger economies is a notable exception). Volatility in financial markets has typically followed a period of tranquillity and a period of turbulence giving rise to the proposition that volatility, as measured by the variance of returns, is *heteroskedastic*, i.e. they are not constant through time. Empirical heteroskedasticity in financial and economic series is also comprehensively documented in 200 empirical journal articles cited by Bollerslev, Chou and Kroner (1992). Thus, the standard deviation may be meaningless as a measure of dispersion or risk, thereby confounding the EMH and all the Quants models based upon the normal distribution that derive from it.

Recall that the standard deviation as a measure of the probability that an observation will be a certain distance from the average observation is only valid if the underlying series is random, i.e. exhibits zero correlation. Yet, three shares with equal volatilities as measured by the standard deviation can exhibit different patterns of return which have serious implications for portfolio management and the mathematical models employed. One may be *normally distributed*, i.e. a random series. Another may display *antipersistent* behaviour, alternatively termed *mean reversion*, whereby a series returns to its long-term mean after a short-term departure. A simple example is where a share which has been up in the previous period is down in the next period or *vice versa*. A third share may reveal *persistent* behaviour: trend-reinforcing characteristics which produce a *biased* random walk.

The quest for mean reversion now occupies a pivotal position in economics and finance. Short-termists are keen to exploit any mean-reverting tendencies in capital markets to generate excess returns. If it exists, a short-term investment holding horizon will be more risky than a long period. This will affect the investors' allocation mix. As Kritzman also observed (1994) active trading strategies will have to be developed to optimise any mean reversion trends which involve the portfolio constituents. Unfortunately, the accepted methodology applied to date, invariably based upon variance ratio analysis, is unable to provide a satisfactory indication as to whether US or UK stock market returns are mean-reverting or not. The existing literature is against the finding of mean reversion, but as Poon (1995) observed this conclusion may be invalid. All the test statistics, variance ratios or otherwise, are Gaussian and still based on a combination of questionable assumptions that the underlying series are independent and identically distributed (IID) variables, a random walk and normal. For examples, see Cochrane (1988), Poterba and Summers (1988 and 1989), Jegadeesh (1991) and Faust (1992).

With regard to persistent behaviour, the empirical evidence looks more promising. The analyses assume that financial markets are not random but have a memory. Investors wait for information which confirms a trend and then react, rather than respond immediately to new information as the EMH assumes. This non-linear view of financial markets supports the observation that the distribution of stock market returns is Paretian, with peaked means and fat tails, following a biased random walk as investors identify a trend reinforcing their outlook, based on changing fundamentals and technical analysis. It has also forced researchers to explore other avenues of mathematics and statistics.

One such area is fractal geometry which permits large system changes to occur through a series of small changes. Large changes can be discontinuous and abrupt which can explain why the October 1987 crash occurred. Fractal statistics also permit the sample variance to be undefined or infinite with an unstable mean. The standard deviation becomes irrelevant as a measure of dispersion or risk and is replaced by H, the *Hurst exponent* (1951) which measures the bias of a system, where:

(*i*) $H = 0.50$ denotes a random series.

(*ii*) $0 \leqslant H \leqslant 0.50$ denotes the strength of antipersistence or mean reversion in a series, depending on how close H is to zero.

(*iii*) $0.50 < H < 1.00$ denotes the strength of persistence of trend reinforcement in a series, with 0.5 as a lower limit signifying a lack of definition or 'noise'.

Peters (1991) brought together the elements of fractal analysis based upon the pioneering work of Mandelbrot (1963 and 1972) to test the Fractal Market Hypothesis (FMH). This states that capital markets follow a Stable Paretian distribution (i.e. H does not equal 0.50). Peters' calculations of the Hurst exponent utilising daily Standard and Poor prices from 1928 to 1990 over different frequencies of time revealed the US equity market to be persistent with a long memory of varying lengths $(0.5 < H < 1.00)$, which elicits a four-year cyclical bias in returns. *Inter alia*, the economy exhibited a five-year bias. He also tested volatility by analysing a monthly series of standard deviation of returns from 1945 to 1990 and discovered one of the few antipersistent series in finance or economics $(H = 0.39)$. If volatility was up in the previous month, it was down in the next month. The FMH was confirmed.

Does all this mean that professional analysts are abandoning EMH techniques which explain changes in security prices and returns? On the contrary, because fractal analysis is descriptive and non-prescriptive, there is still no complete model of investor behaviour to replace the CAPM and its derivatives. Yet, perhaps because of the dangers of bonus-orientated short-termism, new theoretical explanations of non-linearity, the instability of markets and why they have a propensity to crash are being crystallised.

10 THEORIES OF SPECULATIVE BUBBLES

Speculative bubble theory, also termed the 'castle in the air' theory by Malkiel (1985), has a historic pedigree, evidenced by the impressive list supplied by MacKay (1841) which includes the best known example, the South Sea Bubble.

According to theory, stock market behaviour is non-linear and based on inflating and bursting speculative bubbles, rather than economic forecasts. Security prices are bid above their intrinsic prices (which reflect expected cash returns) because a number of investors believe that others will pay more for them in the future. For a while, this behaviour feeds upon itself and prices rise (a bull market). However, at some critical point, investors will react to all their information which they have ignored, lose confidence that prices can rise still further and the market crashes.

Hardouvelis (1988) explains how speculative bubbles can be deflated, as well as initiated, by insignificant extraneous events that are unrelated to fundamental conditions. A group of investors may purchase securities with the expectation of a speculative capital gain. Others follow suit without a proper analysis of all the available information concerning future dividends and interest rates. If such behaviour persists, subsequent demand increases price but the speculative bubble may burst suddenly. The overvalued market is fragile. Much has been ignored and a relatively unimportant piece of bad news may easily create pessimism and trigger an avalanche of selling.

The established test for speculative bubbles identifies abnormal positive returns during the suspected bubble period and assesses the probability of these occurring by chance (Blanchard and Watson 1982). An exceptionally high return is defined in relation to the CAPM, i.e. a return higher than the risk-free rate plus the usual risk premium that is necessary to compensate risk-averse investors for the uncertainty associated with their returns. On the assumption that returns are normally distributed, there is little likelihood that extreme values would occur by chance. Hence, a statistically significant number of very large returns constitute evidence which is consistent with the presence of a bubble.

Given that market returns are not normally distributed but extremely volatile, it is not surprising that the traditional bubble test has low statistical power. Distributions are also negatively skewed which means that abnormal negative returns can mask evidence for a bubble. To resolve this dilemma it is necessary to formulate either a non-normal statistical approach (more of which later) or to provide a more detailed account of the development of the bubble.

Shiller (1989) ignored the distribution of returns and considered the amount of volatility that should be expected in a rational market where security prices are based upon dividend expectations. On the basis of questionnaire data, he asserts that, in the period before October 1987, US price changes were far too volatile to be explained by rational dividend expectations, even when adjusted for inflation. The market was overvalued but investors showed no desire to liquidate their holdings and continued to buy and sell, as they would in the absence of bubbles. In response to one question, Shiller found that 84.3 per cent of institutional investors and 71.7 per cent of individual investors thought that the market was overvalued at the time. Replying to another, only 22.2 per cent and 36.1 per cent respectively described themselves as bullish or optimistic relative to other investors.

Whilst the survey was conducted after the crash, which may have influenced respondents' answers, Shiller maintains that there are two types of investor:

(*i*) 'noise traders' who follow fashion
(*ii*) 'smart money traders' who invest according to value

He also notes that the latter do not necessarily describe professional analysis or financial institutions; conversely noise traders are any investors who tend to over-react to fundamental news concerning future dividends. Smart money then benefits from this.

11 RATIONAL BUBBLE THEORY

Shiller's explanation of stock market volatility challenges both the notion that investors act rationally and that their large numbers ensure efficiency in a rising market. Yet, if investors were not optimistic, it is still difficult to comprehend why they did not liquidate their holdings prior to October 1987.

One explanation by Hardouvelis (1988), which does not depend upon market irrationality, modifies the EMH assumption that people are risk-averse. Recall that, if investors are to accept more risk, they must be compensated with more return. However, if negative returns are involved they will adapt their behaviour to minimise losses.

In the case of a *rational* speculative bubble, investors are aware that the bubble may burst and that they will be locked into their positions once the crash starts. However, there is a good probability that the bubble will continue to expand creating large positive returns. These returns are expected to be higher than the risk-free rate plus the normal risk premium in the absence of bubbles and large enough to offset the probability of the bubble's collapse and an abnormal once-only negative return.

Thus, it is rational for investors to remain in the market. The expected extra return when no bubble crash occurs is termed the bubble *premium*, which increases with the lifetime of the rising market. The bubble premium's time trend derives from the growth behaviour of a security price's bubble *component*. The longer the period, the larger this component becomes relative to a share's fundamental value. This expansion also implies that, with the passage of time, the expected fall in security prices associated with a bubble crash will be more pronounced, necessitating an explosive bubble premium.

Hardouvelis points to a positive and rising bubble premium for approximately eighteen months prior to 1987 on the American and Japanese stock markets. A positive and rising bubble premium was also observable in the UK but did not appear until mid-1987. However, further empirical research is essential. Given the different time trends associated with each bubble, one only has to ask why the Japanese experienced a modest dip in October 1987 share prices (even prior to government intervention) when the UK crash was on a par with the American market.

On the subject of how individuals actually make decisions, more recent research presented by Tversky (1990) appears to support the rational bubble theory. When negative returns are likely, investors tend to be risk-seeking. They will gamble if it can minimise their losses. The longer the period of time it takes for returns to materialise, the more likely people are to gamble. He also asserts that, as a survival technique (given bounded rationality), investors tend to be more confident in their forecasts than is justified by the information in their possession.

12 CHAOTIC SYSTEMS AND CATASTROPHES

Speculative bubble theory is important because it has paved the way for more sophisticated explanations of investor behaviour. It seriously weakens the EMH by suggesting that the capital market is a dynamic non-linear system which possesses important characteristics:

- It is a *feedback* system.
- There are *critical levels* of activity where equilibrium prices breakdown.
- It exhibits *sensitive dependence on initial conditions*, which means that a slight change in current fundamentals can have an explosive impact on future events.

As a consequence, forecasting, let alone prediction, becomes impossible beyond a certain time scale. This lends credibility to short-termism.

In the physical sciences, such a system has long been defined as *chaotic*. The traditional idea that nature always maintains a balance is being replaced continually by *chaos theories* which acknowledge that natural phenomena are interdependent and in a continual state of flux. Nature abhors an equilibrium.

Substantial empirical evidence that financial markets are chaotic has been collated by Peters (1991) including his own analysis of global markets (American, UK, German and Japanese equities) for the period 1959–1990. A number of theoretical models based on natural systems have also been formulated to explain stock market volatility. Two are worthy of consideration here, because they are complementary but draw on the same theory, that of *catastrophe* which is a subset of chaos theory. Moreover, the first was developed many years ago by Zeeman (1974) and is deterministic, whilst the second, set up by Vaga (1991), is a non-linear statistical model which is unique.

Catastrophes can only be observed in non-linear dynamic systems and are characterised by abrupt changes in the systems' dynamic properties due to small shifts in its parameters (recall the Fractal Market Hypothesis). Catastrophe theory is based on the concept of *self-organised criticality* that was originally used to model natural phenomena which tend to be in a *critical state*, i.e. on the edge of stability far from equilibrium. Good examples are volcanoes and earthquakes.

A simple analogy, which has been mathematically modelled by Bak and Chen (1991), involves dropping grains of sand onto a round flat surface. As the pile grows, one grain of sand occasionally causes slides which get larger as the pile gets higher. At some point, sand begins to fall off the edge of the plate and when this equals the sand being dropped the pile stops growing. It has achieved a critical state, since equilibrium would only have been achieved if, originally, the sand had been spread out evenly over a flat surface.

From the critical point, avalanches can vary widely from a few grains to large slides (catastrophes) depending upon the stability of the grains already in place. The distribution of stable and unstable conditions changes frequently around the pile, i.e. local conditions are in a state of flux. However, two phenomena do not change. First, few grains of sand are required for either catastrophes or minor events to occur. Second, because the probabilities of stable or unstable conditions are equal and the distribution of unstable areas frequently changes, even catastrophes do not affect the 'organisation' of the pile. Its precise conical slope does not change significantly.

13 A CATASTROPHE THEORY MODEL

Catastrophe theory's concept of self-organised criticality, where small changes in local conditions can significantly affect the system causing a rapid transition from stable to turbulent behaviour, was first applied to the stock market by Zeeman (1974). He divided all investors into two classes:

(*i*) 'Fundamentalists' who use macro-economic and micro-economic analyses to construct forecasts based on rational expectations to guide their investment strategies.

(*ii*) 'Speculators' whose decisions reflect adaptive behaviour in response to their technical analysis of recent patterns of stock market behaviour.

The two schools of thought are not mutually exclusive. All investors who take risks in order to benefit from disparities in share prices over time are speculators in the normal sense of the word. Thus, fundamentalists can exhibit adaptive behaviour. The essential difference is that fundamentalists tend to pursue a longer-term investment strategy, whereas speculators have a shorter time perspective.

Zeeman classified the activities of these two types of investor by the following variables:

- the proportion of the stock market held by speculators, which is denoted by S
- the excess demand for stock by fundamentalists, which is denoted by F.

The actual market of a stock exchange is represented by an equity price index, such as the Dow Jones or FT-SE 100 and denoted by I. The rate of change in the designated index over time (*t*) is the 'state-variable' of the Zeeman model and is characterised by:

$$\Delta I = dI/dt$$

345

such that:

(*i*) $\Delta I = 0$ represents a static market.

(*ii*) $\Delta I > 0$ characterises a rise in share prices, i.e. a bull market.

(*iii*) $\Delta I < 0$ characterises a bear market.

It is also assumed that equity prices and, therefore, ΔI respond very quickly to any disequilibrium on the stock exchange. However, while ΔI responds swiftly to changes in S and F, ΔI has a much slower feedback effect upon S.

Whereas fundamentalists typically invest in a recuperating bear market (rising F) following a prolonged decline in prices when equity is likely to be undervalued, speculators tend to wait for a period of sustained recovery to establish itself before buying, thereby intensifying any up-trend. Thus, during the bull period the degree of speculation (S) increases and leads to self-fulfilling price rises. Eventually, the disparity between actual share prices and their underlying fundamental values induces fundamentalists to sell equities, causing a fall in F. If the market is about to decline, speculators tracking market trends will start to liquidate their positions as well. This is the transition from a bull to a bear market.

The feedback effects of ΔI on F and S were modelled by Zeeman, as indicated by the dotted lines in Figure 13.1. If the proportion of speculators are in the minority (S is small) then ΔI is a continuously increasing function of F which means that, if fundamentalists induce an excess demand (or excess supply) on the stock exchange, the equity price index I will increase (decrease) monotonically. There is a smooth change from a bull to a bear market.

Conversely, instability is introduced into the market if the proportion of speculators is large (S is substantial). This means that any movement in the equity price index will be amplified by speculation. If the index begins to rise (fall), there will be a rapid move into a bull (bear) market.

Figure 13.1 illustrates the equilibrium surface of the Zeeman model, involving the variables, I, S and F. According to the Classification Theorem of René Thom (1875), this is defined as the *cusp–catastrophe* surface. With a small proportion of speculators in the market, $S < S_0$, the transition from a bull to a bear market results in smooth movements of I. Catastrophe points appear only for a large degree of speculation, when $S > S_0$. Within the catastrophe region, the equilibrium surface consists of three sheets, including two stable *attractors* (bull and bear markets). The middle sheet represents unstable equilibrium points.

The larger the degree of speculation, S, the more pronounced are the possible catastrophe events. During extended bull periods, intensified speculation leads to strong index increases, which indicates a market over-valuation of equities with respect to their fundamentals. Fundamentalists typically begin to disinvest before the market reaches its peak. Price falls are exacerbated as speculators

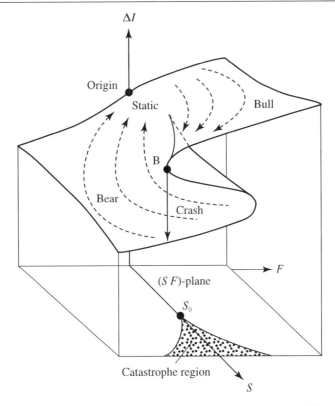

Fig 13.1 Equity price changes in the Zeeman model

adopt their expectations and reinforce the downward trend. In the diagram, point B will be reached if speculation is further amplified by outside events. Only a slight reduction in the excess demand of equity from fundamentalists, F, leads to a 'crash', i.e. an abrupt fall in I, the index.

Thus, instability is introduced into financial markets by speculators who react on the basis of adaptive expectations. During the extended bull period which characterised the US stock market after 1982, speculators seemed to gain prominence (increasing S). This was particularly true during 1987 when the Dow Jones index rose 10 per cent in just three months. At the same time, fundamentals, which were mainly influenced by the huge US budget and current account deficits, tended to point down, indicating a pronounced over-valuation of equity prices generally.

The situation became problematical in the months prior to the crash when the value of long-term debt fell drastically as bond yields rose. These increasing debt yields, accompanied by a growing awareness of economic uncertainly (as evidenced by an unstable exchange rate situation), eventually resulted in a pessimistic (bearish) view of the future. Consequently, the market collapsed. Since then, the Zeeman model has been reconfirmed by market volatility.

14 THE COHERENT MARKET HYPOTHESIS

If financial markets are non-linear chaotic systems with sensitive dependence on initial conditions, forecasting becomes difficult and a more sophisticated statistical analysis than that based on random walks and normality is a matter of urgency.

A unique approach to the problem, termed the Coherent Market Hypothesis (CMH), has recently been developed by Vaga (1991). A non-linear statistical model which also draws upon catastrophe theory, the CMH states that the probability density function of equity returns on the market may be determined by a combination of two factors:

(*i*)   the fundamental bias of the economic environment
(*ii*) group sentiment or the degree of 'crowd behaviour' based upon public opinion.

Depending upon combinations of these two factors the market can be in one of three states:

- Random walk: an efficient market with neutral fundamentals.
- Unstable transition: an inefficient market with neutral fundamentals.
- Chaos, characterised by crowd behaviour with mildly bearish fundamentals.

Vaga draws upon the Theory of Social Imitation developed by Callan and Shapiro (1974) which explains how people follow the dictates of fashion in terms of positive and negative sentiment. At times there is no consensus of public opinion, i.e. an absence of crowd behaviour. At other times there can be strong coherent sentiment. A third possibility is that public opinion may polarise resulting in a chaotic social environment.

Vaga translates the public opinion of social imitation into *market sentiment*. The risk–return trade-off becomes a combination of market sentiment and the fundamental economic environment. Like Zeeman's model of catastrophe theory, the CMH marries the views of fundamental analysts to technical analysts, i.e. those who follow trends.

According to Vaga, true random walk phases with a normal probability density function do exist. Investors react independently of one another to fundamental news which is quickly discounted by the market and reflected in share price. However, unlike the EMH predictions, this state of affairs is the exception rather than the rule.

As public opinion forms, biases in investor sentiment can cause the impact of information to be felt for long periods of time. This persistence of trends, until new information changes them, Vaga termed 'unstable transition' which appears to be the commonest state of markets, i.e. they are inefficient.

If fundamentals remain neutral but crowd behaviour increases, the system becomes very unstable. A classic 'chaotic' market exhibits a high degree of crowd behaviour but no fundamental information to place the bias in either a positive or negative direction. Speculation, rumour or misinterpreted information can cause panics as investors gauge each others' actions, hoping to out-guess the market. Once the market begins to move it can shift rapidly. The slightest information to the contrary can cause wide swings in the opposite direction.

During and after the 1987 crash there was a significant increase in the volatility of share prices, reflecting rapidly changing expectations. Trading volume also increased dramatically. According to Vaga this had little to do with fundamental information. It was pure crowd behaviour characteristic of a chaotic market. In contrast, significant shifts in the fundamental environment in the presence of crowd behaviour can cause a coherent market. For example, optimistic fundamentals result in a coherent bull market where the risk of loss is low and overall volatility declines. This inverts the risk–return trade-off of the CAPM. The probability density function of returns is drastically skewed to the right but retains a long negative tail showing that losses are still possible, even if their likelihood is minimal. Negative information would have a smaller effect in this environment than positive news of the same magnitude. Vaga cites January 1975 and August 1982 as examples of coherent bull markets. Coherent bear markets are also likely if fundamentals are negative but these are rarer still. At the time of writing Vaga considered the period 1973 – 1974 to be the most recent American example. The reader could now cite others.

15 CONCLUSION

The CMH is a significant development in capital market theory because it provides a non-linear statistical model for assessing market risk and how it changes over time in response to fundamental and technical factors.

Although empirical evidence for its support is still sparse and its application is still limited to domestic equity markets, the CMH seems to confirm investor experience in a world that can change abruptly once certain critical levels are reached. It also sits comfortably with the Fractal Market Hypothesis, speculative bubble theory and the Zeeman model of catastrophe, all of which combine the views of fundamental and technical analysts. In each case, the optimal solutions of asset pricing models such as the CAPM and its derivatives, based upon the simplifying assumptions of the EMH, are called into question. However, by offering the possibility of prediction, the CMH may yet provide an alternative explanation of how financial markets operate and, in the presence of stock market inefficiency, an alternative investment strategy to either pure speculation or short-termism.

References

(1) Altman, R.M., *Creating Investor Demand for Company Stock*, Quorum Books 1988.
(2) Arbel, A., Carvell, S. and Strebel, P., 'Giraffes, institutions and neglected firms', *Financial Analysts Journal*, May–June 1983.
(3) Bak, P. and Chen, K., 'Self-organised criticality', *Scientific American*, January, 1991.
(4) Black, F. and Scholes, M., 'The pricing of options and corporate liabilities', *Journal of Political Economy*, Vol. 81, May–June 1973.
(5) Black, F., 'Beta and return', *Journal of Portfolio Management*, Vol. 20, Fall 1993.
(6) Black, F., Jensen, M.C. and Scholes, M., 'The capital asset pricing model: some empirical tests', reprinted in Jensen, M.C. (Ed.), *Studies in the Theory of Capital Markers*, Praeger 1972.
(7) Blanchard, J. and Watson, M.W., 'Bubbles, rational expectation and financial markets', in Wachtel, P. (Ed.), *Crises in the Economic and Financial Structure*, Lexington Books 1982.
(8) Bollerslev, T., Chou, R.Y. and Kroner, K.F., 'ARCH modelling in finance – a review of the theory and empirical evidence', *Journal of Econometrics*, Vol. 52 No. 1–2, 1992.
(9) Brinson, G.P., Hood, R.L. and Beebower, G.L., 'Determinants of portfolio performance', *Financial Analysts Journal*, July–August 1986.
(10) Callan, E. and Shapiro, D., 'A theory of social imitation', *Physics Today*, Vol. 27, 1974.
(11) Campbell, J., 'Index funds – big investors admit defeat', *Investors Chronicle*, November 25, 1988.
(12) Cochrane, H. John, 'How big is the random walk in GNP?', *Journal of Political Economy*, Vol. 96, 1988.
(13) Cootner, P.H. (Ed), *The Random Character of Stock Market Prices*, M.I.T. Press 1964.
(14) Cornell, B. and Roll, R., 'Strategies for pairwise competitions in markets and organisations', *The Bell Journal of Economics*, Spring 1981.
(15) Drucker, P., 'Reckoning with the pension fund revolution', *Harvard Business Review*, March–April 1991.
(16) Elton, E.J., Gruber, M.J. and Mei, J., 'Cost of capital using arbitrage pricing theory: a case study of nine New York utilities', *Financial Markets, Institutions and Instruments*, Vol. 3, August 1994.
(17) Fama, E.F. and French, K.R., 'The cross-section of expected stock returns', *Journal of Finance*, Vol. 47, No.3, June 1992.
(18) Fama, E.F., 'Efficient capital markets: a review of theory and empirical evidence', *Journal of Finance*, Vol. 25, No. 2, May 1970.

(19) Fama, E.F., 'Portfolio analysis in a stable Paretian market', *Management Science*, Vol. 11, No. 3, 1965.

(20) Fama, E.F., 'The behaviour of stock market prices', *Journal of Business*, Vol. 38, 1965.

(21) Faust, J., 'When are variance ratio tests for serial dependence optimal?', *Econometrica*, Vol. 60. No. 5, 1992.

(22) Friedman, B.M. and Laibson, D.I., 'Economic implications of extraordinary movements in stock prices', *Brookings Papers on Economic Activity*, Vol. 2, 1989.

(23) Hardouvelis, G.A., 'Evidence on stock market speculative bubbles: Japan, United States and Great Britain', *Federal Reserve Bank of New York. Research Paper No. 8810*, February 1988.

(24) Hill, R.A. and Meredith, S., 'Insurance institutions and fund management: a UK perspective', *Journal of Applied Accounting Research*, Vol. 1, No. 2, 1994.

(25) Hurst, H.E., 'Long-term storage of reservoirs', *Transactions of the American Society of Civil Engineers*, 116, 1951.

(26) Jegadeesh, N., 'Seasonality in stock price mean reversion: evidence from the US and the UK, *Journal of Finance*, 1991.

(27) Kritzman, M., 'About serial dependence', *Financial Analysts Journal*, Vol. 50, 1994.

(28) Lintner, J., 'The valuation of risk assets and the selection of risk investments in stock portfolios and capital budgets', *Review of Economic Statistics*, Vol. 47, No. 1, December 1965.

(29) Lorie, J.H. and Hamilton, M.T., *The Stock Market: Theories and Evidence*, Richard D. Irwin 1973.

(30) Mackay, L.L.D., *Extraordinary Delusions of the Madness of the Crowds*, Farrar, Straus and Giroux 1932 (Originally published in 1841).

(31) Malkiel, B.G., *A Random Walk Down Wall Street*, W.W. Norton 1985.

(32) Mandelbrot, B., 'Stable Paretian random functions and the multiplicative variation of income', *Econometrica*, Vol. 29, 1961.

(33) Mandelbrot, B., 'Statistical methodology for non-periodic cycles: from the covariance to R/S analysis', *Annals of Economic and Social Measurement*, Vol. 1, 1972.

(34) Mandelbrot, B., 'The stable Paretian income distribution when the apparent exponent is near two', *International Economic Review*, Vol. 4, 1963.

(35) Markowitz, H.M., 'Portfolio selection', *Journal of Finance*, Vol. 13, No. 1, 1952.

(36) Modigliani, F. and Miller, M.H., 'The cost of capital, corporation finance and the theory of investment', *American Economic Review*, Vol. XLVIII, No. 4, June 1958.

(37) Mossin, J., 'Equilibrium in a capital asset market', *Econometrica*, Vol. 34, 1966.

(38) Peters, E.E., *Chaos and Order in the Capital Markets*, Wiley 1991.

(39) Piper, T.R. and Fruhan, W.E., 'Is your stock worth its market price?', *Harvard Business Review*, May–June 1981.

(40) Poon, S.H., 'Persistence and mean reversion in UK stock returns', *Journal of Financial Management*, 1995.

(41) Poterba, J.M. and Summers, L.H., 'Mean reversion in stock prices: evidence and implications', *Journal of Financial Economics*, Vol. 22, No. 1, 1988.

(42) Rappaport, A., *Creating Shareholders' Value*, The Free Press 1986.

(43) Roll, R., 'A critique of the asset pricing theory's tests', *Journal of Financial Economics*, Vol. 4, March 1977.

(44) Ross, S.A., 'Arbitrage theory of capital asset pricing', *Journal of Economic Theory*, Vol. 13, December 1976.

(45) Sharpe, W., 'A simplified model for portfolio analysis', *Management Science*, Vol. 9, No. 2, January 1963.

(46) Sharpe, W., *Investor Wealth Measures and Expected Returns: Quantifying the Market Risk Premium*, Institute of Chartered Financial Analysts (Charlottesville, VA.) 1989.

(47) Shiller, R.J., *Market Volatility*, M.I.T Press 1989.

(48) Taylor, W., 'Can big owners make a difference?', *Harvard Business Review*, September–October 1990.

(49) Treynor, J.L., 'How to rate management of investment funds', *Harvard Business Review*, January–February 1965.

(50) Turner A.L and Weigal E.J., 'An analysis of stock market volatility', *Russell Research Commentaries*, Frank Russell Co. (Tacona, WA.) 1990.

(51) Tversky, A., *The Psychology of Risk in Quantifying the Market Risk Premium Phenomena for Investment Decision Making*, Institute of Chartered Financial Analysts (Charlottesville, VA.) 1990.

(52) Vaga, T., 'The coherent market hypothesis', *Financial Analysts Journal*, December–January 1991.

(53) Wood, A.S., 'Fatal attraction for money managers', *Financial Analysts Journal*, May–June 1989.

(54) Zeeman E.C., 'On the unstable behaviour of stock exchanges', *Journal of Mathematical Economics*, Vol. 1, 1974.

PART SIX

Conclusion

14

Postscript and perspectives

1 INTRODUCTION

This study of corporate finance began with the normative assumption that a company should select investments which maximise shareholders' wealth using NPV criteria. A theoretical picture was painted of the decision-maker as a rational individual who, even under conditions of uncertainty, can formally analyse one course of action in relation to another using a marginal analysis of revenue and cost with a view to securing maximum expected profit in absolute terms at minimum risk.

Because corporate ownership is invariably divorced from control, the choice of an appropriate model, whereby management then gauge the effects of their optimum investment strategies *vis a vis* shareholders' wealth, was considered. A fundamental problem is whether a firm's decision to distribute profits, rather than to retain earnings for reinvestment, has a differential impact on its market price per share. In other words, do shareholders capitalise dividends at a different opportunity cost of capital rate to retained earnings? If so, the firm's financial policy (in this case the dividend decision) as well as its investment policy must be considered when determining the correct discount rates to be incorporated into their NPV analyses.

Of course, corporate finance may be obtained from a variety of sources other than the equity market, each of which requires a return on investment which may be unique. Thus, a further problem which confronts management is how to maximise the wealth of the firm by securing a flexible inflow of funds at a minimum overall cost. This should not only provide shareholders with their desired rate of return, once investment takes place, but simultaneously satisfy the expectations of all the providers of capital.

In this newly leveraged situation, the company's weighted average cost of capital, rather than its cost of equity, becomes the acceptance criterion. Provided a number of conditions are satisfied, projects are then selected which produce a positive NPV when discounted at the firm's opportunity rate. Because different investor returns are now interrelated, to the extent that they may stem from a common investment decision, the impact of financial risk associated with leverage upon the company's cost of capital must also be considered. The question arises as to whether management can divine an optimal capital structure which minimises financial risk and hence its cost of capital. If so, the firm's overall value can be maximised by manipulating its financial policy.

Whether firms can engender an optimum dividend policy or an optimum capital structure which minimises the company's discount rate and maximises share price and overall value is by no means self-evident. If proof be needed, however, the Modigliani–Miller (MM) law of one price is certainly persuasive.

In a perfect capital market they demonstrate that values depend solely upon the profitability of investments and their attendant business risk characteristics. The financial risk, associated with how the firm's earnings are subsequently packaged for distribution to suit the prospective consumption preferences of its shareholders and other suppliers of capital, is an irrelevance.

2 THE PROBLEM OF PERFECT MARKETS

MM maintained that financial policy, i.e. the significance of debt capital and dividends, does not matter. Unfortunately, when they published their papers on the subject (1958 and 1961 respectively) no theory had been developed to allow for the pricing of risk to test their hypothesis. This had to wait until the development of the Capital Asset Pricing Model (Sharpe, 1963 *et al.*) based on Markowitz efficiency.

In theory, the CAPM supports the MM position because it recognises the importance of investment risk and return as a determinant of market price based on similar assumptions. Given identical risk between existing and new investments, the irrelevancy of dividend policy can be confirmed. With regard to capital structure, the incorporation of cheaper financing into the CAPM also leaves total market value unaffected. The sum of returns to shareholders and debenture holders equals the net operating cashflows for an identical all-equity firm. The sum of the covariances of returns of all providers of capital also equates with the covariance of the net operating cashflows.

During the 1970s these normative observations precipitated innumerable empirical CAPM tests concerning the effects of dividend payout on share price and leverage on corporate value (variously reported in Chapters 7 and 10). However, the results were mixed. For example, the study by Litzenberger and Ramaswamy (op.cit. Chapter 7) which analysed the relationship between dividends and security returns concludes that dividends are undesirable. Higher earnings are necessary to compensate investors in order to induce them to hold high yielding shares. In contrast, subsequent work by Miller and Scholes (ibid.) supports the MM conclusion that the value of the firm is independent of dividend yield. And so the debate continues.

Such disparities between theory and practice, however, should no longer surprise the reader. Throughout the text the assumptions of a perfect capital market (upon which the original CAPM and MM hypothesis absolutely depend) have been fundamental to the analyses. When capital markets are perfect, investment and financing decisions can be determined separately (the Separation Theorem). Individuals, firms, financial institutions can all borrow or lend at the market rate of interest to match their own preferences for different combinations of present and future consumption. But when markets are imperfect, borrowing and lending opportunities may differ, even with the same level of risk with important consequences.

In this situation it is not possible for management to appraise their investment decisions and satisfy all parties to any underlying transactions. At one level, for example, the shareholders' perception of future dividends may differ from the firm's own valuation of its income stream. At another, the market may employ an entirely different valuation formula to the firm in assessing its overall investment performance. It will also be recalled that if the market for information is imperfect and costly, or investors do not behave rationally, security prices can be seriously perturbed, irrespective of any changes in corporate investment and financial policies, which may pale into insignificance.

In summary, given the normative objective of corporate finance, management's dilemma is how to select investment projects which represent an efficient use of the firm's assets in relation to the expectations of its shareholders who operate within a capital market which may allocate their own resources inefficiently.

3 THE FORECASTING PROBLEM

Perhaps the ultimate test for corporate finance relates not to its decision models and their refinement but with their voracious appetite for forecast data which is drawn from an imperfect world of uncertainty.

It has been shown that individuals, firms and financial institutions will be certain about few things. Yet it is clear that they all require knowledge of incremental investment and financing opportunities, borrowing and reinvestment rates, probability distributions, utility functions, distribution policies and so on, for every future time period throughout their lives if long-term objectives are to be achieved. Real-world permutations of all the economic variables which impact upon even a single investment decision may be incalculable, whilst varying any simplifying assumptions may produce significantly different conclusions. Thus, it is hardly surprising that for practical decision-making the long-run remains an abstract concept.

One solution to the problem is tacitly to accept that, until theoretical constructions of the long-run are developed in scope and content, one should regard short-run models as indicative of how investment and financial decisions are actually made. Certainly, given the complexity and volatility which now characterises the global capital market there appears to be no *a priori* reason to assume that a long-run equilibrium will ever be attained. Like nature, corporate finance appears to abhor a vacuum.

Thus, rather than speculate on what may or may not materialise in the far distant future, investors and firms should focus on forecasts of what is foreseeable. This is not short-termism in a pejorative sense but an acknowledgement that the short and long-run need not be perceived as either mutually exclusive or inconsistent goals. An implicit assumption of any new models should be that investors seek to increase their long-run stock of wealth, but within practicable horizons.

The gravity of the problems which still confront the short-term decision maker are not to be underestimated. Consider once more the CAPM. If it is assumed that cashflows are normally distributed and the capital market is perfect, there would be no theoretical objection to using such a *single-period* model for the evaluation of a firm's *multi-period* capital projects, provided the risk-free rate of interest, the beta coefficient and the average market rate of return associated with the investment are constant throughout its life.

Given these assumptions, a project's risk-adjusted discount rate is the risk-free rate added to the product of the market premium and the project's beta coefficient. Thus:

Risk-adjusted rate = Risk-free rate

+ (Market rate − Risk-free rate) × beta

The expected net present value is then derived by discounting the average, annual net cash inflows at the risk-adjusted rate, from which the investment's initial cost is subtracted in the usual manner:

$$(1) \qquad E(NPV) = \sum_{t=1}^{n} \frac{\overline{C}_t}{(1 + \bar{r}_j)^t} - I_0$$

where:

I_0 = investment cost at time period zero
$\overline{C}_t$ = average annual net cash inflow at the end of time period t
$\bar{r}_j$ = risk-adjusted discount rate
n = life of project.

Unfortunately, the model's simplicity is deceptive and soon evaporates if the risk-free rate, the market rate and the beta factor are not constant. A different risk-adjusted discount rate (now dated as r_{jt}) would be required period by period, even if only one of its variables changed. Of course, the problem of multiple discount rates is not unique to the CAPM. It is endemic throughout real-world applications of NPV analyses. However, this is to miss the point. The adoption of models, short rather than long, should clarify matters and not produce remedies on a par with the original disease.

4 FUNDAMENTAL DATA

The application of the CAPM to capital budgeting presents further practical difficulties concerning the choice of appropriate data, even if estimators are available.

It will be recalled that a weighted average cost of capital figure correctly applied as a project discount rate should represent the opportunity cost of the firm's existing assets used to value new investments with a commensurate degree of risk. In its most rudimentary form the CAPM, therefore, assumes that a company's capital market beta conforms to the project beta for its average investments.

But if a project involves diversification away from a firm's core activities it will be necessary to use a beta coefficient appropriate to the category of investment. Even if diversification is not contemplated, the beta factor for the project under review may not conform to the firm's archetype. For example, the proposal may exhibit high *operational gearing*, i.e. the proportion of fixed to variable costs, in which case the investment's beta will exceed the average for existing operations. Finally, because the CAPM approaches capital budgeting from the shareholders' viewpoint rather than the firm's there could be a catastrophic conflict of interests. Shareholders with well diversified corporate holdings who dominate a particular company may prefer to accept projects with high risk (high beta coefficients) to balance their portfolios. For the firm in question, however, particularly if it produces few product lines, such a strategy may be tantamount to economic suicide.

Fortunately, one saving grace is that given the investment community's interest in market risk, beta coefficients are regularly published by the financial services industry worldwide. Thus, the management who subscribe to these facilities can estimate their project betas by calculating the average for companies in the same industry as that of the project. The larger the number of comparable beta constituents, the more reliable the estimate of the project beta, or so the argument goes.

Extending the analysis from project risk to financial risk, if it is accepted that the introduction of debt capital increases shareholders' risk then this can also be incorporated into a project's beta coefficient. If debt capital is listed on a stock market then a modified risk-adjusted discount rate can be calculated by a firm using the following formula for the beta coefficient:

Beta = (Equity beta × Proportion of equity to total finance)
+ (Debt beta × Proportion of debt to total finance)

Again, the finance industry provides details, on a commercial basis to investors who are willing to pay for the service, of geared betas from which the coefficient for a project's beta can be estimated.

5 SUMMARY AND CONCLUSIONS

The preceding analysis leads one to conclude that by default, in an inefficient capital market characterised by non-linear events which impact upon its participants who may not act rationally, the MM law of one price, the CAPM and their derivatives still provide a lifeline to the investment community, but at a cost. What then of the future?

Obviously, there will be alternative approaches to corporate finance; their development resting upon how well each satisfies its stated objectives. The effect of alternative objectives must also be studied, if only because current normative theory can only rest on a single objective if there is a measure of acceptance of the concepts implied. Unfortunately, research indicates that, whilst academics still assign importance to the pursuit of shareholders' wealth maximisation, this is still not correlated to the use of the appropriate model, such as investment appraisal based upon the concepts of net present value.

Thus, it remains pertinent to question the sovereignty of the shareholder in financial decision-making and to evaluate alternative techniques on a far simpler basis. Perhaps academics have failed to convince practising decision-makers that their ideas can be made operational under real-world conditions. If their objectives are too broadly based, theoretical models may be dismissed as self-evident. Equally, if they are too specific, the resultant techniques may fail to gain general acceptance. Within the context of practical decision-making, this necessary trade-off between uniformity and flexibility without unnecessary complexity possibly explains why the objective of corporate finance is so readily acknowledged but the conceptual procedures for its achievement are widely ignored.

Appendix 1

Exercises

Chapter 2

The management of Demu plc is considering investment opportunities for the coming year. The details are as follows:

+ *Project A* is a new product launch which is expected to have a three-year life. Annual cash sales are expected to be 10,000 units and the current selling price would be £5.00. The current variable costs per unit are as follows:

Labour	£0.75 ✻ 8'.	10'000 × $5.00 =
Material	£1.50	× 12'%
Overhead	£1.00 +8'.	
	3·25	

Labour and variable overhead costs are expected to increase by 8 per cent per annum. Inventory prices will increase by 12 per cent per annum. To maintain demand, management will restrict increases in selling price to the rate of inflation, which is anticipated to be 5 per cent, year on year.

The cost of the project will be £30,000 which can be depreciated on a straight-line basis for tax purposes. The rate of corporation tax is 20 per cent which is paid one year in arrears.

Project B will involve a current outlay of £50,000 for capital equipment and £15,000 on working capital. At the end of the first year working capital will be increased by £6,000 at today's prices. At the end of year five, the total investment in working capital will be recovered. The following year, the sale of capital equipment will offset any residual corporate tax liability. At current prices, cash profits will be £18,000 per annum after tax for five years. The cashflows associated with the project are expected to be affected by the anticipated inflation rate, which will continue at 5 per cent.

The company's real rate of interest for discounting purposes is 9.52 per cent.

You are required:
To calculate the NPV of both projects and translate these into profitability indices

Chapter 3

A company with manufacturing divisions in the UK and Germany produces studio quality compact discs for the music industry. In response to Japanese competition, top management are convinced that investment in new equipment would yield savings in operating costs vital to its survival.

Two types of equipment are available with a three-year life and negligible resale value.

Model I would cost £5 million and yield a saving of £1.00 per unit.
Model II would cost £12 million and yield a saving of £2.00 per unit.

Current production of CDs is 2 million in each country but new market opportunities, created by a more refined product, might increase sales volumes to 4 million per annum.

The company has traditionally vetted capital projects using IRR, which is currently compared to a 15 per cent cut-off rate for investment. However, the German division is pressing for change and has been given permission to employ NPV allied to an 8 per cent cost of capital for the first time.

You are required:
(a) To advise each division as to which investment is financially beneficial using their preferred investment techniques.
(b) To explain how any anomalies revealed by the analyses can be resolved by the company.

Chapter 4

Although nobody disputes the figures (merely their interpretation), the trustees of the Bosworth Theatrical Company are in disagreement concerning the production of prestigious pantomimes over two successive seasons as a means of recouping the £90,000 cost of refurbishing dilapidated premises.

The Financial Director has produced probablistic estimates relating to audience figures for each of the years as follows:

Probability	Year one	Year two
0.2	80,000	90,000
0.6	60,000	70,000
0.2	50,000	60,000

The following financial data has also been accepted:

(i) Refurbishment costs will be fully met twelve months before the first production.
(ii) Each pantomime will cost £50,000.
(iii) Regional advertising should not exceed £20,000 for the first production and £15,000 for the second.

(*iv*) Ticket prices will be set at £2.00.
(*v*)　The company's cost of capital is 15%.

You are required:
(*a*) To advise the company on the viability or otherwise of the project using NPV and E(NPV) analyses.
(*b*) To explain the implications of differing attitudes towards risk.

Chapter 5

Fortuni Ltd is considering a public quotation to finance future growth. The most recent published accounts reveal the following

Share capital	1 million Ordinary £1.00 shares
Net book value	£3.5 million
Post-tax earnings	£400,000
Dividends (gross)	£100,000

On average the previous four years reported earnings and dividends were only 75 per cent of the latest figures. The company Chairman therefore feels it would be an appropriate time to approach the market.

The following data relates to two companies with a stock exchange listing which are similar to Fortuni in respect to their asset composition, financial structure and product mix:

	Demon plc	*Montfort plc*
	£	£
Current EPS	1.50	2.50
Average EPS	1.00	2.00
Current dividend	0.75	1.25
Average dividend	0.60	1.20
Market price per share	9.00	20.00
Book value per share	6.00	18.00

You are required:
To place a value on the shares of Fortuni making full use of the information.

Chapter 6

Technotronic plc is an electrical wholesaler with a summarised Balance Sheet as noted below. Profit after tax is stable at £1 million and current share price is 800 pence.

Summarised Balance Sheet of Technotronic plc (£000s):

Capital		
1,000,000 Ordinary shares of £1.00 full paid		1,000
Reserves		3,000
		4,000
Liabilities		8,240
		12,240
Represented by		
Fixed assets (net)		
Property	6,000	
Fixtures and fittings	2,000	
Motor vehicles	400	
		8,400
Current asset (net)		3,840
		12,240

Mastermix plc, an electronics manufacturer, regards the acquisition of Technotronic as an ideal opportunity for expanding its distribution network. The following information has been placed before their executive board for consideration:

(*i*)   The rate of return required on an investment of this magnitude is 15% per annum.

(*ii*) The current market valuation of Technotronic property is in the region of £10 million.

(*iii*) The 80-strong fleet of vehicles requires replacement at an average cost of £20,000 each. The current fleet has a market value of £200,000.

(*iv*) A vigorous policy of operational and employee rationalisation, post-acquisition, should produce savings of £1 million per annum.

(*v*)   After five years the brand image of Technotronic should be fully assimilated under the banner of Mastermix.

You are required:
To produce a report which explains a range of values that might be placed upon the shares of Technotronic plc by the executive board of Mastermix.

Chapter 7

The summarised Balance Sheet of L. Stansfield plc as at 31.12.98 is as follows:

	£(000s)
Fixed assets	160
Net current assets	120
	280

Financed by
Share capital
   (fully paid)   200
Reserves   80
                 280

A record of profits before tax and dividend payout are as under:

Year	Profit	Dividend
	£	%
1996	28,000	50
1997	32,000	50
1998	36,000	60

On behalf of your company, *you are required* to calculate possible offer prices for all the share capital of Stansfield based on the following assumptions:

(*i*) Your marginal cut-off rate for investment is 13 per cent.
(*ii*) The purchase transaction will be completed as soon as possible. Thereafter, the year end will still coincide with the end of the calendar year.
(*iii*) Earnings before tax are expected to be £40,000 for the year ending 31.12.99, subsequently rising at an annual compound rate of 5 per cent.
(*iv*) The dividend-payout ratio will absorb 80 per cent of profits after corporation tax at 25 per cent.
(*v*) There will be an immediate asset revaluation loss of £4,000, but an exceptional distribution of £52,000 to shareholders contingent upon a realisation of assets surplus to requirements on 31.12.99.
(*vi*) The anticipated dividend capitalisation rate is expected to be at least 15 per cent to compensate for financial risk.

Chapter 8

The Balance Sheet of Emon plc for 1998 is summarised as follows:

	£000s
Ordinary share capital at £1.00	8,000
18% Preference shares at £1.00	3,000
16% Irredeemable debentures	4,000
12.5% Redeemable debentures (2003)	1,600
10% bank overdraft	200
	16,800

The following information is also available:

(*a*) *Market values:*

	£
Ordinary shares	2.50
Preference shares	1.60
Irredeemable debentures	128.00
Redeemable debentures	90.00

(*b*)	Dividend payout ratio	25%
	Anticipated dividend percentage	20%
	Return on investment	12%
	Rate of corporation tax	20%

You are required
To calculate the weighted average cost of capital for Emon plc based on book values.

Chapter 9

The most recent summarised balance sheet for Giles Limited, a farming consortium, is as follows:

	£000s
Fixed assets	1,630
Current assets	950
Current liabilities	(800)
	1,780
£1 Ordinary shares	750
Reserves	1,030
	1,780

Profits after tax for the year were £370,000 and a dividend per share of 10 pence was paid.

The Company needs to raise £1 million to finance a new venture into industrial property development and is considering three options:

(*i*)   a public issue of ordinary shares at a 10 per cent discount on the market price
(*ii*)   an issue of £1.00, 6 per cent preference shares at £1.50
(*iii*) an issue of irredeemable 8 per cent debentures at par.

You are employed by the company in a consultative capacity to advise on each option and have secured the following information concerning an established player in industrial property development:

EPS	Dividend per share	Book value per share	Market price
£1.65	£0.90	£8.50	£11.00

You are required:

To write a report which contains your advice and explains:

(*a*) A valuation for the ordinary shares of Giles
(*b*) The derivation of possible discount rates for the proposed investment in relation to each financing option
(*c*) The suitability of WACC computations for the purpose of investment appraisal.

The rate of corporation tax is 25 per cent.

Chapter 10

You have just acquired a 10 per cent stake in the equity of T.D.M. plc, whose shares are trading at £5.00. The firm's capital structure comprises 2 million shares issued and fully paid, plus debentures with a market value of £1 million yielding 10 per cent gross. Earnings before interest and tax are £1.5 million. The rate of corporation tax is 25 per cent.

You are now informed of an all-equity company with 2.5 million shares priced at £4.00 each. Because it exhibits identical risk–return characteristics you now wonder whether your recent investment decision was the correct one.

You are required:
To determine an optimal investment strategy in relation to these two companies.

Chapter 11

Alexandre has an investment in Dumas plc which shows an average return of 20 per cent and a standard deviation of 7.75 per cent. He wishes to diversify into two of three other investments on offer. These are:

Athos with a return of 20% and a standard deviation of 7.75%
Porthos with a return of 30% and a standard deviation of 18.44%
Aramis with a return of 40% and a standard deviation of 22.91%

The covariances between the various investments themselves and with Dumas plc are as follows:

Dumas plc with Athos	−60
Dumas plc with Porthos	−100
Dumas plc with Aramis	+90
Athos with Porthos	+100
Athos with Aramis	−90
Porthos with Aramis	−410

Alexandre wishes to invest 80 per cent of his funds in Dumas plc and 10 per cent in each of two of the investments on offer. The question is, which two should be chosen in order to maximise return at the minimum risk? In other words, what is the optimum portfolio, subject to these constraints?

Chapter 12

The following details relate to an investment and a market index for a period of 11 months during the current year.

Month	Investment	Market index
1	100	500
2	102	510
3	106	485
4	106	500
5	103	505
6	108	520
7	114	530
8	110	515
9	115	535
10	120	550
11	125	560

The risk-free rate of interest is 6 per cent per annum throughout this period. For simplicity, the monthly rate is calculated as $6/12 = 0.5$ per cent.

You are required to ascertain the following:

(a) What are the Beta and Alpha factors relating to this investment?
(b) If the investment is in an ungeared company's equity, what is the company's cost of capital?
(c) If the company is geared with 60 per cent equity and 40 per cent debt capital, calculate the asset Beta and the new cost of capital.

Chapter 13

During the period of writing this text the UK stockmarket has soared. For the first time in March 1998 the FT-SE 100 broke through the 6000 mark. In the previous three months it rose 20 per cent; 40 per cent in a year; 100 per cent over three years. Since 1980 the index rose twelvefold, equivalent to a £100,000 investment being worth £1.2 million. American and European markets have also boomed. In the same month the Dow Jones stood at 8900 and the German DAX index moved above 5000 for the first time.

What makes this all the more remarkable is that in the Autumn of 1997 Asian financial markets collapsed by 50 per cent over a few weeks, a crisis which showed no signs of abating six months later. Those who bought shares in Japan in 1989 when the Nikkei index stood just below 40,000 were still confronted with an index which remained below 17,000 in March 1998. Yet, if you bought into the FT-SE 100 at its peak prior to the 1987 crash your investment would have tripled by early 1998. If you bought after the crash it would have quadrupled in one of the greatest bull markets ever seen.

Referring to the latest figures for the indices mentioned above, and with the benefit of hindsight, the final question you might care to consider is whether millions of investors have been living in a fool's paradise. Or have share prices kept on moving up, and if so, by how much?

Suffice it to say, that without perfect foresight, the author cannot provide an answer.

Appendix 2

Answers to exercises

Chapter 2

The best way to deal with *Project A* is to determine the *relevant* real cashflows over the project's life, convert these into money cashflows and calculate the NPV by discounting at the money rate of interest, given by:

$$(1 + m) = (1 + r)(1 + i)$$
$$1.15 = 1.0952 \times 1.05$$
$$m = 15\%$$

(i) DCF analysis at 15% (£000s)

Cashflows	Price index	t_0	t_1	t_2	t_3	t_4	NPV
Investment	0%	(30)	—	—	—	—	
Revenue	5%	—	52.5	55.13	57.88	—	
Labour	8%	—	(8.1)	(8.75)	(9.45)	—	
Material	12%	—	(16.8)	(18.82)	(21.07)	—	
Overhead	8%	—	(10.8)	(11.66)	(12.60)	—	
Tax	Composite	—	—	(1.36)	(1.18)	(0.952)	
Net cashflow		(30.0)	16.80	14.54	13.58	(0.952)	
DCF factor		1.0	0.87	0.76	0.66	0.57	
DCF		(30)	14.62	11.05	8.96	(0.54)	4.09

(ii) Tax computations (£000s)

	t_1	t_2	t_3
Variable cash inflow	16.80	15.90	14.76
Depreciation (tax shield)	(10.00)	(10.00)	(10.00)
Taxable cashflow	6.80	5.90	4.76
Tax at 20%	(1.36)	(1.18)	(0.952)

Note that although depreciation does not enter into the DCF analysis directly (it is

370

a non-cash expense) it does act as a tax shield for corporation tax purposes. The tax liability is then staggered by one year in the analysis until it gives rise to a cash outflow.

Project B is less problematical. The cashflows are already tax adjusted and are affected only by the annual rate of inflation. Thus, real cashflows can be discounted at the real rate of interest. Given the pattern of cashflow, an annuity factor can also be employed to speed the calculation further.

(iii) DCF analysis at 9.52% (£000s)

Cashflows	t_0	t_1	t_{1-5}	t_5	NPV
Investment	(50)				
Profit			18		
Working capital	(15)	(6)	—	21	
Annual cashflow	(65)	(6)	18	21	
DCF factor	1.0	0.91	3.84	0.63	
DCF	(65)	(5.46)	69.12	13.23	11.89

(iv) The NPV index

$$\text{Project A} = \frac{4.09}{30} = 0.136$$

$$\text{Project B} = \frac{11.89}{50} = 0.238$$

Chapter 3

(a) German NPV and UK IRR computations (£000s)

	Model I					
	2			4		
	million	*DCF*		*million*	*DCF*	
Year	*units*	*factor*	*PV*	*units*	*factor*	*PV*
0	(5,000)	1.00	(5,000)	(5,000)	1.00	(5,000)
1	2,000	0.93	1,860	4,000	0.93	3,720
2	2,000	0.86	1,720	4,000	0.86	3,440
3	2,000	0.79	1,580	4,000	0.79	3,160
NPV			160			5,320
IRR using I/C			9.5%			61%
(factor computation)						

	Model II					
	2			4		
	million	*DCF*		*million*	*DCF*	
Year	*units*	*factor*	*PV*	*units*	*factor*	*PV*
0	(12,000)	1.00	(12,000)	(12,000)	1.00	(12,000)
1	4,000	0.93	3,720	8,000	0.93	7,440
2	4,000	0.86	3,440	8,000	0.86	6,880
3	4,000	0.79	3,160	8,000	0.79	6,320
NPV			(1,680)			8,640
IRR using I/C			0%			45%

On the basis of NPV (wealth maximisation), Model I is to be preferred by Germany at the lower level of activity and Model II at the higher level of activity. An indication of probability as applicable to each level of activity would assist further appraisal under conditions of uncertainty. Presumably, the UK division would prefer to proceed with Model I at 4 million units, since this maximises the IRR, even though Model II produces a higher absolute profit at the higher level of activity. Irrespective of the model, the IRR falls short of the cut-off rate at lower production levels.

(b) IRR incremental yield
Because the UK IRR results are anomalous when compared with NPV, an incremental yield approach (which considers the benefits which arise from spending the additional £7 million on Model II using the technique of linear interpolation) could be used to provide a definitive answer.

From the above statements calculate:

Model II cashflows less Model I cashflows for the lower activity.
Model II cashflows less Model I cashflows for the higher activity.

At the lower level of activity, even with a zero rate of interest, the £7 million is not recovered (see below). Model I is preferred, since it does deliver a return in excess of capital cost.

At the higher level of activity on the basis of the original German calculations, the incremental net present value at 8% is given by:

$$
\begin{array}{r}
£ \\
8,640,000 \\
-5,320,000 \\
\hline
2,320,000
\end{array}
$$

This suggests interpolation should begin at a much higher rate of interest, say 30%.

Thus:

Year	Lower level of activity (£000s)	Higher level of activity (£000s)				
	PV 0%	Cashflow	30%	PV	40%	PV
0	(7,000)	(7,000)	1.00	(7,000)	1.00	(7,000)
1	2,000	4,000	0.80	3,200	0.71	2,840
2	2,000	4,000	0.64	2,560	0.51	2,040
3	2,000	4,000	0.51	2,040	0.36	1,460
NPV	(1,000)			800		(680)

So, interpolating:

$$\text{Incremental yield} = 40\% - \frac{£680,000}{£1,480,000} \times 10\% \approx 35\%$$

Of course, an altogether simpler method of establishing where interpolation should begin when incremental cashflows are equal in amount is to calculate the factor to be located in a DCF annuity table:

$$F = I/C = \frac{£7 \text{ million}}{£4 \text{ million}} = 1.75$$

This is found to be smaller than the factor in the 30% column for three years (1.816), which confirms that the incremental investment of £7 million gives an even higher yield Thus, Model II should also be preferred at the higher level of activity by the UK division.

The analyses raise a number of discussion points:

- IRR maximisation selects the investment with the shortest payback.
- If capital investment is variable, IRR fails to maximise wealth.
- IRR is underpinned by unreasonable assumptions concerning borrowing and reinvestment rates.

Chapter 4

(*a*) Your *advice* should be based on:

(*i*) *Most likely outcome* (£000s)

Year	0	1	2	*NPV*
Inflow		120	140	
Outflows				
Refurbishment	(90)			
Production		(50)	(50)	
Advertising		(20)	(15)	
Net cashflow	(90)	50	75	
DCF factor (15%)				
$1/(1 + r)$	1.0	0.87	0.756	
DCF	(90)	43.5	56.7	10.2

(*ii*) *Optimistic outcome* (£000s)

	0	1	2	*NPV*
Inflows		160	180	
Outflows	(90)	(70)	(65)	
Net cashflows	(90)	90	115	
DCF	(90)	78.3	86.94	75.24

Pessimistic outcomes (£000s)

	0	1	2	*NPV*
Inflow		100	120	
Outflows	(90)	(70)	(65)	
	(90)	30	55	Obvious Under Recovery

(*iii*) *Expected outcomes* (£000s)

	0	1	2	*NPV*
Inflow (EMV)		124	144	
Outflows	(90)	(70)	(65)	
Net cashflow	(90)	54	79	
DCF	(90)	46.98	59.77	16.75

Calculation of expected monetary value (£000s)

Year 1	EMV	Year 2	EMV
0.2×80	16	0.2×90	18
0.6×60	36	0.6×70	42
0.2×50	10	0.2×60	12
	62		72
@ £2.00	124	@ £2.00	144

(*b*) Your *explanation* should at least cover:

(*i*) *Annual mean-variance analysis* (£000s)

Year 1: Standard deviation

$(x - \bar{x})$	$(x - \bar{x})^2$	P_i	Certainty cash equivalent
$160 - 124 = 36$	1,296,000	0.2	259,200
$120 - 124 = (4)$	16,000	0.6	9,600
$100 - 124 = (24)$	576,000	0.2	115,200
VAR			384,000
$\sqrt{\text{VAR}} = 19,596$			

Year 2: Standard deviation
Since each $(x - \bar{x})$ and P_i are identical to the first-year values,

$$\sqrt{\text{VAR}} = 19,596$$

The variability around the mean may now be calculated and its associated paradox discussed using:

$$\text{EMV} \pm n\sqrt{\text{VAR}} \qquad \text{where } n = \text{number of standard deviations}$$

For example, at a confidence limit of only one standard deviation below the mean (for a modestly risk-averse trustee), the following emerges (£000s):

Year	0	1	2	E(NPV)
Expected inflow		124	144	
$\sqrt{\text{VAR}}$		19.6	19.6	
$\text{EMV} - \sqrt{\text{VAR}}$		104.4	124.4	
Fixed costs	(90)	(70)	(65.0)	
Net cashflows	(90)	34.4	59.4	
DCF factor 15%	1.0	0.87	0.756	
DCF	(90)	29.93	44.9	(15.17)

375

Thus, the project has a distinct chance of under-recovery

(*ii*) *Lifetime mean-variance analysis* (£000s)
You should also be able to confirm that the discounted mean and standard deviation for the *entire* project are 16.7 and 31.9 respectively. This still reveals that one standard deviation below the mean the pantomimes lose £15,200.

For the more mathematical minded reader, the probability of making an overall loss can be ascertained by reference to the *coefficient of variation* as follows (£000s):

$$\frac{0 - E(NPV)}{\delta}$$

such that:

$$\frac{0 - £16.7}{£31.9} = 0.524 \text{ standard units}$$

$$= 0.1985 \text{ (from normal distribution tables)}$$

Hence:

$$0.5 - 0.1985 = 0.3015$$

Thus, the probability of the investment producing a negative E(NPV) at a 15% discount rate is 30.1%.

Chapter 5

The data can be reformulated as follows:

(*a*) *Fortuni Ltd*

		£	£
Current EPS	$=$	$\dfrac{400,000}{100,000}$	$=$ 4.00
Average EPS	$=$	$\dfrac{320,000}{100,000}$	$=$ 3.20
Current Div PS	$=$	$\dfrac{100,000}{100,000}$	$=$ 1.00
Average Div PS	$=$	$\dfrac{80,000}{100,000}$	$=$ 0.80
Book value per share	$=$	$\dfrac{3.5 \text{ million}}{100,000}$	$=$ 35.00

(*b*) *Calculations*

		Earnings	Dividends
(i)	Current	400,000	100,000
(ii)	Historical average	300,000	75,000
	Total ((i) + 4(ii)/5)	1,600,000	400,000
(iii)	Weighted average	320,000	80,000

(*c*) *Share valuation multipliers*

		Demon plc £	Montfort plc £
Basic EPS	(P/E)	$\dfrac{9.00}{1.50} = 6$	$\dfrac{20.00}{2.50} = 8$
Average EPS	(P/E)	$\dfrac{9.00}{1.00} = 9$	$\dfrac{20.00}{2.00} = 10$
DPS	(P/D)	$\dfrac{9.00}{0.75} = 12$	$\dfrac{20.00}{1.25} = 16$
Average DPS	(P/D)	$\dfrac{9.00}{0.60} = 15$	$\dfrac{20.00}{1.20} = 16.7$
Assets (market price/book value)		$\dfrac{9.00}{6.00} = 1.5$	$\dfrac{20.00}{18.00} = 1.1$

(*d*) *Per share valuations for Fortuni Ltd using comparable multipliers*

	Demon plc £	Montfort plc £
Earnings per share	24.00	32.00
Average earnings per share	28.80	32.00
Dividends per share	12.00	16.00
Average dividends per share	12.00	13.36
Market price/book value	52.50	38.50

(*e*) *Points for discussion*

- Price per share ranges from £12.00 to £52.50.
- Lower prices relate to a value based on dividends, which could be interpreted by the market as a signal for the lowest maintainable future earnings.

- Ignoring dividend valuations, the range is £24.00–£52.50. The market price on book value gives the highest valuation. This might mean something unusual about the asset mix, such as a high proportion of current valued property or investment. Given the deficiencies associated with historical cost accounting, book values usually produce the most conservative valuation for a viable going concern.
- On the P/E ratio range £24.00–£32.00 the average share price is only 53% of book value.
- The question to be asked is why the book value of assets exceeds their earnings power. In other words, is Fortuni a going concern?

Chapter 6

You should explain the rationale behind the following approaches to share valuation:

(*i*) *Asset valuation*

Total assets minus liabilities adjusted for market valuations
Market capitalisation = £7.8 million = £7.80 per share

(*ii*) *Going concern valuation* (which incorporates goodwill)

$$\text{Net assets plus goodwill: (£ million)} = A + \frac{P - rA}{m}$$

$$= 7.8 + \frac{1.17 - 1.0}{0.2}$$

Market capitalisation = £8.65 million = £8.65 per share

where: $P = £7.8 \times 015$, $rA = £1.0$, $m = 20\%$, i.e. 5 years purchase of superprofits. Other assumptions would be acceptable.

(*iii*) *Earnings valuation*

	£million
P (see *ii* above)	1.17
Savings	1.00
Anticipated earnings	2.17

Capitalised at 15%

$$\frac{2.17}{0.15} \quad or \quad 2.17 \times 6.67 \qquad 14.47$$

Less vehicle net replacement cost	1.40
	13.07

Market capitalisation = £13.07 million = £13.07 per share

(*iv*) *Comparison of yields (%)*

Current	Assets	Goodwill	Earnings
$\dfrac{1.00}{800} = 12.5$	$\dfrac{1.17}{7.80} = 15.0$	$\dfrac{1.17}{8.65} = 13.5$	$\dfrac{2.17}{13.07} = 16.6$

(*v*) *Conclusion*
On balance, even in the event of a struggle, Technotronic represents an attractive investment.

Chapter 7

(*i*) *Net asset valuation*
One solution might be:

	1998 £	1999 £
Balance sheet	280,000	
Revaluation	(4,000)	
Excess assets	(52,000)	
Net operating assets	224,000	
Excess assets (PV)	46,018	$= 52{,}000/1.13$
Value	270,018	

The net asset value can also be determined as follows:

$$£276{,}000 - (£52{,}000 \, (1 - 1/1.13)) = \underline{£270{,}018}$$

(*ii*) *Earnings and dividend valuations using the constant growth formula*

	P_0 (1998) £	t_0 (1999) £	t_1 (2000) £	Discounted growth formulae
EARNINGS				
Capitalised earnings		$393{,}750 =$	$\dfrac{31{,}500}{0.08}$	$\dfrac{E_0(1 + 0.05)/(0.13 - 0.05)}{1.13}$
Earnings (t_0)		30,000		
Exceptional distribution		52,000		
VALUE	$421{,}017 =$	$475{,}750/1.13$		

(*continued*)

379

Continued from p. 379

	P_0 (1998) £	t_0 (1999) £	t_1 (2000) £	*Discounted growth formulae*
DIVIDENDS				
Capitalised dividends		252,000 =	$\dfrac{25,200}{0.10}$	$\dfrac{D_0(1 + 0.05)/(0.15 - 0.05)}{1.13}$
Dividend (t_0)		24,000		
Exceptional distribution		52,000		
VALUE	290,265 =	328,000/1.13		

(iii) Modigliani-Miller and the Law of One Price

MM would reconcile the disparity between the preceding earnings and dividend valuations by using 13 per cent as a basis for capitalisation and not 15 per cent. They would also acknowledge that a less than full distribution policy must be compensated by an increase in the *ex div* price. In other words a £6000 retention will produce additional income of £480 in the year 2000. This is confirmed by solving for E, in the following equation:

$$£6000 = \frac{E_1}{0.13 - 0.05}$$

Thus:

	P_0 (1998) £	t_0 (1999) £	t_1 (2000) £
Capitalised earnings		399,750 =	$\dfrac{31,500 + 480}{0.08}$
Dividend (t_0)		24,000	
Exceptional distribution		52,000	
VALUE	421,017 =	475,750/1.13	

(iv) Points to consider

- Given the time-lag between the growth in earnings and the date of acquisition, an element of the net asset valuation and the growth formulae all require discounting back to a present value.
- The dividend capitalisation rate which, according to Gordon, is supposed to compensate for financial risk produces a valuation which conflicts with the MM law of one price. It appears too conservative.
- Given the defects associated with historical cost accounting, one would not

expect a tangible asset valuation to conform with the market capitalisation of equity, irrespective of whether it is based on earnings or dividends.

Chapter 8

(i)   *Component capital costs*   *Notes*

Equity: $\dfrac{0.20}{2.50} + (12\% \times 75\%) = \underline{17\%}$ (incorporate growth)

Preference shares: $\dfrac{0.18}{1.60}$ $= \underline{11.25\%}$

Irredeemable debentures: $\dfrac{16(0.8)}{128}$ $= 10.0\%$ (after tax)

Redeemable debentures: $90 \displaystyle\sum_{t=1}^{n=5} \dfrac{12.5(0.8)}{(1+K_{dt})^{t}} + \dfrac{100}{(1+K_{dt})^{n}}$

K_{dt} $= 13.0\%$ (after tax)

Bank overdraft: $10\% \,(0.8)$ $= \underline{8.0\%}$ (after tax)

(ii) *Weighted average cost of capital*

	Cost %	*Weight*	*WACC*
Equity	17.0	0.476	8.09
Preference shares	11.25	0.178	2.00
Irredeemable debt	10.0	0.238	2.38
Redeemable debt	13.0	0.095	1.23
Overdraft	8.0	0.012	0.10
WACC			13.80

You might care to reformulate the WACC using market values rather than book values which are clearly more appropriate.

Chapter 9

(a) *Valuation of Ordinary shares*

Financial ratios (Giles)	Stock market multipliers	Giles share price
$\text{EPS} = \dfrac{£370,000}{750,000} = £0.493$	$\text{P/E ratio} = \dfrac{£11.00}{£1.65} = 6.67$	£3.29
$\text{DPS} = \dfrac{£75,000}{750,000} = £0.10$	$\text{P/D ratio} = \dfrac{£11.00}{£0.90} = 12.22$	£1.22
$\text{BV/share} = \dfrac{£1,780,000}{750,000} = £2.37$	$\text{MV/BV} = \dfrac{£11.00}{£8.50} = 1.29$	£3.06

Discussion points

- Share price disparities (low dividend pay-out but sound asset backing, plus evidence of goodwill). Appropriate price should be based on earnings (i.e. dividends plus capital gain), say £3.30. Issued at discount, the current price

$$P_0 = £(3.30 - 0.33) = £2.97$$

- Given the disparity between dividend pay-out and earnings, the impact of growth on share price could be discussed.

(b) *Derivation of possible discount rates*

(i) *Marginal cost of capital (project specific)*

Ordinary shares		Preferences shares	Debentures (after tax)
Discount price $\dfrac{\text{EPS}}{P_0} = \dfrac{£0.50}{£2.97} = 16.83\%$		$\dfrac{\text{DPS}}{P_0} = \dfrac{£0.06}{£1.50} = 4\%$	$I(1-t) =$ $8\%\,(0.75) = 6\%$

$$\text{Market price} = \frac{\text{EPS}}{P_0} = \frac{£0.50}{3.30} = \underline{15.15\%}$$

(ii) *WACC (using the market price of equity)*
Given the total market capitalisation of equity = 750,000 × £3.30 = £2.475m, then

Market value of equity + Incremental investment = Corporate value

£2.475m + £1.00 m = £3.475m

so that the WACC for each financing option may be calculated.

Ordinary share issue	Preference issue	Debenture issue
$K = K_e$	$K = f(K_e, K_p)$	$K = f(K_e, K_d)$

Using the market yield from (*i*) above

	$\dfrac{(£2.47m \times 15.15\%)}{+ (£1m \times 4\%)}$	$\dfrac{(£2.475m \times 15.15\%)}{+ (£1m \times 6\%)}$
	£3.457m	£3.475m
= 15.15%	= £11.94%	= £12.52%

(c) *Discussion points on the suitability of WACC*

- The discount rate falls with cheaper financing. As a corollary, corporate value rises (the traditional view).
- Suitability of WACC, given its assumptions and limitations. The proposed investment is more than marginal and a diversification of operations.
- The impact of introducing fixed charges against future income upon investor attitudes.
- The relationship between capital gearing and corporate value and costs (an introduction to MM's law of one price).

Chapter 10

According to MM (1963) in a taxed but otherwise perfect world the value of a geared company (V_G) can be found by adding the capitalised value of the tax savings from debt $(V_D.t)$ to the value of an otherwise identical ungeared firm (V_U). Thus:

$$V_G = V_U + V_D.t$$

If this equality does not hold there is a potential opportunity for arbitrage.

Assume that the all-equity company is correctly valued. It follows that the *theoretical* value of T.D.M. can be compared with its *actual* value as follows:

Theoretical value		Actual value	
	£		£
V_U: £2.5 million × £4.00 =	10 million	Equity: £2.0 million × £5.00 =	10 million
$V_D.t$: £1 million × 25% =	0.25 million	Debt:	1 million
	10.25 million		11 million

T.D.M. plc appears to be overpriced relative to the all-equity company. As a consequence, it is possible to increase investor income through arbitrage by:

- selling the shares of T.D.M.
- increasing personal leverage to the level of corporate leverage in T.D.M. by borrowing
- investing the proceeds of sale and borrowing in the all-equity firm.

Thus:

Disposing of 10% in T.D.M.	£1.0 million
Borrowing (at the market rate)	
10% of the value of debt	£0.1 million
Acquisition of ungeared equity	£1.1 million

The proportionate investment in the ungeared firm is given by:

$$\frac{£1.1 \text{ million}}{£10 \text{ million}} = 11\%$$

The new income position can now be summarised as follows in comparison to the original investment:

	10% share investment in T.D.M.	11% investment in all-equity firm
	£000s	£000s
EBIT	1,500	1,500
Interest	100	—
	1,400	1,500
Tax	350	375
Distributable profit	1,150	1,125
10% of T.D.M.	115	
11% all-equity firm		123.75
Interest on debt (net)		
10% (0.75) × £0.1m		7.50
Investor income	115	116.25

Thus, arbitrage has increased investor income by £1,250, although this ignores market imperfections and real-world considerations such as:

- transaction costs
- differences between personal and corporate tax regimes
- bankruptcy costs
- agency costs
- signalling theory
- pecking order theory.

Chapter 11

In order to solve the problem it is necessary to calculate the standard deviation of each of the following three asset portfolios:

Dumas plc with Athos and Porthos
Dumas plc with Athos and Aramis
Dumas plc with Porthos and Aramis

The equation is taken from the following algebraic formula:

$$(A + B + C)^2 = A^2 + B^2 + C^2 + 2AB + 2AC + 2BC$$

where A, B, and C are the proportions of funds invested in each of the investments.

This is then tempered by using the covariances between the various elements. So the variance of the portfolio mix of Dumas plc with Athos and Porthos will be found using the equation:

$$\text{VAR} = D^2\delta^2(D) + A^2\delta^2(A) + P^2\delta^2(P)$$
$$+ 2DA\ \text{COV}(D, A) + 2DP\ \text{COV}(D, P) + 2AP\ \text{COV}(A, P)$$

where:

D is the proportion of funds invested in the Dumas plc
A is the proportion of funds invested in Athos
P is the proportion of funds invested in Porthos
$\text{COV}(i, j)$ is the Covariance between any two projects i and j
$\delta^2(i)$ is the variance of any investment i

and the sum of the proportions of funds in each investment equals 100 per cent.

Entering the relevant figures we get:

$$\text{VAR} = (0.8)^2(60) + (0.1)^2(60) + (0.1)^2(340)$$
$$+ (2)(0.8)(0.1)(-60) + (2)(0.8)(0.1)(-100) + (2)(0.1)(0.1)(100)$$
$$= 18.8$$

The risk of the portfolio as measured by the standard deviation is given by:

$$\delta = \sqrt{18.8} = 4.34\%$$

The return on this particular portfolio will be in proportion to the funds placed in each of the investments, which is a weighted average of the returns on the portfolio constituents.

80% of the Main business	=	16%
10% of Athos	=	2%
10% of Porthos	=	3%
Return	=	21%

The expected return and risk of the other two possible portfolios can be calculated in the same manner. The following is a summary of the results:

	Return	Risk
Dumas plc with Athos and Porthos	21%	4.34%
Dumas plc with Athos and Aramis	22%	6.87%
Dumas plc with Porthos and Aramis	23%	6.10%

The first mix gives the lowest standard deviation and therefore the least risk. This is because, although Athos and Porthos are positively correlated, they are both negatively correlated with Dumas plc. A risk-averse investor would choose Dumas plc with Porthos and Aramis as the next safest portfolio because it has a higher return and lower standard deviation than Dumas plc with Athos and Aramis.

Chapter 12

(a) The returns on the investment can be calculated by taking the difference between the price at the beginning of the month and that at the end of the month, and expressing it as a percentage of the price at the beginning of the month. For example the return on the investment for the first month is $(102 - 100)/100 = +2.00\%$. The returns from the investment and the market are therefore as follows:

Month	Return on investment % (r_i)	Return on market $(\bar{r}_m)$
1	+2.00	+2.00
2	+4.00	−4.90
3	+0.00	+3.09
4	−2.83	+1.00
5	+4.85	+2.97
6	+5.56	+1.92
7	−3.64	−2.83
8	+4.55	+3.88
9	+4.35	+2.80
10	+4.17	+1.82

The Beta factor is a measure of risk and so it is the risk premiums which are of importance. These are calculated by deducting the risk-free rate of return from the returns shown above. The excess returns over the risk-free rate (the risk premiums) for the investment and the market are therefore as follows:

Month	Investment % $(r_i - r_f)$	Market % $(\bar{r}_m - r_f)$
1	+1.50	+1.50
2	+3.50	−5.40
3	−0.50	+2.59
4	−3.33	+0.50
5	+4.35	+2.47
6	+5.06	+1.42
7	−4.14	−3.33
8	+4.05	+3.38
9	+3.85	+2.30
10	+3.67	+1.32

The Alpha and Beta factors can be found graphically by plotting the excess returns on the investment against the excess returns on the market: $(r_i - r_f)$ on the y axis. The slope of 'the line of best fit' through the points will be the Beta factor and the intersect on the y axis of the graph will be the Alpha factor.

A more accurate calculation of these two factors would be by regression analysis of the excess returns of the investment and the market using the formula:

$$y = a + bx$$

where:
$$x = (\bar{r}_m - r_f)$$
$$y = (r_i - r_f)$$

$$b = \frac{n \, \Sigma \, xy - \Sigma \, x \, \Sigma \, y}{n \, \Sigma \, x^2 - (\Sigma \, x)^2} = \text{Beta}$$

$$a = \frac{1}{n} (\Sigma \, y - b \, \Sigma \, x) = \text{Alpha}$$

Using the above information:

Month	x $(\bar{r}_m - r_f)$	y $(r_i - r_f)$	x^2 $(\bar{r}_m - r_f)^2$	xy $(\bar{r}_m - r_f)(r_i - r_f)$
1	+2.00	+2.00	4.00	+4.00
2	−4.90	+4.00	24.01	−19.60
3	+3.09	0.00	9.55	0.00
4	+1.00	−2.83	1.00	−2.83

(continued)

387

Continued from p. 387

Month	x $(\bar{r}_m - r_f)$	y $(r_i - r_f)$	x^2 $(\bar{r}_m - r_f)^2$	xy $(\bar{r}_m - r_f)(r_i - r_f)$
5	+2.97	+4.85	8.82	+14.40
6	+1.92	+5.56	3.69	+10.68
7	−2.83	−3.64	8.01	+10.30
8	+3.88	+4.55	15.05	+17.65
9	+2.80	+4.35	7.84	+12.18
10	+1.82	+4.17	3.31	+7.59
	+11.75	+23.01	+85.28	+54.37

$$\text{Beta} = \frac{(10 \times 54.37) - (11.75 \times 23.01)}{(10 \times 85.28) - (11.75)^2} = 0.38$$

$$\text{Alpha} = \frac{1}{10}(23.01 - (0.38 \times 11.75)) = 1.85$$

The beta factor is 0.38 which shows that the returns on the investment are 0.38 times as volatile as the returns on the market, i.e. a 100% change in the market return will give a 38% change in the investment return.

The alpha factor, however, is 1.85% for one month which approximates to 22.20% pa. If the investment were correctly priced the alpha factor should equal zero. A negative factor would indicate that the return on the investment is less than that to be expected based on its level of systematic risk.

A positive factor, as above, shows that the share is given a return above that to be expected based on its systematic risk. The above investment is therefore, very valuable returning 22.2% above its risk assessment and moving only very slowly with the market. Its attractiveness should create a demand for it and so eventually its price will increase. The return, therefore, will decrease and at least, theoretically, the alpha factor will approach zero.

(b) The beta factor and the cost of equity capital

If the above investment is in a company's equity, and if, as above, the risk rate is 6% per annum or 0.5% per month and the average return on the market $(\bar{r}_m)$ is 1.175%, then the cost of equity for the above company can be calculated by using the Beta factor as the Equity beta (β_e) of the company:

$$K_e = r_f + (\bar{r}_m - r_f)\beta_e$$

Using the above as an example then:

$$K_e = 0.5 + (1.175 - 0.5)0.38 = 0.7565\% \text{ per month} = 9.078\% \text{ per annum}$$

Any increase in the beta equity will increase the cost of capital because the risk of that capital will be increasing.

(c) Gearing and the CAPM

If a company has a geared capital structure then the overall beta factor is the asset beta (β_0) as distinct from the equity beta (β_e).

With a geared structure:

$$\beta_0 = \beta_e\left(\frac{E}{D+E}\right) + \beta_d\left(\frac{D}{D+E}\right)$$

where:

β_0 = asset beta
β_e = equity beta
β_d = debt beta
D = debt market value
E = equity market value.

As debt-holders are guaranteed a return on their investment they are considered risk-free. Thus:

$$\beta_d = 0$$

$$\beta_0 = \beta_e\left(\frac{E}{D+E}\right)$$

Using the earlier calculation for β_e of 0.38 and assuming that this applies to 60% of the total capital structure:

$$\beta_0 = 0.38(\tfrac{6}{10}) = 0.228$$

Earlier it was shown that:

$$K_e = r_f + (\bar{r}_m - r_f)\beta_e$$

Similarly, WACC is given by:

$$\overline{K} = r_f + (\bar{r}_m - r_f)\beta_0$$

Using the earlier figures:

$$\overline{K} = r_f + (\bar{r}_m - r_f)\beta_0$$
$$= 0.5 + (1.175 - 0.5)0.228 = 0.6539\% \text{ per month.}$$

Alternatively:

$$\overline{K} = 6.0 + (14.1 - 6.0)0.228 = 7.8468\% \text{ per annum.}$$

Proof of this can be carried out by applying the weights to the capital costs:

$$K_e = r_f + (\bar{r}_m - r_f)\beta_e$$
$$= 6 + (14.1 - 6.0)0.38 = 9.078\%$$
$$K_d = r_f = 6.0\%$$

So with a 60 : 40 split:

$$\overline{K} = (0.6)(9.078) + (0.4)(6.00) = 7.8468\% \text{ per annum}$$

The object of the exercise is to find the line which best fits when drawn through the points on the graph. This is a matter of estimation because we are attempting to cut through the points on the scatter diagram using the statistical method of *least squares*.

In this case it can be seen that the line could well pass through the y axis at approximately 1.5% and slopes at approximately 20° degrees. As a slope of 45% would represent a beta factor of 1, so a slope of 20° would give a beta factor of 0.36. Students of trigonometry will realise that this can be found by calculating the tangent of the angle in the following diagram. By using the more accurate regression analysis we found that the alpha factor was 1.85 and the beta factor 0.38.

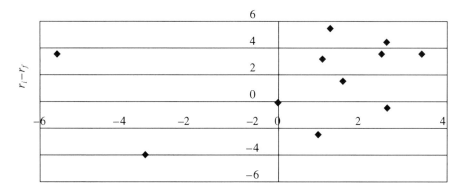

Alpha/beta regression analysis

Appendix 3

DCF tables

Table 1 Future value interest factor (FVIF) (£1 at i% for n years); $FVIF = (1 + i)^n$; $FV_n = PV_0(FVIF_{i,n})$

Period n	1%	2%	3%	4%	5%	6%	7%	8%	9%	10%	11%	12%	13%
0	1.000	1.000	1.000	1.000	1.000	1.000	1.000	1.000	1.000	1.000	1.000	1.000	1.000
1	1.010	1.020	1.030	1.040	1.050	1.060	1.070	1.080	1.090	1.100	1.110	1.120	1.130
2	1.020	1.040	1.061	1.082	1.102	1.124	1.145	1.166	1.188	1.210	1.232	1.254	1.277
3	1.030	1.061	1.093	1.125	1.158	1.191	1.225	1.260	1.295	1.331	1.368	1.405	1.443
4	1.041	1.082	1.126	1.170	1.216	1.262	1.311	1.360	1.412	1.464	1.518	1.574	1.630
5	1.051	1.104	1.159	1.217	1.276	1.338	1.403	1.469	1.539	1.611	1.685	1.762	1.842
6	1.062	1.126	1.194	1.265	1.340	1.419	1.501	1.587	1.677	1.772	1.870	1.974	2.082
7	1.072	1.149	1.230	1.316	1.407	1.504	1.606	1.714	1.828	1.949	2.076	2.211	2.353
8	1.083	1.172	1.267	1.369	1.477	1.594	1.718	1.851	1.993	2.144	2.305	2.476	2.658
9	1.094	1.195	1.305	1.423	1.551	1.689	1.838	1.999	2.172	2.358	2.558	2.773	3.004
10	1.105	1.219	1.344	1.480	1.629	1.791	1.967	2.159	2.367	2.594	2.839	3.106	3.395
11	1.116	1.243	1.384	1.539	1.710	1.898	2.105	2.332	2.580	2.853	3.152	3.479	3.836
12	1.127	1.268	1.426	1.601	1.796	2.012	2.252	2.518	2.813	3.138	3.498	3.896	4.335
13	1.138	1.294	1.469	1.665	1.886	2.133	2.410	2.720	3.066	3.452	3.883	4.363	4.898
14	1.149	1.319	1.513	1.732	1.980	2.261	2.579	2.937	3.342	3.797	4.310	4.887	5.535
15	1.161	1.346	1.558	1.801	2.079	2.397	2.759	3.172	3.642	4.177	4.785	5.474	6.254
16	1.173	1.373	1.605	1.873	2.183	2.540	2.952	3.426	3.970	4.595	5.311	6.130	7.067
17	1.184	1.400	1.653	1.948	2.292	2.693	3.159	3.700	4.328	5.054	5.895	6.866	7.986
18	1.196	1.428	1.702	2.026	2.407	2.854	3.380	3.996	4.717	5.560	6.544	7.690	9.024
19	1.208	1.457	1.754	2.107	2.527	3.026	3.617	4.316	5.142	6.116	7.263	8.613	10.197
20	1.220	1.486	1.806	2.191	2.653	3.207	3.870	4.661	5.604	6.728	8.062	9.646	11.523
24	1.270	1.608	2.033	2.563	3.225	4.049	5.072	6.341	7.911	9.850	12.239	15.179	18.790
25	1.282	1.641	2.094	2.666	3.386	4.292	5.427	6.848	8.623	10.835	13.585	17.000	21.231
30	1.348	1.811	2.427	3.243	4.322	5.743	7.612	10.063	13.268	17.449	22.892	29.960	39.116
40	1.489	2.208	3.262	4.801	7.040	10.286	14.974	21.725	31.409	45.259	65.001	93.051	132.782
50	1.645	2.692	4.384	7.107	11.467	18.420	29.457	46.902	74.358	117.391	184.565	289.002	450.736
60	1.817	3.281	5.892	10.520	18.679	32.988	57.946	101.257	176.031	304.482	524.057	897.557	1,530.05

Table 1 *continued*

Period

n	14%	15%	16%	17%	18%	19%	20%	24%	28%	32%	36%	40%
0	1.000	1.000	1.000	1.000	1.000	1.000	1.000	1.000	1.000	1.000	1.000	1.000
1	1.140	1.150	1.160	1.170	1.180	1.190	1.200	1.240	1.280	1.320	1.360	1.400
2	1.300	1.322	1.346	1.369	1.392	1.416	1.440	1.538	1.638	1.742	1.850	1.960
3	1.482	1.521	1.561	1.602	1.643	1.685	1.728	1.907	2.067	2.300	2.515	2.744
4	1.689	1.749	1.811	1.874	1.939	2.005	2.074	2.364	2.684	3.036	3.421	3.842
5	1.925	2.011	2.100	2.192	2.288	2.386	2.488	2.932	3.436	4.007	4.653	5.378
6	2.195	2.313	2.436	2.565	2.700	2.840	2.986	3.635	4.398	5.290	6.328	7.530
7	2.502	2.660	2.826	3.001	3.185	3.379	3.583	4.508	5.629	6.983	8.605	10.541
8	2.853	3.059	3.278	3.511	3.759	4.021	4.300	5.590	7.206	9.217	11.703	14.758
9	3.252	3.518	3.803	4.108	4.435	4.785	5.160	6.931	9.223	12.166	15.917	20.661
10	3.707	4.046	4.411	4.807	5.234	5.695	6.192	8.594	11.806	16.060	21.647	28.925
11	4.226	4.652	5.117	5.624	6.176	6.777	7.430	10.657	15.112	21.199	29.439	40.496
12	4.818	5.350	5.926	6.580	7.288	8.064	8.916	13.215	19.343	27.983	40.037	56.694
13	5.492	6.153	6.886	7.699	8.599	9.596	10.699	16.386	24.759	36.937	54.451	79.372
14	6.261	7.076	7.988	9.007	10.147	11.420	12.839	20.319	31.961	48.757	74.053	111.120
15	7.138	8.137	9.266	10.539	11.974	13.590	15.407	25.196	40.565	64.359	100.712	155.568
16	8.137	9.358	10.748	12.330	14.129	16.172	18.488	31.243	51.923	84.954	136.969	217.795
17	9.276	10.761	12.468	14.426	16.672	19.244	22.186	38.741	66.461	112.139	186.278	304.914
18	10.575	12.375	14.463	16.879	19.673	22.901	26.623	48.039	85.071	148.023	253.338	426.879
19	12.056	14.232	16.777	19.748	23.214	27.252	31.948	59.568	108.890	195.391	344.540	597.630
20	13.743	16.367	19.461	23.106	27.393	32.429	38.338	73.864	139.380	257.916	468.574	836.683
24	23.212	28.625	35.236	43.297	53.109	65.032	79.497	174.631	374.144	783.023	1,603.00	3,214.20
25	26.462	32.919	40.874	50.658	62.669	77.388	95.396	216.542	478.905	1,033.59	2,180.08	4,499.88
30	50.950	66.212	85.850	111.065	143.371	184.675	237.376	634.820	1,645.50	4,142.07	10,143.0	24,201.4
40	188.884	267.864	378.721	533.869	750.378	1,051.67	1,469.77	5,455.91	19,426.7	66,520.8	219,562	700,038
50	700.233	1,083.66	1,670.70	2,566.22	3,927.36	5,988.91	9,100.44	46,890.4	229,350	*	*	*
60	2,595.92	4,384.00	7,370.20	12,335.4	20,555.1	34,105.0	56,347.5	402,996	*	*	*	*

* These interest factors exceed 1,000,000

393

Table 2 Present value interest factor (PVIF) (£1 at $i\%$ for n years); PVIF $= 1/(1+i)^n$; $PV_0 = FV_n(\text{PVIF}_{i,n})$

Period n	1%	2%	3%	4%	5%	6%	7%	8%	9%	10%	11%	12%	13%
0	1.000	1.000	1.000	1.000	1.000	1.000	1.000	1.000	1.000	1.000	1.000	1.000	1.000
1	0.990	0.980	0.971	0.962	0.952	0.943	0.935	0.926	0.917	0.909	0.901	0.893	0.885
2	0.980	0.961	0.943	0.925	0.907	0.890	0.873	0.857	0.842	0.826	0.812	0.797	0.783
3	0.971	0.942	0.915	0.889	0.864	0.840	0.816	0.794	0.772	0.751	0.731	0.712	0.693
4	0.961	0.924	0.889	0.855	0.823	0.792	0.763	0.735	0.708	0.683	0.659	0.636	0.613
5	0.951	0.906	0.863	0.822	0.784	0.747	0.713	0.681	0.650	0.621	0.593	0.567	0.543
6	0.942	0.888	0.838	0.790	0.746	0.705	0.666	0.630	0.596	0.564	0.535	0.507	0.480
7	0.933	0.871	0.813	0.760	0.711	0.665	0.623	0.583	0.547	0.513	0.482	0.452	0.425
8	0.923	0.853	0.789	0.731	0.677	0.627	0.582	0.540	0.502	0.467	0.434	0.404	0.376
9	0.914	0.837	0.766	0.703	0.645	0.592	0.544	0.500	0.460	0.424	0.391	0.361	0.333
10	0.905	0.820	0.744	0.676	0.614	0.558	0.508	0.463	0.422	0.386	0.352	0.322	0.295
11	0.896	0.804	0.722	0.650	0.585	0.527	0.475	0.429	0.388	0.350	0.317	0.287	0.261
12	0.887	0.788	0.701	0.625	0.557	0.497	0.444	0.397	0.356	0.319	0.286	0.257	0.231
13	0.879	0.773	0.681	0.601	0.530	0.469	0.415	0.368	0.326	0.290	0.258	0.229	0.204
14	0.870	0.758	0.661	0.577	0.505	0.442	0.388	0.340	0.299	0.263	0.232	0.205	0.181
15	0.861	0.743	0.642	0.555	0.481	0.417	0.362	0.315	0.275	0.239	0.209	0.183	0.160
16	0.853	0.728	0.623	0.534	0.458	0.394	0.339	0.292	0.252	0.218	0.188	0.163	0.141
17	0.844	0.714	0.605	0.513	0.436	0.371	0.317	0.270	0.231	0.198	0.170	0.146	0.125
18	0.836	0.700	0.587	0.494	0.416	0.350	0.296	0.250	0.212	0.180	0.153	0.130	0.111
19	0.828	0.686	0.570	0.475	0.396	0.331	0.276	0.232	0.194	0.164	0.138	0.116	0.098
20	0.820	0.673	0.554	0.456	0.377	0.312	0.258	0.215	0.178	0.149	0.124	0.104	0.087
24	0.788	0.622	0.492	0.390	0.310	0.247	0.197	0.158	0.126	0.102	0.082	0.066	0.053
25	0.780	0.610	0.478	0.375	0.295	0.233	0.184	0.146	0.116	0.092	0.074	0.059	0.047
30	0.742	0.552	0.412	0.308	0.231	0.174	0.131	0.099	0.075	0.057	0.044	0.033	0.026
40	0.672	0.453	0.307	0.208	0.142	0.097	0.067	0.046	0.032	0.022	0.015	0.011	0.008
50	0.608	0.372	0.228	0.141	0.087	0.054	0.034	0.021	0.013	0.009	0.005	0.003	0.002
60	0.550	0.305	0.170	0.095	0.054	0.030	0.017	0.010	0.006	0.003	0.002	0.001	0.001

Table 2 *continued*

Period n	14%	15%	16%	17%	18%	19%	20%	24%	28%	32%	36%	40%
0	1.000	1.000	1.000	1.000	1.000	1.000	1.000	1.000	1.000	1.000	1.000	1.000
1	0.877	0.870	0.862	0.855	0.847	0.840	0.833	0.806	0.781	0.758	0.735	0.714
2	0.769	0.756	0.743	0.731	0.718	0.706	0.694	0.650	0.610	0.574	0.541	0.510
3	0.675	0.658	0.641	0.624	0.609	0.593	0.579	0.524	0.477	0.435	0.398	0.364
4	0.592	0.572	0.552	0.534	0.516	0.499	0.482	0.423	0.373	0.329	0.292	0.260
5	0.519	0.497	0.476	0.456	0.437	0.419	0.402	0.341	0.291	0.250	0.215	0.186
6	0.456	0.432	0.410	0.390	0.370	0.352	0.335	0.275	0.227	0.189	0.158	0.133
7	0.400	0.376	0.354	0.333	0.314	0.296	0.279	0.222	0.178	0.143	0.116	0.095
8	0.351	0.327	0.305	0.285	0.266	0.249	0.233	0.179	0.139	0.108	0.085	0.068
9	0.308	0.284	0.263	0.243	0.225	0.209	0.194	0.144	0.108	0.082	0.063	0.048
10	0.270	0.247	0.227	0.208	0.191	0.176	0.162	0.116	0.085	0.062	0.046	0.035
11	0.237	0.215	0.195	0.178	0.162	0.148	0.135	0.094	0.066	0.047	0.034	0.025
12	0.208	0.187	0.168	0.152	0.137	0.124	0.112	0.076	0.052	0.036	0.025	0.018
13	0.182	0.163	0.145	0.130	0.116	0.104	0.093	0.061	0.040	0.027	0.018	0.013
14	0.160	0.141	0.125	0.111	0.099	0.088	0.078	0.049	0.032	0.021	0.014	0.009
15	0.140	0.123	0.108	0.095	0.084	0.074	0.065	0.040	0.025	0.016	0.010	0.006
16	0.123	0.107	0.093	0.081	0.071	0.062	0.054	0.032	0.019	0.012	0.007	0.005
17	0.108	0.093	0.080	0.069	0.060	0.052	0.045	0.026	0.015	0.009	0.005	0.003
18	0.095	0.081	0.069	0.059	0.051	0.044	0.038	0.021	0.012	0.007	0.004	0.002
19	0.083	0.070	0.060	0.051	0.043	0.037	0.031	0.017	0.009	0.005	0.003	0.002
20	0.073	0.061	0.051	0.043	0.037	0.031	0.026	0.014	0.007	0.004	0.002	0.001
24	0.043	0.035	0.028	0.023	0.019	0.015	0.013	0.006	0.003	0.001	0.001	0.000
25	0.038	0.030	0.024	0.020	0.016	0.013	0.010	0.005	0.002	0.001	0.000	0.000
30	0.020	0.015	0.012	0.009	0.007	0.005	0.004	0.002	0.001	0.000	0.000	0.000
40	0.005	0.004	0.003	0.002	0.001	0.001	0.001	0.000	0.000	0.000	0.000	0.000
50	0.001	0.001	0.001	0.000	0.000	0.000	0.000	0.000	0.000	0.000	0.000	0.000
60	0.000	0.000	0.000	0.000	0.000	0.000	0.000	0.000	0.000	0.000	0.000	0.000

Table 3 Future value of an annuity interest factor (FVIFA) (£1 per year at $i\%$ for n years); FVIFA $= ((1 + i)^n - 1)/i$;

$$FVAN_n = PMT(FVIFA_{i,n})$$

Period n	1%	2%	3%	4%	5%	6%	7%	8%	9%	10%	11%	12%	13%
1	1.000	1.000	1.000	1.000	1.000	1.000	1.000	1.000	1.000	1.000	1.000	1.000	1.000
2	2.010	2.020	2.030	2.040	2.050	2.060	2.070	2.080	2.090	2.100	2.110	2.120	2.130
3	3.030	3.060	3.091	3.122	3.152	3.184	3.215	3.246	3.278	3.310	3.342	3.374	3.407
4	4.060	4.122	4.184	4.246	4.310	4.375	4.440	4.506	4.573	4.641	4.710	4.779	4.850
5	5.101	5.204	5.309	5.416	5.526	5.637	5.751	5.867	5.985	6.105	6.228	6.353	6.480
6	6.152	6.308	6.468	6.633	6.802	6.975	7.153	7.336	7.523	7.716	7.913	8.115	8.323
7	7.214	7.434	7.662	7.898	8.142	8.394	8.654	8.923	9.200	9.487	9.783	10.089	10.405
8	8.286	8.583	8.892	9.214	9.549	9.897	10.260	10.637	11.028	11.436	11.859	12.300	12.757
9	9.369	9.755	10.159	10.583	11.027	11.491	11.978	12.488	13.021	13.579	14.164	14.776	15.416
10	10.462	10.950	11.464	12.006	12.578	13.181	13.816	14.487	15.193	15.937	16.722	17.549	18.420
11	11.567	12.169	12.808	13.486	14.207	14.972	15.784	16.645	17.560	18.531	19.561	20.655	21.814
12	12.683	13.412	14.192	15.026	15.917	16.870	17.888	18.977	20.141	21.384	22.713	24.133	25.650
13	13.809	14.680	15.618	16.627	17.713	18.882	20.141	21.495	22.953	24.523	26.212	28.029	29.985
14	14.947	15.974	17.086	18.292	19.599	21.051	22.550	24.215	26.019	27.975	30.095	32.393	34.883
15	16.097	17.293	18.599	20.024	21.579	23.276	25.129	27.152	29.361	31.772	34.405	37.280	40.417
16	17.258	18.639	20.157	21.825	23.657	25.673	27.888	30.324	33.003	35.950	39.190	42.753	46.672
17	18.430	20.012	21.762	23.698	25.840	28.213	30.840	33.750	36.974	40.545	44.501	48.884	53.739
18	19.615	21.412	23.414	25.645	28.132	30.906	33.999	37.450	41.301	45.599	50.396	55.750	61.725
19	20.811	22.841	25.117	27.671	30.539	33.760	37.379	41.446	46.018	51.159	56.939	63.440	70.749
20	22.019	24.297	26.870	29.778	33.066	36.786	40.995	45.762	51.160	57.275	64.203	72.052	80.947
24	26.973	30.422	34.426	39.083	44.502	50.816	58.117	66.765	76.790	88.497	102.174	118.155	136.831
25	28.243	32.030	36.459	41.646	47.727	54.865	63.249	73.106	84.701	98.347	114.413	133.334	155.620
30	34.785	40.568	47.575	56.085	66.439	79.058	94.461	113.283	136.308	164.494	199.021	241.333	293.199
40	48.886	60.402	75.401	95.026	120.808	154.762	199.635	259.057	337.882	442.593	581.826	767.091	1,013.70
50	64.463	84.572	112.797	152.667	209.348	290.336	406.529	573.770	815.074	1,163.91	1,668.77	2,400.02	3,459.51
60	81.670	114.052	163.053	237.991	353.584	533.128	813.520	1,253.21	1,944.79	3,034.82	4,755.07	7,471.64	11,761.9

Table 3 continued

Period n	14%	15%	16%	17%	18%	19%	20%	24%	28%	32%	36%	40%
1	1.000	1.000	1.000	1.000	1.000	1.000	1.000	1.000	1.000	1.000	1.000	1.000
2	2.140	2.150	2.160	2.170	2.180	2.190	2.200	2.240	2.280	2.320	2.360	2.400
3	3.440	3.473	3.506	3.539	3.572	3.606	3.640	3.778	3.918	4.062	4.210	4.360
4	4.921	4.993	5.066	5.141	5.215	5.291	5.368	5.684	6.016	6.362	6.725	7.104
5	6.610	6.742	6.877	7.014	7.154	7.297	7.442	8.048	8.700	9.398	10.146	10.846
6	8.536	8.754	8.977	9.207	9.442	9.683	9.930	10.980	12.136	13.406	14.799	16.324
7	10.730	11.067	11.414	11.772	12.142	12.523	12.916	14.615	16.534	18.696	21.126	23.853
8	13.233	13.727	14.240	14.773	15.327	15.902	16.499	19.123	22.163	25.678	29.732	34.395
9	16.085	16.786	17.518	18.285	19.086	19.923	20.799	24.712	29.369	34.895	41.435	49.153
10	19.337	20.304	21.321	22.393	23.521	24.709	25.959	31.643	38.592	47.062	57.352	69.814
11	23.044	24.349	25.733	27.200	28.755	30.404	32.150	40.238	50.399	63.122	78.998	98.739
12	27.271	29.002	30.850	32.824	34.931	37.180	39.580	50.985	65.510	84.320	108.437	139.235
13	32.089	34.352	36.786	39.404	42.219	45.244	48.497	64.110	84.853	112.303	148.475	195.929
14	37.581	40.505	43.672	47.103	50.818	54.841	59.196	80.496	109.612	149.240	202.926	275.300
15	43.842	47.580	51.660	56.110	60.965	66.261	72.035	100.815	141.303	197.997	276.979	386.420
16	50.980	55.717	60.925	66.649	72.939	79.850	87.442	126.011	181.868	262.356	377.692	541.988
17	59.118	65.075	71.673	78.979	87.068	96.022	105.931	157.253	233.791	347.310	514.661	759.784
18	68.394	75.836	84.141	93.406	103.740	115.266	128.117	195.994	300.252	459.449	700.939	1,064.70
19	78.969	88.212	98.603	110.285	123.414	138.166	154.740	244.033	385.323	607.472	954.277	1,491.58
20	91.025	102.444	115.380	130.033	146.628	165.418	186.688	303.601	494.213	802.863	1,298.82	2,089.21
24	158.659	184.168	213.978	248.808	289.494	337.010	392.484	723.461	1,322.66	2,443.82	4,450.00	8,033.00
25	181.871	212.793	249.214	292.105	342.603	402.042	471.981	898.092	1,706.80	3,226.84	6,053.00	11,247.2
30	356.787	434.745	530.321	647.439	790.948	966.712	1,181.88	2,640.92	5,873.23	12,940.9	28,172.3	60,501.1
40	1,342.03	1,779.09	2,360.76	3,134.52	4,163.21	5,529.83	7,343.86	22,728.8	69,377.5	207,874	609,890	*
50	4,994.52	7,217.72	10,435.6	15,089.5	21,813.1	31,515.3	45,497.2	195,373	819,103	*	*	*
60	18,535.1	29,220.0	46,057.5	72,555.0	114,190	179,495	281,733	*	*	*	*	*

* These interest factors exceed 1,000,000

Table 4 Present value of annuity interest factor (PVIFA) (£1 per year at *i*% for *n* years); PVIFA $= (1 - (1/(1 + i)^n))/i$;

$$\text{PVAN} = PMT(\text{PVIFA}_{i,n})$$

Period *n*	1%	2%	3%	4%	5%	6%	7%	8%	9%	10%	11%	12%	13%
1	0.990	0.980	0.971	0.962	0.952	0.943	0.935	0.926	0.917	0.909	0.901	0.893	0.885
2	1.970	1.942	1.913	1.886	1.859	1.833	1.808	1.783	1.759	1.736	1.713	1.690	1.668
3	2.941	2.884	2.829	2.775	2.723	2.673	2.624	2.577	2.531	2.487	2.444	2.402	2.361
4	3.902	3.808	3.717	3.630	3.546	3.465	3.387	3.312	3.240	3.170	3.102	3.037	2.974
5	4.853	4.713	4.580	4.452	4.329	4.212	4.100	3.993	3.890	3.791	3.696	3.605	3.517
6	5.795	5.601	5.417	5.242	5.076	4.917	4.766	4.623	4.486	4.355	4.231	4.111	3.998
7	6.728	6.472	6.230	6.002	5.786	5.582	5.389	5.206	5.033	4.868	4.712	4.564	4.423
8	7.652	7.325	7.020	6.733	6.463	6.210	5.971	5.747	5.535	5.335	5.146	4.968	4.799
9	8.566	8.162	7.786	7.435	7.108	6.802	6.515	6.247	5.995	5.759	5.537	5.328	5.132
10	9.471	8.983	8.530	8.111	7.722	7.360	7.024	6.710	6.418	6.145	5.889	5.650	5.426
11	10.368	9.787	9.253	8.760	8.306	7.887	7.499	7.139	6.805	6.495	6.207	5.938	5.687
12	11.255	10.575	9.954	9.385	8.863	8.384	7.943	7.536	7.161	6.814	6.492	6.194	5.918
13	12.134	11.348	10.635	9.986	9.394	8.853	8.358	7.904	7.487	7.103	6.750	6.424	6.122
14	13.004	12.106	11.296	10.563	9.899	9.295	8.745	8.244	7.786	7.367	6.982	6.628	6.302
15	13.865	12.849	11.938	11.118	10.380	9.712	9.108	8.559	8.061	7.606	7.191	6.811	6.462
16	14.718	13.578	12.561	11.652	10.838	10.106	9.447	8.851	8.312	7.824	7.379	6.974	6.604
17	15.562	14.292	13.166	12.166	11.274	10.477	9.763	9.122	8.544	8.022	7.549	7.120	6.729
18	16.398	14.992	13.754	12.659	11.690	10.828	10.059	9.372	8.756	8.201	7.702	7.250	6.840
19	17.226	15.678	14.324	13.134	12.085	11.158	10.336	9.604	8.950	8.365	7.839	7.366	6.938
20	18.046	16.351	14.877	13.590	12.462	11.470	10.594	9.818	9.128	8.514	7.963	7.469	7.025
24	21.243	18.914	16.936	15.247	13.799	12.550	11.469	10.529	9.707	8.985	8.348	7.784	7.283
25	22.023	19.523	17.413	15.622	14.094	12.783	11.654	10.675	9.823	9.077	8.422	7.843	7.330
30	25.808	22.397	19.600	17.292	15.373	13.765	12.409	11.258	10.274	9.427	8.694	8.055	7.496
40	32.835	27.355	23.115	19.793	17.159	15.046	13.332	11.925	10.757	9.779	8.951	8.244	7.634
50	39.196	31.424	25.730	21.482	18.256	15.762	13.801	12.233	10.962	9.915	9.042	8.304	7.675
60	44.955	34.761	27.676	22.623	18.929	16.161	14.039	12.377	11.048	9.967	9.074	8.324	7.687

Table 4 *continued*

Period n	14%	15%	16%	17%	18%	19%	20%	24%	28%	32%	36%	40%
1	0.877	0.870	0.862	0.855	0.847	0.840	0.833	0.806	0.781	0.758	0.735	0.714
2	1.647	1.626	1.605	1.585	1.566	1.547	1.528	1.457	1.392	1.332	1.276	1.224
3	2.322	2.283	2.246	2.210	2.174	2.140	2.106	1.981	1.868	1.766	1.674	1.589
4	2.914	2.855	2.798	2.743	2.690	2.639	2.589	2.404	2.241	2.096	1.966	1.849
5	3.433	3.352	3.274	3.199	3.127	3.058	2.991	2.745	2.532	2.345	2.181	2.035
6	3.889	3.784	3.685	3.589	3.498	3.410	3.326	3.020	2.759	2.534	2.399	2.168
7	4.288	4.160	4.039	3.922	3.812	3.706	3.605	3.242	2.937	2.678	2.455	2.263
8	4.639	4.487	4.344	4.207	4.078	3.954	3.837	3.421	3.076	2.786	2.540	2.331
9	4.946	4.772	4.607	4.451	4.303	4.163	4.031	3.566	3.184	2.868	2.603	2.379
10	5.216	5.019	4.833	4.659	4.494	4.339	4.193	3.682	3.269	2.930	2.650	2.414
11	5.453	5.234	5.029	4.836	4.656	4.486	4.327	3.776	3.335	2.978	2.683	2.438
12	5.660	5.421	5.197	4.988	4.793	4.611	4.439	3.851	3.387	3.013	2.708	2.456
13	5.842	5.583	5.342	5.118	4.910	4.715	4.533	3.912	3.427	3.040	2.727	2.469
14	6.002	5.724	5.468	5.229	5.008	4.802	4.611	3.962	3.459	3.061	2.740	2.478
15	6.142	5.847	5.575	5.324	5.092	4.876	4.675	4.001	3.483	3.076	2.750	2.484
16	6.265	5.954	5.669	5.405	5.162	4.938	4.730	4.033	3.503	3.088	2.758	2.489
17	6.373	6.047	5.749	5.475	5.222	4.990	4.775	4.059	3.518	3.097	2.763	2.492
18	6.467	6.128	5.818	5.534	5.273	5.033	4.812	4.080	3.529	3.104	2.767	2.494
19	6.550	6.198	5.877	5.584	5.316	5.070	4.844	4.097	3.539	3.109	2.770	2.496
20	6.623	6.259	5.929	5.628	5.353	5.101	4.870	4.110	3.546	3.113	2.772	2.497
24	6.835	6.434	6.073	5.746	5.451	5.182	4.937	4.143	3.562	3.121	2.776	2.499
25	6.873	6.464	6.097	5.766	5.467	5.195	4.948	4.147	3.564	3.122	2.776	2.499
30	7.003	6.566	6.177	5.829	5.517	5.235	4.979	4.160	3.569	3.124	2.778	2.500
40	7.105	6.642	6.233	5.871	5.548	5.258	4.997	4.166	3.571	3.125	2.778	2.500
50	7.133	6.661	6.246	5.880	5.554	5.262	4.999	4.167	3.571	3.125	2.778	2.500
60	7.140	6.665	6.249	5.882	5.555	5.263	5.000	4.167	3.571	3.125	2.778	2.500

Appendix 4

Areas under the standard normal curve from 0 to *z*

z	0	1	2	3	4	5	6	7	8	9
0.0	0.0000	0.0040	0.0080	0.0120	0.0160	0.0199	0.0239	0.0279	0.0319	0.0359
0.1	0.0398	0.0438	0.0478	0.0517	0.0557	0.0596	0.0636	0.0675	0.0714	0.0754
0.2	0.0793	0.0832	0.0871	0.0910	0.0948	0.0987	0.1026	0.1064	0.1103	0.1141
0.3	0.1179	0.1217	0.1255	0.1293	0.1331	0.1368	0.1406	0.1443	0.1480	0.1517
0.4	0.1554	0.1591	0.1628	0.1664	0.1700	0.1736	0.1772	0.1808	0.1844	0.1879
0.5	0.1915	0.1950	0.1985	0.2019	0.2054	0.2088	0.2123	0.2157	0.2190	0.2224
0.6	0.2258	0.2291	0.2324	0.2357	0.2389	0.2422	0.2454	0.2486	0.2518	0.2549
0.7	0.2580	0.2612	0.2642	0.2673	0.2704	0.2734	0.2764	0.2794	0.2823	0.2852
0.8	0.2881	0.2910	0.2939	0.2967	0.2996	0.3023	0.3051	0.3078	0.3106	0.3133
0.9	0.3159	0.3186	0.3212	0.3238	0.3264	0.3289	0.3315	0.3340	0.3365	0.3389
1.0	0.3413	0.3438	0.3461	0.3485	0.3508	0.3531	0.3554	0.3577	0.3599	0.3621
1.1	0.3643	0.3665	0.3686	0.3708	0.3729	0.3749	0.3770	0.3790	0.3810	0.3830
1.2	0.3849	0.3869	0.3888	0.3907	0.3925	0.3944	0.3962	0.3980	0.3997	0.4015
1.3	0.4032	0.4049	0.4066	0.4082	0.4099	0.4115	0.4131	0.4147	0.4162	0.4177
1.4	0.4192	0.4207	0.4222	0.4236	0.4251	0.4265	0.4279	0.4292	0.4306	0.4319
1.5	0.4332	0.4345	0.4357	0.4370	0.4382	0.4394	0.4406	0.4418	0.4429	0.4441
1.6	0.4452	0.4463	0.4474	0.4484	0.4495	0.4505	0.4515	0.4525	0.4535	0.4545
1.7	0.4554	0.4564	0.4573	0.4582	0.4591	0.4599	0.4608	0.4616	0.4625	0.4633
1.8	0.4641	0.4649	0.4656	0.4664	0.4671	0.4678	0.4686	0.4693	0.4699	0.4706
1.9	0.4713	0.4719	0.4726	0.4732	0.4738	0.4744	0.4750	0.4756	0.4761	0.4767
2.0	0.4772	0.4778	0.4783	0.4788	0.4793	0.4798	0.4803	0.4808	0.4812	0.4817
2.1	0.4821	0.4826	0.4830	0.4834	0.4838	0.4842	0.4846	0.4850	0.4854	0.4857
2.2	0.4861	0.4864	0.4868	0.4871	0.4875	0.4878	0.4881	0.4884	0.4887	0.4890
2.3	0.4893	0.4896	0.4898	0.4901	0.4904	0.4906	0.4909	0.4911	0.4913	0.4916
2.4	0.4918	0.4920	0.4922	0.4925	0.4927	0.4929	0.4931	0.4932	0.4934	0.4936
2.5	0.4938	0.4940	0.4941	0.4943	0.4945	0.4946	0.4948	0.4949	0.4951	0.4952
2.6	0.4953	0.4955	0.4956	0.4957	0.4959	0.4960	0.4961	0.4962	0.4963	0.4964
2.7	0.4965	0.4966	0.4967	0.4968	0.4969	0.4970	0.4971	0.4972	0.4973	0.4974
2.8	0.4974	0.4975	0.4976	0.4977	0.4977	0.4978	0.4979	0.4979	0.4980	0.4981
2.9	0.4981	0.4982	0.4982	0.4983	0.4984	0.4984	0.4985	0.4985	0.4986	0.4986
3.0	0.4987	0.4987	0.4987	0.4988	0.4988	0.4989	0.4989	0.4989	0.4990	0.4990
3.1	0.4990	0.4991	0.4991	0.4991	0.4992	0.4992	0.4992	0.4992	0.4993	0.4993
3.2	0.4993	0.4993	0.4994	0.4994	0.4994	0.4994	0.4994	0.4995	0.4995	0.4995
3.3	0.4995	0.4995	0.4995	0.4996	0.4996	0.4996	0.4996	0.4996	0.4996	0.4997
3.4	0.4997	0.4997	0.4997	0.4997	0.4997	0.4997	0.4997	0.4997	0.4997	0.4998
3.5	0.4998	0.4998	0.4998	0.4998	0.4998	0.4998	0.4998	0.4998	0.4998	0.4998
3.6	0.4998	0.4998	0.4999	0.4999	0.4999	0.4999	0.4999	0.4999	0.4999	0.4999
3.7	0.4999	0.4999	0.4999	0.4999	0.4999	0.4999	0.4999	0.4999	0.4999	0.4999
3.8	0.4999	0.4999	0.4999	0.4999	0.4999	0.4999	0.4999	0.4999	0.4999	0.4999
3.9	0.5000	0.5000	0.5000	0.5000	0.5000	0.5000	0.5000	0.5000	0.5000	0.5000

Index

yes, I'm still the one

by close

(Any

2) * promotional price can be reduced.
   * reduce cost
   _____

First we eat meals

then go alone